# A CRITICAL AND GRAMMATICAL COMMENTARY ON ST. PAUL'S EPISTLES TO THE THESSALONIANS.

WITH A

REVISED TRANSLATION.

BY

CHARLES J. ELLICOTT, B.D.,

DEAN OF EXETER, AND PROFESSOR OF DIVINITY, KING'S COLLEGE, LONDON.

Wipf & Stock
PUBLISHERS
Eugene, Oregon

Wipf and Stock Publishers
199 West 8th Avenue, Suite 3
Eugene, Oregon 97401

A Critical & Grammatical Commentary on St. Paul's Epistle to the Thessalonians
By Ellicott, Charles J.
ISBN: 1-57910-082-1
Publication date 11/12/1997
Previously published by Warren F. Draper, 1998

# PREFACE TO THE FIRST EDITION.

THE present volume forms the fifth part of my Commentary on St. Paul's Epistles, and is constructed as nearly as possible on the same plan as the portion which appeared last year, viz., that containing the Epistles to the Philippians, Colossians, and Philemon. I peculiarly specify this, as I have been informed by friends on whose judgment I can rely, that the last portion of my labors is an improvement on those which preceded it.

If I may venture to assume that this is really the case, I cannot help feeling that it is to be attributed not only to increased experience, but also to the cautious but somewhat freer admixture of exegesis which two of the three Epistles that formed the volume seemed more especially to require. This slight modification, and so to say dilution, of the critical and grammatical severity which distinguished the earlier parts of the work, has been continued in the present volume; but it has been done so both watchfully and cautiously, and will be found really more in the way of slight addition than in actual change. Time and experience seem both to show that the system of interpretation that I have been enabled to pursue is substantially sound, that plain and patient accuracy in detail does in most cases lead to hopeful results, and serves not unfrequently to guide us to far loftier and more ennobling views of the Word of Life, than such an unpretending method might at first prepare us to expect.

The modifications, then, or rather additions and expansions, are really slight, and may be briefly summed up under *two* heads: on the one hand, an attempt to elucidate more clearly the connection of clauses and the general sequence of thought; and, on the other hand, an attempt to develop more completely the dogmatical significance of passages of a more profound and more purely theological import. Neither of these portions of sacred interpretation was neglected in the early parts of this Commentary, but in the present a deepening sense of their extreme importance has suggested this further expansion and development.

A few slight additions to other departments of the Commentary may be briefly noticed.

To the ancient Versions which I have been in the habit of consulting, viz., the Old Latin, the Peschito, the Gothic, the Coptic, the Philoxenian Syriac, and the two Ethiopic Versions, I did not think it would be necessary for me ever to make any addition. I have been convinced, however, by the able notice of the Armenian Version in Horne's *Introduction*, by my learned acquaintance Dr. Tregelles, that this venerable Version has greater claims on our attention than I had before believed. In spite of the excellent edition of Zohrab, I had shared the opinion entertained by the majority of critics, that the once-called "Queen of the Versions" had but slender claims to that supremacy, and had suffered so much from Latinizing recensions as to be but of doubtful authority. The charges brought against the labors of King Haithom in the thirteenth century, and the admissions of the collator Uscan at a more recent period, tended of late years to awaken the suspicions of critical scholars. It is fair, however, to say that the charges of Latinism do not appear to be well founded, and that this ancient version deserves the attention of the critic and commentator; still, if I am not presumptuous in hazarding an opinion, I do seem to myself to perceive a generally Occidental tinge in its interpretations, and I have more than once verified the observation of Loebe and De Gabelentz, that there are coincidences and accordances with the Gothic Version that do not seem wholly accidental. My knowledge, however, is at present too limited to enable me to speak with confidence.

I have, then, deemed it my duty to make use of this Version, and to acquire such a knowledge of the language as should enable me to state faithfully its opinion in contested passages. To the student who may feel attracted towards this interesting, highly inflected, yet not very difficult language, I will venture to recommend the grammar and dictionary of Aucher.[1] The former is now selling at a low price, and can easily be procured. Its great defect is in the syntax, which I cannot think very clearly or scientifically arranged; and in the Chrestomathy, which is not at first sufficiently easy and progressive. The present extracts, though curious, are not well suited for a beginner, and are not introduced by any elementary lessons in parsing and grammatical application. . . . . A strong sense of the

1 Since the above was written a much more useful and scientifically arranged grammar has come under my notice, viz. '*Brevis Linguæ Armeniacæ Grammatica*' of J. H. Petermann (Berol. 1841). It has a simple Chrestomathy and good glossary, but no syntax. The standard grammar of a larger size appears to be that of Cirbied.

value of such aids reminds me that I may not unsuitably take this opportunity of recommending the *Coptic Grammar* of Uhlemann. It is extremely well arranged, is brief and perspicuous, and, besides a good progressive Chrestomathy, is furnished with a small but very useful Vocabulary.

I again venture to commend these ancient Versions to the attention of all students who have leisure, and an aptitude for the acquisition of languages. It is startling to find how little we really know of these ancient witnesses, how erroneous are the current statements of their mere readings, how neglected their authority in interpretation. And yet we see on all sides critical editions of the sacred volume multiplying, and, in at least one instance (I regret to say that I allude to the otherwise useful edition of Dr. Tischendorf), can abundantly verify the fact that Latin translations, not always trustworthy or exact, have been the main authorities from which the readings have been derived. Is it too much to demand of a *critical* editor, of one who is by the very nature of his work free from the many distractions of thought that are the lot of the commentator, — is it too much to demand that he should consider it a part of his duties *himself* to acquire such a knowledge of these languages as to be able to tell us, plainly and unmistakably, what are and what are not the true readings of these early and invaluable witnesses? Nay, more, it is, and it will ever be found, of paramount importance that the loyal critic should use no eyes but *his own*. He may endeavor to procure collations from others, he may try to proceed on the principle of division of labor, but he will, I firmly believe, ultimately be forced to admit that this is one of those cases in which labor cannot be well divided, and in which the mechanically-made comparisons of the associated collator can never be put in the same rank with the results of the intelligent search of the professed critic. The very interest that the latter feels in what he is looking for protects him, to a great degree, from those inaccuracies which the mere collator can never hope entirely to escape; added to which his exact knowledge of the variations of the reading at issue will save him, as nothing else can, from confounding a merely greater inclusiveness of meaning with evidences of distinct textual change. To cite a single and familiar instance, — how often must the critical scholar have observed that Oriental Versions are adduced on one side or other, in such cases of prepositional variation as ἐν and διά, when the plain fact is that the greater inclusiveness of the Beth or the Bet of the Version leaves the actual reading which the translator had before him a matter of complete uncertainty. Are, then, our scholars, and more especially our critics, to shrink from such a useful and even necessary duty as the study of the ancient Versions? Are a certain number of weary hours, more or less, to be set in comparison with the ability and the privilege of making clearly known to others the critical characteristics of Versions of the Book of Life, that have been the blessed media of salvation to early churches and to ancient nations?

One word, and one word only, as to my own humble, most humble efforts in this particular province. Time, toil, and patience have done something; and though, alas! my knowledge is still limited, yet I may at length venture to hope that in most of these versions the student may fully rely on my statements, and that the number of those statements that may hereafter be reversed by wiser and better scholars than myself will not be very large. I am forced to say this, as I have observed in one or two reviews with which I have been favored, that avowals of inexperience, which seemed the more suitable and becoming in proportion as the means of detecting it were in fewer hands, have been understood to imply that my citations from these ancient authorities could not confessedly be relied on. This, however, has not been, and is not the case. While I sensitively shrink from dragging into notice the amount of my own labors, I still perceive that I must beware of leading the reader to pass over what may be of real use to him, and of feeling distrust where actually there may be no just ground for it. The intelligent scholar will see at a glance that to state fairly and *correctly* the translation of words of which the subject is familiarly known, is a task which certainly does not lie beyond the reach of ordinary patience and industry.

Among other additions, the reader will, I trust, be benefited by the still increasing attention to our best English divinity. I have made it my study to refer especially to sermons on all more interesting and difficult verses, and it is unusually cheering to find that no portion of my labors has been more kindly appreciated, or has apparently been of more real service to theological students. Without drawing any unfair comparison between English and German divinity, it does not seem one whit too much to say, that if we are often indebted to the latter for patient and laborious exegesis, it is to the former alone that we must go if we would fain add to our mere contextual knowledge some true perceptions of the analogy of Scripture, and are really and sincerely interested in striving to comprehend all the profound and mysterious harmonies of Catholic Truth.

With regard to matters of textual criticism, the student will observe in this volume the same persistent attention to the principal differences of reading, even in the grammatical notes. My constant effort is to popularize this sort of knowledge, to make exegesis lend it a helping hand, and to insensibly decoy the student into examining and considering for himself what human words seem to have the best claims to be regarded as the earthly instruments by which the adorable mercies of God have been made known to the children of men. These notices, it must be remembered, are merely selected, and neither are, nor are intended to be, enumerations of *all* the differences of reading; still I have good hope that in the present volume no reading that may be thought to deserve attention has been wholly overlooked.

I have now only to conclude with a few notices of those works to which I am especially indebted. This list is now gradually becoming shorter. I have been enabled to use so many more first-class authorities than when I commenced this work, that it does not seem disrespectful to such as can only be fairly considered as second-class, to silently omit them from pages where text and notes only too often stand in an undesirable though unavoidable disproportion.

In these Epistles, as in the Pastoral Epistles, I have lost the sagacious guidance of Dr. Meyer; I have not, however, so much to lament the change of editor as in the Epistles above alluded to. Though distinctly inferior to Meyer, especially in the critical and grammatical portion of his work, Dr. Lünemann is still a commentator of a very high order. His exegesis is commonly sound and convincing, and none, I am sure, can beneficially study these two beautiful Epistles without having at hand the Commentary of this able editor.

The larger and more comprehensive Commentaries will be found specified in former portions of this work, but I must pause to express my hearty sense of the continued excellence of my friend Dean Alford's Commentary. As our readers will see, we occasionally break a friendly lance, more especially in matters of detail. These gentle encounters, however, are not only unavoidable, but even desirable. It is by all such amicable conflicts of opinion that the truth, often lying midway between those engaged in her defence, is most surely seen and recognized.

Of the separate editions of these Epistles I desire to specify the very able Commentaries of Pelt and Schott. The former of these two writers has the great merit of being one of the first of later times who distinctly felt the importance of using the exegetical works of the Greek Fathers, and the latter supplies a good specimen of that patient mode of grammatical interpretation which has now obtained such general currency. Though both these works have been many years before the world, and though in many cases their opinions have been reversed by more modern expositors, they can neither of them be justly considered as superseded or antiquated.

Last of all, I come to the edition of Professor Jowett. And here I would rather that our differences of opinion appeared in their respective places than were thus specifically alluded to. I feel it, however, a duty to speak, and it is with pain that I must record my fixed opinion that the system of interpretation pursued by Professor Jowett is as dangerous as I believe it to be inaccurate and untenable. Surely expressions that would be thought hard if applied to Pindar or Thucydides seem sadly out of place when directed against the diction of the inspired Saul of Tarsus. After making every possible allowance for the obvious fact that our systems of interpretation are completely and persistently antagonistic, after willingly making in my own case every correction for bias, I still feel morally convinced that the objections to Professor Jowett's system of Interpretation are such as cannot be evaded or explained away. . . . . After having thus performed a very painful duty, I trust I may be permitted to express my full recognition of the genius that pervades his writings, the ease, finish, and, alas! persuasiveness of the style, the kindly though self-conscious spirit that animates his teaching, and the love of truth that, however sadly and deeply wounded by paradoxes and polemics, still seems to be ever both felt and cultivated. May these good gifts be dedicated anew to the service of Divine Truth, and be overruled to more happy and more chastened issues.

It now only remains for me, with all humility and lowliness of heart, to lay this work before the Great Father of Lights, imploring his blessing on what I may have said aright, and his mercy where mine eyes have been holden, and where I have not been permitted to see clearly all the blessed lineaments of Divine Truth.

ΤΡΙΑΣ, ΜΟΝΑΣ, ʼΕΛΕΗΣΟΝ.

LONDON, August 4th, 1858.

THE

# FIRST EPISTLE TO THE THESSALONIANS.

# ADVERTISEMENT TO THE SECOND EDITION.

The present edition differs but little from the first. There will be found, however, traces of a regular and deliberate revision on every page. Scriptural references have been again verified; readings and interpretations have been carefully reconsidered, and the grammatical principles on which the interpretations appear to rest, tested by fresh investigation. Though the result is a *very* small amount of change, yet the amount of time thus spent in reconsideration, has not been wholly thrown away; as the commentary is now presented anew to the reader with a humble yet increased confidence in the general soundness of the principles on which it is based.

Exeter, December, 1861.

# INTRODUCTION.

THIS calm, practical, and profoundly consolatory epistle was written by the apostle to his converts in the wealthy and populous city of Thessalonica (see notes on ch. i. 1) not long after his first visit to Macedonia (Acts. xvi. 9), when, in conjunction with Silas and Timothy, he laid the foundations of the Thessalonian Church (Acts xvii. 1 sq.; comp. notes *on* 1 *Thess.* i. 1).

The exact *time* of writing the epistle appears to have been the early months of the apostle's year-and-a-half stay at Corinth (Acts xviii. 11), soon after Timothy had joined him (1 Thess. iii. 6) and reported the spiritual state of their converts, into which he had been sent to inquire (ch. iii. 2), probably from Athens; see notes on ch. iii 1. We may thus consider the close of A. D. 52, or the beginning of A. D. 53, as the probable date, and, if this be correct, must place the epistle first in the chronological list of the apostle's writings.

The arguments in favor of a later date, are based either on passages which have been thought to imply that the apostle had preached the gospel for some time elswhere (ch. i. 8), or on statements in the epistle (ch. iv. 13, v. 12; 2 Thess. iii. 17), which have been judged more in accordance with a greater interval between the time of the first preaching at Thessalonica and the date of the epistle than is usually assigned. These have all been satisfactorily answered by Davidson (*Introd.* Vol. II. p. 435), and have met with no acceptance at the hands of recent expositors, or chronologers; comp. Lünemann, *Einleitung*, p. 6, Wieseler, *Chronol.* p. 40 sq.

The main *object* of the apostle in writing this epistle can easily be gathered from some of the leading expressions. It was designed alike to console and to admonish; — to console, with reference both to recent external trials and afflictions (ch. ii. 14 sq.), and still more to internal trials arising from anxieties as to the state of their departed friends (ch. iv. sq.), — to admonish, with reference to grave moral principles (ch. iv. 1 sq.), Christian watchfulness (ch. v. 1 sq.), and various practical duties (ch. v. 14) which had been neglected, owing to the feverish expectations and anxieties which appear to have prevailed at Thessalonica even from the first: comp. ch. iv. 11, and see notes *in loc.* St. Paul had heard of all these things from Timothy; and this information, combined with the apostle's full consciousness that there were many points, both in knowledge and practice, in which they were deficient (ch. iii. 10), and on which he would fain have further instructed them personally (comp. ch. ii. 17 sq.), appears to have called forth this instructive and strengthening epistle.

The *authenticity* and *genuineness* of the epistle are placed beyond all reasonable doubt, both by clear external testimonies (Irenæus, *Hær.* v. 6. 1, Clem.-Alex. *Pædag.* I. p. 109, ed. Pott., Tertullian, *de Resurr. Carn.* cap. 24), and by still stronger internal arguments derived from the style and tone of thought. The objections that have been urged, like those advanced against the authenticity and genuineness of the second epistle (see *Introd.*), may justly be pronounced as rash, arbitrary, and unworthy of serious consideration. They will be found fully answered in Davidson, *Introd.* Vol. II. 454 sq.

THE

# FIRST EPISTLE TO THE THESSALONIANS.

## CHAPTER I. 1.

Apostolic address and salutation.

1 ΠΑΥΛΟΣ καὶ Σιλουανὸς καὶ Τιμόθεος, τῇ ἐκκλησίᾳ Θεσσαλονικέων ἐν Θεῷ

1. Παῦλος] The absence of the official designation ἀπόστολος in these Epp. is not due to their early date, nor to the fact that the title had not yet been assumed by St. Paul (compare Jowett), but simply to the terms of affection that subsisted between St. Paul and his converts at Thessalonica, and their loving recognition of his office and authority; compare Beng. *in loc.*, and see notes *on Phil.* i. 1. The reason of Chrys., followed by Theoph. and Œcum., διὰ τὸ νεοκατηχήτους εἶναι τοὺς ἄνδρας, καὶ μηδέπω αὐτοῦ πεῖραν εἰληφέναι, does not seem sufficient. That it was 'propter reverentiam Silvani' (Cajet., Est.), is far from probable, for compare 1 and 2 Cor. i. 1. Σιλουανός] Identical with Silas mentioned in the Acts (comp. Acts xvi. 19 sq. with 1 Thess. ii. 1, 2, and Acts xv. 32 with 2 Cor. i. 19), a προφήτης (Acts xviii. 5), and one ἡγούμενος ἐν τοῖς ἀδελφοῖς in the Church of Jerusalem (ver. 22): he was sent by the Apostles and elders of that Church with St. Paul and St. Barnabas to Antioch, and accompanied the former on his second missionary journey (Acts xv. 40) through Asia Minor to Macedonia. There he coöperates with the Apostle (Acts xvii. 4) and Timothy (comp. Acts xvi. 3, xvi. 14, 1 Thess. iii. 6) in founding the Church of Thessalonica, and after staying behind at Berœa (Acts xvii. 14), rejoins St. Paul at Corinth, and actively preaches the Gospel in that city (2 Cor. i. 19). It does not seem improbable that he afterwards joined St. Peter, and is identical with the Silvanus mentioned 1 Pet. v. 12; compare Bleek *on Hebr.* Vol. I. p. 408. He is here placed before Timothy (so also Acts xvii. 14, 15, xviii. 5, 2 Cor. i. 19, 2 Thess. i. 1) as being probably the older man, and certainly the older associate of St. Paul. According to tradition, Silas was afterwards Bishop of Corinth, and Silvanus of Thessalonica (compare the list in Fabric. *Lux Evang.* p. 117); the former name, however, though paroxytone, is, in all probability, only a contracted form of the latter; see Winer, *Gr.* § 16. 1, p. 93. For further and legendary notices of Silas, see *Acta Sanct.* July 13, Vol.

πατρὶ καὶ Κυρίῳ Ἰησοῦ Χριστῷ. χάρις ὑμῖν καὶ εἰρήνη.

III. p. 476, and for an attempt to identify Silas with St. Luke, see *Journal Sacr. Lit.*, Oct. 1850, p. 328 sq.

Τιμόθεος] The name of this convert is too well known to need more than a brief notice. He was the son of a Greek father (Acts xvi. 1) and a Jewish mother (Eunice, 2 Tim. i. 5), most probably from Lystra, and *perhaps* converted by St. Paul on his first visit to that city (Acts xiv. 8 sq.). He accompanied the Apostle on his second missionary journey to Macedonia, remains behind at Berœa (Acts xvii. 14), is summoned by St. Paul when at Athens; probably rejoins him *there* (comp. 1 Thess. iii. 1, and see Neander, *Planting*, Vol. I. p. 195), is despatched to Thessalonica, and returns to the Apostle at Corinth (Acts xviii. 5). After an interval, he reappears in St. Paul's third missionary journey, and is sent from Ephesus to Macedonia (Acts xix. 22) and Corinth (1 Cor. iv. 17). He was with St. Paul when he wrote 2 Cor. (ch. i. 1) and Rom. (ch. xvi. 21), accompanied him from Corinth to Asia (Acts xx. 4), and subsequently was with him when he wrote Phil (i. 1), Col. (i. 1), and Philem. (ver. 1). He appears afterwards to have been left in charge of the Church at Ephesus (1 Tim. i. 3), and finally, is summoned by St. Paul to Rome, at the close of the Apostle's second imprisonment. He is named by Eusebius (*Hist. Eccl.* III. 4, comp. *Const. Apost.* VII. 46) as first Bishop of Ephesus, and is said to have suffered martyrdom under Domitian; see Phot. *Biblioth.* CCLIV. p. 1402 (ed. Hoesch.), *Acta Sanct.* Jan. 24, Vol. II. p. 562, and *Menolog. Græc.* Vol. II. p. 128. It may be remarked that Silvanus and Timothy are here named with St. Paul, not merely as being then with him (Gal. i. 2), or as the 'socii salutationis' (comp. notes *on Phil.* i. 1), but also as having coöperated with him in founding the Church of Thessalonica.

τῇ ἐκκλ. Θεσσαλ. κ. τ. λ.] '*to the Church of the Thessalonians in God the Father*,' etc.; not 'scribunt aut mittunt hanc epistolam' (Est.), but in the usual elliptical form of greeting (Lucian, *Conviv.* § 22), the χαίρειν (James i. 1) being involved and implied in the wish (χάρις κ. τ. λ.) which forms the second period of the salutation; see notes *on* 1 *Tim.* i. 2. Thessalonica was a large (Lucian, *Asin.*, § 46), wealthy, and populous city (Strabo, *Geogr.* VII. 7, 4, Vol. II. p. 60, ed. Kramer) at the northeast corner of the Sinus Thermaicus. It was built on the site of, or near to (Pliny, *Hist. Nat.* IV. 10 (17), ed. Sillig), the ancient Therme (Herod. VII. 121, Thucyd. I. 61), by Cassander, in honor of his wife Θεσσαλονίκη (Strabo, *Geogr.* VII *Fragm.* 21, Vol. II. p. 79, ed. Kram.), and under the Romans was of sufficient importance to be chosen as the capital of the second district of Macedonia; see Livy, XLV. 29. It retained its importance through the middle ages (see Conyb. and Howson, *St. Paul*, Vol. I. p. 345 sq., ed. 1), and even at the present day, under the name of Saloniki, is one of the chief cities of European Turkey; see Leake, *N. Greece*, Vol. III. p. 238 sq. For further notices, see the good account of Conyb. and Hows. *l. c.*, Winer, *RWB.* Vol. II. p. 608, Pauly, *Real Encycl.* Vol. VI. p. 1880, and especially the learned and comprehensive treatises of Tafel, *Histor. Thessalon.* Tubing. 1835, and *de Thessal. ejusque agro*, Berol. 1839.

ἐν Θεῷ πατρὶ κ. τ. λ. must be closely joined with τῇ ἐκκλ. Θεσσ., to which it stands in the relation of a kind of tertiary predication (Donalds. *Gr.* § 489), and which it serves to distinguish from the πολλαὶ ἐκκλησίαι καὶ Ἰουδαϊκαὶ καὶ Ἑλληνικαί (Chrys.), which were in that

We thank God for your spiritual progress. The manner in which we preached, and ye heard the Gospel is now well known unto all men.

2 Εὐχαριστοῦμεν τῷ Θεῷ πάντοτε περὶ πάν-

city; ἐν Θεῷ πατρί, as De W. suggests, distinguishing it from the latter, καὶ Κυρ. κ. τ. λ., from the former. To connect these words with what follows (Koppe), or to understand χαίρειν λέγουσιν (Schott, — not Winer [Alford], who expressly adopts the right view) is arbitrary and untenable, and to supply τῇ or τῇ οὔσῃ (De W., Alf., compare Chrysost., Syr.), unnecessary, and even inexact, such unions without an article being by no means uncommon in the N. T.; see cxx. in Winer, *Gr.* § 20. 2, p. 123, and for the principle of such combinations, notes *on Eph.* i. 15. Commentators call attention to the fact, that the term ἐκκλ. occurs only in the addresses to Thess., 1 and 2 Cor., and Gal., while in the supposed later Epp. Rom., Eph., Phil., Col., the more individualizing τοῖς ἁγίοις κ. τ. λ. is adopted. The variation is slightly noticeable; it does not, however, seem to point to gradually altered views with regard to the attributes of the Church (Jowett), but merely to the present comparative paucity of numbers (compare Chrysost.), and their aggregation in a single assembly; compare Koch, p. 56, note. On the meaning and application of the term, see Pearson, *Creed*, Art. IX. Vol. I. p. 397, Jackson, (ed. Burt.) *Creed*, XII. 2. 1 sq.

χάρις ὑμῖν κ. τ. λ.] Scil. εἴη not ἔστω Schott); see notes *on Ephesians* i. 2. On the blended form of Greek and Hebrew greeting, see notes *on Galat.* i. 2, *Ephesians* i. 2. The reading is somewhat doubtful: *Rec.* adds ἀπὸ Θεοῦ πατρὸς ἡμῶν καὶ Κυρίου Ἰησοῦ Χριστοῦ on good external authority [AC (apparently) DEKL; Tol., Coptic, Syriac, (Philox., but with asterisk), Æthiop. (Platt); Chrysostom, al.]; the omission, however, is fairly supported [BFG; 47. 73. 115; Vulgate, Syriac, Æthiopic, Armenian; Chrysost. (comm.), Theophylact, al.], and, on critical grounds, decidedly preferable, as the uniqueness of the form in St. Paul's Epp. would be likely to suggest interpolation; comp. Col. i. 2.

2. εὐχαριστοῦμεν] '*We give thanks;*' compare Phil. i. 3, Col. i. 3, Philem. 4. It has been doubted whether the plural is to be understood of the Apostle alone (Koch, Conyb.), as in ch. ii. 18, iii. 1 sq., or to be referred also to Silvanus and Timothy. As the plural is elsewhere used in reference to the Apostle *and* his συνεργοί (comp. 2 Cor. i. 19, and notes *on Col.* i. 3), and as Silv. and Tim. stood in a very close relation to the Church of Thessalonica, it seems most natural here to adopt the latter view; so Lünem., and Alford, who, however, appears inexact in claiming all the ancient commentt., as Chrys. and the Greek expositors seem clearly, though indirectly, to adopt the former view. On the late use of the verb εὐχαριστεῖν in the sense of 'gratias agere,' see notes *on Phil.* i. 3, and esp. *on Col.* i. 12: the more correct χάριν ἔχω occurs 1 Tim. i. 12, 2 Tim. i 3, and Philem. 7 (*Tisch.*). These thanks are returned to God (the Father, compare Col. i. 3), ὡς αὐτὸς ἐργασάμενος τὸ πᾶν, Chrysost.; so 2 Thess. i. 3, 2 Tim. i. 3, and with the addition of μου, Rom. i. 8, 1 Cor. i. 4, Phil. i. 3, Philem. 4. πάντοτε κ. τ. λ. here obviously belongs to the finite verb (1 Cor. i. 4, 2 Thess. i. 3, comp. Eph. i. 16) not to the participle (Phil. i. 4, Col. i. 3, Philem. 4, compare Rom. i. 10). Even if the second ὑμῶν be omitted (*Lachm.*), the connection with the participle will be almost equally untenable, as the expression μνείαν ποιεῖσθαι περί τινος (though not unclassical, Plato, *Protag.* 317 E) is not elsewhere found in St. Paul's Epp.; so Syr., Æth., the Greek expositors (silet Theod.), and nearly all modern editors. On the allit-

των ὑμῶν, μνείαν ὑμῶν ποιούμενοι ἐπὶ τῶν προσευχῶν ἡμῶν,
3 ἀδιαλείπτως μνημονεύοντες ὑμῶν τοῦ ἔργου τῆς πίστεως καὶ τοῦ

eration πάντοτε περὶ πάντων, comp. notes *on Phil.* i. 4. περὶ πάντων ὑμῶν] '*concerning you all;*' not without slight emphasis, and affectionate cumulation; the Church of Thessalonica, like that of Philippi, presented but few unfavorable developments. The very εὐχαριστία was tacitly commendatory (τὸ εὐχαριστεῖν κ. τ. λ., μαρτυροῦντός ἐστιν αὐτοῖς πολλὴν προκοπήν, Chrys.), the inclusive nature of it still more expressly so. The difference between the use of περὶ (1 Cor. i. 4) and ὑπὲρ (Eph. i. 16) in this and similar formulæ in the N. T. is scarcely appreciable; see notes *on Eph.* vi. 19. Perhaps, as a general rule, we may say that in the former the attention is more directed to the object or circumstances to which the action of the verb extends, in the latter more to that action itself; see notes *on Gal.* i. 4, and *on Phil.* i. 7. μνείαν ὑμῶν ποιούμ.] '*making mention of you;*' not a limitation of the preceding εὐχαρ. πάντοτε, but a definition of the circumstances under which it took place; compare Rom. i. 9, Eph. i. 16, Philem. 4. For further remarks on the formula (not 'making mention of, *or* remembering,' Jowett, but simply the former, — as often in Aristotle, al.), see notes *on Philem.* 4, and for a distinction between μνήμη (γενικὴ τύπωσις ψυχῆς) and μνεία (λόγος κατ' ἀνανέωσιν λεγόμενος), Ammonius, *Voc. Diff.* p. 95 (ed. Valck.). The reading is slightly doubtful; *Lachm.* omits ὑμῶν with AB; 3 mss.; Amit., Harl.**, but apparently on insufficient evidence. It does not seem improbable that the presence of the former ὑμῶν suggested a supposed emendatory omission. ἐπὶ τῶν προσευχῶν] '*in my prayers,*' 'in orationibus,' Vulg., Copt. (compare Syr., Æth.), — not merely 'at the time I offer them,' but, with a tinge of local reference, 'in my performance of that duty;' see Bernhardy, *Synt.* v. 23 a, p. 246, and notes *on Eph.* i. 16. In such cases perhaps the prep. marks the object to which the action has reference, its point, so to say, of application; see Krüger, *Sprachl.* § 68. 40. 5.

3. ἀδιαλείπτως] '*unremittingly;*' used in the N. T. only by St. Paul, ch. ii. 13, v. 17, Rom. i. 9, and in all cases in direct (ch. v. 17) or indirect connection with prayer. The adverb is referred by Syr., Æth., Arm., and some modern expositors to the preceding participle, but far more naturally by Chrys. and the Greek commentators to μνημονεύοντες, each new clause serving to enhance and expand what had preceded; so *Lachm.*, *Tisch.*, *Buttm.*, and perhaps Copt., Vulg. Alford urges Rom. i. 9, but there the order is different. μνημονεύοντες] '*remembering,*' Auth. Ver., 'memores,' Vulg., Clarom.; participial clause parallel to the preceding μνείαν ποιούμενοι, and defining, not the cause (Schott), but the circumstances and *temporal* concomitants of the action: the εὐχαριστία found its utterance in the prayers, and owed its persistence (πάντοτε) to the unceasing continuance of the μνήμη. The first participle has thus more of a modal, the second of a temporal tinge; οὐ μόνον, φησίν, ἐπὶ τῶν προσευχῶν μου μέμνημαι ὑμῶν ἀλλὰ καὶ ἄλλοτε πάντοτε, Theoph. It has been doubted whether μνημον. is here 'commemorare' (Beza), or 'memor esse' (Vulg., Syr., Æth., Arm., and appy. Copt.), as in Heb. xi. 22 (but with περὶ and a gen.). The context (ἔμπροσθεν Θεοῦ κ. τ. λ.) seems slightly in favor of the former (De W., Alf.), but St. Paul's use of the verb, and the case after it (gen. not accus.), somewhat decidedly in favor of the latter; see Winer, *Gr.* § 30. 10, p. 184 (ed. 6),

κόπου τῆς ἀγάπης καὶ τῆς ὑπομονῆς τῆς ἐλπίδος τοῦ Κυρίου ἡμῶν

Jelf, *Gr.* § 512. obs., notes on ch. ii. 9, and *on* 2 *Tim.* ii. 8. The three objects of the Apostle's remembrance then follow in their natural order (so ch. v. 8, Col. i. 4, comp. Tit. ii. 2; aliter 1 Cor. xiii. 13), ἀγάπη being the result and exemplification of πίστις, and ἔλπις the link between the present and the future; see Reuss, *Théol. Chrét.* IV. 20, Vol. II. p. 219, and esp. Usteri, *Lehrb.* II. 1. 4, p. 238. ὑμῶν τοῦ ἔργου κ. τ. λ.] '*your work of faith,*' *i. e.*, 'which characterizes, is the distinctive feature of, faith;' compare Rom. ii. 15, and in point of sentiment, Gal. v. 6, πίστις δι' ἀγάπης ἐνεργουμένη. The precise meaning and connection of these words has been much contested. The simplest view seems to be as follows:—(1) Ὑμῶν is not immediately dependent on μνημον. (Œcum.), as this would involve an untenable ellipse of a prep. before the succeeding words (see Herm. *Viger*, p. 701, Lond. 1824), but is a possess. gen. in connection with τοῦ ἔργου, and also (as its slightly emphatic position suggests) τοῦ κόπου and τῆς ὑπομονῆς; see further exx. in Winer, *Gr.* § 22. 7. 1, p. 140 (2) Τοῦ ἔργου is certainly not pleonastic, but must stand in parallelism both in force and meaning (hence not 'veritas,' Kypke, *Obs.* Vol. II. p. 332) with the succeeding τοῦ κόπου (Winer, *Gr.* § 65. 7, p. 541), and has probably here not so much a collective (Syr. ܥܒ̈ܕܐ [opera]), as a *tinge* of active force, imparted both by the context and the following τοῦ κόπου; comp. Eph. iv. 12, Knapp, *Scripta Var. Arg.* Vol. II. p. 491, note, and Usteri, *Lehrb.* II. i. 4, p. 238. (3) Τῆς πίστεως is certainly not a gen. of *apposition* (Alf.), as it would thus lose all parallelism with the succeeding genitives, but is either (*a*) a gen. of the *origin* (Hartung, *Casus*, p. 17, comp. *on Col.* i. 23), 'quod ex fide proficiscitur,' Grot., or perhaps more simply (*b*), a *possessive* genitive, τοῦ ἐργοῦ being the prevailing feature and characteristic of the πίστις, and that by which it evinces its vitality; compare Chrys., ἡ πίστις διὰ τῶν ἔργων δείκνυται, who, however, with Theod., al., doubtfully limits τὸ ἔργον to endurance in sufferings, τὸ ἐν κινδύνοις βέβαιον, Theod. τοῦ κόπου τῆς ἀγάπης] '*the toil of love,*' *i. e.* (retaining the same genitival relation as in the preceding words) 'the toil which characterizes and evinces the vitality of love;' 'multum est per se *dilectio*, sed multo magis, si accedunt *molesti labores*, id enim κόπος,' Grot.; see notes *on* 1 *Tim.* iv. 10. The ἀγάπη is here not in reference to God, or to God *and* one another (compare Œcum.), but simply to the latter (Col. i. 4, Heb. vi. 10); and that, as evinced,—not merely in teaching (comp. De W.), or in bearing a brother's faults (Theod.), or in ministering to the sick, etc. (Alf.),—but, as the forcible κόπος seems to suggest, in ministering to, laboring for, and if need be, suffering for, a brother-Christian; comp. Chrysost. *in loc.* On the theological meaning and application of ἀγάπη (Vulgate 'caritas' or 'dilectio;' appy. never 'amor,' but consider August. *de Civ. Dei.* XIV. 7), see Reuss, *Théol. Chrét.* IV. 19, Vol. II. p. 203 sq., and comp. Barrow, *Serm.* XXVII. Vol. II. p. 44 sq. τῆς ὑπομ. τῆς ἐλπ.] '*the patience of Hope,*' *i. e.*, as before, 'the patience which is,'—not exactly the product (De W.), or the cause (Œcum.), but the distinguishing and characterizing feature of your hope; ὑπομένειν δὲ προσήκει τὸν ταύτην δεξάμενον τὴν ἐλπίδα, καὶ φέρειν γενναίως τὰ προσπίπτοντα σκυθρωπά, Theod. In the noble word ὑπομόνη, there always appears (in the N. T.) a background of ἀνδρεία (comp.

Ἰησοῦ Χριστοῦ ἔμπροσθεν τοῦ Θεοῦ καὶ πατρὸς ἡμῶν, 4 εἰδότες,

Plato, *Theæt.* p. 177 B, where ἀνδρικῶς ὑπομεῖναι is opp. to ἀνάνδρως φεύγειν); it does not mark merely the *endurance*, the 'sustinentiam' (Vulg.), or even the 'patientiam' (Clarom.), but the 'perseverantiam' (see Cicero, *de Invent.* II. 54 [163]), the *brave* patience with which the Christian contends against the various hindrances, persecutions (Chrysost.), and temptations (Theophyl.), that befall him in his conflict with the inward and outward world; compare Rev. ii. 3, and see notes *on* 2 *Tim.* ii. 10, and *on Tit.* ii. 2, and Neander, *Planting*, Vol. I. p. 479 (Bohn). In some cases it seems almost to occupy the place of ἐλπίς; compare 2 Thess. i. 4, 1 Tim. vi. 11, Tit. ii. 2, and for a full notice of other shades of meaning, Barrow, *Serm.* XLII. Vol. II. p. 525 sq. τοῦ Κυρίου κ. τ. λ. does not refer to the three preceding substantives (Olsh.), but merely to the immediately foregoing ἐλπίδος: our Lord was the object of that hope; His second coming was that to which it ever turned its gaze; comp. ver. 10, and see Reuss, *Théol. Chrét.* IV. 20, Vol. II. p. 221. For. exx. of this accumulation of genitives, esp. in St. Paul's Epp., see Winer, *Gr.* § 30. 3. 1, p. 172. ἔμπροσθεν κ. τ. λ.] '*before God and our Father*,' scil. μνημονεύοντες (Syr., Theoph. 1, Alf), not with τοῦ ἔργου τῆς πίστεως κ. τ. λ. (Theod., Theoph. 2, Jowett), as in such a case the article could *scarcely* be dispensed with. The formula ἔμπρ. τοῦ Θεοῦ, which only occurs in this Ep. (ch. iii. 9, 13, compare ch. ii. 19), and in Acts x. 4 (*Lachm.*, *Tisch.*), is scarcely distinguishable in meaning from the more usual ἐνώπιον τοῦ Θεοῦ, Rom. xiv. 22, Gal. i. 20, al., or the less usual ἔναντι τοῦ Θεοῦ, Luke i. 8, and Acts viii. 21 (*Lachm. Tisch.*): it serves to hint at the more solemn circumstances (of prayer) under which the remembrance took place, and to mark its sincerity and earnestness; it was no accidental or pretended μνεία, but one entertained in His presence, and in which His eyes saw no insincerity; comp. Calv. *in loc.*, and on the phrase generally, Frankel, *Vorstud. z. LXX.* p. 159. On the formula Θεὸς καὶ πατήρ, see notes *on Gal.* i. 4.

4. εἰδότες] '*seeing we know*,' or '*knowing as we do*;' ܝܕܥܝܢ ܓܝܪ [novimus enim], Syr.; participial clause parallel to μνημονεύοντες, and similarly dependent on εὐχαριστοῦμεν, serving to explain the reasons and motives which led to the εὐχαριστία. The finite verb has thus three participial clauses attached to it; the first serves principally to define the *manner*, the second the *time* and circumstances, the third the *reasons* and motives of the action. These delicate uses of the Greek participle deserve particular attention; comp. Krüger, *Sprachl.* § 56. 10 sq. It is somewhat singular that so good a commentator as Theodoret should refer εἰδότες to the Thessalonians; so also Grot., who refers the clause to the remote ἐγενήθητε, ver. 6. There is no trace of such a connection in any of the ancient Vv., except in Æth. (Polygl.). ἠγαπημένοι ὑπὸ Θεοῦ] '*beloved by God*;' comp. 2 Thess. ii. 13; so rightly Syr., Vulgate, Clarom., Copt., Æth. (Pol.), and inferentially Chrys. (ὑπὲρ γὰρ τῶν τοῦ Θεοῦ ἀγαπητῶν τί οὐκ ἄν τις πάσχοι). To connect ὑπὸ Θεοῦ with τὴν ἐκλογήν, as Æth. (Platt), Theophyl., and our own Auth. Ver., involves a disturbance of the natural order, and an ellipse of εἶναι that is here highly improbable. τὴν ἐκλογὴν ὑμῶν] '*your election*;' scil. out of others not ἐκλεκτοί, with reference to the sovereign decree of God made before the foundation of the world; see Eph. i. 4, and

ἀδελφοὶ ἠγαπημένοι ὑπὸ Θεοῦ, τὴν ἐκλογὴν ὑμῶν, 5 ὅτι τὸ εὐαγ-

notes *in loc.* To refer this merely to the *manner* of their election to the Gospel (Baumg.—Crus., Jowett 2), or to any internal renewing of the Spirit (Pelt), is in a high degree forced and unsatisfactory. On the use of the terms ἐκλέξασθαι, ἐκλογή, and ἐκλεκτοί, in St. Paul's Epp. see Reuss, *Theol. Chrét.* IV. 14, Vol. II. p. 132, and on the doctrine generally, the clear and mainly satisfactory statements of Ebrard, *Dogmatik*, § 560, 561; compare also the very valuable remarks of Hooker, *on Predest.* Vol. II. p. 705, sq. (ed. Keble), especially p. 711, 712.

5. ὅτι] '*in that*,' '*because*,' ܡܛܠ ܕ Syr., 'quia,' Vulg., and sim. Coptic Æthiopic, Armenian; reason for this knowledge on the part of St. Paul and his companions, ὅτι having here its causal force (Winer, *Gr.* § 53. 8. a., p. 395), and, with its regular objective characteristics (Krüger, *Sprachl.*, § 65. 8. 1), referring to known facts as confirmatory of a preceding assertion. The Apostle argues they must be elect, because (ver. 5) he and his companions were enabled to preach the Gospel among them with such power, and, secondly (ver. 6), because they received it with such joy; ἐκ τούτου φησί, δῆλον ὅτι ἐκλεκτοί ἐστε, ἐκ τοῦ τὸν Θεὸν τὸ κήρυγμα ἐν ὑμῖν δοξάσαι, Theoph. Others, as Beng., Schott, give ὅτι its expository force, 'that,' 'to wit that' (see Krüger, *Sprachl.* § 61. 1. 3), and place only a comma after ὑμῶν; in which case ver. 5 becomes an objective sentence (Donalds. *Gr.* § 584 sq), dependent on εἰδότες, and more distinctly explanatory of the nature of the ἐκλογή. This is grammatically tenable, but certainly not exegetically satisfactory, as the whole context seems to have more of a direct and argumentative than of a dependent and explanatory nature.

τὸ εὐαγγ. ἡμῶν] '*our gospel*,' 'the gospel which we preached;' the gen. being appy. that of the (mediate) *source* or *origin* (Hartung, *Casus*, p. 23), or perhaps rather the (mediate) *causa efficiens*; see notes on ver. 6.

ἐγενήθη εἰς ὑμᾶς] '*came unto you*;' not 'erga vos,' Calv., but simply 'ad vos,' Vulg., Copt., the preposition not having here its ethical force (compare Philem. 6), but simply marking the *direction* which was taken by the εὐαγγέλιον; compare Donaldson, *Cratyl.* § 170, and notes *on Galatians* iii. 14. The reading is very doubtful. Πρὸς is well supported, viz. by AC²DEFG; 5 mss.; Chrys., Theoph., (*Lachm.*, *Tisch.* ed. 1). As, however, εἰς appears a less probable correction for πρὸς than the converse, and is fairly supported by external authority [B, perhaps C¹, JK; nearly all mss.; Chrysostom (ms.), Theod., al., *Rec.*, *Griesb.*], we retain the reading of *Tisch.* (ed. 2). If πρὸς be adopted, the same meaning will be admissible (comp. 2 John 12, *Lachm.*, *Tisch.*), but will seem less probable than 'apud' (Clarom.; comp. 1 Cor. xvi. 10), as the general reference of the context is rather to the development of the Gospel among them than the circumstances of its first arrival; for this meaning of γίνεσθαι πρὸς in the N. T., which Alford seems to doubt, see Meyer *on* 1 *Cor.* ii. 3, and Fritz. *on Mark*, p. 201. On the passive *form* ἐγενήθη, which occurs noticeably often in this Epistle, but does not appy. involve any passive *meaning* (Alford), see Lobeck, *Phryn.* p. 108, Thomas M. p. 189 (ed Bern.), and notes *on Col.* iv. 11. ἐν λόγῳ] '*in word*;' not merely equivalent to λόγος (compare Jowett), but, as usual, with a reference to the sphere or domain of its action, 'non stetit intra verba,' Grot.; compare Winer, *Gr.* § 48. a, p. 345.

γέλιον ἡμῶν οὐκ ἐγενήθη εἰς ὑμᾶς ἐν λόγῳ μόνον, ἀλλὰ καὶ ἐν δυνάμει καὶ ἐν Πνεύματι ἁγίῳ καὶ ἐν πληροφορίᾳ πολλῇ, καθὼς

ἐν δυνάμει κ. τ. λ.] '*in power and in the Holy Ghost;*' 'in an element of power and, — to specify a yet higher principle (καὶ being not so much explanatory as slightly *climactic*, see on ver. 6), in the influence of the Holy Ghost;' the preposition, as before, defining the sphere, and thence *inferentially* the manner, in which the preaching took place; see notes on ch. ii. 3. Δυνάμει does not appear to refer specially to 'miraculous powers' (Theod., Theophyl., al.), but, as in the similar passage, 1 Cor. ii. 4, to the reality, energy, and effective earnestness with which the Apostle and his followers preached among the Thessalonians. Jowett defends the reference of ἐν δυν. to the influence produced on the Thess., but is thus led into an interpr. of ἐν Πνεύμ. ἁγίῳ, — 'the inspiration of the speaker caught by the hearers,' which, as tending to obscure the reference to the personal Πνεῦμα ἅγιον seems in a high degree precarious and unsatisfactory. On the use of Πνεῦμα as a proper name, see notes *on Galat.* v. 5, and compare Winer, *Gr.* § 19. 1, p. 111 (ed. 6). πληροφορίᾳ πολλῇ] '*much assurance,*' *i. e.* 'much confidence, much assured persuasion,' on the part of the preachers; *subjective*, corresponding to the more *objective* side presented in the preceding clause; comp. Heb. x. 22, πληροφορίᾳ πίστεως, which latter subst. Alford here unnecessarily inserts in translation. Of the *three* explanations which Jowett proposes, (*a*) certainty, (*b*) fulness of spiritual gifts, Corn. a Lap., al., (*c*) effect, fulfilment, Thom, Aq. 2, the first alone seems in harmony with the context, *if* limited to the Apostle and his companions. To refer it to the Thess. (Musc., compare Zanch. ap. Pol. *Syn.*), or to them *and* the Apostle (Vorst., Schott) seems to mar the correct sequence of thought, and to introduce notices of the state of the recipients which only come first into view in ver. 6. The word πληροφορία (Hesych. βεβαιότης) appears confined to the N. T. (Col. ii. 2, Heb. vi. 11, x. 22) and the ecclesiastical writers. καθὼς οἴδατε] '*even as ye know;*' 'appeal for confirmation to the knowledge of the readers themselves,' Olsh.; ὑμεῖς φησί, μάρτυρες πῶς ἐν ὑμῖν ἀνεστράφημεν, Theoph. To place a colon or period at πολλῇ, and to regard καθὼς οἴδατε as the antecedent member of a sentence of which καὶ ὑμεῖς is the consequent ('qualem me vidistis ..... tales etiam vos estis,' Koppe), involves untenable meanings of οἴδατε and ἐγενήθητε, and is well refuted by Lünemann *in loc.* οἷοι ἐγενήθημεν] '*what manner of men we proved;*' not 'quales fuerimus,' Vulg., nor yet quite so much as 'facti simus,' Alf. (who throws undue emphasis on the passive *form*), but with the more certain and natural sense, 'came to be, proved to be;' see above, and *on Col.* iv. 11. The ποιότης was not evinced merely in confronting dangers (Theod. compare Chrys.), but in the power and confidence with which they delivered their message. δι' ὑμᾶς] '*on your account,*' '*for your sake;*' 'propter vos,' Vulg.; not with so specific a force as ὑπὲρ ἡμῶν (compare Theod., who uses this latter formula in connection with κινδύνους ὑφεστάναι), nor yet one so undefined as περὶ ὑμῶν, but with a clear and distinct reference to the *cause* and best *interests* [sake, — Sax. *sac*, Germ. *Sache*] of those to whom the Apostle preached; τῆς ἐμῆς [ἡμετέρας] σπουδῆς τῆς εἰς ὑμᾶς ἢ ὑμῶν παρὰ Θεοῦ ἐκλογὴ πρόφασις γέγονεν, Œcum. The ἐν ὑμῖν, it need scarcely be said, is simply 'among you;' ἀνεστράφημεν ἐν ὑμῖν, Theoph.

οἴδατε οἷοι ἐγενήθημεν ἐν ὑμῖν δι' ὑμᾶς· 6 καὶ ὑμεῖς μιμηταὶ ἡμῶν

6. καὶ ὑμεῖς κ. τ. λ.] *'and ye became imitators of us;'* second ground for knowing that the Thess. were ἐκλεκτοί; the καὶ not being ascensive (compare *on Eph.* ii. 1), or equivalent to '*sic*, more Hebræo' (Grot.), but simply copulative, and the verse remaining, if not structurally, yet logically, under the vinculum of the preceding ὅτι. It thus seems best to place neither a period (*Tisch.*, *Alf.*) nor a comma (*Lachm.*, *Buttm.*), but a colon, after ver. 5. Here, as in ver. 5, Lün. and Alf. lay a stress on the passive form ἐγενήθητε, 'ye were made to receive.' This, however, is lexically doubtful; the Apostle is rather dwelling on the effects produced among them, on what they *came to be*, and thus significantly adopts not the simple verb μιμεῖσθαι, but the more definitive μιμηταὶ γίνεσθαι; see 1 Cor. iv. 16, xi. 1, Eph. v. 1, Phil. iii. 17. καὶ τοῦ Κυρίου] *'and of the Lord,'* tacit avoidance of any misunderstanding by means of the slightly climactic καί, see Hartung, *Partik* καί, 5. 4, Vol. I. p. 145. This use of the particle, which is strictly in accordance with its supposed derivation [*tshi*, 'cumulare,' comp. Pott, *Etym. Forsch.* Vol. II. p. 320], forms the sort of connecting link between its simply copulative and simply ascensive uses, and may perhaps be termed its *climactic* use, compare Fritz. *on Mark*, i. 5, p. 11. For a brief analysis of the leading distinctions in the use of this particle, see notes *on Phil.* iv. 12. The exact manner in which the Thessalonians became imitators of their founders — and of the Lord, is defined in the concluding words of the verse, ἐν θλίψει πολλῇ μετὰ χαρᾶς Πν. ἁγίου: joy *amid suffering and affliction* is the 'tertium comparationis;' comp. Acts v. 41, Heb. x. 34.

δεξάμενοι τὸν λόγον] *'having received the word:'* *temporal* use of the participle (see notes on *Ephesians* iv. 8), marking here the contemporaneousness of the action with that of the finite verb: the predication of *manner* is given in the following words; compare Romans iv. 20. It is scarcely necessary to add that τὸν λόγον is here practically equivalent to τὸν λόγον τοῦ Κυρίου (verse 8), τοῦ Θεοῦ (2 Corinthians ii. 17), or τῆς ἀληθείας (Ephesians i. 13), and refers to the preaching of the *gospel*, which was the λόγος, κατ' ἐξοχήν; comp. Luke viii. 13, Acts xvii. 11. On the force of δέξασθαι τὸν λόγον, and its probable distinction from παραλαβεῖν τ. λόγ., see notes on ch. ii. 13.

θλίψει πολλῇ] *'much affliction.'* The affliction of the Thessalonians dated back as early as their first reception of the gospel (see Acts xvii. 6), and, as this Epistle incidentally shows, continued both while the Apostle was with them (ch. ii. 14), and after he had left them (ch. iii. 2, 3). χαρᾶς Πνεύματος] *'joy of the Spirit;'* certainly not 'lætitiam de Spiritu,' Fritz. (*Nova Opusc.* p. 271), still less χαρὰ πνευματική (Jowett), but 'joy inspired by and emanating from the Spirit:' gen. of the *originating cause;* see notes *on Col.* i. 23. Between the two usual forms of the gen. of ablation, viz. (*a*) the stronger gen. of the *causa efficiens*, and (*c*) the weaker gen. *originis*, which forms the point of transition to the partitive genitive, it is perhaps not hypercritical in the N. T. to insert (*b*), a gen. of the *originating cause*, or, if the expression be permissible, the *originating agent*, — in which the two ideas of source and agency are blended and intermixed; consider the exx. cited in Scheuerl. *Synt.* § 17. 1, p. 126. With the present case, which appears to fall under form (*b*), — the Spirit being not only an external giver, but an internal source of the χαρά — contrast on the

ἐγενήθητε καὶ τοῦ Κυρίου, δεξάμενοι τὸν λόγον ἐν θλίψει πολλῇ
μετὰ χαρᾶς Πνεύματος ἁγίου,
7 ὥστε γενέσθαι ὑμᾶς τύπον πᾶσιν
τοῖς πιστεύουσιν ἐν τῇ Μακεδονίᾳ καὶ ἐν τῇ Ἀχαΐᾳ.
8 ἀφ' ὑμῶν

one hand, 2 Thess. ii. 13, ἁγιασμὸς Πνεύματος, where the verbal in -μος suggests the form (*a*), and on the other, Gal. v. 22, ὁ καρπὸς τοῦ Πνεύμ., where, if the gen. be not possessive, the image seems to suggest the weaker form (*c*). Such distinctions, which are not wholly without importance in the N. T., are really due as much to doctrinal, as to grammatical considerations; compare Winer, *Gr.* § 30. 1, p. 167 sq.

7. ὥστε γεν. τύπον.] '*so that ye became an ensample:*' spiritual progress of the Thessal. converts; they were not only imitators of the example of their teachers, but themselves (regarded as a collective body; comp. Winer, *Gr.* § 27. 1, p. 157 note) an example to others. This could hardly apply to those who had received the Gospel before them (οἱ προλαβόντες, Chrys., Theoph.), for, as Lünemann observes, the church of Philippi was the only one in Europe which received the Gospel before that of Thessalonica; comp. ch. ii. 2, Acts xvi. 12 sq. The reading is very doubtful; the plural τύπους is well supported [AC FGKL; Boern., Syriac (Philox.); many Ff.], but seems so much more likely to have been changed from the singular than vice versâ (Schott), that on the whole τύπον, though with less external authority [BD¹(D³E, and 1 mss. read τύπος); 3 mss.; Claromanus Sangerm., Vulg., Syr., Æthiop. (both), al, *Lachm.*, *Tisch.*,] is here to be preferred. πᾶσιν τοῖς πιστ.] '*to all the believers;*' πιστεύουσιν not having here a pure participial force, τοῖς ἤδη πιστεύουσι, Chrys., but, as often in the N. T., coalescing with the article to form a substantive; see Winer, *Gr.* § 45. 7, p. 316. Μακεδ. καὶ Ἀχ.] '*Macedonia and Achaia,*' *i. e.*, the whole of Greece; Acts xix. 21, Rom. xv. 26. comp. 2 Cor. ix. 2. Macedonia was at first (B. C. 167) divided by the Romans into four provinces, but subsequently (B. C. 142) reunited into one, comprising all the northern portion of Greece. Achaia proper was united with Hellas and the rest of the Peloponnese (B. C. 142) in one province, and as the leading state at that time gave the name to the whole southern portion of Greece; see Winer, *RWB.* Vol. I. p. 16, and Vol. II. p. 44. The omission of ἐν before τῇ Ἀχαΐᾳ (*Rec.*) has against it all the uncial MSS. except K and L; see *Tisch. in loc.*

8. ἀφ' ὑμῶν γάρ] '*For from you;*' proof and amplification of the preceding assertion. The preposition is here simply *local* (Alf.),—not ethical ('vobis efficientibus,' Storr; a very questionable paraphrase), nor both combined (Schott),—and marks the Thess. as the simple terminus a quo of the ἐξηχεῖσθαι. It may be observed that appy. in all cases in the N. T. where ἀπὸ is said to be equivalent to ὑπό, the action implied in the verb is represented as emanating from, rather than wrought by, the assumed agent; compare Luke vi. 18 (*Lachm.*, *Tisch.*), James i. 13, see Winer, *Gr.* § 47. b, p. 331, and notes *on Gal.* i. 1. ἐξήχηται] '*hath sounded forth;*' an ἅπ. λεγόμ. in the N. T. (Hesychius, ἐξῆλθεν· ἐκηρύχθη), but found in the LXX (Joel iii. 14, comp. Ecclus. xl. 13) and occasionally in later writers, *e. g.* Polyb. *Hist.* XXX. 4. 7, τὸ κύκνειον ἐξηχήσαντες. The word forcibly marks both the clear and the pervasive nature of the λόγος τοῦ Κυρίου; ὡς ἐπὶ σάλπιγγος λαμπρὸν ἠχούσης καὶ ἐπὶ πολὺ φθανούσης, Theoph. ὁ λόγος τοῦ Κυρίου] '*the word of the Lord,*' *i. e.* the gospel (see above, ver. 6) as received by

γὰρ ἐξήχηται ὁ λόγος τοῦ Κυρίου οὐ μόνον ἐν τῇ Μακεδονίᾳ καὶ

the Thess., not 'the report that it was received by them' (De W.), still less 'the message from the Lord' (Alf.),—both of which meanings seem needlessly artificial. The gospel was received by them with such eager zeal, its words were so constantly in their mouths, and so wrought in their hearts, that it swelled as it were into a mighty trumpet-call that was heard of all men sounding forth from Thessalonica. ἐν τῇ Μακ. καὶ 'Αχ.] Here the omission of the article and prepp. before 'Αχαΐᾳ is not only permissible (on the ground that the previous more exact specification of each would preclude any misconception), but really grammatically exact: Macedonia and Achaia now form a whole in antithesis to all the rest of the world; compare Winer, *Gr.* § 19. 4, p. 116 sq. The reading, however, is very doubtful; *Lachm.* inserts ἐν τῇ with strong external testimony [CDEFGKL; 30 mss.; Vulg., Clarom., Syr. (both), al.], but as the insertion of the ἐν τῇ would seem so much more likely to have been a conformation to ver. 7, than its omission to have been accidental, we retain the reading of *Tischend.*, though only with AB; majority of mss., some Vv; Chrysostom, Theod., al. ἀλλ' ἐν παντὶ κ. τ. λ.] There is some little difficulty in the exact connection, as ἀλλ' ἐν κ. τ. λ. seems clearly in immediate antithesis to οὐ μόνον κ. τ. λ. (opp. to Lünem., who places a colon after Κυρίου), but yet stands associated with a new nominative. The most simple explanation appears that of Rückert (*Loc. Paul Expl.* Jen. 1844), according to which the Apostle is led by the desire of making a forcible climax into a disregard of the preceding nominative, and in fact puts a sentence in antithesis to οὐ μόνον—'Αχαΐᾳ instead of a simple local clause, ἐν παντὶ τόπῳ, or ἐν ὅλῳ τῷ κόσμῳ (Rom. i. 8), as the strict logical connection actually required. *Rec.* inserts καὶ after ἀλλά, but on decidedly insufficient authority—viz. CD[3]EKL; Vulgate, Æthiopic, (both), and several Ff. On the distinction between this latter form ('ubi prior notio, non per se, sed quatenus sola est, negatur') and οὐ μόνον—ἀλλά ('ubi posterior notio, ut gravior, in locum prioris substituitur, priore non plane sublato') see the good note of Kühner on Xenoph. *Mem.* I. 6. 2, and correct accordingly in Jelf, *Gr.* § 762. 1; see also Klotz, *Devar.* Vol. II. p. 8. ἡ πρὸς τὸν Θεόν] '*which is toward God,*' '*to Godward,*' Auth.: more exact definition of the πίστις by means of the repeated article; compare Tit. ii. 10, notes *on Gal.* iii. 26, and Winer, *Gr.* § 20. 1. p. 119 sq. The less usual preposition πρὸς is here used with great propriety, as there is a tacit contrast to a previous faith, πρὸς τὰ εἴδωλα (see ver. 9), in which latter case the deeper πίστ. εἰς (faith *to* and *into,*—surely not 'on,' Alf.) would seem theologically unsuitable. On the meaning of πίστ. πρός, see notes *on Philem.* 5, and on the force of πίστις and πιστεύειν with different prepp., Reuss, *Théol. Chrét.* IV. 14, Vol. II. p. 129, and notes *on* 1 *Tim.* i. 16. ἐξελήλυθεν] '*is gone forth;*' so, with reference to a report, Matth. ix. 26, Mark i. 28, Rom. x. 18: Koch compares the Hebrew יָצָא, Ezek. xvi. 14. The currency of the report was probably much promoted by the commercial intercourse between Thess. and other cities, both in Greece and elsewhere; see Koch *in loc.*, and Wieseler, *Chronol.* p. 42, who suggests that Aquila and Priscilla, who had lately come from Rome (Acts xviii. 2), might have mentioned to the Apostle the prevalence of the report even in that more distant city. If this be so, the justice and truth of the

Ἀχαΐᾳ, ἀλλ' ἐν παντὶ τόπῳ ἡ πίστις ὑμῶν ἡ πρὸς τον Θεὸν ἐξελήλυθεν, ὥστε μὴ χρείαν ἔχειν ἡμᾶς λαλεῖν τι· 9 αὐτοὶ γὰρ

Apostle's hyperbole is still more apparent; to be known in Rome was to be known everywhere; contrast Baur, *Paulus*, p. 484. λαλεῖν τι] '*to speak anything*,' scil. about your πίστις, or, as Syr. ܥܠܝܟܘܢ [de vobis]; προὔλαβεν ἡμᾶς ἡ φήμη καὶ παρ' ἄλλων ἀκούομεν ἃ λέγειν ἐθέλομεν, Theodoret. On the difference between λαλεῖν and λέγειν, compare notes *on Tit.* ii. 1. The fundamental distinction that λαλεῖν (Hesych. φθέγγεσθαι) points merely to *sound* and *utterance*, λέγειν to *purport*, is mainly observed in the N. T. with this exception, that λαλεῖν is *sometimes* used where λέγειν would appear more natural, but never vice versâ; see esp. the good note of Lücke *on John*, viii. 43. The position of ἡμᾶς after ἔχειν is supported by overwhelming uncial authority.

9. αὐτοί] '*they themselves*;' *i. e.* the people in Macedonia and Achaia and elsewhere; a very intelligible 'constructio ad sensum;' see Winer, *Gr.* § 22. 3, p. 131, and notes *on Gal.* ii. 2. The interpr. of Pelt, 'sponte,' αὐτομαθῶς, is here artificial and unnecessary; αὐτοὶ stands in somewhat emphatic antithesis to the preceding ἡμᾶς; '*we* have no need to say anything about you, for *they* to whom otherwise we might have told it, themselves speak of it and spread it; οὐ παραμένουσιν ἀκοῦσαι περὶ ὑμῶν ἀλλὰ τοὺς παρόντας καὶ τεθεαμένους τὰ ὑμέτερα κατορθώματα, οἱ μὴ παρόντες μηδὲ τεθεαμένοι παραλαμβάνουσιν, Chrys. περὶ ἡμῶν] '*about us*,' scil. the Apostle and his helpers; not 'de me et vobis simul,' Zanch. (compare Lünem., — well answered by Alf.), as the studied prominence of περὶ ἡμῶν and the real point of the clause are thus completely overlooked; instead of our telling about our own success, they do it for us; ἃ γὰρ αὐτοὺς ἐχρῆν παρ' ἡμῶν ἀκούειν, ταῦτα αὐτοὶ προλαβόντες λέγουσι, Chrys. ὁποίαν εἴσοδ. ἔσχ.] '*what manner of entering in we had unto you*;' fuller explanation of the preceding περὶ ἡμῶν. The reference of the qualitative ὁποίαν to the dangers and sufferings undergone by St. Paul and his followers in their first preaching at Thess. (Chrys., Theoph., Œcum.) is rightly rejected by most modern commentators; the ποιότης is rather evinced in the power and confidence with which they preached, and serves to illustrate ver. 5. Εἴσοδος has here no ethical meaning, 'indolem nostram,' Æth. (Pol.), comp. Olsh., but, as always in the N. T. (ch. ii. 1, Acts xiii. 24, Heb. x. 19, 2 Pet. i. 11), is simply local in its reference, 'introitus,' Vulg., Arm., 'ingressus,' Copt., 'quomodo venimus ad vos,' Æth. (Platt): so too, inferentially, the Greek commentators, and after them most modern writers. The present ἔχομεν (*Rec.*) appy. rests only on the authority of cursive mss., and is rejected by all modern editors. πῶς ἐπεστρέψατε] '*how ye turned*;' illustration of ver. 6. The πῶς does not necessarily involve εὐκόλως, μετὰ πολλῆς σφοδρότητος, Chrysost., 'quantâ facilitate,' Calv., but simply points to the fact of ἐπιστροφή (Alf.), the clause not being modal, but objective; compare Donalds. *Gr.* § 584. In the verb ἐπιστρέφειν the prep. does not *here* seem to mark regression (comp. *on Gal.* iv. 2), but simply *direction*; both meanings are lexically admissible (see Rost u. Palm, *Lex.* s. v., and s. v. ἐπί, c), but the second seems most in accordance with the context. πρὸς τὸν Θεὸν marks the conversion in its general, rather than its specifically Christian aspects, with reference to the former heathen and Gentile condition of the

περὶ ἡμῶν ἀπαγγέλλουσιν ὁποίαν εἴσοδον ἔσχομεν πρὸς ὑμᾶς, καὶ
πῶς ἐπεστρέψατε πρὸς τὸν Θεὸν ἀπὸ τῶν εἰδώλων δουλεύειν Θεῷ
ζῶντι καὶ ἀληθινῷ,
10 καὶ ἀναμένειν τὸν υἱὸν αὐτοῦ ἐκ τῶν οὐρανῶν, ὃν ἤγειρεν ἐκ τῶν νεκρῶν, Ἰησοῦν τὸν ῥυόμενον ἡμᾶς ἀπὸ τῆς ὀργῆς τῆς ἐρχομένης.

Thessalonians: if they had been Jews, the appropriate formula, as Olsh. well observes, would have been πρὸς τὸν Κύριον. On this and the following verse, a sound sermon will be found by Sherlock, *Serm.* LIII. Vol. III. p. 56 (ed. Hughes). δουλεύειν κ. τ. λ.] '*to serve the living and true God;*' infinitive of the purpose or intention, εἰς τὸ δουλεύειν κ. τ. λ., Chrys., — a form of the final sentence (Donalds. *Gr.* § 606) not uncommon in St. Paul's Epp.; see 1 Cor. i. 17, Eph. i. 4, Col. i. 22. On the difference between this and the infin. with ὥστε (consecutive sentence), see notes *on Col. l. c.*, and compare Winer, *Gr.* § 44. 1 (ed. 6), but more fully, § 45. 3 (ed. 5). God has here the appropriate title of ζῶν (Acts xiv. 15), in contrast with the dead (Wisdom xiv. 29, 5, comp. Habak. ii. 9) and practically non-existent (1 Cor. viii. 4, see Meyer *in loc.*) gods of the heathen, — and that of ἀληθινός (John xvii. 3, 1 John v. 20, comp. 2 Chron. xv. 3), in contrast to their false semblance (Gal. iv. 8) and ματαιότης (אֱלִילִם Lev. xix. 4, xxvi. 1). On the omission of the art. with Θεός, compare Winer, *Gr.* § 19. 1, p. 110.

10. ἀναμένειν] '*to await;*' second great purpose involved in the ἐπιστροφή; hope of the nature here described, as Lünem. observes, involves and includes faith, and forms a suitable preparation for the allusions in the latter portion of the Epistle. If χαρὰ be said to be the key-note of the Ep. to the Phil. (iii. 1), ἐλπὶς may truly be termed that of the present Ep. The verb ἀναμένειν, an ἅπ. λεγόμ. in the N. T., does not here involve any reference to awaiting one who is to *return* (comp. Beng.), nor yet any specific notion of eagerness or joy (Flatt), but simply that of patience ('*er*harren,' Winer) and confidence; the ἀνὰ having that modified intensive force (προσμένειν, Theod. [1 Tim. i. 3], περιμένειν, Theoph. [Acts i. 4]), which is so hard to convey without paraphrase; see esp. Winer, *de Verb. Comp.* III. p. 15, and comp. Rost u. Palm, *Lex.* s. v. ἀνά, E. b. ἐκ τῶν οὐρανῶν belongs to ἀναμένειν, involving a slight, but perfectly intelligible, form of brachyology, scil. ἐρχόμενον ἐκ τῶν οὐρ.; compare Winer, *Gr.* § 66. 2, p. 547. ὃν ἤγειρεν κ. τ. λ.] '*whom He raised from the dead:*' relative-sentence placed emphatically before Ἰησοῦν as involing an 'argumentum palmarium' (Beng.) of His sonship; see Rom. i. 4, and compare Pearson, *Creed,* Art. V. Vol. I. p. 313 (ed. Burton). The article before νεκρῶν is omitted by *Rec.* with ACK.: mss.; Œc., but is supported by preponderating external evidence [BDEFGL.; majority of mss.; Ff.], and by the probability of a confirmation to the more usual ἐγείρειν ἐκ νεκρῶν. Ἰησοῦν τὸν ῥυόμ.] '*Jesus who delivereth us.*' The present participle has not the force of an aor. ('qui eripuit,' Vulg., Arm.) or future part. ('qui eripiet,' Clarom., 'qui liberabit,' Copt.), but may serve (*a*) to mark the action as commenced and continuing (Vorst.), or (*b*) as 'rem *certo* futuram' (Schott), or still more probably, (*c*) is associated with the article in a substantival character, 'our deliverer,' Alf.; see Winer, *Gr.* § 45. 7, p. 316. τῆς ἐρχομένης] '*which is coming;*' more specific definition of

Our entrance was not empty; we neither beguiled you nor were burdensome, but toiled bravely, and encouraged you both by actions and words.

II. Αὐτοὶ γὰρ οἴδατε, ἀδελφοί, τὴν εἴσοδον
ἡμῶν τὴν πρὸς ὑμᾶς, ὅτι οὐ κενὴ γέγονεν,
2 ἀλλὰ προπαθόντες καὶ ὑβρισθέντες καθὼς

the ὀργή; εἶπε τὴν ἀνάστασιν, λέγει καὶ τὴν ἀνταπόδοσιν, ἣν ἡμέραν ὀργῆς καλεῖ, Œcum. The present participle has no future tinge, *e. g.* = μελλούσης (Olsh., Koch), but marks the certainty of the coming (Bernhardy, *Synt.* x. 2, p. 371), and hints at the enduring principles of the moral government of God; comp. Eph. v. 6, Col. iii. 6. The powerful term ὀργὴ is not merely synonymous with κόλασις or τιμωρία (Orig. *Cels.* IV. p. 211; compare Lünem.), but implies definitely the holy anger of God against sin, — that anger which, deeply considered, only serves to evince His love; see esp. Müller, *Doctr. of Sin,* I. 2. 2, Vol. I. p. 265 (Clark).

CHAPTER II. 1. Αὐτοὶ γὰρ οἴδατε] *'For ye yourselves know;'* explanatory confirmation of the first part of ch. i. 9, by an appeal to the knowledge and experience of his readers. In ch. i. 9, two distinct subjects are alluded to, (*a*) the power and confidence of the preachers, (*b*) the obedience and receptivity of the hearers, compare Chrys.; the former is amplified in the present and eleven following verses, the latter in ver. 13—16. Γὰρ is thus certainly not resumptive, nor yet explicative, but what Hartung (*Partik.* γάρ, § 2) terms 'argumentativ-explicativ,' the ἄρα element of the particle referring to what had preceded ('quasi pro re natâ jam recte atque ordine hoc ita se habere dicitur,' Klotz), the γὲ element adding an explanatory asseveration; see esp. Klotz, *Devar.* Vol. II. p. 235. If the distinction of Hand (*Tursell.* Vol. II. p. 375) be correct, 'nam ipsi,' Vulg., is here a judicious correction of 'ipsi enim, Clarom. ὅτι οὐ κενὴ γέγ.] *'that it was not empty,'* *i. e.* void of power and earnestness; 'non inanis, sed plena virtutis,' Beng. In this form of the objective sentence, — by no means uncommon after verbs of 'knowledge, perception,' etc., there is an idiomatic anticipation of the object, which serves to awaken the reader's attention to the subsequent predications; see esp. Krüger, *Sprachl.* § 61. 6. 2. For other forms of the objective sentence, see Donalds. *Gr.* § 592. The exact meaning of κενὴ has been somewhat differently estimated: it can scarcely involve any ethical reference ('deceitful,' Hammond, μῦθοι ψευδεῖς καὶ λῆροι, Œcum.), or any allusion to accompany dangers (Theod., Theophyl.), or yet the results of the εἴσοδος (De Wette 1), as these belong to the second part of ver. 9, — but, as γέγονεν and the leading idea in the following words (ἐπαῤῥησ. ἐν τῷ Θεῷ κ. τ. λ.) both suggest, to the essential character of the εἴσοδος, its fulness of power and purpose and reality; οὐκ ἀνθρωπίνη οὐδὲ ἡ τυχοῦσα, Chrys. So rightly De Wette 2, Lünem., and Alf.

2. ἀλλὰ introduces the antithesis to the preceding οὐ κενὴ γέγονεν; see 1 Cor. xv. 10. προπαθ. καὶ ὑβρισθ.] *'having suffered previously and having been injuriously treated,'* Acts xvi. 20, 21 sq.; 'id quod alios a prædicando deterrere potuisset,' Beng. It is doubtful whether the participle is here concessive ('although we had,' etc., Lünem.; see Plato, *Rep.* II. p. 376), or simply temporal. If καὶ (*Rec.*) were to be admitted in the text before the part., the former meaning would seem more probable, as in such cases the καὶ (though not = καίπερ, De W.) serves to sharpen the antithesis involved in the concession (see Krüger, *Sprachl.* § 56. 13. 1 seq.); as, however, καὶ has no uncial authority,

οἴδατε ἐν Φιλίπποις, ἐπαρρησιασάμεθα ἐν τῷ Θεῷ ἡμῶν λαλῆσαι πρὸς ὑμᾶς τὸ εὐαγγέλιον τοῦ Θεοῦ ἐν πολλῷ ἀγῶνι. 3 ἡ γὰρ

3. οὐδὲ (2nd)] So *Lachm.* with ABCD¹FG; 6 mss.; Copt. (*Tisch.* ed. 1). The reading is, however, very doubtful. *Tisch.* (ed. 2, 7) reads οὔτε with D³EJK; nearly all mss.; Chrys. (aliquoties), Theod. (οὔτε—οὔτε), Dam., al. (*Rec.*, *Alf.*), and with some plausibility, as οὐδὲ might be thought a correction for οὔτε, which, though unusual, is here deemed not indefensible (comp. *Schott*, *Alf.*); still, as this defence rests mainly on a doubtful use of ἐν, — as a recognition of the change of prepp. *might* have suggested a change from οὐδὲ to οὔτε nearly as probably as a non-recognition of it the converse, — and lastly, as the uncial authority *very* distinctly preponderates in favor of οὐδέ, we revert to the reading of *Tisch.* (ed. 1). So *Winer* (*Gr.* § 55. 6, p. 437), *Olsh.*, *De W.*, *Lünem.*, *Koch.*

the simple participle seems here more naturally regarded as temporal; comp. Xenoph. *Mem.* II. 2. 5. So Auth., and appy. Syr., Copt. The verb προπάσχειν is an ἅπ. λεγόμ. in the N. T., though not uncommon elsewhere (Thucyd. III. 67, Xenoph. *l. c.*, Plato, *l. c.*), and serves clearly to define the relation of time; ἀπὸ κινδύνων ἐκφυγόντες πάλιν εἰς ἑτέρους κινδύνους ἐνεπέσομεν; compare Syr. and Æth. (Platt). To this ὑβρισθ. gives an additional force and circumstantiality.

ἐπαρρησιασάμεθα] '*we were bold of speech;*' so distinctly Æth. (Pol., but not Platt). It seems more exact to retain this primary meaning: for though παρρησία has indisputably in the N. T. the derivative meaning of *confidence*, *boldness* (see *on Eph.* iii. 12), still, by comparing Eph. vi. 20, and Acts xxvi. 26 (a speech of St. Paul's), the idea of bold *speech*, even though reiterated in λαλῆσαι, can scarcely be excluded. This παρρησία was ἐν τῷ Θεῷ ἡμῶν; it was *in Him* (not exactly 'per Deum,' Schott 1), as the causal sphere and ground of its existence, that the παρρησία was felt and manifested. On the particularizing ἡμῶν, see notes *on Philem.* 6, and *on Phil.* i. 3.

λαλῆσαι] '*so as to speak;*' explanatory infinitive, defining still more clearly the *oral* nature of the boldness; see Winer, *Gr.* § 44. 1, p. 285; so rightly De W., Meyer (*on Eph.* vi. 20), and Koch, who, however, by his reference to Winer, *Gr.* p. 379 (ed. 5), confounds this use with that of the inf. with the art. τοῦ. Lünem., Alf., and others, far less plausibly, consider the inf. as a simple object infin. after ἐπαρρησ. The ancient Vv. here give no distinct opinion, except, perhaps, Syr. (Philox.), 'in fiducia (?) in Deo nostro, loqui,' etc., where the inf. seems clearly regarded as explanatory: so too (appy.) Chrys.

τὸ εὐαγγ. τοῦ Θεοῦ] '*the Gospel of God;*' the Gospel which cometh from Him, and of which He is the origin; gen. not of the object (Chrys. *on Rom.* i. 1), but of the *origin* or *originating cause;* see notes on ch. i. 6. On the various genitives associated wlth εὐαγγ., comp. Reuss. *Théol Chrét.* IV. 8, Vol. II. p. 81.

ἐν πολλῷ ἀγῶνι] '*in much conflict;*' not without emphasis: it was this fortitude amidst external dangers that peculiarly evinced that the εἴσοδος οὐ κενὴ γέγονεν. It does not seem necessary here to refer ἀγὼν to any internal conflict (compare *on Col.* ii. 1), but simply, in accordance with the context, to the *external* dangers by which they were surrounded; so Theophyl., Œcum.: Chrys. appears to unite both.

3. ἡ γὰρ παράκλ. ἡμῶν] '*for our exhortation;*' explanatory confirmation (see on ver. 1) of ἐπαρρ. κ. τ. λ., especially of the concluding words; οἱ

παράκλησις ἡμῶν οὐκ ἐκ πλάνης οὐδὲ ἐξ ἀκαθαρσίας οὐδὲ ἐν
δόλῳ, 4 ἀλλὰ καθὼς δεδοκιμάσμεθα ὑπὸ τοῦ Θεοῦ πιστευθῆναι

πλανῶντες οὐκ εἰς κινδύνους ἑαυτοὺς ἐκδιδόασιν, Œcum., compare Chrys. There is here, as Bengel acutely observes, an 'ætiologia duplex,' the present γὰρ introducing a reference to the apostle's regular habit, the second γὰρ (ver. 5) to that habit as specially evinced among the Thessalonians. The word παράκλησις here includes 'totum præconium evangelicum' (Beng.), and approaches in meaning to διδαχή (Chrys.), or διδασκαλία (Theod.), from both of which, however, it is perhaps distinguishable, as directed more to the feelings than the understanding: compare notes *on* 1 *Tim*. iv. 13. A good dissertation on παρακαλεῖν, παράκλησις, and παράκλητος, will be found in Knapp, *Scripta Var. Argum.* No. IV.; see esp. p. 134.

οὐκ ἐκ πλάνης] '*is not of error;*' not, 'grounded on,' Alf. 1, but, 'having its source in,' Alf. 2, the prep. retaining its usual and primary force of *origination from;* see notes *on Gal.* ii. 16, Winer, *Gr.* § 47. b, p. 329 (ed. 6). The verb to be supplied is not ἦν (Syr., Æth.), but ἐστίν (Copt.); as the apostle is here referring to his general and habitual mode of preaching; see above. Lastly, πλάνη is not transitive, 'impostura,' Beza, 'seducendi studium,' Grot. (compare Theoph.), but, as appy. in nearly all passages in the N. T., intransitive, 'error,' Vulg., ܛܘܥܝܐ [error] Syr., the context serving to show whether it is in the more abstract sense of 'mentis error' ('Irrthum'), as in Eph. iv. 14, or as here in the more general meaning of 'being deceived' (Irrwhan, delusion), whether by oneself or others; comp. Theod., οὐκ ἔοικε τὰ παρ' ἡμῶν προσφερόμενα τῇ μυθολογίᾳ τῶν ποιητῶν, ἃ πολλοῦ μὲν ψεύδους πολλῆς δὲ ἀκολασίας ἐμπέπλησται.

ἀκαθαρσίας] '*impurity,*' almost '*impure motives;*' not apparently with any reference to the *unclean* and licentious teaching of μάγων καὶ γοήτων, Theoph. (compare Chrys.), but, as ἐν προφάσει πλεονεξίας (ver. 5) seems to suggest, with reference to moral impurity, more especially as evinced in coveteousness (Olsh.) and desire of gain (Lünem., Alf.); comp. the term αἰσχροκερδής in ref. to Christian teachers, 1 Tim. iii. 8, Tit. i. 7, and the charges that appear to have been brought against the apostle himself, 2 Cor. xi. 8 sq.

οὐδὲ ἐν δόλῳ] '*nor in guile,*' *i. e.* 'in any deliberate intention to deceive;' not so much with reference to 'the *manner* in which' (Alf.), as to the (ethical) sphere in which the παράκλησις was found, and by which it was, as it were, environed; comp. 2 Cor. iv. 2, μὴ περιπατοῦντες ἐν πανουργίᾳ μηδὲ δολοῦντες τὸν λόγον τοῦ Θεοῦ, a somewhat instructive parallel. The use of ἐν, especially with abstract or non-personal substantives, is always somewhat debateable in the N. T., and can only be fixed by the context; it sometimes librates *towards* διά, both with gen. (1 Pet. i. 5) and acc. (Matth. vi. 7), sometimes, towards μετά (Col. iv. 2, see notes), sometimes, but appy. very rarely, towards κατὰ (Heb. iv. 11),—but is commonly best referred to the imaginary sphere in which the action takes place; see Winer, *Gr.* § 48, a, p. 345, and Rost u. Palm, *Lex.* s. v., where this prep. is very fully discussed. On the reading of this passage, see crit. note, and on the most suitable transl. of οὐ—οὐδέ, notes to *Transl.*

4. καθὼς δεδοκιμ.] '*according as we have been approved;*' οὐκ αὐτοχειροτόνητοι διδάσκαλοι καθεστήκαμεν, ἀλλ' ὑπὸ τοῦ Θεοῦ τὸ εὐαγγέλιον ἐπιστεύθημεν, Theod. Καθὼς (see *on Gal.* iii. 6)

τὸ εὐαγγέλιον, οὕτως λαλοῦμεν, οὐχ ὡς ἀνθρώποις ἀρέσκοντες
ἀλλὰ Θεῷ τῷ δοκιμάζοντι τὰς καρδίας ἡμῶν. 5 Οὔτε γάρ ποτε

has here no argumentative force (Eph. i. 3, see notes), but stands in correlation to οὕτως, marking the measure or proportion existing between their approval by God to preach the Gospel, and their actual performance of the commission. The idea of a recognition of any worth on the part of God in the δεδοκιμασμένοι (Chrys., Theoph., Œcum.) is certainly here not necessarily involved in the word. Δοκιμάζειν is properly,(*a*) 'to put to the test' (Eph. v. 10, 1 Tim. iii. 10), thence, by an easy gradation, (*b*) 'to choose after testing,' which again passes insensibly into (*c*) 'to approve of what is so tested:' comp. Rom. xiv. 22, 1 Cor. xvi. 3, and notes *on Phil.* i. 10. In the present case, the appended notice of the subject in respect of which the δοκιμασία was exercised, seems clearly to limit the meaning to (*b*): ἐπειδὴ ἔδοξεν αὐτῷ καὶ ἐδοκίμασε πιστεῦσαι ἡμῖν, Theod. πιστευθῆναι τὸ εὐαγγ.] *'to have the Gospel entrusted to us,'* compare 1 Tim. i 11, Tit. i. 3: explanatory infinitive serving to define more nearly that to which the δοκιμασία was directed, see Winer, *Gr.* § 44. 1, p. 285; compare Madvig, *Synt.* § 148. For remarks on, and exx. of the idiomatic construction of the accus. *rei* with πιστεύομαι and similar verbs, see Winer, *Gr.* § 32. 5, p. 204.

ὡς ἀνθ. ἀρέσκοντες] *'as busied in pleasing men;'* the present tense having here its fullest force, and marking that which they were engaged in, were seeking to do; ἀρέσκειν θέλοντες, Theoph.; see Scheuerl. *Synt.* § 31. 2, p. 313, and comp. notes *on Gal.* i. 10. The particle ὡς, as usual, serves to characterize the action, and to define the *aspect* in which the whole was to be regarded, 'not as striving to please men, but (as striving to please) God,' etc.; compare Bernhardy, *Synt.* VII. 2, p. 333, and notes *on Col.* iii. 23.

τῷ δοκιμ. κ. τ. λ.] *'who proveth, trieth our hearts;'* δοκιμ. here relapsing back to its primary meaning, see above. The plural ἡμῶν can here scarcely be referred otherwise than to St. Paul *and* his fellow preachers at Thessalonica: if the sentence had been general, it would have been omitted (Rom. viii. 27); if the reference were simply to St. Paul, the plurals καρδίας and ψυχὰς (ver. 8) would seem wholly inappropriate. The insertion of the art. before Θεῷ (*Rec.*), though well attested [AD³EFG KL], seems due to grammatical corection, and is rightly rejected by *Tisch.* and [*Lachm* ].

5. Οὔτε γὰρ κ. τ. λ.] Confirmation of this general character of his and their apostolic teaching by a special appeal to the experience of his readers; compare ver. 3. ἐγενήθημεν ἐν] *'did we take part in,' 'came we to share in;'* scarcely 'were we found employed in,' Alf. (compare Lünem.), as the more distinct passive meaning cannot safely be maintained; see notes *on Eph.* iii. 7. The Greek commentators (Chrys., Theoph.) paraphrase it simply by ἐκολακεύσαμεν; this, however, somewhat falls short of the idiomatic γίγνομαι ἐν, 'in aliquâ re versor' (Matth. *Gr.* § 577. 5, Vol. II. p. 1004), and fails to mark the entrance into, and existenee in the given thing or condition; see notes *on* 1 *Tim.* ii. 14.

λόγῳ κολακείας] *'speech of flattery,'* 'sermone adulationis,' Vulg., Syr., 'verbo adulationis,' Copt., 'blanditiis usi sumus in voce,' Æth. (Platt); λόγος having here its simple and proper meaning of 'speech,' 'teaching' (not coextensive with Heb. דָבָר, — a use apparently not found in the N. T.), and κολακείας being a gen. — not of quality ('assentatorio,' Beza), nor of origin ('ex adulandi studio profecto,' Schott),

ἐν λόγῳ κολακείας ἐγενήθημεν, καθὼς οἴδατε, οὔτε ἐν προφάσει
πλεονεξίας, Θεὸς μάρτυς, 6 οὔτε ζητοῦντες ἐξ ἀνθρώπων δόξαν,
οὔτε ἀφ' ὑμῶν, οὔτε ἀπ' ἄλλων, δυνάμενοι ἐν βάρει εἶναι ὡς Χρισ-

but of the *substance* and *contents;* comp. 2 Cor. vi. 7, Eph. i. 13, al.; and see Scheuerl. *Synt.* § 12. 1, p. 182, Hartung, *Casus*, p, 21. The word κολακεία [possibly connected with κλείειν, Pott, *Etymol. Forsch.* Vol. I. p. 233, or with κόλος, κλάω in sense of broken-spiritedness, *cringing*] is an ἅπ. λεγόμ. in the N. T., and is defined in Pseud.-Plat. *Def.* Vol. IX. p. 272 (ed. Bekk.), as ὁμιλία ἡ πρὸς ἡδονὴν ἄνευ τοῦ βελτίστου; compare Theoph. *Charact.* 2. It serves here more specifically to illustrate the ἐν δόλῳ of ver. 3, and forms a natural transition to the next words, the essence of κολακεία being self-interest; ὁ δὲ ὅπως ὠφέλειά τις αὐτῷ γίγνηται εἰς χρήματα καί ὅσα διὰ χρημάτων, κόλαξ, Aristotle, *Ethic. Nicom.* IV. 12 (ad. fin.), compare VIII. 9. ἐν προφάσει πλεον.] '*in a cloak of coveteousness;*' 'prætextu specioso quo tegeremus avaritiam,' Beng. The exact meaning of these words is not perfectly clear. Πρόφασις is not here 'occasio,' Vulg., Clarom., nor 'accusatio,' Hamm, nor even 'species,' Wolf, still less is otiose, Loesn. (*Obs.* p. 376), but has its simple and usual meaning of 'prætextus' comp. Copt.; ܥܠܬܐ Syr. is somewhat indef.), while the gen. πλεονεξίας is a gen. *objecti* (compare Scheuerl. *Synt.* § 17. 1, p. 126) serving to define that to which the πρόφασις was applied, and which it was intended to mask and conceal; comp. Xenoph. *Cyr.* II. 1. 25, πρόφασις μειονεξίας, and see exx. in Rost u. Palm, *Lex.* s. v. (b), Vol. II. p. 1251. The apostle and his companions used no λόγος which contained κολακεία, nor any pretext which was intended to cloak their πλεονεξία. On the true meaning of πλεονεξία, see notes *on Eph.* iv. 19, and on its distinction from φιλαργυρία, Trench, *Synon.* § 24. Θεὸς μάρτυς] '*God is* (*our*) *witness;*' strong confirmation of the declaration immediately preceding; comp. Rom. i. 9, Phil. i. 8. The Greek commentators pertinently remark, that, in what men could judge of, he appeals to his readers, but, in what they could not so distinctly recognize, he appeals to God; ὅπερ ἦν δῆλον, αὐτοὺς καλεῖ μάρτυρας· εἰ ἐκολακεύσαμεν ὑμεῖς οἴδατε, φησίν· ὅπερ δὲ ἄδηλον ἦν, τὸ ἐν τρόπῳ (?) πλεονεξίας, Θεὸν καλεῖ μάρτυρα, Chrys.

6. οὔτε ζητοῦντες κ.τ.λ.] '*neither seeking glory from men;*' continued notice, on the negative side, of his characteristics of his own and the companions' ministry; ζητοῦντες being dependent on the preceding ἐγενήθημεν, and the clause serving to illustrate οὐχ ὡς ἀνθρ. ἀρέσκ., ver. 4. It is very difficult *here* to substantiate any real distinction between ἐξ and ἀπὸ. The assertion of Schott and Olsh. that ἐκ refers to the immediate, ἀπὸ to the more remote, origin is true (see *on Gal.* ii. 16), but here inapplicable; that of Lünem. and Alf.,—that ἐκ points to what is abstract and general, ἀπὸ to what is concrete and special,—is artificial and precarious. It would really seem more probable that they are here synonymous (Winer, *Gr.* 50. 2, p. 365), and that while in the first clause ἐκ might seem more idiomatic in immediate union with ζητεῖν, the disjunctive clauses into which it is expanded might admit and be lightened by the change to ἀπό. St. Paul's love of prepositional variation has often been noticed; compare Winer, *Gr.* § 50. 6, p. 372, notes *on Gal.* i. 1. δυνάμενοι ἐν βάρει εἶναι] '*though we could be of weight;*' concessive participial clause subordinated to the preceding part. ζη-

τοῦ ἀπόστολοι· 7 ἀλλ' ἐγενήθημεν ἤπιοι ἐν μέσῳ ὑμῶν, ὡς ἐὰν

τοῦντες; comp. Krüger, *Sprachl.*. § 56. 13. 1, Donalds. *Gr.* § 621. The meaning of these words is somewhat doubtful. Two interpretations deserve consideration: (*a*) 'oneri esse,' Vulg., Æth. (Copt. *baros*, uncertain), βάρος retaining its more simple meaning, and referring to the apostolic right of being sustained by converts (Theod.); comp. ἐπιβαρῆσαι, ver. 9, 2 Thess. iii. 8, κατεβάρησα, 2 Cor, xii. 16, and the converse, ἀβαρῆ ἐτήρησα, 2 Cor. xi. 9: (*b*) 'in gravitate [honore] esse,' Clarom., and appy. Syr. ܡܝܩܪ̈ܐ [honorabiles; see Schauf, *Lex.* s. v.], βάρος having its derivative sense of 'weight,' 'authority;' comp. Diod. Sic. IV. 61, τὸ βάρος τῆς πόλεως (τὴν ἰσχύν, Suid.), esp. XVI. 8 (where it is associated with ἀξίωμα), and somewhat similarly Polyb. *Hist.* IV. 32. 7, XXX. 15. 1; see esp. Suidas, s. v. Of these (*a*) is plausible on account of ἐπιβαρ., ver. 9: as, however, the concessive clause is closely appended to one in which δόξα is the prevalent notion, and as the reference to ἠπιότες serves to enhance the same idea by contrast, it seems more exegetically correct, and more in harmony with the immediate context to adopt (*b*); so Chrys., πολλῆς ἀπολαῦσαι τιμῆς, and less decidedly, Theophyl. and Œcum. ὡς Χρ. ἀπόστολοι) '*as Christ's Apostles;*' the (possessive) genitive marking, with slight emphasis, whose ministers they were (see *on Eph.* i. 2, *Col.* i. 1), and the term ἀπόστολοι receiving its more extended sense (see *on Gal.* i. 1), and including Sylvanus and Timothy. De Wette, Koch, al., refer the plural solely to St. Paul, but without sufficient reason. Though a reference to the apostle's coadjutors must not, perhaps, be strongly pressed in every case where the plural occurs, yet, in the present passage, καρδίας, ver. 4, and ψυχάς, ver. 8, seem distinctly to favor the more extended application.

7. ἀλλ' ἐγενήθημεν] Statement, on the positive side, of the behavior of the apostle and his helpers, the ἀλλὰ introducing an antithesis, not merely to the last clause, but to the whole of the preceding verse: they did not seek δόξαν as διδάσκαλοι, but, what was very different (see Klotz, *Devar.* Vol. II. p. 2), evinced the affection of a parent; οὐ βάρυ οὐδὲ κόμπον ἔχον ἀπεδειξάμεθα, Chrys. ἤπιοι] '*gentle;*' a δὶς λεγόμ. in the N. T., here and 2 Tim. ii. 24. The epithet is similarly applied to a father (Hom. *Od.* II. 47), to a ruler (Herod. III. 89), to the gods (Eur. *Androm.* 741), as marking 'animi lenitatem in aliis ferendis' (Tittm.), and pointing to an outward exhibition of an inward πραότης: compare *Etym. M.*, ἤπιος· ὁ ἐν λόγῳ πάντα ποιῶν καὶ μὴ πάθει, ἐκ μεταλήψεως δὲ καὶ ὁ διὰ λόγου προσηνὴς καὶ πρᾶος (where, however, the derivation seems too much pressed), see Tittm. *Synon.* I. p. 140, and notes *on* 2 *Tim. l. c.* The reading is doubtful: νήπιοι is well supported [*Lachm.* with BC¹D¹FG; mss.; Vulg., Clarom., Copt., Æth. (both), al.], but as a repetition of the N, owing to the somewhat common use of νήπιος in St. Paul's Epp. is more probable than that of an omission, and as νήπιος mars both the sense and metaphor, we seem fully justified in adopting ἤπιος, with AC²D³EKL.; great majority of mss.; Sah., Basm., Syr. (both). So *Tisch.*, and the majority of recent editors. ἐν μέσῳ ὑμῶν] '*in the midst of you;*' scarcely by an anticipation of the image, 'sicut gallina pullis circumdata,' Beng.,—but, with a hint at the absence of all assumption of authority, 'as one of yourselves,' 'ut æquales idque cum omnibus,' Zanch.;

τροφὸς θάλπῃ τὰ ἑαυτῆς τέκνα, 8 οὕτως ὁμειρόμενοι ὑμῶν εὐδοκοῦμεν μεταδοῦναι ὑμῖν οὐ μόνον τὸ εὐαγγέλιον τοῦ Θεοῦ, ἀλλὰ

ὡς ἂν εἴποι τις, ἐξ ὑμῶν, οὐχὶ τὴν ἄνω λαβόντες λῆξιν, Chrys. ὡς ἐὰν τροφὸς κ. τ. λ.] *'as a nurse (nursing mother) doth cherish her own children;'* the particle ὡς having here not a temporal, but simply a comparative force (Klotz, *Devar.* Vol. II. p. 757) ܐܝܟܢܐ ܕ [sicut] Syr., 'tanquam si,' Vulg., Clarom., 'sicut,' Copt., Æth., — and combining with ἐὰν and the *pres.* subj. in marking the habitude, or, perhaps rather, continuance of the objectively-possible event; see Winer *Gr.* § 42. 3. b, p. 274, and compare Herm. *de Part.* ἄν, p. 275, Green, *Gr.* p. 57 sq. For exx. of somewhat similar usages of τροφός, see the list collected by Loesner, *Obs.* p. 377, and on the meaning of θάλπειν [fostering warmth of the breast, comp. Deut. xxii. 6], see Krebs, *Obs.* p. 345, and notes *on Eph.* v. 29. The tenderness conveyed in the τὰ ἑαυτῆς τέκνα should not be overlooked: τὴν φιλοστοργίαν αὐτοῦ δείκνυσιν, Theoph. The present clause must not be separated by a colon (Lünem.), but regarded both as an illustration of the preceding words, and as the protasis to the following, οὕτως ὁμειρόμενοι ὑμῶν εὐδοκοῦμεν, ver. 8.

8. ὁμειρόμενοι] *'earnestly, affectionately desiring you,' 'having a fond affection for you;'* ἐπιθυμοῦντες, Hesych., Photius (*Lex.* p. 242). This form, though not found in the current lexicons (Rost u. Palm not excepted), is supported by all the uncial, and more than 30 cursive mss., and rightly retained by *Lachm.*, *Tisch.*, and most modern commentators. It is not compounded of ὁμοῦ and εἴρειν (Theoph., Phot.), but is either, (*a*) a form of the shorter μείρομαι (comp. δύρομαι, ἀδόρομαι), Winer, *Gr.* § 16. 4, p. 92, or (*b*) a late and perhaps coarsely-strengthened form of the more usual ἱμείρομαι, comp. Fritz. 1, *on Mark* p. 792. As it seems probable that μείρομαι (Nicander, *Theriaca*, 402) is not an independent verb, but only an apocopated form of ἱμείρομαι, 'metri causâ' (see Rost u. Palm, *Lex.* s. v. μείρομ.), it seems safer to adopt (*b*), and to consider ὁμειρομ. a corrupted and perhaps strengthened form of the more usual verb. οὕτως — εὐδοκ.] *'So — had we good will;'* the οὕτως being connected, not with the participle, but with the finite verb. The verb εὐδοκ. is here not present, 'cupimus,' Clarom., but imperf., 'cupide volebamus,' Vulg. (comp. Copt., *an-temat*), the past tenses being commonly found in the N. T. with the more Attic εὐ (comp. Lobeck, *Phryn.* p. 140, 456), not with ηὐ as B here, and a few MSS. elsewhere, 1 Cor. x. 5 [ABC], Col. i. 19 [ADE], al. The verb εὐδοκ. is only found in writers after the time of Alexander (see Sturz, *de Dial. Maced.* p. 167), and appears commonly used in the N. T., not as a mere equivalent for δοκέω (compare Koch), but, as conveying the idea either of the 'propensa voluntas' (Fritz.), or of the free. unconditioned, and gracious will (Luke xii. 32, Gal. i. 15, comp. 1 Thess. iii. 1) of the subject; compare notes *on Eph.* i. 5, and esp. see Fritz. *on Rom.* x. 1, Vol. II. p. 369 sq For a notice of the constructions of εὐδοκ. in the N. T., see notes *on Col.* i. 19. μεταδοῦναι] *'to impart;'* properly and specially in connection with τὸ εὐαγγ., but also, by a very intelligible zeugma, with τὰς ἑαυτῶν ψυχάς, the compound verb being in the latter case understood in its simple form; compare δοῦναι τὴν ψυχήν, Mark x. 45. The use of μεταδιδόναι with a dat. and acc., though less usual than with a dat.

καὶ τὰς ἑαυτῶν ψυχάς, διότι ἀγαπητοὶ ἡμῖν ἐγενήθητε. 9 μνημο-
νεύετε γάρ, ἀδελφοί, τὸν κόπον ἡμῶν καὶ τὸν μόχθον· νυκτὸς καὶ
ἡμέρας ἐργαζόμενοι, πρὸς τὸ μὴ ἐπιβαρῆσαί τινα ὑμῶν, ἐκηρύξαμεν

and gen. (Jelf, *Gr.* § 535), is not without example, especially when the partitive notion is by the context inadmissible; see Krüger, *Sprachl.* § 47. 15. ἀλλὰ καὶ κ. τ. λ.] '*but even our own souls,*' 'nostras animas,' Clarom.; not with any Hebraistic tinge (=נַפְשֹׁתֵינוּ) 'nosmet ipsos' (Koppe), nor even *merely* 'nostras vitas,' but perhaps with a faint reference to the deeper meaning of ψυχή, as pointing to the centre of the personality (Olshaus. *Opusc.* p. 144, Beck, *Seelenl.* § 1), our lives and souls (Fell), our very existences, and all things pertaining to them. On the plural, see above on ver. 4, and on the use of ἑαυτῶν with an included reference to the third person, Winer, *Gr.* § 22. 5, p. 136. The force of the strong antithesis οὐ μόνον — ἀλλὰ καὶ is noticed on ch. i. 8. διότι ἀγαπ. ἡμῖν ἐγεν.] '*because ye became very dear (beloved) to us;*' surely here with no reference to the agent by whom they were made so (Alf.), but simply to their having *become* so, owing to their eager and earnest reception of the apostolic message; see on ch. i. 5. On the pronominal conjunction διότι, here used in its slightly modified sense of διὰ τοῦτο ὅτι (*eo quod*), 'quoniam,' Vulg., 'quia,' Clarom., see Fritz. *on Rom.* i. 19, Vol. I. p. 58, but correct the very doubtful statement (endorsed by Koch) that διότι is there equivalent to γὰρ or 'nam,' see Meyer *in loc.* The reading ἐγενηθ. is supported by all the uncial MSS. except K (γεγένησθε); the latter reading may have been a correction to harmonize the clause with the supposed present εὐδοκ.

9. μνημονεύετε γάρ] '*For ye remember;*' confirmation of the main declaration of ver. 8 (μετα)δοῦναι τὰς ἑαυτῶν ψυχάς, not of the more remote ἤπιοι ἐγενήθητε (compare Olsh.), still less of the subordinate causal member διότι κ. τ. λ. (Lünem.; comp. Just., Alf.), — a doubtful reference of γὰρ appy. suggested by an undue limitation of the term ψυχάς, and, still more, by finding no allusion in the present verse to actual dangers. This, however, is not necessary: the apostle and his followers practically gave up their existences to their converts, when they spent night and day in toil rather than be a burden to any of them. τὸν κόπον καὶ τὸν μόχθον] '*our toil and our travail,*' the article being repeated to give emphasis to the enumeration, and to enhance the climax; comp. Winer, *Gr.* § 19, 5, p. 117. The words κόπος and μόχθος are again found in connection in 2 Thess. iii. 8, and 2 Cor. xi. 27: the former perhaps marks the toil on the side of the *suffering* it involves (see *on* 1 *Tim.* iv. 10), the latter, as derivation seems to suggest [connected with μόγις, and perhaps allied to μέγας, see Pott, *Etym. Forsch.* Vol. I. p. 283], on the side of the *magnitude* of the obstacles it has to overcome: the connection of μόχθος with ἄχθος (Koch, Rost u. Palm, *Lex.* s. v.) seems philologically doubtful; comp. Pott, *l. c.* No. 373. νυκτὸς καὶ ἡμ. ἐργαζ.] '*laboring night and day;*' modal participial clause defining the circumstances under which the κήρυγμα was delivered. On the (secondary) predication of time, νυκτὸς καὶ ἡμέρας, and on the strict grammatical force of the gen. as pointing to some indefinite point of the continuous time expressed by the subst. (contrast 2 Thess. iii. 8), see notes *on* 1 *Tim.* v. 5. There is perhaps some emphasis in the collocation of the whole expression, but appy. none in that of νυκτός (Alf.), as St. Paul

εἰς ὑμᾶς τὸ εὐαγγέλιον τοῦ Θεοῦ. 10 ὑμεῖς μάρτυρες καὶ ὁ Θεός,
ὡς ὁσίως καὶ δικαίως καὶ ἀμέμπτως ὑμῖν τοῖς πιστεύουσιν ἐγενή-

always adopts this order; see further *on* 1 *Tim. l.c.*, and comp. Lobeck, *Paralipom.* p. 62 sq. The addition of γὰρ after νυκτός [*Rec.* with D³EKL; mss.; Chrys. (Text), Theod], though partially defended by De W., seems to have been an insertion 'nexus causâ,' and is rightly rejected by most modern editors.

ἐργαζόμενοι has here a special reference to the manual labor (Schott) of the apostle and his associates; comp. Acts xviii. 3. In 1 Cor. iv. 12 (comp. Eph. iv. 28) the verb is enhanced by the addition ταῖς χερσίν. πρὸς τὸ μὴ ἐπιβ.] '*with a view of not being burdensome to any of you;*' object contemplated in the νυκτὸς καὶ ἡμ. ἐργαζ. On this use of πρός, comp. Winer, *Gr.* § 44. 6, p. 295 (ed. 6), and on its possible distinction from εἰς, comp. notes *on Eph.* iv. 12, and *on Tit.* i. 2. The late form ἐπιβαρεῖς (2 Cor. ii. 5, 2 Thess. iii. 8, comp. Dion. Halic. IV. 9, VIII. 73) is nearly, but not quite equivalent in meaning to καταβαρεῖν (2 Cor. xii. 16), the prep. in the former case being mainly directive (onus imponere), in the latter mainly intensive; comp. ἐπιβαρύνειν, Exod. xxi. 30. The inference of Chrys., Theoph. that the Thessalonians were ἐν πενίᾳ, is very questionable; consider Acts xvii. 4, γυναικῶν τε τῶν πρώτων οὐκ ὀλίγαι, and comp. Baumgarten, *Acts*, Vol. II. p. 208 sq. (Clark). ἐκηρύξ. εἰς ὑμᾶς] '*we preached unto you,*' ܠܟܘܢ Syr., Æth.; not 'in vobis,' Vulg., Clarom., Copt., the preposition being not equivalent to ἐν, but indicative of the direction, so to say, which the κήρυγμα took; see Matth. *Gr.* § 578. b. It is singular that Winer (*Gr.* p. 191. ed. 6) should have been induced merely by the plural to adopt the less probable translation 'unter,' especially as in ed. 5 (p. 241) he has added the more exact rendering, 'Botschaft an die Völker gebracht;' compare Mark xiii. 10, Luke xxiv. 47, 1 Pet. i. 25.

10. ὑμεῖς μάρτ. καὶ ὁ Θεός] '*Ye are witnesses, and God:*' statement in a collected form of what had previously been expanded in particulars. As the summary involves what could not be adequately judged of by man, the apostle subjoins an appeal to God; τοῦ δὲ Θεοῦ τὴν μαρτυρίαν προστέθεικεν· ἐπειδὴ τοῖς ἀνθρώποις δῆλα τὰ ὁρώμενα μόνα, τῷ δὲ Θεῷ καὶ τὰ τοὺς ἀνθρώπους λανθανόμενα, Theod. ὡς ὁσίως κ.τ.λ.] '*how holily and righteously and blamelessly we behaved to you that believe;*' characteristics of the behaviour of the apostle and his associates, the adverbs ὁσίως κ.τ.λ. not being merely adjectival, but serving as secondary predicates (Donalds. *Gr.* § 436 sq.) to define the form and manner of the 'comparatum esse' involved in the γίγνεσθαι; see Winer, *Gr.* § 54. 2, p. 341, Krüger, *Sprachl.* § 62. 2. 3. The adverbs are grouped together somewhat cumulatively, to express, both on the positive and negative side, the complete faithfulness of the ministry. The ordinary distinction between the two former (περὶ μὲν ἀνθρώπους τὰ προσήκοντα πράττων δίκαι' ἂν πράττοι, περὶ δὲ Θεοὺς ὅσια, Plato, *Gorg.* p. 507 B; comp. Chariton, I. 10), urged *here* with some plausibility (Theoph., Alf., al.) on account of the preceding ὑμεῖς καὶ ὁ Θεός, is still always precarious in the N. T.; see notes *on Eph.* iv. 24, *Tit.* i. 8. Perhaps it is safer to say that ὁσίως and δικαίως form on the positive side a compound idea of holy purity and righteousness, whether towards God or towards men, while ἀμέμπτως states on the negative side the general blamelessness in both aspects and relations. To

θήμεν, 11 καθάπερ οἴδατε, ὡς ἕνα ἕκαστον ὑμῶν, ὡς πατὴρ τέκνα

refer ἀμέμπτως to themselves (Beng.), or to regard it as merely the negative reiteration of δικαίως in ref. to men (Olsh.), seems too restrictive; comp. Luke i. 6. ὑμῖν τοῖς πιστεύουσιν] '*to you that believe;*' objects in whose interest the behaviour was shown; dative of *interest*, see Krüger, *Sprachl.* § 48. 4. Lünem. and Alf., following Œcum. and Theoph., and swayed by the position of the words and *supposed* passive force of ἐγενήθ., regard ὑμῖν as a dat. *judicii;* comp. Winer, *Gr.* § 31. 3. b, p. 245 (ed. 5,—omitted in ed. 6). This, however, seems very doubtful; the apostle would scarcely have appealed to God in ref. to the judgment of the Thessalonians; nor would an allusion to their estimate of a former line of conduct have been so pertinent as one to their consciousness that they were the interested objects of it. The addition τοῖς πιστ. is not otiose (Jowett), nor suggestive of different relations with unbelievers (compare Theoph.), but enhances the appeal to the conduct towards the Thess., by showing that their spiritual state was such as would naturally evoke it.

11. καθάπερ οἴδατε] '*even as ye know;*' confirmatory appeal to the individual experience of his hearers; the general ὁσιότης, δικαιοσύνη, and ἀμεμφία of the apostle and his companions was verified by its strict accordance (καθάπερ) with what was observable in special cases. The genuine and expressive form καθάπερ (καθὰ marking the comparison, περ the latitude of the application, 'ambitum rei majorem vel quamvis maximum,' Klotz, *Devar.* Vol. II. p. 722) is only used in the N. T. by St. Paul (ten or eleven times), and by the author of the Ep. to the Hebrews (ch. iv. 2, v. 4 [*Rec.*]), the later καθὼς (see *on Gal.* iii. 6) being greatly the predominant form. The simple καθὰ only occurs once, Matth. xxvii. 10. ἕνα ἕκαστον] '*as regards each one of you,*' 'unumquemque, nemine omisso,' Schott; accus. governed by the participles, and put prominently forward to mark the individualizing reference of the acts; βαβαί, ἐν τοσούτῳ πλήθει μηδένα παραλιπεῖν, Chrys. The collective ὑμᾶς follows, as serving still more clearly to define that all were included: it is thus not so much a mere pleonastic repetition of the pronoun (Col. ii. 13, compare Bernhardy, *Synt.* p. 275), as a defining and supplementary accusative, *somewhat* allied to the use of that case in the σχῆμα καθ' ὅλον καὶ μέρος, Jelf, *Gr.* § 584. ὡς πατήρ] Appropriate change from the image of a mother (ver. 7) to that of a father; the reference not being here to the tenderness of the love, but to its manifestation in instruction and education. The remark of Theoph. (suggested by Chrys.), ἄνω μὲν οὖν τροφῷ ἑαυτὸν ἀπείκασε νῦν δὲ πατρί, τὴν ἀγάπην δεικνύων, καὶ τὴν προστασίαν, is thus not wholly appropriate.

παρακαλ. ὑμᾶς καὶ παραμυθ.] '*exhorting you and encouraging you;*' more exact specification of the behaviour previously described. The participles are certainly not directly (Copt.), nor even indirectly (by an assumed omission of ἦμεν, Beza, al.) equivalent to finite verbs, but are either (*a*) dependent on ἐγενήθημεν supplied from the preceding clause (Lünem., Alf.), or (*b*) are used ἀνακολούθως, as modal clauses to a finite verb (= ἐγενήθ. ὑμῖν) that has been omitted, but is readily suggested by the context; 'ye know how *we did so*, exhorting you,' etc.; so appy. Theod., ταῦτα δὲ ἐποίουν προτρέπων κ.τ.λ., and probably Vulg., Goth., which simply retain the participle. Between (*a*) and (*b*) the difference is practically not great; in the former case the participles form part of the primary,

ἑαυτοῦ, παρακαλοῦντες ὑμᾶς καὶ παραμυθούμενοι 12 καὶ μαρτυ-
ρόμενοι εἰς τὸ περιπατεῖν ὑμᾶς ἀξίως τοῦ Θεοῦ τοῦ καλοῦντος
ὑμᾶς εἰς τὴν ἑαυτοῦ βασιλείαν καὶ δόξαν.

in the latter of the modal and secondary predication: (*b*), however, seems preferable, both from the special consideration that thus the secondary predications of manner in ver. 10 find a parallelism in ver. 11, and from the general consideration that these participial anacolutha are common in St. Paul's Epp.: compare 2 Cor. vii. 5, and Winer, *Gr.* § 45. 6, p. 313. The verb παραμυθ. seems here to imply not so much direct 'consolation' (John xi. 31), compare Syr. ܡܡܠܠܝܢ ܒܠܒܟܘܢ [loquentes in cordibus vestris], Copt., Æth., as 'encouragement,' yet not specially to meet dangers bravely (Œcum.), but, as the context suggests,—to perform generally their duties as Christians.

12. μαρτυρόμενοι] '*charging*,' '*conjuring*,' 'quasi testibus adhibitis' (comp. Eph. iv. 17,—not, however, = διαμαρτυρόμ. (De Wette, Lünem.), which is obviously a stronger form; see notes *on* 1 *Tim.* v. 12. This sense of μαρτυρ. is abundantly confirmed by the use of the verb not only in later (Polyb. *Hist.* XIII. 8. 6), but even in earlier writers, *e. g.* Thucyd. VI. 80, δεόμεθα δὲ καὶ μαρτυρόμεθα, and VIII. 53, μαρτυρομένων καὶ ἐπιθειαζόντων (Goëll.),—and is similar to, though not, as the context shows, perfectly identical with (Koch), its use in Gal. v. 3, Eph. iv. 17, where it approaches more nearly to μαρτυροῦμαι; see notes *in locc.* The reading is slightly doubtful: *Rec.*, *Lachm.*, read μαρτυρούμ. with D[1]FG; most mss.; Theod., Theoph., al., but as the external evidence in favor of μαρτυρόμ. [BD[2] (appy.) D[3]KL; 30 mss; Chrys., Œc.) is more than of equal weight, and as μαρτυρεῖσθαι is always used passively in St. Paul's Epp., we adopt μαρτυρόμ. with *Tisch.* and the majority of modern critics; see Rinck, *Lucubr. Crit.* p. 91.

εἰς τὸ περιπατ. ὑμᾶς] '*that ye should walk worthy*,' Col. i. 10; dependent on the preceding participles, and indicating not merely the subject (Lünem.) or direction (Alf.), but, as εἰς τὸ with the infin. nearly always indicates, the *purpose* of the foregoing exhortation and appeal: compare Chrys., who paraphrases by ἵνα with the subj., and contrast Theod., who paraphrases with a simple infin. The form εἰς τὸ with the infin. is commonly used by St. Paul simply to denote the *purpose* (compare Winer, *Gr.* § 44. 6, p. 295, Meyer, *on Rom.* i. 20, note), and probably in no instance is simply indicative of *result* (ecbatic); still, as perhaps in the present case, there appear to be several passages in which the purpose is so far blended with the subject of the prayer, entreaty, etc., or the issues of the action, that it may not be improper to recognize a secondary and weakened force in ref. to purpose, and analogous to that in the parallel use of ἵνα; comp. *on Eph.* i. 17. The present περιπατεῖν is rightly adopted by most modern editors on preponderant uncial authority [ABD[1]FG; many mss.]. τοῦ καλοῦντος) '*who is calling*;' not καλέσαντος, as in Gal. i. 6, and here in A and 8 mss.: the calling was still continuing as relating to something which, in its fullest realization, was future. It has been before observed that in St. Paul's Epistles, the gracious work of calling is always ascribed to the Father; compare notes *on Gal. l. c.*, Reuss, *Théol. Chrét.* IV. 15, p. 144 sq., Usteri, *Lehrb.* II. 2. 3, p. 269 sq. On the 'vocatio externa' and 'interna,' see the good distinctions of Jackson, *Creed*, XII. 7. 1, 2. βασι-

We thank God that ye received our preaching. Ye suffered from your own people as we did from the Jews.

13 *Διὰ τοῦτο καὶ ἡμεῖς εὐχαριστοῦμεν τῷ*

13. Διὰ τοῦτο] So *Rec.* with DEFGKL; appy. all mss.; Syr., Vulg., Clarom., Goth., Æth. (both); Chrys., Theod., Theoph., Œcum. (*De W.*, *Lünem.*, *Wordsw.*). *Tisch.* and *Lachm.* prefix καὶ with AB; Copt., Syr. (Philox.); Theod. (ms. B), Ambrosiaster (*Alf.*), — but certainly not on sufficient authority, especially as it is by no means unreasonable to suppose that the καὶ was prefixed to help out the difficulty of connection.

λείαν καὶ δόξαν] '*kingdom and glory:*' not an ἓν διὰ δυοῖν for βασιλεία ἔνδοξος (Olsh.), but, as all the Vv. rightly maintain (Syr., Copt., Æth. even repeat the pronoun), two separate substantives, the common article being accounted for by the inserted genitive; see Winer, *Gr.* § 19. 4. d, p. 116. The βασιλεία τοῦ Θεοῦ is the kingdom of His Son, the βασιλεία τῶν οὐρανῶν (Chrys.), of which even while here on earth the true Christian is a subject, but the full privileges and blessedness of which are to be enjoyed hereafter; comp. Ruess, *Théol. Chrét.* IV. 22, Vol. II. p. 244 sq., and the long treatise of Bauer (C. G.) in *Comment. Theol.* Part II. p. 107—172. The δόξα to which He calls us is His own eternal glory, of which all the true members of the Messianic kingdom shall be partakers; comp. Rom. v. 2, and see Reuss, *l. c.*, p. 253, Usteri, *Lehrb.* II. 2. B, p. 351.

13. Διὰ τοῦτο] '*For this cause;*' as we have displayed this zeal and earnestness, we thank God that ye received our message in an accordant spirit. The exact reference of these words is somewhat doubtful. Schott and others refer the words to the 'effectum admonitionis' implied in εἰς τὸ περιπ. κ. τ. λ. (compare Jowett); De W., al., to the purpose and object of the preaching which the same words seem to imply, but thus introduce a greater or less amount of tautology which it seems impossible to explain away. It would seem, then, as Lünem. correctly observes, that we can only logically refer them (*a*) to the *specific* declaration involved in the clause immediately preceding, scil. ὅτι λαλεῖ ὑμᾶς ὁ Θεὸς εἰς κ. τ. λ., Olsh., Lünem., Alf.: or (*b*) to the *general* subject of the preceding verses, — the earnestness and zeal of the apostle and his associates. Of these (*a*) deserves consideration, but is open to the grave objection that thus διὰ τοῦτο is made to refer to a mere appended clause, rather than, as usual, to the tenor of the whole preceding sentence. We therefore with (as it would seem) the Greek expositors, adopt (*b*); οὐκ ἔστιν εἰπεῖν ὅτι ἡμεῖς μὲν πάντα ἀμέμπτως πράττομεν, ὑμεῖς δὲ ἀνάξια τῆς ἡμετέρας ἀναστροφῆς ἐποιήσατε, Chrys. καὶ ἡμεῖς] '*we also,*' not, as Alf. and Lünem., 'we, as well as πάντες οἱ πιστεύοντες' (ch. i. 7), — a reference far too remote, — but, 'we, as well as you who have so much to be thankful for;' the καὶ involving some degree of *contrast* (see *on Phil.* iv. 12), and delicately marking the corresponsiveness of the feeling between οἱ περὶ τὸν Παῦλον and the twice repeated ὑμεῖς in the preceding verse; see especially notes *on Eph.* i. 15. De W. and Koch (so also Auth.) refer καὶ to διὰ τοῦτο, — a connection decidedly at variance with the usage of the particle in demonstrative clauses, but involving a less error than the counter-assertion of Lünem., that we should then expect διὰ καὶ τοῦτο: such collocations are very rare; see *on Phil.* iv. 3, and comp. Hartung, *Partik.* καί, 4. 3, Vol, I. p. 143. εὐχαριστοῦμεν τῷ Θεῷ] '*we give thanks to God.*' On the meaning and usages of

Θεῷ ἀδιαλείπτως, ὅτι παραλαβόντες λόγον ἀκοῆς παρ' ἡμῶν τοῦ Θεοῦ ἐδέξασθε οὐ λόγον ἀνθρώπων ἀλλὰ καθώς ἐστιν ἀληθῶς

εὐχαρ. see notes *on Phil.* i. 3, and esp. *on Col.* i. 12. ὅτι παραλαβόντες κ.τ.λ.] *'that when ye received;'* objective sentence (Donald. *Gr.* § 584 sq.) defining the matter and grounds of the εὐχαριστία. The participle is here temporal, and specifies the more external act that was either contemporaneous with, or, rather, immediately prior to, the more internal ἐδέξασθε; compare *on Eph.* iv. 8, but transpose 'subsequent to' and 'preceding.' The distinction between παραλαμβάνειν and δέχεσθαι, stated by Lünem. and Koch, viz. that παραλαμβάνειν points rather to an *objective* (Gal. i. 12, see notes), δέχεσθαι to a subjective *reception* (2 Cor. viii. 17, seems substantially correct, but must be applied with caution; see *on Col.* ii. 6. λόγον ἀκοῆς] *'the word of hearing;'* *i. e.* 'the word which was heard,' or 'the word of preaching,' ἀκοὴ being used in its prevailing (N. T.) passive sense (see *on Gal.* iii. 2; comp. Heb. iv. 2, and the Heb. קוֹל שְׁמוּעָה, Jer. x. 22), and the gen. being that of *apposition* or *identity;* Winer, *Gr.* § 59. 8, p. 470 (ed. 6), Scheuerl. *Synt.* § 12), 1, p. 82, 83. The gen. ἀκοὴ is probably here subjoined to λόγος to introduce a slight contrast between the λόγος in its first state, as heard by the ear, and the same λόγος in its subsequent state, as ἐνεργούμενος in the hearts of believers; comp. Rom. x. 17. παρ' ἡμῶν thus naturally belongs to παραλαβόντες (ch. iv. 1, 2 Thess. iii. 6, compare Gal. i. 12), from which it is only separated by the somewhat emphatic object-accusative; so Vulg., Syr., Copt., Goth. (Æth. omits παρ' ἡμῶν), Œcum., and a few modern commentators. The construction adopted by the majority of expositors, and *perhaps* Clarom., Syr. (Philox.), ἀκοῆς παρ' ἡμῶν, is defensible, — but harsh and unnatural, and probably only suggested by the unusual but significant position of the following τοῦ Θεοῦ. On the force of παρὰ as denoting the more immediate source, see *on Gal.* i. 12, and esp. Schultz, *Abendm.* p. 218, sq. τοῦ Θεοῦ] *'of God,'* sc. 'which cometh from God;' Θεοῦ not being a gen. *objecti* ('de Deo,' Grot.), nor the possessive gen. ('belonging to,' Alf. 1), but a gen. of the *author* (De Wette, Alf. 2), or even more simply, of the *source* from which the λόγος ἀκοῆς really and primarily came; see on ch. i. 6, and *on Col.* i. 23. The unusually placed τοῦ Θεοῦ seems added correctively, the words being appended, almost 'extra structuram,' to mark that though the ἡμεῖς were the immediate *human* source of the ἀκοή, its real and proper source was *divine.* οὐ λόγον ἀνθρ.] *'not the word of men,'* *i. e.* which cometh from them, and of which they are the true source; see above. It is incorrect to supply tacitly ὡς: the apostle, as Lünem. observes, is not stating what the Thessalonians regarded the message, but, as the next clause still more clearly shows, what it was as a matter of fact. The importance of this clause as asserting the direct inspiration of the spoken words must not be overlooked. ὃς καὶ ἐνεργεῖται] *'which also worketh,'* *'is operative,'* scil. the λόγος Θεοῦ (Clarom., Goth., Theophyl., Œcum.), not Θεός (Vulg., Theod.), — a substantive which, in St. Paul's Epp., is never found with the middle ἐνεργεῖσθαι, but always with the act.; see 1 Cor. xii. 6, Gal. ii. 8, iii. 5, Eph. i. 11, al. On the constructions of ἐνεργ., see notes *on Gal.* ii. 8, and on the distinction between the active ('vim exercere') and the intensive middle ('ex se vim suam exercere'), see

λόγον Θεοῦ, ὃς καὶ ἐνεργεῖται ἐν ὑμῖν τοῖς πιστεύουσιν. 14 ὑμεῖς
γὰρ μιμηταὶ ἐγενήθητε,ἀδελφοί, τῶν ἐκκλησιῶν τοῦ Θεοῦ τῶν οὐσῶν
ἐν τῇ Ἰουδαίᾳ ἐν Χριστῷ Ἰησοῦ, ὅτι τὰ αὐτὰ ἐπάθετε καὶ ὑμεῖς
ὑπὸ τῶν ἰδίων συμφυλετῶν, καθὼς καὶ αὐτοὶ ὑπὸ τῶν Ἰουδαίων

notes *on Gal.* v. 6, Winer, *Gr.* § 38. 6, p. 231, and comp. Krüger, *Sprachl.* § 52. 8. 1 sq. The καὶ must not be omitted in transl. (Alf.), or associated with the relative (De W., Koch), but connected with ἐνεργ., which it enhances by suggesting a further property or characteristic of the inspired word, and perhaps a *contrast* with its inoperative nature when merely heard and not believed. On this use of καί, see notes *on Eph.* i. 11, Klotz, *Devar.* Vol. II. p. 636, and comp. Krüger, *Sprachl.* § 69. 32. 12. ἐν ὑμῖν τοῖς πιστ.] '*in you that believe*,' not 'in vobis qui credidistis,' Vulg., which would require τοῖς πιστεύσασιν, nor 'propterea quod fidem habetis,' Schott (comp. Olsh., Koch), which would require the omission of the article (comp. Donalds. *Gr.* § 492), but 'vobis qui creditis,' Goth., Syr. (Philox), τοῖς πιστεύουσιν adding a spiritual characteristic that serves indirectly to illustrate and verify the preceding declarations of the verse.

14. ὑμεῖς γάρ] Confirmation, not of their reception of the word (Œcum), nor of the predication of their belief (Olsh.), but of the ἐνέργεια displayed in them by the λόγος Θεοῦ: 'your imitation of the churches of Judæa in your sufferings is a distinct evidence of the ἐνέργεια of the word within you.' On the words μιμηταὶ ἐγενήθ., see notes on ch. i. 6. τῶν οὐσῶν ἐν Ἰουδ.] '*which are in Judæa*;' not 'præsens pro præterito,' Grot., but with a direct reference to the churches that were still existing in Judæa; comp. Gal. i. 22. Why the apostle peculiarly specifies these churches has been very differently explained. The most probable reason seems to be that as the Jews were at present the most active adversaries of Christianity, he specifies that locality where this opposition would be shown in its most determined aspects, and under circumstances of the greatest social trial; see Wordsw. *in loc.* ἐν Χρ. Ἰ.] '*in Christ Jesus*;' 'in union and communion with Him;' comp. *on Gal.* i. 22. Both here and Gal. *l. c.* this spiritual definition is suitably subjoined as still more clearly separating them even in thought from the συναγωγαὶ τῶν Ἰουδαίων (Œcum.) which might be ἐν Θεῷ, but were far indeed from being ἐν Χριστῷ. ὑπὸ τῶν ἰδίων συμφυλ.] '*at the hands of your own countrymen*;' closely dependent on ἐπάθετε, — ὑπὸ being used correctly with neuter verbs which involve a passive reference, see Winer, *Gr.* 47. b, p. 330: the reading ἀπὸ [D¹FG; Or (1), in some ed.] is probably only due to a grammatical corrector. The supererogatory compound συμφυλ. ('contribulis,' Vulg., ὁμοεθνής Heysch.) is an ἅπ. λεγόμ. in the N. T.; it is not found in earlier writers (πολίτης, δημότης, φυλέτης, ἄνευ τῆς σύν, Herodian, p. 471, ed. Lobeck), and is an instance of the observable tendency in later Greek to compound forms without adequate increase of meaning; compare συμπολίτης, Eph. ii. 19, and see Thiersch, *de Pentat.* II. 1, p. 83. These συμφυλέται, as the contrast requires, must have been *Gentiles*; it is, however, not unreasonable to suppose that they might have been instigated by Jews (De W.); compare Acts xvii. 5, 13. καθὼς καὶ αὐτοί] '*even as they also*;' not a grammatically exact, though a perfectly intelligible

15 τῶν καὶ τὸν Κύριον ἀποκτεινάντων Ἰησοῦν καὶ τοὺς προφήτας,
καὶ ἡμᾶς ἐκδιωξάντων, καὶ Θεῷ μὴ ἀρεσκόντων καὶ πᾶσιν ἀνθρώ-

apodosis; comp. Demosth. *Phil.* I. p. 51, and Heindorf on Plato, *Phædo*, § 79, Jelf, *Gr.* § 869. 2. On the repetition of καὶ in both members of the sentence, by which, 'per aliquam cogitandi celeritatem,' a double and reciprocal comparison is instituted, see Fritz. *on Rom.* i. 13, Vol. I. p. 37, 38, and notes *on Eph.* v. 23. The αὐτοὶ obviously does not refer to the apostle and his helpers (Goth., Æth. [Pol. — but not Platt], Copt.), but, by a 'constructio ad sensum,' to the persons included in the more abstract ἐκκλησιῶν (Syr., Vulg., Clarom., Arm.); compare Gal. i. 22, 23, and Winer, *Gr.* § 22. 3, p. 131.

15. τῶν καὶ τὸν Κύρ. κ. τ. λ.] *'who slew both the Lord Jesus, and,'* etc.: warning notice of the true character of the unbelieving Jews, suggested probably by recent experiences; comp. Acts xvii. 5, 13, xviii. 6. The particle καὶ is not ascensive, 'qui ipsum Dominum occiderunt,' Clarom., nor connected with τῶν (Lünem.),—a *most* questionable connection, as τῶν, properly considered, has no relatival force — but simply correlative to the following καί, 'et Dominum ..... et prophetas' (Vulg., Copt. omits first καί), and introductory of the first of two similar and co-ordinate members; see Winer, *Gr.* § 53. 4, p. 389, and notes *on* 1 *Tim.* iv. 10. The position of τὸν Κύριον is obviously emphatic, and serves more forcibly to evince the heinous nature of their sin. καὶ τοὺς προφήτ.] *'and the prophets;'* clearly governed by the preceding ἀποκτειν. (Chrys., Theoph., Œcum.), not by the succeeding ἐκδιωξάντων (De W., Koch). The counter-argument that *all* the prophets were not killed is of little weight, as, 'mutatis mutandis,' it can be nearly as strongly urged against the connection with ἐκδιωξάντων. The addition of this second member serves indirectly to weaken the force of the plea of ignorance (comp. Acts iii. 17): ἀλλ' ἠγνόησαν αὐτὸν ἴσως. Μάλιστα μὲν οὖν ᾔδεσαν. Τί δαί; οὐχὶ καὶ τοὺς ἰδίους προφήτας ἀπέκτειναν, Chrys. The reading is somewhat doubtful: ἰδίους is inserted by *Rec.* with $D^2D^3E^2KL$; appy. Syr., Goth., al.; Chrysost., Theod., al., but is not found in $ABD^1E^1FG$; 7 mss. Vulg., Clarom., Copt., Orig. (2) Tertull. (who inscribes the insertion to Marcion), and was perhaps suggested by the preceding ἰδίων in ver. 14. It is thus apparently rightly omitted by nearly all modern editors. καὶ ἡμᾶς ἐκδιωξ.] *'and drove us out;'* *i.e.* not merely St. Paul and his helpers, but the apostles generally. The force of the compound ἐκδιώκειν is somewhat doubtful: ἐκ does not seem otiose (De W.), nor even simply intensive (Lünem.), but has appy. a *semi-local* reference, 'qui persequendo ejecerunt,' Beng., Alf.; comp. Luke xi. 49, and consider Acts xviii. 6. This meaning of ἐκδιώκειν does not seem to have been clearly recognized either by Chrys., al., or any of the best Vv., but is somewhat strongly supported by the prevailing use of the verb in the LXX; see Deut. vi. 19, 1 Chron. viii. 13, xii. 15, Joel ii. 20, al. Θεῷ μὴ ἀρεσκ.] *'do not please God;'* not 'placere non quærentium,' Beng., nor aoristic 'non placuerunt,' Clarom., but, with the proper force of the tense, 'are not pleasing,' are pursuing a course displeasing to, — the present marking the result of a regular and continuing course of behaviour; comp. Winer, *Gr.* § 45. 1, p. 304. The μὴ here does not seem to imply so much as 'Deo placere non curantium,' Alf., but is simply used to mark the aspects under which their conduct leads them to be presented to the

ποις ἐναντίων, 16 κωλυόντων ἡμᾶς τοῖς ἔθνεσιν λαλῆσαι ἵνα

reader; compare Winer, *Gr.* § 55. 5, p. 429, and esp. Gayler, *de Part. Neg.* cap. IX. p. 275 sq. In estimating the force of μὴ with a participle in the N. T, two things should always be borne in mind, (1) that μὴ with the participle is so decidedly the prevailing combination, that while the force of οὐ with the part. will commonly admit of being pressed; that of μὴ will not; see Green, *Gr.* p. 122; (2) that it is not correct always to find in the μὴ (as Alf. here) a reference to the feelings or views of the *subject* connected with the participle (compare *on Gal.* iv. 8), but that it sometimes refers to the *aspect* in which the facts are presented by the writer, and regarded by the reader; see esp. Winer, *Gr. l. c.*, and Herm. *Viger*, No. 267. πᾶσιν ἀνθρ. ἐναντίων] '*contrary to all men;*' scil. 'quia saluti generis humani per invidiam et malitiam obsistebant,' Est. 2, and in effect Chrys. and the Greek commentators. The usual reference of the τὸ ἐναντίον to the 'adversus omnes alios hostile odium,' Tacit. *Hist.* v. 5 (Olsh., De W., Jowett), has been recently called in question by Lünem., and satisfactorily refuted, (1) on the ground that this exclusiveness, which had originally, a monotheistic reference, would hardly have received from the apostle such unqualified censure; (2) on the grammatical principle that the (causal) participle κωλυόντων does not add any new fact, but explains the meaning of the appy. 'generaliter dictum' of the preceding words; so also Schott and Alford.

16. κωλυόντων] '*seeing they hinder;*' not ܕܟܳܠܶܝܢ [qui prohibent] Syr., compare De W., but ܟܰܕ ܟܳܠܶܝܢ [dum prohibent] Syr. (Philox.), 'prohibentes,' Vulg., the participle being anarthrous, and supplying the causal explanation of the foregoing assertion; compare Donalds. *Gr.* § 492 sq. There is no idea of 'conatus' (De W.) involved in κωλυόντων; the present simply states what they were actually doing, as far as circumstances permitted; comp. Lünem. λαλῆσαι ἵνα σωθῶσιν] '*to speak that they might be saved;*' not 'evangelium prædicare ut ('qua,' Erasm.) salvæ fiant,' Menoch. ap. Pol. *Syn.*, but simply, 'gentibus loqui ut serventur,' Beza, — λαλῆσαι preserving its ordinary meaning, and appy. coalescing with ἵνα σωθῶσιν to form an emphatic periphrasis of εὐαγγελίζεσθαι (Olsh.). Ἵνα will perhaps thus have a somewhat weakened force (see *on Eph.* i. 17) and the final sentence will to some extent merge into the objective. On the nature of these forms of sentence, see Donalds. *Gr.* § 584 sq., and 605 sq. εἰς τὸ ἀναπληρ.] '*in order to fill up (the measure of) their sins;*' final clause appended, not merely to κωλυόντων, but to the whole preceding verse, and marking with the full force of εἰς τὸ (see notes on ver. 12) the *purpose* contemplated in their course of action. This purpose, viewed grammatically, must be ascribed to the Jews, — whether as conscious and wilful (σκοπῷ τοῦ ἁμαρτάνειν ἐποίουν, Œcum.), or as blinded and unconscious agents (De W.): considered, however, theologically, it mainly refers to the eternal purpose of God which unfolded itself in this wilful, and at last, judicial blindness on the part of His chosen people; comp. Olsh. and Lünem. *in loc.* The compound ἀναπλ. is not synonymous with πληροῦν, but marks the existence of a *partial* rather than an entire vacuum; the Jews were always blind and stubborn, but when they slew their Lord, and drove forth His apostles, they filled *up* (supplebant) the measure of

σωθῶσιν, εἰς τὸ ἀναπληρῶσαι αὐτῶν τὰς ἁμαρτίας πάντοτε.
ἔφθασεν δὲ ἐπ' αὐτοὺς ἡ ὀργὴ εἰς τέλος.

**I endeavored to see you, but was hindered by Satan. Ye truly are our crown and glory.**

17 Ἡμεῖς δέ, ἀδελφοί, ἀπορφανισθέντες ἀφ'

their iniquities; see notes *on Phil.* ii. 30, and Winer, *de Verb. Comp.* III. p. 11 sq. πάντοτε] '*at all times*,' ܒܟܠܙܒܢ [omni tempore] Syr., not only in the times before Christ (ἐπὶ τῶν προφητῶν), but when he came, and after he left them (ἐπὶ τῶν ἀποστόλων). There is no exegetical necessity for assuming that πάντοτε = παντελῶς (Bretschneider, Olsh.); the Jews were *always*, in all periods of their history, acting in a manner that tended to fill up the continually diminishing vacuum. ἔφθασεν δὲ ἐπ' αὐτούς] '*but there is come upon them*;' contrast between their course of evil and its sequel of punishment. It is scarcely necessary to say that δὲ is not here equivalent to γάρ ('enim,' Vulg.), but with its usual and proper force (Syr. ܕܝܢ, Clarom., 'autem') marks the antithesis between the procedure and its issue; 'alii rei aliam adjicit, ut tamen ubivis quædam oppositio declaretur,' Klotz, *Devar.* Vol. II. p. 362. On the meaning of the verb φθάνειν in later Greek (not *præ*venit,' Clarom., but ܡܛܬ [advenit] Syr., and, with εἰς, 'pervenit,' Vulg.), see notes *on Phil.* iii. 30, and Fritz. *Rom.* ix. 31, Vol. II. pp. 356, 357. The aorist ἔφθασεν, 'came' (but see notes to *Transl.*), is certainly not equivalent either to a present (Grot.) or to a future (Schott), but marks the event as an historical fact that belongs to the past, without, however, further specifying '*quam late pateat* id quod actum est;' see esp. Fritz. *de Aor. Vi*, p. 17. The perfect ἔφθακεν [*Rec.*, *Lachm.*, with BD] was appy. an intepr. suggested by a supposed inappropriateness in the use of the aorist. The perf. contemplates an endurance in the present, the aorist leaves this fact unnoticed, but does not deny it. ἡ ὀργή] '*the anger*,' scil. τοῦ Θεοῦ, — as actually added in DEFG; Vulg., Clarom., Goth.; comp. Rom. v. 9. The article either marks the ὀργὴ as προωρισμένη καὶ προφητευομένη (Chrys. 2, 3), or perhaps rather as ὀφειλομένη (Chrys. 1, Œcum.), or even simply ἐρχομένη; compare ch. i. 10. εἰς τέλος] '*to the end*,' '*to the uttermost*;' 'usque ad finem,' Clarom.; in close connection with ἔφθασεν, not with ὀργή, — a construction that would certainly require the insertion of the article. Εἰς τέλος is not used adverbially (Jowett, — comp. Job xx. 7), whether in the sense of 'postremo' (Wahl, compare Beng.) or 'penitus' (Homb.), but, in acccordance with the ordinary construct. of φθάνειν εἰς τί, marks the issue to which the ὀργὴ had arrived: it had reached its extreme bound, and would at once pass into inflictive judgments. As the cup of the ἁμαρτία had been gradually filling, so had the measures of the divine ὀργή. It can scarcely be doubted that in these words the apostle is pointing prophetically to the misery and destruction which in less than fifteen years came upon the whole Jewish nation. To regard the present clause as specifying what had already taken place (Baur, *Paulus*, p. 483), is wholly inconsistent with the context: see Lünem. *in loc.*, who has well refuted the arguments urged by Baur, *l. c.*, against the genuineness of the Ep., as derived from this and the preceding verses.

17. Ἡμεῖς δέ] '*But we*;' return after the digression to the subjects and

ὑμῶν πρὸς καιρὸν ὥρας, προσώπῳ οὐ καρδίᾳ, περισσοτέρως ἐσπουδάσαμεν τὸ πρόσωπον ὑμῶν ἰδεῖν ἐν πολλῇ ἐπιθυμίᾳ.

leading thought of ver. 13, the δὲ not being simply resumptive, but reintroducing the apostle and his associates with *contrasted* reference to the Jewish persecuters just alluded to: compare the remarks on this participle, *Gal.* iii. 8.

ἀπορφανισθέντες ἀφ' ὑμῶν] '*bereaved in our separation from you*,' 'desolati a vobis,' Vulg., ܝܬܡ̈ܐ ܡܢܟܘܢ [orphani a vobis] Syr., — *temporal*, not concessive (Theod.) use of the participle, marking an action prior to that of the finite verb; comp. Winer, *Gr.* § 45. 6. b. p. 315. In this expressive compound, the ἀπὸ (reiterated before the pronoun) serves to mark the idea of *separation* (Winer, *Gr.* § 47, p. 331), and the term ὀρφανός, ὀρφανίζω, the feeling of desolation and *bereavement* which the separation involved. The further idea, παίδων πατέρας ζητούντων, Chrys. (Æsch. *Choëph.* 246), or conversely, 'orbati ut parentes liberis absentibus,' Beng., is not necessarily involved in the term, as ὀρφανὸς [cognate with 'orbus,' and perhaps derived from Sansc. *rabh*, the radical idea of which is 'seizing,' etc.; see Pott, *Etym. Forsch.* Vol. I. p. 259] is not unfrequently used with some latitude of reference; compare Pind. *Isthm.* VII. 16, ὀρφανοὶ ἑταίρων, Plato, *Republ.* p. 495 C, ὀρφανὴν συγγενῶν, and the good collection of exx. in Rost u. Palm, *Lex.* s. v. Vol. II. p. 542. The idea of separation *from those we love*, seems, however, always involved in the term, when in personal references: compare Plato, *Phædr.* p. 239 E, τῶν φιλτάτων . . . . . ὀρφανόν.

πρὸς καιρὸν ὥρας] '*for the season of an hour*;' a more emphatic expression than the usual πρὸς ὥραν (2 Cor. vii. 8, Gal. ii. 5, Philem. 15), or the less defined πρὸς καιρόν (Luke viii. 13, 1 Cor. vii. 5), serving to mark the shortness of the time that elapsed between the bereavement and the feeling of the longing to return; comp. the Latin 'horæ momento,' Hor. *Sat.* I. 1. 7. On the use of πρὸς in these temporal formulæ, as properly serving to mark motion toward an epoch, conceived as before the subject, see notes *on Philem.* 15, and compare Donalds. *Cratyl.* § 177.

προσώπῳ οὐ καρδίᾳ] '*in face, not in heart*;' scil. τῆς αἰσθητῆς ὑμῶν ἐστέρημαι θέας, τῆς δὲ νοητῆς ἀπολαύω διηνεκῶς, Theod.: datives, certainly not of manner (Alf.), but of *relation* (of 'reference to'), marking with the true limiting power of the case the metaphorical place to which the action is restricted; comp. 1 Cor. v. 3, Col. ii. 5, see notes *on Gal.* i. 22, and esp. Scheuerl. *Synt.* § 22, p. 179 sq., where the difference between the local, modal, and instrumental uses of this case is well illustrated.

περισσοτ. ἐσπουδασ.] '*were the more abundantly zealous*,' 'eo amplius [magis] studuimus,' Beza, — viz. because our heart was with you, and our longing consequently greater. The exact reference of the comparative is somewhat doubtful. It is certainly not merely an intensified positive (Olsh., Just. 2, comp. Goth.); for though frequently used by St. Paul (2 Cor. i. 12, ii. 4, vii. 13, xi. 23, xii. 15, Gal. i. 14, Phil. i. 14; compare Heb. ii. 1, xiii. 19), it has appy. in every case its proper comparative force; see Winer, *Gr.* § 35, 4, p. 217. The most plausible ref. is not to the mere fact of the ἀπορφανισμός (Winer, *l. c.*), nor to the briefness of the time as suggestive of a less obliterated remembrance (Lünem., compare Alf, Jowett), still less to the comparative length of it (περισσοτ. ἢ ὡς εἰκὸς ἦν τοὺς πρὸς ὥραν ἀπολειφθέντας, Theoph., comp. Chrys.), but to the fact

18 διότι ἠθελήσαμεν ἐλθεῖν πρὸς ὑμᾶς, ἐγὼ μὲν Παῦλος καὶ ἅπαξ

18. Διότι] So *Lachm.* with ABD[1]FG; 7 mss. (*Tisch.* ed. 1, 7, *Lünem.*, *Alf.*). *Tisch.* has here rightly returned to the reading of his first edition, as the external authority for διό (*Rec.*, *De W.*, *Tisch.* ed. 2) — viz. D[2]D[3]EKL; great majority of mss.; Chrys., Theod., Dam., al., is not strong, and, owing to the unusual position of διότι, the probability of correction very great.

that the separation was προσώπῳ οὐ καρδίᾳ; 'quo magis corde præsens vobiscum fui, hoc abundantius faciem vestram videre studui,' Musc. The form περισσοτέρως (περισσότερον, Heb. vi. 17, vii. 15) is appy. rare in classical Greek, compare however, Isocr. p. 35 E (ed. Coray). πρόσωπον ὑμῶν ἰδεῖν] '*to see your face;*' not 'exquisite positum' for ὑμᾶς ἰδεῖν, with reference to the preceding προσώπῳ (Schott, Jowett), but appy. an expressive Hebraistic periphrasis (רְאוֹת אֶת־פְּנֵי), marking the personal face-to-face nature of the meeting; compare ch. iii. 10, Col. ii. 1. ἐν πολλῇ ἐπιθ.) '*with great desire;*' appended clause specifying the ethical sphere *in* which the σπουδή was evinced 'in multo desiderio,' (Clarom., Copt., Goth.), or perhaps more simply the concomitant feeling ('cum multo desiderio,' Vulg., compare Arm.) *with* which it was associated; see notes *on Col.* iv. 2, and compare above, on ver. 3.

18. διότι] '*On which account,*' scil. of our longing to come and see you. The particle διότι is here used in a sense little different from διό (compare Lat. 'quare'), and stands at the beginning of the period, — a usage in which Jowett appears to have felt a difficulty, as he here unnecessarily alters the correct punctuation of *Lachm.*, and places only a comma after ἐπιθυμίᾳ. On the reading, see the critical note. ἠθελήσαμεν] '*we wished,*' '*would fain:*' not ἐβουλήθημεν, which would have expressed 'ipsam animi propensionem' (Tittm.) with a greater force than would be consistent with the context; comp. Philem. 13, 14. On the distinction between θέλω and βούλομαι, see notes *on* 1 *Tim.* v. 14, and Donalds. *Cratyl.* § 463, but in applying it in St. Paul's Epp. observe that the use of θέλω is seven to one compared with that of βούλομαι. This perhaps suggests that we may commonly safely press the latter, but must be cautious with regard to the former. ἐγὼ μὲν Παῦλος] '*even I, Paul,*' 'ipse ego, Paulus,' Æth. The μὲν 'solitarium' serves to enhance the distinctive use of the personal pronoun (Hartung, *Partik.* μὲν, 3. 3, Vol. II. p. 413) by faintly hinting at the others from whom, for the sake of emphasis — not of contrast in conduct (κἀκεῖνοι μὲν γὰρ ἤθελον μόνον, ἐγὼ δὲ καὶ ἐπεχείρησα, Chrys.) — he is here detaching himself; compare Devar. *de Partic.* Vol. I. p. 122 (ed. Klotz). On the proper force of μέν (incorrectly derived by Klotz and Hartung from μήν), and its connection with the first numeral, see Donalds. *Cratyl.* § 154, and comp. Pott, *Etym. Forsch.* Vol. II. p. 324. καὶ ἅπαξ καὶ δίς] '*both once and twice,*' *i. e.* 'not once only, but twice;' see Phil. iv. 16, and notes *in loc.* The first καὶ is not otiose (Raphel, *Annot.* Vol. II. p. 522), but adds an emphasis to the enumeration; contrast Nehem. xiii. 20, 1 Macc. iii. 30, where the omission of the καὶ leaves the formula scarcely stronger in meaning than 'aliquoties.' καὶ ἐνέκοψεν κ. τ. λ.] '*and Satan hindered us.*' The καὶ has here no adversative force ('sed,' Vulg., De W.), but simply places in juxtaposition with the intention

καὶ δίς, καὶ ἐνέκοψεν ἡμᾶς ὁ Σατανᾶς. 19 τίς γὰρ ἡμῶν ἐλπὶς ἢ

the actual issue ('et impedivit,' Clarom., and all the other Vv.), the opposition lying really in the *context*. On this practically contrasting use of *καί*, see notes *on Phil.* iv. 12, and Winer, *Gr.* § 53. 3, p. 388. On the primary meaning of the verb *εγκόπτειν* (Hesych. *ἐνοκοπτόμην· ἐνεποδιζόμην*), 'to hinder by breaking up a road,' see notes *on Gal.* v. 7. ὁ Σατανᾶς] '*Satan*,' Heb. שָׂטָן the personal evil Spirit, the 'adversary' *κατ' ἐξοχήν* (*ὁ ἐχθρός*, Luke x. 19); compare notes *on Eph.* iv. 27. To refer this term to human adversaries (De W.), or to some inward impediment (Jowett, who most inaptly compares Acts xvi. 7), is in a high degree doubtful and precarious: St. Paul here plainly says that *the Devil* was the hindrance; what peculiar agencies he used are not revealed. Without here entering into controversy, it seems not out of place to remark, that the language of the N. T., if words mean anything, does ascribe a personality to the Tempter so distinct and unmistakeable, that a denial of it can be only compatible with a practical denial of Scripture inspiration. To the so-called charge of Manicheism, it is enough to answer that if an inspired apostle scruples not to call this fearful Being *ὁ θεὸς τοῦ αἰῶνος τούτου* (2 Cor. iv. 4), no sober thinker can feel any difficulty in ascribing to him permissive powers and agencies of a frightful extent and multiplicity; see Hofmann, *Schriftb.* Vol. I. p. 389 sq., and Ebrard, *Dogmatik*, § 240, Vol. I. p. 290.

19. τίς γὰρ ἡμῶν] Interrogative confirmation of the apostle's earnest desire to see his converts: 'who is so if ye are not so,' Olsh., 'quid mirum si tanto tenear vestri desiderio? nam quid aliud est in hoc mundo quo mihi placeam, quo me jactem, quo fretus mihi promittam felicitatem,' Calv.

ἐλπὶς ἢ χαρά] '*hope or joy;*' not exactly 'causa spei et materies lætandi,' Schott, but the subjects and substratum of both one and the other, — the subjects in whom both reside; comp. Phil. iv. 1, and, more significantly and emphatically, 1 Tim. i. 1 (notes). Examples of similar uses in pagan writers are collected by Wetst. *in loc.*; the most pertinent seems Livy, XXVIII. 39, 'Scipionem — spem omnem salutemque nostram.' στέφανος καυχήσεως] '*crown of boasting;*' comp. Prov. xvi. 31, Ezek. xvi. 12, עֲטֶרֶת תִּפְאֶרֶת [*στέφ. καυχήσεως*, LXX], and somewhat similarly Isaiah lxii. 3, *ἔσῃ στέφανος κάλλους καὶ διάδημα βασιλείας*: the Thessalonians were to the apostle as it were a chaplet of victory, of which he might justly make his boast in the day of the Lord. It is scarcely necessary to add that *καυχήσεως* is not merely = *δόξης λαμπρᾶς* (Theoph.), but implies *ἐφ' ᾧ ἀγάλλομαι* [*καυχῶμαι*], Chrys. the genitive being not the gen. 'appositionis' (Koch), nor even of the metaphorical substance (comp. Rev. xii. 1), but, as the termination in *-σις* seems to require, that of the 'remoter object;' see exx. in Winer, *Gr.* § 30. 2. β, p. 170. ἢ οὐχὶ καὶ ὑμεῖς] '*or are not ye also;*' not 'nonne,' Vulg., but 'aut [an] non,' Clarom., ܐܘ ܠܐ Syr. (Philox.), the particle *ἢ* retaining its proper disjunctive force (see Devar. *de Part.* Vol. I. p. 101, ed. Klotz), and introducing a second and negative interrogation, explanatory and confirmatory of what is implied in the first; comp. Winer, *Gr.* § 57. 1, p. 451, and esp. compare the good remarks of Hand, *Tursell.* Vol. I. p. 349. The ascensive *καὶ* serves to place the Thessalonians in gentle contrast with other converts, 'ye, as well as my other converts;' *οὐ γὰρ εἶπεν*

χαρὰ ἢ στέφανος καυχήσεως, ἢ οὐχὶ καὶ ὑμεῖς, ἔμπροσθεν τοῦ
Κυρίου ἡμῶν Ἰησοῦ ἐν τῇ αὐτοῦ παρουσίᾳ; 20 ὑμεῖς γάρ ἐστε
ἡ δόξα ἡμῶν καὶ ἡ χαρά.

**As we could not forbear any longer, we sent Timothy to reassure you in your affliction.**

III. Διὸ μηκέτι στέγοντες εὐδοκήσαμεν

ὑμεῖς, ἁπλῶς, ἀλλά, καὶ ὑμεῖς, μετὰ τῶν ἄλλων, Chrys. [How accurate is this great commentator's observation of the details of language.] ἔμπροσθεν τοῦ Κυρίου κ. τ. λ.] '*in the presence of our Lord Jesus at his coming?*' There is some little difficulty in the connection of this member with what precedes. We clearly must not assume a transposition, and connect it with τίς γὰρ—καυχήσεως (Grot.), nor again closely and exclusively unite it with ἢ οὐχὶ καὶ ὑμεῖς (Olsh.), but, as the context seems to require, append it to the whole foregoing double question, to which it imparts its specifically Christian aspect. The apostle might have paused at καὶ ὑμεῖς, and proceeded with ver. 20, but feeling that the ἐλπίς, χαρά, κ. τ. λ. needed characterizing, he subjoins the circumstances of place and time. Ἐν τῇ παρουσίᾳ obviously refers to the Lord's second coming,—not merely and exclusively 'to establish his Messianic kingdom'. (Lünem., compare the objectionable remarks of Usteri, *Lehrb.* p. 352), but—to judgment; compare ch. iii. 13, iv. 15, v. 23. The addition Χριστοῦ (*Rec.* with FGL; many Vv.) is rightly rejected by *Lachm.*, *Tisch.*, and most modern editors.

20. ὑμεῖς γὰρ κ. τ. λ.] '*Yea verily ye are our glory and our joy.*' The γὰρ does not appear here to be argumentative,—*i. e.* it does not subjoin a reason of greater universality (Alford, citing Soph. *Philoct.* 746, but see Buttm. *in loc.*), but seems rather confirmatory and explanatory ('confirmat superiorem versum *seriâ asseveratione*,' Calv.), the γὲ element having here the predominance; see notes *on Gal.* ii. 6, and Winer, *Gr.* § 53. 8. b, p. 396. For a complete investigation of the primary meaning and principal uses of this particle, the student is especially referred to Klotz, *Devar.* Vol. II. p. 231 sq.

Chapter III. 1. Διό] '*On which account:*' not exactly διὰ τὸ εἶναι ὑμᾶς τὴν δόξαν ἡμῶν καὶ τὴν χαράν (Lünem.), which seems too restricted, but, on account of the affectionate but abortive desire expressed in the three preceding verses; ἐπειδὴ ἡμεῖς δραμεῖν πρὸς ὑμᾶς ἐκωλύθημεν ἀπεστείλαμεν Τιμόθεον, Theodor. On the use of διό, see notes *on Gal.* iv. 31, and grammatical reff. *on Philem.* 5. μηκέτι στέγοντες] '*no longer able to forbear;*' 'no longer able to control my longing to see, or at least hear, about you;' 'cum desiderio vestri impares essemus,' Just. Lünemann (approved by Winer, *Gr.* § 55. 5, p. 529, ed 6) rightly objects to the assertion of Rückert that μηκέτι is here incorrectly used for οὐκέτι, as μηκέτι can be properly and accurately explained as involving the subjective feelings of the writer ('being in a state that I could not,' 'as one that could not'); still, as has been before said (notes on ch. ii. 15), the tendency of later Greek to adopt the subjective form of negation with participles is very noticeable, and must always be borne in mind; comp. Madvig, *Synt.* § 207, and see also the notes and reff. on ch. ii. 15. The verb στέγειν (βαστάζειν, ὑπομένειν, Hesych.; φέρειν, ὑπομένειν, καρτερεῖν, Chrys. *on* 1 *Cor.* ix. 12) is only used in the N. T. by St. Paul, twice with (1 Cor. ix. 12, xiii. 7), and twice without (here and ver. 5) an accus. objecti: see, how-

καταλειφθῆναι ἐν Ἀθήναις μόνοι, 2 καὶ ἐπέμψαμεν Τιμόθεον τὸν ἀδελφὸν ἡμῶν καὶ συνεργὸν τοῦ Θεοῦ ἐν τῷ εὐαγγελίῳ τοῦ Χριστοῦ, εἰς τὸ στηρίξαι ὑμᾶς καὶ παρακαλέσαι ὑπὲρ τῆς πίστεως

ever, the list of exx. in Wetst. *on* 1 *Cor. l. c.*, and those in Kypke, *Annot.* Vol. II. p. 213, the most pertinent of which in ref. to this place is Philo, *in Flacc.* § 9, Vol. II. p. 527 (ed. Mang.), μηκέτι στέγειν δυνάμενοι τὰς ἐνδείας.

εὐδοκήσαμεν] '*we thought it good;*' Auth., compare Arm., 'placuit nobis,' Vulg., Clarom., 'galeikaida uns.,' Goth., not 'enixe voluimus' (*ahedarna*] Æth., comp. Syr., as the idea of a 'libera' (εἰλόμεθα, προεκρίναμεν, Theoph.) rather than a 'propensa voluntas' seems here more suitable to the context; see notes on ch. ii. 8, and Fritz. *Rom.* Vol. II. p. 369 sq. The plural here seems clearly to refer, not to St. Paul and Silas (Beng.), but to St. Paul alone, the subject of the verse being in close connection with the concluding verses of ch. ii., where the apostle expressly limits the reference to himself. καταλειφθ. ἐν Ἀθήν. μόνοι] '*to be left behind at Athens alone,*'—*alone*, not without some emphasis, as its position seems to indicate; alone, and that at Athens, 'urbe videlicet a Deo alienissimâ,' Beng. There is some little difficulty in reconciling this passage with Acts xvii. 13 sq. From the latter passage compared with xviii. 5, it would seem that Timothy and Silas first rejoined St. Paul at Corinth, and so, that the former was not with the apostle at Athens; from the present words (καταλειφθῆναι, ἐπέμψαμεν, ver. ii.; ἔπεμψε, ver. 5), however, it seems scarcely doubtful that Timothy was despatched from Athens. Omitting untenable suppositions of a second visit to Athens (Schrader), or of St. Luke's 'ignorance,' or 'that only Silas was left behind' (Jowett),—we must either suppose (*a*) that St. Paul despatched Tim. before his own arrival to Athens (Wieseler, *Chronol.* p. 246 sq.), or perhaps more naturally, (*b*) that Timothy, having been able to obey the apostle's order (Acts xvii. 15) more quickly than Silas, did actually come to Athens, and was at once despatched to Thessalonica. The apostle then continued waiting for both where he was (Acts xvii. 16), but ultimately left the city, and was rejoined by them both after his arrival at Corinth; see Neander, *Planting*, Vol. I. p. 195, note (Bohn).

2. συνεργὸν τοῦ Θεοῦ] '*fellow-worker with God,*' 'adjutorem Dei,' Clarom.; compare 1 Cor. iii. 9. The σὺν does not refer to others not named, but, in accordance with the regular construction of the word in the N. T. (Rom. xvi. 3, 9, 21, Phil. ii. 25, iv. 3, compare 2 Cor. i. 24), to the expressed and associated genitive Θεοῦ; comp. Bernhardy, *Synt.* III. 49, p. 171, Jelf, *Gr.* § 519. The reading is somewhat doubtful, and the variations very numerous (see Tisch. *in loc*), but all probably to be referred to the supposed difficulty of the expression. *Rec.* reads καὶ διάκονον τοῦ Θεοῦ καὶ συνεργὸν ἡμῶν with DE (confusedly) KL; mss.; Syr. (omits καί), Philox. (but with asterisk), al.; Chrysost., Theod. The text as it stands [*Griesb.*, *Lachm.*, *Tisch.*, and most modern editors] is only found in D[1]; Clarom., Sangerm., Ambrosiast., but is supported indirectly by A, some mss., and several Vv. (Copt., Goth., Æth.), which have διάκονον instead of συνεργόν, and FG, al. which have both, and also to some extent by B, which omits τοῦ Θεοῦ. ἐν τῷ εὐαγγελίῳ defines more precisely the sphere in which his co-operation was exhibited; see Rom. i. 9, Phil. iv. 3. εἰς τὸ στηρίξαι κ. τ. λ.] '*to establish you and to exhort in behalf of your*

ὑμῶν ³ τὸ μηδένα σαίνεσθαι ἐν ταῖς θλίψεσιν ταύταις· αὐτοὶ

*faith that etc:'* purpose of Timothy's mission; he was, in the unavoidable absence of the apostle, to strengthen them, and to exhort them to be steadfast; compare Acts xv. 32. These expressions do not seem in accordance with the timid character which Alf. *in loc.* and *on* 2 *Tim.* i. 7, 8, al. ascribes to the apostles faithful fellow-worker. παρακαλέσαι] '*to exhort,*' 'ad exhortandos,' Vulg.; not here 'to comfort,' Auth., Syr. (Philox.), al. (Eph. vi. 22, Col. iv. 8 [correct *on ib.* ii. 2, Eng. ed. 1]), still less ܢܒܥܐ ܡܢܟܘܢ ܥܠ [roget vos de] Syr., but, as the next verse seems to require, in the more usual sense of 'encouraging,' or 'exhorting;' ἵνα παρακέσῃ φέρειν γενναίως τὰς τῶν ἐναντίων ἐπιβουλάς, Theod. The second ὑμᾶς which *Rec.* here adds with D³KL; mss.; Vv., is rightly rejected by *Lachm.*, *Tisch.*, with distinctly preponderating external evidence [ABD¹FG; mss.; Vv.; Chrys., Theod.] ὑπὲρ τῆς πίστεως] Not identical in meaning with περὶ τῆς πίστεως (De W.), which *Rec.* adopts on weak external authority [D³E²L; mss.], but appy. more distinctly expressive of the benefit to, and furtherance of, the faith, which was contemplated in the παράκλησις; see Winer, *Gr.* § 47. 1, p. 343, and comp. notes *on Phil.* ii. 13.

3. τὸ μηδένα σαίνεσθαι] '*that no one be disturbed;'* objective sentence (Donalds. *Gr.* § 584) dependent on παρακαλέσαι, explaining and specifying the subject-matter of the exhortation; comp. Winer, *Gr.* § 44. 5, p. 294 (ed. 6), but more fully p. 375 (ed. 5). Of the different explanations of this infinitival clause, this seems far the most simple and grammatically tenable. That of Schott, — according to which τὸ μηδένα κ. τ. λ. is an accus. of 'reference to,' is defensible (see Krüger, *Sprachl.* § 50. 6. 8, compare notes *on Phil.* iv. 10), but, in the case of transitive verbs like παρακαλεῖν, of precarious application: that of Lünem. and Alf., — according to which τὸ μηδ. is in opposition to the whole preceding sentence, and dependent on the preceding εἰς, more than doubtful; the regimen is remote, and the assumption that τουτέστι might have been written for τό (Alf.), extremely questionable, if not inconsistent with the assumed dependence on εἰς. The only objection to the construction here advocated — that παρακαλέσαι would thus be associated with a simple accus. *rei* — is of no real weight; for (1) such a construction *is* possible (compare 1 Tim. vi. 2), and (2) the dependence of such explanatory or accusatival infinitives on the governing verb is appy. not so definite and immediate as that of simple substantives; comp. Matth. *Gr.* § 543, obs. 2, 3, Scheuerl. *Synt.* § 45. 4, p. 478. The only real difficulty in these and similar constructions is correctly to define the difference between the infin. when with, and when without the article: perhaps it amounts to no more than this, that in the former case, the infinitival clause is more emphatic, aggregated, and substantival, in the latter more merged in the general structure of the sentence; see Winer, *Gr.* § 44. 2, p. 286 (ed. 6), Krüger, *Sprachl.* § 50. 6. 3, Matth. *Gr. l. c.* obs. 2. The reading of *Rec.*, τῷ μηδένα κ. τ. λ., is not either exegetically or grammatically admissible (opp. to Green, *Gr.* p. 277; see Winer, *l. c.*, p. 294), and is wholly unsupported by uncial authority; see Tisch. *in loc.* σαίνεσθαι] '*be disturbed,*' '*be disquieted.*' This verb (ἅπ. λεγόμ. in the N. T.) properly signifies 'to be fawned on' (σαίνειν, ἐπὶ ζώων ἀλόγων, ὅ ἐστι σείειν τὴν οὐράν, Eustath. p. 393,

γὰρ οἴδατε ὅτι εἰς τοῦτο κείμεθα· 4 καὶ γὰρ ὅτε πρὸς ὑμᾶς ἦμεν,
προελέγομεν ὑμῖν ὅτι μέλλομεν θλίβεσθαι, καθὼς καὶ ἐγένετο καὶ

9), and metaphorically 'soothed' (Æsch. *Choëph.* 186), but is occasionally found in later writers in the stronger sense of κινεῖσθαι, σαλεύεσθαι (Heysch.); comp. Diog. Laert. VIII. 41 (cited by Elsner), σαινόμενοι τοῖς λεγομένοις ἐδάκρυον καὶ ᾤμωζον. So rightly Chrys. (θορυβεῖσθαι), Theod., Zonaras, *Lex.* p. 1632 (κλονεῖσθαι), al., most of the ancient Vv. (Syr. ܢܬܬܙܝܥ [succideretur], Vulg., 'moveatur'), and nearly all modern commentators. Wolf, Tittmann (*Synon.* I. p. 189), and appy. Jowett, retain the more usual sense of 'pellici,' scil. 'ad officium deserendum,' but with little plausibility, and in opposition to the consent of both Ff. and Vv. The derivation, it need scarcely be said, is not from ΣΑΝ- or ΞΑΝ- (Benfey, *Wurzellex.* Vol. I. p. 191), but from σείω; comp. Donalds. *Cratyl.* § 473. ἐν ταῖς θλίψεσιν ταύταις] '*in these afflictions;*' not merely those endured by the apostle (compare Œcum.), but those in which both he and his readers had recently shared, and which, though appy. over for a time (ver. 4), would be almost certain to recur. The ἐν is certainly not instrumental, or even temporal (Lünemann), but merely *local*, with ref. to the circumstances *in* which they were, and by which they were (so to say), environed; compare Winer, *Gr.* § 48. a, p. 345. αὐτοὶ γὰρ οἴδατε] '*for yourselves know;*' reason for the foregoing exhortation τὸ μὴ σαίνεσθαι κ. τ. λ.: both their own experiences and the apostle's words (ver. 4) taught them this practical lesson. εἰς τοῦτο κείμεθα] '*we are appointed thereunto;*' scil. τὸ θλίβεσθαι (comp. ver. 4), not τὸ ὑπομένειν θλίψεις, Koch 1, the τοῦτο referring laxly to the preceding θλίψεσιν. On the meaning of κείμεθα (Vulg., 'positi,' Syr. ܣܝܡܝܢܢ, Goth. 'ratidai,' but?), see notes *on Phil.* i. 17, and with respect to the sentiment, which is here perfectly general (περὶ πάντων λέγει τῶν πιστῶν, Chrys.), see 2 Tim. iii. 12 (notes), and compare Ruess, *Théol. Chrét.* IV. 20, Vol. II. p. 224 sq.

4. καὶ γὰρ ὅτε κ. τ. λ.] '*for verily when we were with you,*' 'nam et,' Vulg., Clarom., ܐܦ ܟܕ Syr.; proof of the preceding assertion, γὰρ introducing the reason, καὶ throwing stress upon it; see Winer, *Gr.* § 53, p. 397, and notes *on Phil.* ii. 27, where this formula is briefly discussed. On the use of πρὸς with acc. with verbs implying rest, etc., see notes *on Gal.* i. 18, iv. 18. μέλλομεν θλίβεσθαι] '*we are to suffer persecution;*' here not merely a periphrasis of the future, but an indirect statement of the fixed and appointed decree of God; comp. ver. 3. The verb μέλλω has three constructions in the N. T.; (*a*) with the present, — in the Gospels and the majority of passages in the N. T.; (*b*) with the aor., Gal. iii. 23, Rev. iii. 2, iii. 16, — a construction found also in Attic Greek (Plato, *Crit.* p. 108 A. *Gorg.* p. 525 A, al.): (*c*) with a future, — only in a few passages (Acts xi. 28, xxiv. 15), though the prevailing use in earlier Greek: see Winer, *Gr.* § 44. 7, p. 298, Krüger, *Sprachl.* § 53. 8. 3 sq. καὶ οἴδατε] '*and know,*' scil. from your own experiences. The first καὶ does not here seem correlative to the second, καὶ—καὶ (see *on* 1 *Tim.* v. 10), but appears rather to have an ascensive force, while the second is simply copulative; οὐχ ὅτι ἐγένετο τοῦτο λέγει μόνον. ἀλλ' ὅτι πολλὰ καὶ ἄλλα προεῖπε, καὶ ἐξέβη, Chrysostom.

οἴδατε.
5 διὰ τοῦτο κἀγὼ μηκέτι στέγων ἔπεμψα εἰς τὸ γνῶναι
τὴν πίστιν ὑμῶν, μήπως ἐπείρασεν ὑμᾶς ὁ πειράζων καὶ εἰς κενὸν
γένηται ὁ κόπος ἡμῶν.

**When he came to us and reported your faith, we were greatly comforted, and are deeply thankful.**

6 Ἄρτι δὲ ἐλθόντος Τιμοθέου πρὸς ἡμᾶς ἀφ'

5. διὰ τοῦτο] '*On this account;*' scil. because the foretold tribulation had now actually come upon you. In the following κἀγὼ the καὶ does not belong to the sentence (the argument of Lünem., however, that it would then be διὰ καὶ τοῦτο is of no weight, see *on Phil.* iv. 3) but to the pronoun, which it puts in gentle contrast with the ὑμεῖς, both expressed and involved in the preceding verse: as they had felt for the apostle (more fully to in ver. 6), so he, on his part, felt for them; comp. notes on ch. ii. 13. μηκέτι στέγων] '*no longer forbearing, able to contain;*' see notes on ver. 1. εἰς τὸ γνῶναι] '*with a view of learning;*' design of the ἔπεμψα, comp. ver. 2. It does not seem right to supply mentally αὐτόν (Olsh.; 'ut cognosceret,' Æth.-Platt, sim. Pol.); the subject of the principle verb is naturally the subject of the infinitive. So rightly Syr. ܕܐܕܥ [ut cognoscerem]: the other Vv. adopt the inf., or an equivalent ('ad cognoscendam fidem vestram,' Vulg., Clarom.), and are thus equally indeterminate with the original. μήπως ἐπείρασεν κ. τ. λ.] '*lest haply the tempter hath tempted you;*' aor. indic. specifying a fact regarded as having actually taken place already: the temptation was a fact, its results, however, were uncertain (comp. Chrys.); see Winer, *Gr.* § 56. 2, p. 448, and compare notes on the similar passage Gal. ii. 2. It may be observed that Green (*Gr.* p. 81), Fritzsche (*Fritz. Opusc.* p. 176 note), and Scholef. (*Hints*, p. 114) regard μήπως as dubitative in the first clause, and expressive of apprehension in the second, '*an forte* Satanas tentasset ..... *ne forte* labores irriti essent,'—but with little plausibility. The argument of Fritz., that the μήπως (metuentis) in the first clause would have required γενήσεται in the second ('atque ita labores irriti essent futuri'), is certainly not valid: the future would have represented something to occur at some indefinite future time, the aor. subj. is properly used of a transient state occurring in particular cases; see Matth. *Gr.* § 519. 7, and compare Madvig, *Synt.* § 124. 1, who correctly observes that μὴ with fut., after verbs of fearing, etc., always gives a prominence to the notion of futurity. On the substantival form ὁ πειράζων, see exx. in Winer, *Gr.* § 45. 7, p. 316, compare Bernhardy, *Synt.* VI. 22, p. 316. εἰς κενὸν γένηται] '*prove in vain;*' comp. Gal. ii. 2, and the exx. collected by Kypke, *Obs.* Vol. II. p. 275. The primary force of the prep. is somewhat similarly obscured in the adverbial formulæ, εἰς κοινόν, εἰς καιρόν, κ. τ. λ.; see Bernhardy, *Synt.* V. 11, p. 221. On the meaning of κόπος, compare notes on ch. ii. 9.

6. Ἄρτι δὲ is most naturally connected with the participle (Æth. [Pol], —distinctly), not with the remote verb παρεκλήθημεν, ver. 7 (Lünem., Koch), which has its own adjunct, διὰ τοῦτο; so appy. Syr., and probably all the other Vv., but the uncertainty as to punctuation precludes their being confidently cited on either side. The adverb ἄρτι [ἄρω, connected with ἀρτίως, ἁρμοῖ], which properly stands in opp. as well to immediately present (νῦν, Plato *Meno*, p. 89) as remotely past time (πάλαι, *Crit.* p. 43), is often used in the N. T. and in later writers in reference to purely

ὑμῶν καὶ εὐαγγελισαμένου ἡμῖν τὴν πίστιν καὶ τὴν ἀγάπην ὑμῶν,
καὶ ὅτι ἔχετε μνείαν ἡμῶν ἀγαθὴν πάντοτε, ἐπιποθοῦντες ἡμᾶς
ἰδεῖν καθάπερ καὶ ἡμεῖς ὑμᾶς, 7 διὰ τοῦτο παρεκλήθημεν, ἀδελ-

present time; see esp. Lobeck, *Phryn.* p. 18 sq. εὐαγγελισαμένου] '*having told the good tidings of;*' comp. Luke i. 19: οὐκ εἶπεν ἀπαγγείλαντος, ἀλλ', εὐαγγελισαμένου· τοσοῦτον ἀγαθὸν ἡγεῖτο τὴν ἐκείνων βεβαίωσιν καὶ τὴν ἀγάπην, Chrys. The verb εὐαγγελ. is used in the N. T. both in the active (Rev. x. 7, xiv. 6), passive (Gal. i. 11, Heb. iv. 6, al.), and middle. In the last form its constructions in the N. T. are singularly varied; it is used (*a*) absolutely, Rom. xv. 20, 1 Cor. i. 17; (*b*) with a dat. *personæ*, Rom. i. 15; (*c*) with an accus. *personæ*, Acts xvi. 10, 1 Pet. i. 12; (*d*) with an accus. *rei*. Rom x. 15, Gal. i. 23; (*e*) with an accus. *personæ* and *rei*, Acts xiii. 32; and lastly (*f*) — the most common construction — with a dat. *personæ* and acc. *rei*, Luke i. 19, al. Of these (*b*), and occasionally (*c*), are the forms in use in the earlier writers; see Lobeck, *Phryn.* p. 267, Thom.-Mag. p. 379, ed. Bern. τὴν πίστιν καὶ τὴν ἀγ.] '*your faith and your love,*' the faith which you have, and the love which you evince to one another (ver. 12); δηλοῖ ἡ μὲν πίστις τῆς εὐσεβείας τὸ βέβαιον, ἡ δὲ ἀγάπη τὴν πρακτικὴν ἀρετήν, Theod. The third Christian virtue, ἐλπίς, is not here specified (compare 1 Tim. i. 14, 2 Tim. i. 13, al.), but obviously included; comp. Usteri, *Lehrb.* II. 1. 4, p. 241, Reuss, *Théol. Chrét.* IV. 22, Vol. II. p. 259, 260. ὅτι ἔχετε μνείαν κ. τ. λ.] '*that ye have good remembrance of us always;*' not exactly, μνημονεύετε ἡμῶν μετὰ ἐπαίνων καὶ εὐφημίας, Theoph. (comp. Chrys.), but simply, 'that ye retain a good, *i. e.*, as the following words more fully specify, a faithful (βεβαίαν, Œcum.) and affectionate remembrance of us,' 'ut nostra memoria bona sit in vobis,' Copt., compare Syr. The μνεία ἀγαθὴ formed the third item in the good tidings; τρία τέθεικεν ἀξιέραστα, τὴν πίστιν, τὴν ἀγάπην, καὶ τοῦ διδασκάλου τὴν μνήμην, Theod. πάντοτε seems here more naturally joined with the preceding verb (Syr., Æth.), as in ch. i. 2, 1 Cor. i. 4, 2 Thess. i. 3, al., than with the participle (Copt.); the μνεία was not only ἀγαθή, but ἀδιάλειπτος; see 2 Tim. i. 4. So Auth., Arm., and appy. the majority of modern commentators. ἐπιποθ. ἡμᾶς ἰδεῖν] '*longing to see us;*' further expansion of the preceding words; comp. 2 Tim. i. 4. On the force of the ἐπί, here not intensive but *directive*, see Fritz. *on Rom.* i. 11, Vol. I. p. 31, and notes *on* 2 *Tim. l. c.* καθάπερ καὶ ἡμεῖς ὑμᾶς] '*even as we also are longing to see you;*' τὸ γὰρ μαθεῖν τὸν φιλοῦντα ὅτι τοῦτο οἶδεν ὁ φιλούμενος, ὅτι φιλεῖται, πολλὴ παραμυθία καὶ παράκλησις, Chrys. On the meaning and use of καθάπερ, see notes on ch. ii. 11, and on the use of καὶ with comparative adverbs, notes *on Eph.* v. 23.

7. διὰ τοῦτο] '*for this cause:*' in reference to the three preceding specifications, which are here grouped together in one view. The resumed διὰ τοῦτο is not superfluous (compare De W.); the length of the preceding sentence, and the fact that ἄρτι ἐλθόντος involved mainly the predication of time, make a recapitulatory and causal formula here by no means inappropriate. παρεκλ. ἐφ' ὑμῖν] '*we were comforted over you;*' you were the objects which formed the substratum of our comfort; compare 2 Cor. vii. 7. The prep. ἐπὶ is not exactly equivalent to 'in,' Vulg., 'ex,' [fram] Goth., or even 'propter,' Æth. (Pol.), — still less to 'quod attinet ad,' Lünem., — but with its usual and proper

φοί, ἐφ' ὑμῖν ἐπὶ πάσῃ τῇ ἀνάγκῃ καὶ θλίψει ἡμῶν διὰ τῆς
ὑμῶν πίστεως, 8 ὅτι νῦν ζῶμεν ἐὰν ὑμεῖς στήκητε ἐν Κυρίῳ.

force points to the basis *on* which the παράκλησις rested, 'fundamentum cui veluti superstructa est,' Schott; see Winer *Gr.* § 48. c, p. 351. The reading παρακεκλήμεθα, though found only in A and 3 mss., has been adopted by Koch, as according better with his connection of ἄρτι with the finite verb. Surely this is most rash criticism.

ἐπὶ πάσῃ κ. τ. λ.] '*in all our necessity and tribulation;*' certainly not 'in quâvis augustiâ et afflictione,' Schott, — a translation distinctly precluded by the presence of the article, which here represents the ἀνάγκη καὶ θλίψις as a collective whole; compare 2 Cor. i. 4, vii. 4. The use of ἐπὶ is here only slightly different from that above; it has appy. neither a temporal (Lünem.) nor a causal (2 Cor. i. 4, but obs. the accompanying ἐν τῇ θλ.), but a *semi-local* force (compare 2 Cor. vii. 4, and Mey. *in loc.*), marking that with which the παράκλησις stands in immediate contact and connection; comp. Bernhardy, *Synt.* v. 24. b, p. 248 sq., and notes *on Phil.* i. 3. In the former use the idea of ethical superposition seems mainly predominant, in this latter, that of ethical contact; compare Krüger, *Sprachl.* § 68. 41. 5. There is some little doubt as to what the ἀνάγκη καὶ θλίψις are to be referred. On the whole, the force of ἀνάγκη [connected with ΑΓΧ-, Pott, *Etym. Forsch.* Vol. I. p. 134; 'vim omnem significat quæ evitari non potest,' Wunder, Soph. *Trach.* 823] and the tenor of the context seem to imply, not any inward distress (De W.), but rather some *outward* trial and trouble (Alf. compares Acts xviii. 5—10) under which the apostle was then suffering; see Lünem. *in loc.* The order of the words is inverted in *Rec.* (θλίψ. κ. ἀνάγκῃ), but only on the authority of JK; mss.; several Ff. διὰ τῆς πίστεως] '*through your faith;*' the medium by which this comfort was realized by the apostle, was the faith on the part of the Thess. of which he had received tidings; αὕτη ἀσάλευτος μείνασα τὴν παράκλησιν ἡμῖν εἰργάσατο, Œcum.

8. ὅτι νῦν ζῶμεν] '*because now we live;*' reason for the preceding statement of the comfort which he received from hearing of the faith of his converts. The contrast shows that the apostle regards the ἀνάγκη καὶ θλίψις as a kind of death, from which he is raised to the full powers of life (comp. Rom. viii. 7) by the knowledge of the firm posture of the Thess.; τὴν γὰρ ὑμετέραν βεβαίωσιν ζωὴν ἡμετέραν ὑπολαμβάνομεν, Theod.; compare Pearson, *Creed*, Vol. II. p. 319 (ed. Burt.). The conditional member, ἐὰν ὑμεῖς κ. τ. λ., shows that νῦν (like the Lat. 'nunc') is not here used in a purely temporal (comp. Jowett), but in a logical and argumentative sense, approaching in meaning to 'in hoc rerum statu,' 'rebus sic se habentibus;' see Hartung, *Partik.* νῦν, 2. 2, Vol. II. p. 25, Jelf. *Gr.* § 719. 2. The true principle of the usage is well explained by Hand; 'sæpe in his duæ rerum conditiones collocantur, quarum altera aut præcessit, aut cogitatur esse posse, eique ex adverso opponitur ea quæ vera ac *præsens* adest et valet,' *Tursell.* Vol. IV. p. 340.

ἐὰν ὑμεῖς στήκητε] '*if ye stand (fast);*' hypothetically stated, as the faith of the Thessalonians was not yet complete (comp. ver. 10); experience was yet to show whether the assumption was correct. On the force of ἐὰν with the subj. ('sumo hoc, et potest omnino ita se habere, sed utrum vere futurum sit, necne, id nescio, verum experientiâ cognoscam,' Herm.), and on its general distinction from εἰ with the indic., see

9 τίνα γὰρ εὐχαριστίαν δυνάμεθα τῷ Θεῷ ἀνταποδοῦναι περὶ ὑμῶν ἐπὶ πάσῃ τῇ χαρᾷ ᾗ χαίρομεν δι' ὑμᾶς ἔμπροσθεν τοῦ Θεοῦ

notes *on Gal.* i. 9, Winer, *Gr.* § 41. 2, p. 260, and Herm. *Viger*, No. 312. The solecistic reading στήκετε [AFGKL; mss.; Chrys. ms.] is maintained by Koch and *Tisch.* (ed. 7), — but on insufficient authority, as such permutations of similar vowels are occasionally found even in the best MSS.; comp. Scrivener, *Introd. to N. T.* p. 10. On the meaning of this late form στήκειν, not *per se* 'to stand *fast*' (comp. Rom. xiv. 4], see notes *on Phil.* i. 27. In the N. T. it occurs only in St. Paul's Epp., and Mark xi. 25. ἐν Κυρίῳ] '*in the Lord*,' — in Him, as the element of their true life, and the sphere of its practical manifestations; comp. Phil. iv. 1, and see notes *on Eph.* iv. 17, vi. 1.

9. τίνα γὰρ κ.τ.λ.] Confirmation of the preceding conditioned declaration, ὅτι νῦν ζῶμεν κ. τ. λ.; 'we live, I say, for what sufficient thanks can be rendered to God for our plenitude of joy on your account;' τοσαύτη, φησίν, ἡ δι' ὑμᾶς χαρά, ὅτι οὐδὲ εὐχαριστεῖν κατ' ἀξίαν εὑρίσκομεν, Œcum., comp. Theoph. ἀνταποδοῦναι] '*render*,' — properly, 'in return,' 'retribuere,' Vulg., ܠܡܦܪܥܘ, Syr.; εὐχαριστία is regarded as a kind of return for the mercies and blessings of God: Grot. aptly compares Ps. cxvi. 12, מָה־אָשִׁיב לַיהוָה. The binary compound ἀνταποδιδόναι is used by the apostle both 'in bonam' and 'in malam partem' (2 Thess. i. 6, comp. Rom. xii. 19), in the sense of rendering back a due; the ἀντὶ marking the idea of return, the ἀπὸ hinting at that of the debt incurred, 'ubi dando te exsolvis debito,' Winer, *de Verb. Comp.* IV. p. 12. περὶ ὑμῶν '*concerning you*,' '*for you*;' compare ch. i. 2, 1 Cor. i. 4, 2 Thess. i. 3, ii. 13. The difference between περὶ and ὑπὲρ (Eph. i. 16, compare Phil. i. 4) in such combinations as the present is scarcely appreciable; see notes *on Col.* iv. 3, and comp. *on Phil.* i. 7. ἐπὶ πάσῃ τῇ χαρᾷ] '*on account, for, all the joy*;' ἐπὶ having here more of its causal and derivative sense, and marking the ground and reason of the ἀνταπόδοσις εὐχαριστίας: comp. 1 Cor. i. 4, 2 Cor. ix. 15, Polyb. *Hist.* XVIII. 26. 4, see notes *on Phil.* i. 5, and Krüger, *Sprachl.* § 68. 41. 6. The present use of ἐπὶ is nearly allied to the common use of the prep. with verbs denoting affections of the mind, θαυμάζειν, ἀγαλλιᾶν, κ. τ. λ., but perhaps recedes a shade farther from the idea of 'ethical basis,' to which both this and all similar uses of the prep. are to be ultimately referred; see notes on ver. 7, and Winer, *Gr.* § 48. c. p. 351. It is scarcely necessary to say that πᾶσα ἡ χαρὰ is not, except by reference, 'summa lætitia' (Schott, — who, however, fails to observe the article), but 'all the joy,' Copt., — 'joy taken in its whole extent;' see Winer, *Gr*, § 18. 4, p. 101: the apostle's joy wanted nothing to make it full and complete. ᾗ χαίρομεν] '*which we joy*:' attraction for ἣν χαίρομεν (Winer, *Gr.* § 24. 1), the construction being appy. here χαίρειν χαρὰν (Matth. ii. 10), not χαίρειν χαρᾷ (John iii. 29), which, though analogous, would be scarcely so natural with the simple relative. On these intensive forms, see Winer, *Gr.* § 32. 2, p. 201, § 54. 3, p. 341, Lobeck, *Paralipom.* p. 224 sq. ἔμπροσθεν κ. τ. λ.] '*before our God*;' further definition of the pure nature of the joy: it was such as could bear the scrutiny of the eye of God, 'illo videlicet teste atque inspectore, et ut arbitror probatore,' Just., comp. Calv. On the formula ἔμπροσθεν τοῦ Θεοῦ, only used

ἡμῶν; [10] νυκτὸς καὶ ἡμέρας ὑπερεκπερισσοῦ δεόμενοι εἰς τὸ ἰδεῖν ὑμῶν τὸ πρόσωπον καὶ καταρτίσαι τὰ ὑστερήματα τῆς πίστεως ὑμῶν.

May God direct my way to you. May he make you abound in love, and stablish you in holiness.

11 Αὐτὸς δὲ ὁ Θεὸς καὶ πατὴρ ἡμῶν καὶ ὁ

by St. Paul in this Ep. (ch. i. 3, iii. 13, comp. ii. 19), see notes on ch. i. 3. The clause obviously belongs, not to χαρᾷ (Pelt), still less to ver. 10 (Sy.-Pesh., but not Philox.), but to verb χαίρομεν.

10. νυκτὸς καὶ ἡμέρας] '*night and day;*' καὶ τοῦτο τῆς χαρᾶς σημεῖον, Chrys. On this formula, see notes on ch. ii. 9, and *on* 1 *Tim.* v. 5. ὑπερεκπερισσοῦ δεόμενοι] '*above measure praying;*' participial adjunct, not to χαίρομεν, which is only part of a subordinate clause, but to the leading thought τίνα — ἀνταποδοῦναι (Lünem., Alf., Jowett), the participle not having so much a causal (Lünem.) as a circumstantial ('praying as we do,' Alf.), or perhaps rather a simply temporal reference; compare Krüger, *Sprachl.* § 56. 10. 1. On the rare cumulative form ὑπερεκ. (ch. v. 13, Eph. iii. 20, Daniel iii. 23 (Theod.), compare Clem., Rom. 1 *Cor.* 20), and St. Paul's noticeable use of compounds of ὑπέρ, see notes *on Eph. l. c.* εἰς τὸ ἰδεῖν] '*that we may see,*' 'ut videamus,' Vulg., Clarom.; purpose and object (ἵνα ἴδῃ αὐτούς, Theoph.) of the prayer, with perhaps an included reference to the subject of it; comp. 2 Thess. ii. 2, and see notes on ch. ii. 12. καταρτίσαι] '*make complete,*' 'ut suppleamus,' Clarom. The verb καταρτίζειν (Hesych. κατασκευάζειν, στερεοῦν, Zonar. ἁρμόζειν) properly signifies 'to make ἄρτιος' — the κατὰ having appy. a slightly intensive force (see Rost u. Palm, *Lex.* s. v. κατά, IV. 4), — thence 'to re-adjust and restore,' whether in a simple (Matth. iv. 21) or an ethical sense (Gal. vi. 1), what had been previously out of order; and thence, with a somewhat more derivative sense (as here), 'to supply what is lacking or deficient,' πληρῶσαι, Theod., ἀναπληρῶσαι. Œcum. For exx. see Wetst. Vol. I. p. 278, Elsner, *Obs.* Vol. II. p. 70, and notes *on Gal. l. c.* τὰ ὑστερήματα κ. τ. λ.] '*the lacking measures of your faith,*' 'that in which your faith was yet deficient;' compare Col. i. 24. These defects are referred by Olsh. to their faith, not on the side of its power, but of its knowledge. This seems substantially true (οὐ πάσης ἀπέλαυσαν τῆς διδασκαλίας, οὐδὲ ὅσα ἐχρῆν μαθεῖν ἔμαθον, Chrys., compare ch. iv. 13); it does not, however, seem correct to exclude defects on the side of *practice,* which ch. iv. 1 sq. seem mainly intended to supply; see Lünem. *in loc.*

11. Αὐτὸς δὲ κ. τ. λ.] '*Now may God Himself and our Father;*' transition by the δὲ μεταβατικὸν [see notes *on Gal.* iii. 8) to good wishes and prayers for their progress in holiness. The αὐτὸς does not seem here to suggest any antithesis between God and the δεόμενοι, ver. 10 (De W.), but merely to enhance the power of God in respect of κατευθύνειν τὴν ὁδόν (Lünem.), and to place in contrast the human agent with his earnest but foiled efforts (ch. ii. 18), and God, who, if He willed, could instantly and surely accomplish all; ὡσεὶ ἔλεγεν, ὁ Θεὸς ἐκκόψαι τὸν Σαταν͂αν τὸν πανταχοῦ ἡμῖν διὰ τῶν πειρασμῶν ἐμποδίζοντα, ἵνα ὀρθὴν ὁδὸν πρὸς ὑμᾶς ποιησώμεθα, Œcum. On the meaning of the august title, ὁ Θεὸς καὶ πατήρ, and the probable connection of ἡμῶν with only the latter subst. (so also Lünem.), see notes *on Gal.* i. 4. It may be remarked that the copula is omitted in Syr., Copt., Æth. (both), and retained in Vulg., Clarom.

*Κύριος ἡμῶν Ἰησοῦς κατευθύναι τὴν ὁδὸν ἡμῶν πρὸς ὑμᾶς.*
12 *ὑμᾶς δὲ ὁ Κύριος πλεονάσαι καὶ περισσεύσαι τῇ ἀγάπῃ εἰς*

Goth., Arm., Syr. (Philox.), but that in these latter Vv., where it thus occurs, there is no trace of the explanatory force here ascribed to it by many modern commentators. καὶ ὁ Κύριος ἡμῶν Ἰησ.] Union of the Son with the Father in the apostle's prayer. The language of some of the German expositors is here neither clear nor satisfactory: we do not say with Lünem., that Christ, as sitting at the right hand of God, has a part in the government of the world, 'nach paulinischer Anschauung' (compare Usteri, *Lehrb.* II. 2. 4, p. 315), still less with Koch, that the apostle regards Christ 'als die Weisheit und Macht Gottes,'—but assert simply and plainly, that the Eternal Son is here distinguished from the Father in respect of His Personality, but mystically united with Him (observe the significant singular, κατευθύναι) in respect of his Godhead, and, as God, rightly and duly addressed in the language of direct prayer; see esp. Athan. *contr. Arian.* III. 11, Waterl. *Defence*, Qu. XVII. Vol. I. p. 423, Qu. XXII. p. 467. The addition Χριστός (*Rec.*), though supported by D³EFGKL; mss.; Vv.; Ath., and many Ff., is appy. rightly rejected by most modern editors with ACD²; 5 mss.; Clarom., Sangerm., Amit., Æth. (Pol.,—but not Platt), al., as a conformation to the more usual formula. κατευθύναι] *'direct;'* optative, not infinitive,—which, though occasionally found in older, and esp. poetical writers in ref. to wishes and prayers (Appollon. *de Synt.* III. 14, Bernhardy, *Synt.* IX. 3, p. 357), has no place in the language of the N. T.; see Winer, *Gr.* § 43. 5, p. 283. The singular is certainly very noticeable both here and 2 Thess. ii. 17; no reasons, except those founded on the true relation of the Father and Son, seem in any way to account for the enallage of number. The verb κατευθύνειν (Luke i. 79, 2 Thess. iii. 5) properly signifies 'to make straight,' thence (as here) 'to direct' ('dirigat,' Vulg., ܢܬܪܘܨ, Syr.), the κατὰ being appy. not so much intensive (Koch) as directive, and the appended πρὸς specifying the *terminus ad quem;* comp. Winer, *Gr.* § 52. 4, p. 383.

12. ὑμᾶς δὲ] *'But you,'—you*—whatever it may please God to appoint with respect to *us* and our prayer: 'aliud votum quo optat Paulus ut interea dum obstructum illi est iter, se tamen absente Dominus illos confirmet in sanctitate,' Calv. ὁ Κύριος] Not the First Person of the blessed Trinity (Alf.),—still less the Third (Basil, ap. Pearson, *Creed*, Vol. II. p. 265, ed. Burt), but, in accordance with the application of the title both in ver. 11 and ver. 13, and the prevailing usage in St. Paul's Epp., the *Second;* compare Winer, *Gr.* § 19. 1, p. 113. The subject ὁ Κύριος [ὁ Θεός, A, 73; ὁ Κύριος Ἰησοῦς, D¹E¹FG; Clarom., Sangerm., al.] is omitted in Syr., Arab. (Erp.), and is rejected by *Mill* (*Prolegom.* p. cxxx), De W., Koch, al.), as an interpolation. The external authority for its insertion is too preponderant to be safely reversed; so, *Lachm.*, *Tisch.* πλεονάσαι καὶ περισσεύσαι] *'make you to increase and to abound,'* 'multiplicet et abundare faciat,' Vulg., Clarom.; both verbs transitive, and nearly synonymous; the former referring not to mere numerical increase (τῷ ἀριθμῷ πλεονάσαι, Theod.), but to spiritual enlargement, the second to spiritual abundance, and having more of a superlative meaning; comp. Fritz. *Rom.* Vol. I. p. 351. Πλεονάζειν is not transitive elsewhere in the N. T., see,

ἀλλήλους καὶ εἰς πάντας, καθάπερ καὶ ἡμεῖς εἰς ὑμᾶς· 13 εἰς τὸ
στηρίξαι ὑμῶν τὰς καρδίας ἀμέμπτους ἐν ἁγιωσύνῃ ἔμπροσθεν
τοῦ Θεοῦ καὶ πατρὸς ἡμῶν, ἐν τῇ παρουσίᾳ τοῦ Κυρίου ἡμῶν
Ἰησοῦ μετὰ πάντων τῶν ἁγίων αὐτοῦ.

however, Psalm lxx. 21, ἐπλεόνασας τὴν δικαιοσύνην, 1 Macc. iv. 35, πλεονάσας τὸν στρατόν; the latter περισσ. is also commonly intrans., but see 2 Cor. iv. 15, iv. 8, Eph. i. 8 (notes). τῇ ἀγάπῃ κ. τ. λ.] '*in your love one toward another, and toward all;*' instrumental or rather ablatival dative, specifying that *with* which they were to be enlarged and to abound; see Hartung, *Casus*, p. 94, Scheuerl. *Synt.* § 22, p. 178, 182. This love was to be shown both in the form of brotherly love (φιλαδελφία, ch. iv. 9) and, in its more extended form, to all mankind, whether ὁμόπιστοι (Theod.) or not; τοῦτο γὰρ τῆς κατὰ Θεὸν ἀγάπης ἴδιον τὸ πάντας περιπλέκεσθαι, Theoph. καθάπερ καὶ ἡμεῖς εἰς ὑμ.] '*even as we also do toward you;*' scil. πλεονάζομεν καὶ περισσεύομεν τῇ ἀγάπῃ [περὶ ὑμᾶς διετέθειμεν, Theod.], the verbs which were previously transitive now relapsing into their usual intransitive meaning: τὸ μὲν ἡμέτερον ἤδη ἐστί· τὸ δὲ ὑμέτερον ἀξιοῦμεν γενέσθαι, Chrys. This mode of supplying the ellipsis, though open to the objection of causing two different meanings to be assigned to πλεον. and περισσ. in the same verse, seems less arbitrary than that of Syr. (comp. Copt., al., ἀγάπην ἔχομεν, Grot.) '*sumus*, more Hebræo,' etc., and is supported by the analogy of simple verbs being supplied from compound verbs, affirmative from negative; comp. Jelf, *Gr.* § 895. f, h. On the meaning of καθάπερ, see notes on ch. ii. 11, and on the use of καί, notes on ch. iv. 5.

13. εἰς τὸ στηρίξαι] '*in order to establish,*' '*to the end he may establish,*' Auth.-Ver.; not the result (Baumg.-Crus.), but the end and aim of the πλεον. καὶ περισσ. τῇ ἀγάπῃ: ἂν γὰρ αὐτὴ περισσεύῃ, στηριγμός ἐστι τῶν κεκτημένων αὐτήν, Œcum.; love being, as De W. observes, the fulfilling of the law (Rom. xiii. 10) and the bond of perfectness (Col. iii. 14). The subject of the inf., it need scarcely be said, is not ἡμᾶς (Corn. a Lap. 1), nor ἀγάπην (Œcum.), nor even Θεόν (a Lap. 2), but the subject of the foregoing verse, τὸν Κύριον. ἀμέμπτους ἐν ἁγιωσύνῃ] '*so as to be unblameable in holiness;*' proleptic use of the adjective; compare 1 Cor, i. 8, Phil. iii. 21, see Winer, *Gr.* § 66. 3, p. 550, Jelf, *Gr.* § 439. 2, Schæfer, Demosth. Vol. I. p. 239, and the long and elaborate note of Koch, *in loc.* The *hearts* (ἐκ τῆς καρδίας ἐξέρχονται διαλογισμοὶ πονηροί, Chrys.) were to be blameless, and that not simply, but in a sphere and element of holiness. On the orthographically correct but late form ἁγιωσύνη (Rom. i. 4, 2 Cor. vii. 1), not ἁγιοσύνη, as B[1]DEFG, see Fritz. *Rom.* Vol. I. p. 10, Buttm. *Gr.* § 118. 11. In meaning it differs but little from ἁγιότης (2 Cor. i. 12 [*Lachm.*], Heb. xii. 10), except perhaps that it represents more the condition than the abstract quality, while ἁγιασμός, as its termination shows, points primarily to the process (2 Thess. ii. 13, 1 Pet. i. 2), and thence, with that gradual approach of the termination in -μος to that in -σύνη which is so charactertisic of the N. T., the state (1 Tim. ii. 15, see notes), frame of mind, or holy disposition (Waterland, *on Justif.* Vol. VI. p. 7), in which the action of the verb is evinced and exemplified; see Usteri, *Lehrb.* II. 1. 3, p. 226, and compare ἀγαθωσύνη, ἀγαθότης, and notes *on Gal.* v. 22. ἔμπροσθεν τοῦ Θεοῦ does not belong exclusively either to ἐν ἁγιωσύνῃ (Pelt) or to ἀμέμπτους

Abound ye, according to my commands. God's will is your sanctification, wherefore be chaste and continent.

IV. Λοιπὸν οὖν, ἀδελφοί, ἐρωτῶμεν ὑμᾶς καὶ παρακαλοῦμεν ἐν Κυρίῳ Ἰησοῦ, ἵνα καθὼς

1. ἵνα καθώς] So *Lachm.* with $BD^1E^1FG$; 8 mss.; Syr., Vulg., Clarom., Copt., Goth. [but does not repeat it in last clause], Æth.-Pol. (appy., but ? Platt), Arm.; Chrys. (1 ms.), Lat. Ff. (*Tisch.* ed. 1, *Lünem.*, *Alf.*). In his second ed. *Tisch.* omits the conjunction with $AD^3E^2KL$; great majority of mss.; Syr. (Philox.), appy. Æth. (Platt); Chrys., Theod., Dam., al. (*Rec.*, *Scholz*), but has now (ed. 7) rightly (as it would seem) returned to the reading of *Lachmann.*

(De W.), but to both (Lünem.); their ἀμεμφία ἐν ἁγιωσ. was to be such as could bear the searching eye of God; see notes on ver. 9, and on ch. i. 3. ἐν τῇ παρουσίᾳ Ἰησοῦ] '*at the coming of Jesus;*' καὶ γὰρ ὑπ' αὐτοῦ κρινόμεθα ἔμπροσθεν τοῦ Πατρός, Theoph.; see notes on ch. ii. 19. The addition Χριστοῦ is rightly rejected by *Lachm.*, *Tisch.*, with ABDEK; 20 mss.; Clarom., Sangerm., Amit., Æth. (Pol.,—but not Platt); Dam., Ambr.: the appearance of Ἰησοῦ without Χριστοῦ seems somewhat noticeably frequent in this Epistle (nine times out of sixteen); compare i. 10, ii. 15, 19, iii. 11, iv. 1, 2, 14 (bis). μετὰ πάντων κ.τ.λ.] '*accompanied with all His Saints;*' not σύν, but μετά; they are here represented not so much united with Him as attending on Him and swelling the majesty of His train; compare notes *on Eph.* vi. 23, and contrast Col. iii. 4, where, on the contrary, the context shows that the idea is mainly that of coherence. It is very doubtful whether οἱ ἅγιοι are, with Pearson (*Creed*, Vol. II. p. 296), to be referred to the Holy Angels (2 Thess. i. 7, Matth. xvi. 27, xxv. 31, al.; compare Heb. קְדֹשִׁים Psalm lxxxix. 6, Zech. xiv. 5, al.), or, with Hofmann (*Schriftb* Vol. II. 2, p. 595), to the Saints in their more inclusive sense (ch. iv. 14, comp. 1 Cor. vi. 2): perhaps the addition πάντες may justify us in referring the term to both; so Beng., Alf. The ἀμὴν at the end of the verse [bracketed by *Lachm.*, with $AD^1E$; mss.; Clarom., Sang., Vulg.] seems a mere liturgical addition.

CHAPTER IV. 1. Λοιπὸν οὖν] '*Furthermore then,*' in consequence of, and in accordance with the issue prayed for in the preceding verse; the οὖν having here its *collective* force, and introducing an appeal to the Thessalonians on their side, grounded on what the apostle had prayed for them from God; they were to do *their* part, Olsh. On the two uses of οὖν (*collective* and *reflexive*), see Klotz, *Devar.* Vol. II. p. 717, compared with Hartung, *Partik.* Vol. II. p. 9. The transl. of Vulg., 'ergo' (Clarom. less correctly, 'autem'), is judiciously altered by Beza to 'igitur,' the former being properly used only 'in graviore argumentatione,' Hand, *Tursell.* Vol. III. p. 187. The exact meaning of λοιπὸν has been somewhat contested. By observing its use (2 Cor. xiii. 11) and that of the more specific τὸ λοιπὸν (Eph. vi. 10, Phil. iii. 1, iv. 8, 2 Thess. iii. 1) in St. Paul's Epp., it does not appear either simply temporal (ἀεὶ μὲν καὶ εἰς τὸ διηνεκές, Chrys., Theoph), or simply ethical (ἀποχρώντως, Œcum. 2), but rather marks the transition to the close of the Ep., and to what remains yet to be said ('de cætero,' Vulg.), whether much (Phil. iii. 1) or little (2 Cor. xiii. 11); τὸ εἰς παραίνεσιν ἐλθεῖν, Œcum. 1: compare notes *on Phil.* iii. 1. The omission of τὸ is here supported by all the MSS. except $B^2$ [mss.; Chrys., Theod.], and acqui-

παρελάβετε παρ' ἡμῶν τὸ πῶς δεῖ ὑμᾶς περιπατεῖν καὶ ἀρέσκειν Θεῷ, καθὼς καὶ περιπατεῖτε ἵνα περισσεύητε μᾶλλον. 2 οἴδατε

καθὼς καὶ περιπατεῖτε] So *Lachm.* with ABDEFG; 8 mss.; Amit., Harl., Clarom., Copt., Goth., Syr. (Philox.), Æth. (both), Arm. (*Tisch.* ed., 1 *Lünem.*, *Alf.*, *Wordsw.*). The clause was omitted by *Tisch.* (ed. 2) with D³E²KL; great majority of mss; Syr.; Chrys., Theod., Dam. (*Rec.*, *Mill*, *Scholz*, *De W.*), but is now (ed. 7) properly restored, the authority for the omission being obviously insufficient.

esced in by *Lachm.*, *Tisch.*, and appy. all modern editors: that of οὖν [only B¹; 8 mss.; Syr., Copt.; Chrys.], though approved by *Mill* (*Prolegom.* p. xcv) and *Tisch.* ed. 1, is, on the contrary, by no means probable. ἐρωτῶμεν] '*we beseech:*' comp. v. 12, Phil. iv. 3, 2 Thess. ii. 1: a derivative and non-classical use of ἐρωτᾶν, perhaps suggested by the double use of שָׁאַל (Schott), of which in the LXX it is not uncommonly a translation; see Psalm cxxii. 6, ἐρωτήσατε (שַׁאֲלוּ) δὴ τὰ εἰς εἰρήνην τῇ Ἱερουσαλήμ. παρακαλοῦμεν ἐν Κυρίῳ] '*exhort you in the Lord;*' our παράκλησις is only in Him (see Phil. ii. 1, and notes); He is the sphere and element in which alone all we say and do has its proper existence and efficacy: see notes *on Eph.* iv. 17, vi. 1. The gloss διὰ τοῦ Θεοῦ, Chysost. (τὸν Χριστὸν παραλαμβάνει, Theophyl., '*per* Christum rogat et obsecrat,' Schott 2), involves needless departures from the almost regular meaning of this significant formula: all the ancient Vv. retain the simple and primary meaning of the preposition. ἵνα καθὼς κ. τ. λ.] '*that, even as ye received from us;*' subject of the prayer blended with the purpose of making it, introduced by the partially final ἵνα; see notes *on Eph.* i. 17. On the meaning of παρελάβετε, here unduly extended by Chrys., Theoph. to the teaching of examples (οὐχὶ ῥημάτων μόνον ἐστὶν, ἀλλὰ καὶ πραγμάτων), see notes on ch. ii. 13. τὸ πῶς δεῖ κ. τ. λ.] '*how ye ought to walk;*' literally 'the how,' etc., the τὸ giving to the whole clause a substantival character, and bringing the two members into a single point of view: comp. Luke ix. 46, Rom. iv. 13, viii. 26, see Winer, *Gr.* § 20. 3, p 162 (ed. 5,—omitted or placed elsewhere in ed. 6), Fritz. *on Mark*, p. 372, and the numerous exx in Matth. *Gr.* § 280. καὶ ἀρέσκειν Θεῷ] '*and* (*by so doing*) *to please God.*' The καὶ does not seem either explanatory (Schott 2) or Hebraistic ('vim consilii aut effectus describens,' Storr, cited by Schott) but, with its not uncommon consecutive force, marks the ἀρέσκειν as the result of the περιπατεῖν; comp. notes *on Phil.* iv. 12. On the insertion of the following clause, καθὼς καὶ περιπατεῖτε, which we can hardly say is 'vitiose et parum ad rem' (Just.), see critical notes, the terms of the concluding exhortation seem to render an allusion to their present state, if not necessary, yet certainly natural and appropriate. For a sound sermon on this text, see Beveridge, *Serm.* CXXIII. Vol. v. p. 347 sq. περισσεύητε μᾶλλον] '*ye may abound still more,*' scil. in your walking and pleasing God. The omission of an οὕτως corresponding to the first καθώς, and the conclusion of the sentence in terms not wholly symmetrical to what had preceded, involve no real difficulty, and are characteristic of the apostle's style.

2. οἴδατε γάρ] '*For ye know.*' Appeal to the memory of the Thess. in confirmation of the foregoing declaration καθὼς παρελάβετε, 'quasi dicat, accepisse vos a nobis dico,' Est.; comp. 1 Cor. xv. 1, 2, Gal. iv. 13. τίνας παραγγ.] '*what command;*'

γὰρ τίνας παραγγελίας ἐδώκαμεν ὑμῖν διὰ τοῦ Κυρίου Ἰησοῦ.
3 τοῦτο γάρ ἐστιν ϑέλημα τοῦ Θεοῦ, ὁ ἁγιασμὸς ὑμῶν, ἀπέχεσ-

not 'evangelii prædicationem,' Pelt, — but, in accordance with the regular meaning of the word and the tenor of the context, 'præcepta,' scil. 'bene sancteque vivendi,' Est., 'vitæ præcepta,' Calv.; compare Acts v. 28, xvi. 24, 1 Tim. i. 5, 18, and see notes *in locc.* The emphasis, as Lünem. observes, rests on τίνας, and prepares the reader for the following τοῦτο, ver. 3. διὰ τοῦ Κυρ. Ἰησ.] '*by the Lord Jesus,*' 'per Dominum,' Vulg., Clarom., 'þairh,' Goth.; not equivalent to ἐν Κυρίῳ (Pelt), but correctly designating the Lord as the 'causa medians' through which the παραγγελίαι were declared; they were not the apostle's own commands, but Christ's (οὐκ ἐμὰ γὰρ, φησίν, ἃ παρήγγειλα, ἀλλ' ἐκείνου ταῦτα, Theoph.), by whose blessed influence he was moved to deliver them; comp. 2 Cor. i. 5, and see Winer, *Gr.* § 47. 1, p. 239 (note). The addition does not, thus, seem designed so much to vindicate the authority of the apostle (Olsh.) as to enhance the importance of the commands; comp. 1 Cor. vii. 10.

3. τοῦτο γὰρ κ. τ. λ.] '*For this is the will of God,*' — 'this that follows, this that I am about to declare to you;' further explanation of the τίνας παραγγελίας, γὰρ having here more of its explanatory ('quippe hæc,' Schott) than its argumentative force; see notes *on Gal.* ii. 6. Τοῦτο is obviously not the predicate (De Wette), but the subject, placed somewhat emphatically forward to echo the preceding τίνας, and to direct the reader's attention to the noun in apposition that follows. Lünem. and Alf. compare Rom. ix. 8, Gal. iii. 7; but the passages are not perfectly analogous, as there the demonstrative pronoun is retrospective, here mainly prospective; compare notes *on Gal. l. c.* ϑέλημα τοῦ Θεοῦ] '*the will of God;*' 'id quod Deus vult,' Fritz. *Rom.* Vol. II. p. 33. The omission of the article (AFG [*Lachm.*] insert it) is not to be accounted for by the non-distribution of the predicate ϑέλ. τοῦ Θεοῦ (Alf.), nor because what follows does not exhaust the conception (Lünem.), but simply on the principle noticed by the Greek grammarians (Apollon. *de Synt.* I. 31, p. 64, ed. Bekk.), that 'after verbs substantive or nuncupative,' the article is frequently omitted: see Middleton, *Gr. Art.* III. 3. 2, p. 43 (ed. Rose), but observe that the rule is by no means so universal as Middl. seems to think; see Winer, *Gr.* § 18. 7, p. 104. When the subject is a demonstrative pronoun, and the verb omitted (Rom. ix. 8), the exceptions are naturally fewer, as the insertion of the article might often leave it uncertain whether the demonstr. pronoun was intended to be predicative or no; see Stalb. on Plato, *Apol.* p. 18 A, and Engelhart on Plato, *Lach.* § 1.

It may be noticed that the useful and common form ϑέλημα is appy. confined to the LXX, N. T., and late writers; comp Lobeck, *Phryn.* p. 7.

ὁ ἁγιασμὸς ὑμῶν] '*your sanctification;*' appositional member to the preceding ϑέλημα τοῦ Θεοῦ, further defined both negatively and positively in the following clauses, and more specially exemplified in the subsequent appositional member τὸ μὴ ὑπερβαίνειν, ver. 6. The late substantive ἁγιασμός, — which, as the defining clauses seem to show, has here somewhat of a special meaning (Beng.), — is not equivalent to ἁγιωσύνη (comp. Olsh., Usteri, *Lehrb.* p. 225, note), but, in accordance with its termination ('action of verb proceeding from subject,' Donalds. *Cratyl.* § 254), still retains its active force, ὑμῶν

ϑαι ὑμᾶς ἀπὸ τῆς πορνείας, 4 εἰδέναι ἕκαστον ὑμῶν τὸ ἑαυτοῦ

being a simple gen. *objecti*, 'sanctificatio vestri,' *i. e.* 'ut sanctitati studeatis,' Menoch. ap. Pol. *Syn.:* comp. Krüger, *Sprachl.* § 47. 7. 1 sq., and see note on ch. iii. 13. ἀπέχεσϑαι ὑμᾶς κ. τ. λ.] '*to wit, that ye abstain from fornication;*' explanatory infinitive, defining on the negative side the preceding term ὁ ἁγιασμός, which otherwise must have been regarded as simply general in its signification; see Krüger, *Sprachl.* § 57. 10. 6 sq., Winer, *Gr.* § 44. 1, p. 284, and comp. Madvig, *Synt.* § 153, who, however, has not sufficiently illustrated this not uncommon use of the infinitive. Even Winer (*Gr.* § 44. 2) seems to regard the present as a subject-inf. in apposition to ϑέλημα τοῦ Θεοῦ (comp. too Syr., Æth.), but appy. with but little plausibility. The insertion (ch. v. 22) or omission of ἀπὸ (1 Tim. iv. 3), after the compound ἀπέχεσϑαι involves no real change of meaning (compare Acts xv. 20, 29), but differs at most only thus much, —'ut in priori formula [with ἀπὸ] sejunctionis cogitatio ad rem, in posteriore autem ad nos ipsos referatur,' Tittmann, *Synnon.* I. p. 225. τῆς πορνείας] '*Fornication;*' abstract, and perhaps here with a somewhat comprehensive meaning [F and a few mss. insert πασης; others, Chrys., Theod., al. (compare Syr.), substitute it for the art.], 'quicquid est rerum venerearum,' Calv., or more suitably to the present context, 'omnem illicitum concubitum' (comp. Est.). It must be always remembered that the deadly sin of πορνεία in its usual and general sense ever formed the subject of special prohibition, as being one of those things which the Gentile world regarded as ἀδιάφορα; see Meyer *on Acts* xv. 20.

4. εἰδέναι ἕκαστον] '*that each one of you know* (*how*) *etc.;*' explanatory infinitive, defining on the positive side of the preceding ἁγιασμός: so (as far as can be inferred from the collocation of words and form of expression), Copt., Goth., Arm., and, in spite of modern punctuation, Vulg. Alford and others (comp. Clarom. 'abstinere — ut sciat — ut nequis') regard the whole εἰδέναι — διεμαρτυράμεϑα as a further specification of what immediately precedes; this, however, tends to obscure the distinction between the infinitival clauses with and without the article (see below on ver. 6), and, exegetically considered, has nothing particularly to recommend it. For a similar comprehensive force of εἰδέναι, see Phil. iv. 12; δείκνυσι ὅτι ἀσκήσεως καὶ μαϑήσεώς ἐστι τὸ σωφρονεῖν, Theoph. τὸ ἑαυτοῦ σκεῦος κτᾶσϑαι] '*to get himself his own vessel;*' so, it would seem, Syr., Copt. (*e-chphof naf*), Armen. (*sdānāl*); — but, as in these and other languages the ideas of acquisition and possession are expressed by the same word, discrimination is not easy. The meaning of the clause, and especially of the word σκεῦος, has been much debated. Setting aside all arbitrary and untenable interpretations, we have two explanations of τὸ ἑαυτοῦ σκεῦος; (*a*) '*his body;*' σκεῦος τὸ σῶμα φησίν, Theoph., Œcum.; so Chrysost., Theod. (who notices and rejects the other expl.), Tertull. (*de Resurr.* 16), Ambrosiast., Olsh., and some modern commentators; (*b*) '*his wife:*' σκεῦος τὴν ἰδίαν ἑκάστου γαμέτην ὀνομάζει, Theod.-Mops., August. *contra Jul.* IV. 10, — or more generally (De Wette), his lawful 'copartner and recipient' in fulfilling the divine ordinance (Gen. i. 28), with a reference to the similar use of the Heb. כְּלִי (see the pertinent ex. *Megill. Est.* i. 11, 'vas meum quo ego utor,' cited by Schoettg. *Hor.* Vol. I. p. 727, and most commentt.) and the generally appropriate nature of the trope (see *Sohar. Levit.* xxxviii. 152,

σκεῦος κτᾶσθαι ἐν ἁγιασμῷ καὶ τιμῇ, 5 μὴ ἐν πάθει ἐπιθυμίας
καθάπερ καὶ τὰ ἔθνη τὰ μὴ εἰδότα τὸν Θεόν, 6 τὸ μὴ ὑπερβαί-

cited by Schoettg.): so Aquin., Est., more recently Schott, De Wette, and appy. the majority of recent expositors. Of these two interpretations (*a*) is plausible, but open, as Lünem. clearly states, to four objections, — (α) the inaccurate meaning 'possidere' (Vulg.) thus assigned to κτᾶσθαι; (β) the absence of any adj. (2 Cor. iv. 7) or defining gen. (Barnab. *Epist.* § 17) which might warrant such a meaning being assigned to σκεῦος, — unsuccessfully evaded (Olsh.) by the assumption that ἑαυτοῦ practically = ψυχῆς; (γ) the emphatic position of ἑαυτοῦ (compare 1 Cor. vii. 2), which is hardly to be explained away as a mere equivalent of a possess. pronoun; (δ) the context, which seems naturally to suggest, not a mere periphrasis of what had preceded, but a statement on the positive and permitted side antithetical to the prohibition on the negative. These objections are so strong that we can scarcely hesitate in adopting (*b*), towards which both lexical usage (κτᾶσθαι γυναῖκα, Ecclus. iv. 4, Xenoph. *Symp.* II. 10) and exegetical arguments very distinctly converge. While πορνεία is prohibited on the negative side, chastity and holiness in respect of the primal ordinance are equally clearly inculcated on the positive. For further details see the elaborate notes of De W., Koch, and Lünem. *in loc.* ἐν ἁγιασμῷ καὶ τιμῇ] '*in sanctification and honor;*' ethical element in which τὸ κτᾶσθαι was to take place: the union of man and woman was to be in sanctification and honor, not, as in the case of πορνεία, in sin and shame. Here, as the associated abst. subst. suggests, ἁγιασμῷ passes from its act. into its neutral meaning; comp. notes on ch. iii. 14.

5. μὴ ἐν πάθει ἐπιθ.] '*not in the lustfulness of desire;*' not in that sinful and morbid state (comp. Cicero, *Tusc. Disp.* III. 4. 10) in which ἐπιθυμία becomes the ruling and prevailing principle, and the κοίτη ceases to be ἀμίαντος (Heb. xiii. 4, 5). On the meaning of πάθος, see Suicer, *Thesaur.* s. v. Vol. II. p. 542, and notes *on Col.* iii. 5. καθάπερ καὶ τὰ ἔθνη] '*even as the Gentiles also;*' the καὶ having here its comparative force, and instituting a comparison between the Gentiles and the class implied in the ἕκαστον ὑμῶν; comp. ch. iii. 6, and see notes *on Eph.* v. 23, where this usage is fully discussed. Alford cites Xenoph. *Anab.* II. i. 22, καὶ ἡμῖν ταὐτὰ δοκεῖ ἅπερ καὶ βασιλεῖ, but not with complete pertinence, as there the καὶ appears in both clauses, here only in the relative clause; see Klotz, *Devar.* Vol. II. p. 635. The remark of Fritz. (*Rom.* Vol. I. p. 114) on the presence or absence of the article, 'ubi de paganis in universum loquitur, articulum addit; ubi de gentilium parte, eundem omittit,' is substantially correct, but must not be over-pressed; compare 1 Cor. i. 23 (*Lachm.*, *Tisch.*). τὰ μὴ εἰδότα τὸν Θεόν] '*which know not God;*' who as a class are so characterized, the subjective negation being rightly used both in harmony with the oblique and infinitival character of the preceding clauses, and with the fact that the Gentiles are here not historically described as 'ignorantes Deum' (see *on Gal.* iv. 8), but only so regarded by the writer; see Winer, *Gr.* § 55. 5, p. 428 sq. The article is here appropriately added to Θεόν, but this is one of the many words in the N. T. on which no precise rules can be laid down: see Winer, *Gr.* § 19. 1, p. 110.

6. τὸ μὴ ὑπερβαίνειν] '*that no one go beyond,*' 'that there be no going beyond,' — the subject-accus. not being

*νειν καὶ πλεονεκτεῖν ἐν τῷ πράγματι τὸν ἀδελφὸν αὐτοῦ, διότι ἔκδικος Κύριος περὶ πάντων τούτων, καθὼς καὶ προείπομεν ὑμῖν*

ἕκαστον (Alf.), but τινα (comp. Krüger, *Sprachl.* § 55. 2. 6) supplied from the following αὐτοῦ, and suggested by the general character of the prohibition. The clause is thus not merely parallel to the anarthrous εἰδέναι, but reverts to the preceding ἁγιασμός, of which it presents a specific exemplification (comp. Krüger, *Sprachl.* § 50. 6. 3) more immediately suggested by the second part of ver. 4. First, πορνεία is prohibited; then a holy use of its natural remedy affirmatively inculcated; and lastly, the heinous sin of μοιχεία, especially as regarded in its social aspects, formally denounced. So rightly Chrys. (ἐνταῦθα περὶ μοιχείας φησίν· ἀνωτέρω δὲ καὶ περὶ πορνείας πάσης), and after him Theod., Theophyl., Œcum., and the majority of modern commentators. To regard the verse with Calv., Grot., and recently De W., Lünem., Koch, as referring to the fraud and coveteousness in the affairs of life, is (α) to infringe on the plain meaning of τῷ πράγματι, — see below; (β) to obscure the ref. to the key-word of the paragraph, ἀκαθαρσία ver. 7; (γ) to mar the contextual symmetry of the verses; and, lastly, to introduce an exegesis so frigid and unnatural, as to make us wonder that such good names should be associated with an interpretation so seemingly improbable.

ὑπερβαίνειν καὶ πλεονεκτεῖν] '*go beyond and over-reach,*' 'supergrediatur et circumveniat,' Vulg., both words associated with the following accus., — and both of them significantly and appositely chosen. Ὑπερβαίνειν (an ἅπ. λεγόμ. in the N. T.) with an accus. *personæ* properly signifies a 'passing beyond,' thence derivatively a 'leaving unnoticed,' whether simply (Isæus, 38. 6, 43. 34) or contemptuously (Plutarch, *de Amore Prol.* § 3; comp. Kypke, *Obs.* Vol. II. 337), as appy. Æth. *taähaja* [extulit se], — with which, perhaps, in the present case, there may be associated a reference to an ὑπέρβασις of another, in respect of the ὅροι appointed by God and by nature; see Chrysost. and the Greek commentators, who, however, seem to have taken ὑπερβαίνειν absolutely; compare Raphel, *Annot.* Vol. II. 542. Πλεονεκτεῖν with an accus. *personæ* properly signifies 'lucri causâ fraudem facere alicui' (2 Cor. vii. 2, xii. 17), thence with a slightly more general reference 'circumvenire aliquem' (comp. 2 Cor. ii. 11), 'bifaih(o),' Goth., the idea of selfish and self-seeking fraud rather than mere wrong or injury (comp. Syr., Copt., Arm.) being always involved in the word; see Suicer, *Thesaur.* s. v. Vol. II. p. 746, and compare Meyer *on 2 Cor.* vii. 2.

ἐν τῷ πράγματι] '*in the matter,*' Copt. (definitely expressing the art.), and similarly, but too strongly, Syr. ܒܗܕܐ ܨܒܘܬܐ [in hoc negotio], — not exactly ἐν τῇ μίξει, Theoph., Œcum., but more generally, in *the* matter of which we are now speaking (compare 2 Cor. vii. 11), which, however, obviously involves reference to carnality and adultery; see Middleton, *Gr. Art.* p. 377 (ed. Rose), Green, *Gram.* p. 156. To regard ΤΩ as enclitic (Koppe) is contrary to the language of the N. T., and to assume that τῷ πράγματι — τοῖς πράγμασιν (De W., comp. Winer, *Gr.* § 18. 3, p. 105), or that it can imply 'the business in question' (Lünem.), when nothing has preceded sufficient to mark what the πρᾶγμα really is, must respectively on grammatical and logical grounds be pronounced wholly untenable.

τὸν ἀδελφὸν αὐτοῦ] '*his brother,*' — not merely 'his neigh-

καί διεμαρτυράμεθα. 7 οὐ γὰρ ἐκάλεσεν ἡμᾶς ὁ Θεὸς ἐπὶ ἀκα-
θαρσίᾳ ἀλλ' ἐν ἁγιασμῷ. 8 τοιγαροῦν ὁ ἀθετῶν οὐκ ἄνθρωπον

bor' (Schott), but 'his Christian brother, him, whom so to wrong and defraud is doubly flagitious; ἀδελφὸν καλεῖς καὶ πλεονεκτεῖς, καὶ ἐν οἷς οὐ χρή, Chrys. διότι ἔκδικος Κύριος] '*because that the Lord is the avenger;*' οὐδὲ γὰρ ἀτιμωρητὶ ταῦτα πράξομεν, Chrys.; see Eph. v. 6, Col. iii. 6, where similar prohibitions are accompanied by a similar minitatory reason. The term ἔκδικος, a δὶς λεγόμ. in the N. T. (here and Rom. xiii. 4) primarily denotes τὸν ἔξω τοῦ δικαίου ὄντα (Suid. s. v., Zonar. *Lex.* p. 651), 'lawless,' 'unjust' (comp. Soph. *Œd. Col.* 917); thence, in later writers, it passes over to the meaning of 'an avenger;' comp. Suid. s. v. Ἴβυκος (ἴδε αἱ Ἰβύκου ἔκδικοι), Wisdom xii. 12, Ecclus. xxx. 6. On the still later use in eccl. writers to denote 'Defensores' or 'Syndics' of the church, see Suicer, *Thesaur.* s. v. Vol. I. p. 1045, Bingham, *Antiq.* III. 11. 5. On διότι, comp. note and reff. on ch. ii. 8. περὶ πάντων τούτων] '*concerning, in the matter of, all these things,*'—not merely cases of ὑπερβασία and πλεονεξία (Alf.), but, as the comprehensive expression seems to require, all the sins of the flesh previously mentioned; see Chrys., Theoph., Œcum., who, by the inclusive nature of their language, appy. adopt the latter view. As illustrative of the use of ἔκδικος with περί, comp. 1 Macc. xiii. 6, ἐκδικήσω περὶ τοῦ ἔθνους μου.

καθὼς καὶ προείπ. κ. τ. λ.] '*as also we before told you and solemnly testified;*' the first καὶ being comparative and associated with καθώς (see on ver. 6), the second simply copulative. The πρὸ appears merely to point to a time prior to the ἐκδίκησις taking place: comp. Gal. v. 21, and notes *in loc.* On the stronger and more emphatic διαμαρτύρ. (not simply = μαρτύρομαι, Olsh.), see notes *on* 1 *Tim.* v. 21, and on the form εἴπαμεν [*Griesb.* and *Sholz* εἴπομεν, with AKL; majority of mss.; Chrys., Theod.], comp. Winer, *Gr.* § 15, p. 78. In the N. T. the 1st aor. form seems to prevail in the 2nd person (Matth. xxvi. 25, 64, Mark xii. 32, Luke xx. 39, John iv. 17), the other 2nd aor. forms in the other persons, but in the latter instances, esp. in the case of the 3rd pers. plural, there is much difference of reading.

7. οὐ γὰρ κ. τ. λ.] '*For God called us not;*' confirmation of the preceding statement, διότι ἔκδικος κ. τ. λ., derived from the object contemplated in the κλῆσις. On the act of calling, scil. εἰς τὴν ἑαυτοῦ βασιλείαν καὶ δόξαν (ch. ii. 12) as specially attributed to God the Father, see notes *on Gal.* i. 6. ἐπὶ ἀκαθαρσίᾳ] '*for uncleanness:*' object or purpose for which they were (not) called, the primary meaning of the prep. ('nearness or approximation,' Donald. *Crat.* § 172) not being wholly obliterated; see Krüger, *Sprachl.* § 68. 41. 7, Jelf, *Gr.* § 634. 3, notes *on Gal.* v. 13, and exx. in Raphel, *Annot.* Vol. II. p. 546. ἐν ἁγιασμῷ] '*in sanctification;*' not 'in sanctificationem,' Vulg., but 'in sanctificatione,' Clarom.; ἐν being neither equivalent to εἰς (Pisc), nor yet used brachyologically, scil. ὥστε εἶναι ἡμᾶς ἐν (Winer, *Gr.* § 50. 5, p. 370), but simply marking the sphere *in which* Christians were called to move; see *on Gal.* i. 6, *on Eph.* iv. 4, and comp. Green, *Gram.* p. 292.

8. τοιγαροῦν] '*Wherefore then;*' logical conclusion from the preceding verse. The compound particle τοιγάροῦν (only here and Heb. xii. 1) is not simply synonymous with τοιγάρτοι (Hartung, *Partik.* s. v. τοί, 3. 5, Vol. I. p. 354), but while differing from the simpler τοιγάρ, 'hâc de causâ igitur'

*ἀθετεῖ ἀλλὰ τὸν Θεὸν τὸν καὶ δόντα τὸ Πνεῦμα αὐτοῦ τὸ ἅγιον εἰς ὑμᾶς.*

(Klotz), in imparting a more syllogistic and ratiocinative character to the sentence, differs also from τοιγάρτοι, 'qua propter sane,' in having not an affirmative (τοί), but a collective and retrospective (οὖν) force; see Klotz, *Devar.* Vol. II. p. 748. ὁ ἀθετῶν] '*the despiser,*' '*the rejecter;*' substantival use of the present participle; see Winer, *Gr.* § 45. 7, p. 316, and Middleton, *Gr. Art.* p. 159. Any definite insertions after ἀθετῶν, *e. g.* Vulg. (Amit.) 'hæc,' Arm. ὑμᾶς, Beza 'hæc, scil. præcepta,' are wholly unnecessary. It is clear that the commands recently given must form the objects of the ἀθέτησις; these, however, the apostle does not specify, his object being to call attention not so much to what is set at nought as to the person who does so, and the personal risk that he incurs. On the verb ἀθετεῖν, used in the N. T., both with persons (Mark vi. 26, Luke x. 16, John xii. 48) and things Mark vii. 9, Gal. (iii. 15, al.), comp. notes *on Gal.* ii. 21. οὐκ ἄνθρωπον κ. τ. λ.] '*rejecteth not man but God,*' not one whom it might be thought in some degree excusable to despise, — but, τὸν Θεόν. The antithesis οὐκ — ἀλλὰ is thus not to be explained away, 'non tam hominem . . . . . quam Deum,' Est., but retained with its usual and proper force, 'non hominem . . . . . sed Deum,' Vulg.; see esp. Winer, *Gr.* § 55. 8, p. 439 sq. (ed. 6), and notes *on Eph.* vi. 12. On the exact difference between this formula ('ubi prior notio tota tollitur, et in ejus locum posterior notio substituitur'), οὐ μόνον — ἀλλά, and οὐ μόνον — ἀλλὰ καί, see Kühner on Xenoph. *Mem.* II. 6. 2, comp. also notes on ch. i. 8. The omission of the article before ἄνθρωπον, 'a man,' 'any man,' — with a latent reference to the apostle, not to τὸν πλεονεκτηθέντα (Œcum.), — and its insertion before Θεόν (almost 'ipsum Deum'), though not capable of being conveyed in translation, must not be overlooked. τὸν καὶ δόντα] '*who also gave;*' who in addition to having called us ἐν ἁγιασμῷ, has also been pleased to furnish us with the blessed means of realizing it; compare Reuss, *Théol. Chrét.* IV. 15, Vol. II. p. 150. The only difficulty is the reading: καί is omitted by *Lachm.* with ABD[3]E; 10 mss.; Clarom., Sangerm., Goth., al.: Athan., Did., Chrys., Theod. (ms.), Theoph., al., — but, as the insertion is well supported [D[1]FGKL; great majority of mss.; Boern., Syr. Philox.); al.; Clem., Theod., Dam., Œcum.], and far less easy to be accounted for than the omission, we retain καί with *Rec.*, *Tisch.* ed. 2, 7, Alf., and the bulk of recent editors. It is much more difficult to decide between δόντα [*Rec.*, *Tisch.* ed. 2, 7, with AKL; great majority of mss.; apparently all Vv.;] Clement, Chrysostom, Theodosius.] and διδόντα [*Lachmann* with BDEFG; 10 mss.; Athan., Did.]. The latter deserves great consideration as having such strong uncial authority, still as the Vv. appear all to favor the aorist, and as it also certainly does seem probable that the correction might have arisen from a desire to represent that the gift of the Spirit was still going on (comp. Luke xi. 13), we retain (with *Tisch.*) the aorist participle. τὸ Πν. αὐτοῦ τὸ ἅγιον] Not without great emphasis and solemnity (comp. Eph. iv. 3), — 'His Holy Spirit,' the blessed Spirit which proceeds from Him (see notes *on Phil.* i. 19), whose attribute is holiness, and whose office especially 'consists in the sanctifying of the servants of God,' Pearson, *Creed*, Vol. I. p. 387 (ed. Burt.). To dilute this distinct personal expression into 'the gift of spiritual

On brotherly love I need say nothing. I beseech you to be quiet, industrious, and orderly.

9 Περὶ δὲ τῆς φιλαδελφίας οὐ χρείαν ἔχετε γράφειν ὑμῖν· αὐτοὶ γὰρ ὑμεῖς θεοδίδακτοί ἐστε

insight,' etc. (Olsh.), is by no means satisfactory; see notes *on Gal.* iv. 6. εἰς ὑμᾶς] *'unto you;'* not merely equivalent to a transmissive dative, nor yet with any idea of diffusion (Alf., — see) notes on ch. ii. 6), but, with the usual and proper meaning of local direction, 'in vos,' Clarom., Copt., (*ekhrei*): they were the objects to whom that blessed gift was directed; comp. Gal. iv. 6. The reading of *Rec.* ἡμᾶς has but weak external support [A; mss.; Vulg., Syr. (Philox.), Æth. (Pol., but not Platt); Chrys., al.], and on internal grounds is not free from some suspicion.

9. Περὶ δὲ κ. τ. λ.] *'Now concerning etc.;'* transition by means of the δὲ μεταβατικὸν to a fresh exhortation. On this force of δέ, see notes *on Gal.* iii. 8. φιλαδελφίας] *'brotherly love,'* love to their fellow Christians; Rom. xii. 10, Heb. xiii. 1, 1 Pet. i. 22, 2 Pet. i. 7, comp. 1 Pet. iii. 8. This love was to be no passive virtue, but, as ver. 10. suggests, was to display itself in acts of liberality and benevolence towards their poorer and suffering brethren: so Theod., though perhaps a little too definitely, φιλαδελφίαν ἐνταῦθα τὴν τῶν χρημάτων φιλοτιμίαν ἐκάλεσεν. It is unnecessary to exclude wholly a reference to a love εἰς πάντας (Theoph.): the Christian ἀδελφοὶ were the primary objects (comp. 1 Pet. iii. 8, where φιλαδελφία is distinguished from, and prevenient to, the general ἀγάπη), but the great brotherhood of mankind was still not to be forgotten; comp. Gal. vi. 10. οὐ χρείαν ἔχετε γράφειν ὑμῖν] *'ye have no need that I write to you:'* rhetorical turn, technically termed 'præteritio,' or παράλειψις, in which what might be said is partly suppressed, to conciliate a more loving acceptance of the implied command; κατὰ παράλειψιν δὲ τὴν παραίνεσιν τίθησι, δύο ταῦτα κατασκευάζων· ἓν μὲν ὅτι οὕτως ἀναγκαῖον τὸ πρᾶγμα ὡς μηδὲ διδασκάλου δεῖσθαι· ἕτερον δὲ μᾶλλον αὐτοὺς ἐντρέπει, διεγείρων ἵνα μὴ δεύτεροι ἔλθωσι τῆς ὑπολήψεως ἣν ἔχει περὶ αὐτῶν, νομίζων αὐτοὺς ἤδη κατωρθωκέναι, Theoph. On this rhetorical form, see notes *on Philem.* 19, and Wilke, *N. T. Rhetorik*, p. 365. The reading is scarcely doubtful: *Lachm.* indeed adopts ἔχομεν with D[1]FG; 6 mss.; Vulg., Clarom., Goth., Syr., (Philox.); Chrys., Theoph., but the external authority is not sufficiently strong, and the probability of a correction to obviate the difficulty of construction very great. γράφειν] *'that I write.'* The object-inf. has here practically the sense of a passive (comp. ch. v. 1), but differs from it in suggesting the supplement of some accusative, — 'that I or any one should write to you;' see Winer, *Gr.* § 44. 8. 1, p. 303, Jelf, *Gr.* § 667. 3. To deny this on the ground that the context precludes an indefinite reference, and practically limits the supplied accus. to the apostle (Lünem.), seems distinctly hypercritical, and is rightly rejected by Alford *in loc.* αὐτοὶ γὰρ ὑμεῖς] *'for you yourselves;'* not 'vos ipsi sponte,' Schott, but 'your*selves*,' — in sharp contrast to the subject involved in the infinitive; comp. 1 John ii. 20. θεοδίδακτοι] *'taught of God,'* — not in marked opposition to any other form of teaching (οὐ δεῖσθε φησί, παρὰ ἀνθρώπου μαθεῖν, Chrys., comp. Olsh.), but with the principal emphasis on the fact of their being already taught, and with only a subordinate emphasis on the source of the teaching. The chief moment of thought, as Lünem well observes, rests on the second, and not on the first, half of the compound verbal θεοδίδακτοι. The form itself is an ἅπαξ λεγόμ. in the

εἰς τὸ ἀγαπᾶν ἀλλήλους· 10 καὶ γὰρ ποιεῖτε αὐτὸ εἰς πάντας τοὺς
ἀδελφοὺς τοὺς ἐν ὅλῃ τῇ Μακεδονίᾳ. παρακαλοῦμεν δὲ ὑμᾶς,
ἀδελφοί, περισσεύειν μᾶλλον, 11 καὶ φιλοτιμεῖσθαι ἡσυχάζειν

N. T.; compare however, John vi. 45, διδακτοὶ τοῦ Θεοῦ, and add Barnab. *Epist.* § 21, γίνεσθε δὲ θεοδίδακτοι, ἐκζητοῦντες, τί ζητεῖ Κύριος ἀφ' ὑμῶν.

εἰς τὸ ἀγαπῶν ἀλλήλους] '*to love one another,*' 'ut diligatis invicem,' Vulg.; practical tendency and purpose of the διδαχή, with perhaps an included reference to the purport and subject of it; see notes on ch. ii. 12.

10. καὶ γὰρ κ. τ. λ.] '*for indeed ye do it;*' confirmatory explanation of the preceding clause; γὰρ introducing the historical fact on which the confirmation rested (οἶδα ἀφ' ὧν ποιεῖτε, Theoph.), καὶ enhancing the ποιεῖτε, and putting it in gentle contrast with the θεοδίδακτοί ἐστε. Thus neither the καὶ nor the γὰρ (Syr. Æth.-Pol., — but not Syr.-Philox., and Æth.-Platt) is otiose: both fully retain their proper force (Copt., Goth., Arm.), their association being due to the early position which γὰρ regularly assumes in the sentence; see notes and reff. *on Phil.* ii. 27, and comp. Winer, *Gr.* § 53. 8. b, p. 397. αὐτό] '*it,*' scil. τὸ ἀγαπᾶν ἀλλήλους (Lünem., Alf.), not τὸ τῆς φιλαδελφίας (Koch), — a reference needlessly remote. εἰς πάντας τοὺς ἀδελφ.] '*toward all the brethren;*' direction and destination of the action; not, observe, with any marked universality, εἰς πάντας τοὺς ἁγίους, but — εἰς πάντας τοὺς ἀδ. τοὺς ἐν ὅλῃ τῇ Μακεδ., the last definition fairly justifying the remark of Lünem. (opp. to Baur, *Paulus*, p. 484), that there is no reason for assuming any longer period between the conversion of the Thessalonians and the time of writing the Epistle (one and one-half or two years) than is assumed in the ordinary chronology. The arguments of Baur, according to which this beautiful and most genuine Ep. is to be considered a 'matte Nachbild' of 1 Cor., have been recently reiterated in Zeller, *Theol. Jahrb.* for 1855, p. 151, but (it is not too much to say) without even — plausibility.

The second and definitive τοὺς (Winer *Gr.* § 20. 1, p. 119) is omitted by *Lachm.* with AD[1]FG; Chrys. (ms.), but appy. rightly retained by *Tisch.* with BD[2]D[3]E KL; nearly all mss.; many Ff.

παρακαλοῦμεν δέ] '*but we beseech you;*' continuation of the implied command in ver. 9 in a slightly antithetical form; not only is the duty of φιλαδελφία tacitly and delicately inculcated, and an expansion of it in the form of general ἀγάπη (ver. 9) distinctly suggested, but further, an increase in the same set forth as the subject of direct hortatory entreaty. On the pres. infin. after παρακαλῶ, which is here rightly used as marking the continuance and permanence of the act, see Winer, *Gr.* § 44. 7, p. 298, but observe that the use of the pres. inf. or aor. inf. after commands, etc., depends much on the peculiarity of the writer, and the subjective aspects under which the command was contemplated; comp. Bernhardy, *Synt.* x. 9, p. 383, and the good note and distinctions of Mätzner on Antiphon, p. 153 sq.

11. καὶ φιλοτιμεῖσθαι κ. τ. λ.] '*and to study, etc.;*' exhortation in close grammatical, though somewhat more lax logical, connection with what immediately precedes. The close union of these appy. different subjects of exhortation has been variously explained. On the whole, it seems most natural to suppose that their liberality involved some elements of a restless, meddling, and practically idle spirit, that exposed them to the comments of οἱ ἔξω. It is perhaps not wholly improbable that mistaken ex-

*καὶ πράσσειν τὰ ἴδια καὶ ἐργάζεσθαι ταῖς χερσὶν ὑμῶν, καθὼς ὑμῖν παρηγγείλαμεν,* 12 *ἵνα περιπατῆτε εὐσχημόνως πρὸς τοὺς ἔξω καὶ μηδενὸς χρείαν ἔχητε.*

pectations in respect of the day of the Lord had led them into a neglect of their regular duties and occupations, and was marring a liberality, of which the true essence was ἐργαζόμενοι ἑτέροις παρέχειν, Chrys. φιλοτιμεῖσθαι ἡσυχάζειν] '*make it your aim to be quiet*,' 'et operam detis ut quieti sitis,' Vulg. (sim. Clarom.), 'biarbaidjan anaqal,' Goth. It is somewhat doubtful whether (*a*) the primary meaning of φιλοτιμ., 'gloriæ cupiditate accensum aliquid facere' (comp. Copt., Æth.-Pol.), or (*b*) the secondary meaning, 'magno studio anniti,' 'operam dare' (Vulg, Clarom., Syr., Goth., Arm.) is here to be adopted. As both meanings rest on good lexical authority (comp. Xenoph. *Mem.* II. 9, 3, with *Œcon.* IV. 24, in which latter passage φιλοτιμ. is associated with μελετᾶν), the context will be our safest guide. Of the three passages in which it is used in the N. T., Rom. xv. 20, 2 Cor. v. 9, and *h. l.*, the first alone seems to require (*a*); comp. Fritz. *Rom.* Vol. III. p. 277, and even Meyer, *on* 2 *Cor. l. c.*, who, while affecting to retain (*a*), translates in accordance with (*b*), 'beeifern wir uns u. s. w.' In all, perhaps, some idea of τιμὴ may be recognized, but in 2 Cor. *l. c.* and in the present passage that meaning recedes into the background; see the numerous exx. in Wetst. Vol. II. p. 94, 95, and Kypke, *Obs.* Vol. II. p. 189. To consider φιλοτ. an independent inf. (Copt., Theophyl. 1; compare Theod., Calv.) seems very unsatisfactory. ἡσυχάζειν marks the sedate and tranquil spirit (compare 1 Tim. ii. 2), which stands in contrast to the excited and unquiet bustle (περιεργάζεσθαι, 2 Thess. iii. 11) that often marks ill-defined or mistaken religious expectation; see esp. 2 Thess. iii. 11, 12, which forms an instructive parallel to the present exhortations. πράσσειν τὰ ἴδια] '*to do your own business*,' 'to confine yourselves to the sphere of your own proper duties.' The correct formula according to Phrynichus is τὰ ἐμαυτοῦ κ. τ. λ. πράττειν, or τὰ ἴδια ἐμαυτοῦ κ. τ. λ. πράττειν; see exx. collected by Lobeck, p. 441, and Kypke, *Obs.* Vol. II. p. 338. The form ἰδιοπραγεῖν occurs in Polyb. (*Hist.* VIII. 28. 9) and later writers. ἐργάζ. ταῖς χερσὶν ὑμῶν] '*work with your hands*,' *i. e.* 'follow your earthly callings,' which, as the words imply, were those of handicraftsmen and artificers; 'ad populum scribit, in quo plurimorum est ea quæ manibus fiunt opera exercere,' Est. The numbers engaged in mercantile and industrial calling at Thessalonica are alluded to by Tafel, *Hist. Thessal.* p. 9. The inserted ἰδίαις [*Rec.* with AD³KL; mss.: Theod., Dam.] is rightly struck out by *Lachm.*, *Tisch.*, and most modern editors, on the preponderant authority of BD¹E(?)EG; 10 mss.; appy. all Vv.; Bas., Chrysost., Theoph. and Latin Ff. καθὼς ὑμῖν παρηγγ.] '*according as we commanded you*,' scil. when personally present with you; with reference not merely to the last, but to all the preceding clauses. The very first publication of Christianity in Thessal. seems to have been attended with some manifestations of restlessness and feverish expectation.

12. ἵνα περιπατ. εὐσχημόνως] '*in order that ye may walk seemly*,' Rom. xiii. 13, 1 Cor. xiv. 40; purpose of the foregoing παράκλησις, the present member referring mainly to ἡσυχάζειν καὶ πράσσειν τὰ ἴδια, the following to ἐργαζ. ταῖς χερσὶν ὑμῶν. The adverb εὐσχημ. (associated with κατὰ τάξιν

Do not grieve for those that sleep. We shall not anticipate them, but at the last trump they will be raised, and we translated.

13 Οὐ θέλομεν δὲ ὑμᾶς ἀγνοεῖν, ἀδελφοί,
περὶ τῶν κοιμωμένων, ἵνα μὴ λυπῆσθε καθὼς

1 Cor. *l. c.*) stands in partial contrast to ἀτάκτως, 2 Thess. iii. 6 Lünem.); the general idea, however, of that decent gravity and seemly deportment (εὐλαβῶς· σεμνῶς, Zonar. s. v.) which should ever be the characteristic of the true Christian, ought not to be excluded. On the use of περιπατεῖν as commonly implying the 'agendi vivendique rationem quam quis *continenter* et ex animo sequitur,' see Winer, *Comment. on Eph.* IV. 1, p. 5 (cited by Koch), Fritz. *Rom.* xiii. 13, Vol. III. p. 140 sq., Suicer, *Thesaur.* s. v. Vol. II. p. 679, and compare notes *on Phil.* iii. 18. πρὸς τοὺς ἔξω] '*toward them that are without;*' πρὸς pointing to the social relation in which they were to stand, or the general demeanor they were to assume toward those who were not Christians. On this use of πρός, in which the primary meaning of ethical *direction* is still apparent, see reff. in notes *on Col.* iv. 5, where the same expression occurs. Οἱ ἔξω is the regular designation of those who were not Christians; see 1 Cor. v. 12, 13, Col. *l. c.*, and notes *on* 1 *Tim.* iii. 7. μηδενὸς χρείαν ἔχ.] '*have need of no man;*' the contrast being ἐπαιτεῖν καὶ ἑτέρων δεῖσθαι, Chrys., comp. Theod. It is somewhat doubtful whether μηδενὸς is here to be regarded as masc. with Syr., Vulg., Æth., and the Greek commentt., or neuter with Copt. (appy.; Goth., Clarom. uncertain) and several modern commentators. On the whole, the masc. seems most in accordance with the context; they were not, by the neglect of their proper occupations, to live dependent upon others, whether heathens or (more probably) fellow-Christians; comp. Chrys., Theod. The argument of Lünem., repeated by Alf., 'that to stand in need of no man is for man an impossibility,' is not of much weight, as the general statement will naturally receive its proper limitations from the context.

13. Οὐ θέλομεν δὲ κ. τ. λ.] '*Now we would not have you to be ignorant;*' transition by means of the δὲ μεταβατικόν (Hartung, *Partik.* Vol. I. p. 165, notes *on Gal.* iii. 8), and the impressive οὐ θέλομεν ὑμᾶς ἀγνοεῖν (Rom. i. 13, xi. 25, 1 Cor. x. 1, xii. 1, 2 Cor. i. 8), to a new and important subject, the state of the departed. Most modern expositors seem rightly to coincide in the opinion that in the infant Church of Thessalonica there had prevailed, appy. from the very first, a feverish anxiety about the state of those who had departed, and about the time and circumstances of the Lord's coming. They seem especially to have feared that those of their brethren who had fallen on sleep before the expected advent of the Lord would not participate in its blessings and glories (ver. 15). Thus their apprehensions did not so much relate to the resurrection generally (Chrysost., Theod., Theoph.), as to the share which the departed were to have in the παρουσία τοῦ Κυρίου; see Hofmann, *Schriftb.* Vol. II. 2, p. 596, compare Wieseler, *Chronol.* p. 249. The reading θέλομεν [*Rec.* θέλω] has the support of all the MSS. and the majority of the mss., the bulk of the Vv. and Ff., and is rightly adopted by *Lachm.*, *Tisch.*, and all modern editors. περὶ τῶν κοιμωμένων] '*concerning those that are sleeping;*' *i. e.* those that are dead, according to the significant synonym found not only in Scripture (1 Kings ii. 10, John xi. 11, Acts vii. 60, 1 Cor. xi. 30, al.) but in Pagan writers (Callim. *Fragm.* x. 1), yet here, as the following verses clearly show, to be specially restricted to the *Christian* dead; compare

καὶ οἱ λοιποὶ οἱ μὴ ἔχοντες ἐλπίδα. 14 εἰ γὰρ πιστεύομεν ὅτι
Ἰησοῦς ἀπέθανεν καὶ ἀνέστη, οὕτως καὶ ὁ Θεὸς τοὺς κοιμηθέντας

οἱ νεκροὶ ἐν Χριστῷ, ver. 16, and see Suicer, *Thesaur.* s. v. Vol. II. p. 121. All special doctrinal deductions, however, from this general term (Weizel, *Stud. u. Krit.* 1836, p. 916 sq., compare Reuss, *Théol. Chrét.* IV. 21, Vol. II. p. 239) must be regarded as extremely precarious, especially those that favor the idea of a ψυχοπαννυχία in the intermediate state; see esp. Bull, *Serm.* III. p. 41 (Oxf. 1844), Delitzsch, *Bibl. Psychol.* VI. 4, p. 360 sq., Zeller, *Theol. Jahrb.* for 1847, p. 390—409, and a long and careful article by West, *Stud. u. Krit.* for 1858, esp. p. 278, 290; compare also Burnet, *State of the Departed*, ch. III. p. 49 sq. (Transl.), and notes *on Phil.* i. 23. Death is rightly called sleep as involving the ideas of continued existence (Chrys.), repose, and ἐγρήγορσις (Theod.); comp. Theopyl. *on John* xi. 11, and the eloquent sermon of Manning, *Serm.* XXI. Vol. I. p. 308 sq.

The reading is doubful: *Rec.* with DE FG(FG κεκοιμηνων)KL; mss.; many Ff., reads κεκοιμημένων,—a form well supported, but not improbably a conformation to Matth. xxvii. 52, 1 Cor. xv. 20. We retain, therefore, the less usual κοιμωμένων with AB; many mss.; Orig., Chrys. (1 ms.), Dam. (*Lachm.*, *Tisch.*). ἵνα μὴ λυπῆσθε] '*that ye sorrow not;*' purpose and object of the οὐ θέλομεν ὑμᾶς ἀγνοεῖν. The λύπη in this particular case was called out not merely by the feeling of having lost their departed brethren, but by anxieties in regard to their participation in Christ's advent. The reading λυπεῖσθε (*Tisch.* ed. 7) is appy. not sufficiently supported for us to admit so great a deviation from the usual construction.

καθὼς καὶ οἱ λοιποί] '*even as the rest also*,' scil. λυποῦνται. The καθὼς does not introduce any comparison between the sorrow of Christians and that of οἱ λοιποί, as if a certain amount of sorrow *was* permissible (οὐ παντελῶς κωλύει τὴν λύπην, ἀλλὰ τὴν ἀμετρίαν ἐκβάλλει, Theod.), but simply contrasts with Christians those in whom λύπη might naturally find a place, οἱ μὴ ἔχοντες ἐλπίδα. Christians, as the antithesis implies, were not to mourn at all; σὺ δὲ ὁ προσδοκῶν ἀνάστασιν, τίνος ἕνεκεν ὀδύρῃ, Chrys. The οἱ λοιποὶ (Eph. ii. 3) obviously includes all, whether sceptical Jews or unenlightened heathen (Chrys.), who had no sure hope in any future resurrection. On the use of καὶ with adverbs of comparison, see notes *on Eph.* v. 23. οἱ μὴ ἔχοντες ἐλπίδα] '*who have no hope*,' who form a class that is so characterized; compare notes on ver. 5, and Winer, *Gr.* § 55. 5, p. 428 sq., but observe also that the comparative member is under the vinculum of ἵνα. The hope here alluded to is obviously in reference to the resurrection; τίνος ἐλπίδα; ἀναστάσεως. οἱ γὰρ μὴ ἔχοντες ἐλπίδα ἀναστάσεως οὗτοι ὀφείλουσι πενθεῖν, Theoph. The true hopelessness of the old heathen world finds its saddest expression in Æsch. *Eumen.* 638, ἅπαξ θανόντος οὔτις ἐστ' ἀνάστασις; see more in Lünem. and Jowett, and in answer to the quotation of the latter from the O. T., the pertinent remarks of Alford *in loc.*

14. εἰ γὰρ πιστεύομεν] '*For if we believe;*' reason for the purpose expressed in the preceding verse, ἵνα μὴ λυπῆσθε κ. τ. λ., based on the fundamental truth that as Christ the Head died and rose again, even so shall all the members of His body; comp. Pearson, *Creed*, Art. XI. Vol. I. p. 450 (ed. Burt.), Jackson, *Creed*, XI. 16. 8 sq. The εἰ here obviously involves no element of doubt, but is simply logical ('εἰ particula

διὰ τοῦ Ἰησοῦ ἄξει σὺν αὐτῷ. 15 τοῦτο γὰρ ὑμῖν λέγομεν ἐν

est plane logica,' Herm. *Viger*, No. 312,) and virtually assertory; comp. notes *on Phil.* i. 22, and *on Col.* iii. 1. ἀπέθανεν καὶ ἀνέστη] '*died and rose again;*' the two foundations of Christian faith united in one enunciation. It is noticeable that the apostle here, as always, uses the direct term ἀπέθανεν in reference to our Lord, to obviate all possible misconception: in reference to the faithful he appropriately uses the consolatory term κοιμᾶσθαι; see esp. Theod. *in loc.* οὕτως κ.τ.λ.] '*so also shall God;*' slightly inexact apodosis: the rigidly correct sequel would be καὶ πιστεύειν δεῖ, ὅτι κ.τ.λ. (Lünem., Jowett), or some similar formula. The οὕτως is not pleonastic (Olsh.), but, as Lünem. correctly observes, marks the complete accordance of the lot of Christians with that voluntarily assumed by their Lord, while the καὶ serves to enhance and to give force to the comparison; see Winer, *Gr.* § 60. 5, p. 478, and on this use of καὶ after relative or demonstrative particles, Klotz, *Devar.* Vol. II. p. 636. τοὺς κοιμηθέντας διὰ τοῦ Ἰησ.] '*those laid to sleep through Jesus;*' certainly not equiv. to ἐν Ἰησ. (Jowett), but, with the usual and proper force of the prep., those who through His mediation are now rightly accounted as 'sleeping.' It must remain to the last an open question whether διὰ τοῦ Ἰησ. is to be connected (*a*) with the finite verb ἄξει, or (*b*) with the participle. Chrysost. and the Greek commentators (silet Theod.) admit both, but prefer the latter; modern writers mainly adopt the former. There is confessedly a difficulty in (*b*) which the exx. adduced by Alf. scarcely tend to diminish; for the meaning τῇ πίστει τοῦ Ἰησοῦ κοιμηθ. (Chrysost.), or the more exact meaning advocated above, is but in lax parallelism with εἰρήνην ἔχειν δι' αὐτοῦ (Rom. v. 1), καυχᾶσθαι δι' αὐτοῦ (Rom. v. 11), al. Still the negative arguments against (*a*),—viz. (1) that thus ἄξει would have two prepositional adjuncts, (2) that the natural emphasis would then suggest the order διὰ τοῦ Ἰησ. τοὺς κοιμηθ., (3) that the sentence would thus be harsh (De W.) and awkward in the extreme—seem so unanswerable, that with the earlier interpreters, Æth., and (as the rigid preservation of the order seems to hint) the remaining Vv., we adopt the more simple and logical connection κοιμηθέντας δι' αὐτοῦ. The two contrasted subjects Ἰησοῦς and κοιμηθέντας διὰ τοῦ Ἰησοῦ thus stand in clear and illustrative antithesis, and the fundamental declaration of the sentence ἄξει σὺν αὐτῷ, remains distinct and prominent, undiluted by any addititious clause. ἄξει σὺν αὐτῷ] '*will bring with Him.*' The more natural word would have been ἐγερεῖ (compare 2 Cor. iv. 14), but the apostle probably uses the more significant ἄξει, as marking that blessed association of departed Christians with their Lord at His παρουσία, in which the Thess. feared their sleeping brethren would have no part; see above on ver. 13.

15. τοῦτο γὰρ λέγομεν] '*For this we say;*' confirmation, not (by an 'ætiologia duplex') of the foregoing ἵνα μὴ λυπῆσθε (Koch), but of the words immediately preceding; the relation of the faithful living to the faithful departed is explained, first negatively in this verse, then positively in ver. 16, 17. ἐν λόγῳ Κυρίου] '*in the word of the Lord,*' in coincidence with a declaration received directly from him, 'quasi Eo ipso loquente,' Beza. The prep. is here neither equivalent to κατὰ (Zanch.) nor to διά (Auth., comp. De W.), but has appy. its usual and prevalent meaning

λόγῳ Κυρίου, ὅτι ἡμεῖς οἱ ζῶντες οἱ περιλειπόμενοι εἰς τὴν παρουσίαν τοῦ Κυρίου οὐ μὴ φθάσωμεν τοὺς κοιμηθέντας,

'in the sphere of:' the declaration was couched in language of the Lord Himself, and gained all its force from coincidence with his words; see Winer, *Gr.* § 48. a, p. 345, who, however, by comparing 1 Cor. ii. 7, λαλοῦμεν . . . . . ἐν μυστηρίῳ, 1 Cor. xiv. 6, λαλήσω ἐν ἀποκαλύψει, gives ἐν more of a reference to the *form* or *nature* of the revelation than seems fully in accordance with the context. The meaning is simply 'edicit me interprete Dominus,' Fritz, *Rom.* Vol III. p. 34; compare בִּדְבַר יְהוָה 1 Kings xx. 35. This revelation is certainly not to be referred to Matth. xxiv. 31 (Schott 1, comp. Usteri, *Lehrb.* II. 2. B, p. 325) nor to any traditional 'effatum Christi' (Schott 2, and appy. Jowett), but was directly received by the apostle from the Lord himself; οὐκ ἀφ' ἑαυτῶν, ἀλλὰ παρὰ τοῦ Χριστοῦ μαθόντες λέγομεν, Chrys.; see Gal. i. 12, ii. 2, Eph. iii. 2, and compare 2 Cor. xii. 1, With these passages before us, can we say with Jowett, that 'St. Paul nowhere speaks of any special truths or doctrines as imparted to himself?' The language of Usteri, *l. c.* is equally unsatisfactory; not so that of De W. *in loc.* ἡμεῖς οἱ ζῶντες κ. τ. λ.] '*we the living who are remaining.*' The deduction from these words, 'that St. Paul himself expected to be alive,' Alf., with Jowett, Lünem., Koch, and the majority of German commentt., must fairly be pronounced more than doubtful. Without giving any undue latitude to ἡμεῖς (οὐ περὶ ἑαυτοῦ φησὶν . . . . . ἀλλὰ τοὺς πιστοὺς λέγει, Chrys.), to ζῶντες (ζῶντας τὰς ψυχάς, κοιμηθέντας δὲ τὰ σώματα λέγει, Method. *de Resurr.* ap. Œcum.), or to περιλειπόμενοι ('præsens loco futuri, more Hebraico,' Calv., 'superstites,' Bretsch.), it seems just and correct to say that περιλειπόμενοι is simply and purely present, and that St. Paul is to be understood as classing himself with 'those who are *being left* on earth' (compare Acts ii. 47), without being conceived to imply that he had any precise or definite expectations as to his own case. At the time of writing these words he was one of the ζῶντες and περιλειπόμενοι, and as such he distinguishes himself and them from the κοιμηθέντες, and naturally identifies himself with the class to which he then belonged. It does not seem improper to admit that in their ignorance of the day of the Lord (Mark xiii. 32) the apostles might have imagined that He who was coming would come speedily, but it does seem over hasty to ascribe to inspired men *definite* expectations, since proved to be unfounded, when the context. calmly weighed and accurately interpreted, supplies no certain elements for such extreme deductions; see notes *on* 1 *Tim.* vi. 14, and compare the long note of Wordsw. on ver. 17. On the verb περιλείπεσθαι, see notes, ver. 17 (*Transl.*).

οὐ μὴ φθάσωμεν] '*shall not prevent,*' Auth.. *i. e.* shall not arrive into the presence of the Lord, and share the blessings and glories of His advent, before others The verb φθάνειν (Hesych. προήκειν, προλαμβάνειν) has here its regular meaning of 'prævenire,' involving the idea of a priority in respect of *time,* and thence, derivatively, of privilege; οὕτω, φησίν, ὀξέως καὶ ταχέως καὶ ἐν ἀκαρεῖ οἱ τετελευτηκότες ἅπαντες ἀναστήσονται, ὡς τοὺς ἔτι κα ἐκεῖνον τὸν καιρὸν περιόντας προλαβεῖν, καὶ προαπαντῆσαι τῷ σωτῆρι τῶν ὅλων, Theod. On the strengthened negation οὐ μὴ with the aor. subjunct., see Winer, *Gr.* § 56. 3, p. 450; and observe that the usually

16 ὅτι αὐτὸς ὁ Κύριος ἐν κελεύσματι, ἐν φωνῇ ἀρχαγγέλου καὶ
ἐν σάλπιγγι Θεοῦ καταβήσεται ἀπ' οὐρανοῦ, καὶ οἱ νεκροὶ ἐν

recognized distinction between these particles with the fut. and with the aor. (Hermann on Soph. *Œd. Col.* 853) must not be pressed in the N. T. (opp. to Koch), the prevalence of οὐ μὴ with the subj. being much too decided to justify a rigorous application of the rule; see notes *on Gal.* iv. 30.

16. ὅτι] '*because*,' ܡܛܠ ܕ [propterea quod] Syr., 'quia,' Clarom., quoniam,' Vulg., 'unte,' Goth., sim. Æth. (Platt, — Pol. omits), Arm.; reason for the declaration immediately preceding, derived from the circumstances of detail. To regard ὅτι as 'that' (Koch), and as dependent on the preceding τοῦτο ὑμῖν λέγομεν (ver. 15), mars the logical evolution of the passage, and is opposed to the opinion of the Greek expositors (γάρ, Theod., Theoph.), and, as is shown above, of the best ancient Versions. αὐτὸς ὁ Κύριος] '*the Lord Himself;*' obviously not 'He the Lord' (De W.), nor yet 'Himself,' with ref. to His glorified body (Olsh.), but simply with ref. to His own august personal presence, αὐτὸς γὰρ πρῶτος τῶν ὅλων ὁ Κύριος ἐκ τῶν οὐρανῶν ἐπιφανήσεται κατιών, Theod. ἐν κελεύσματι] '*with a shout of command*,' 'in jussu,' Vulg., Clarom., Goth., sim. Copt. [*ouah-sahni*], Syr., Arm. The word κέλευσμα (sometimes, though doubtfully, κέλευμα, Lobeck on Soph. *Ajax*, 704, p. 323), an ἅπ. λεγόμ. in the N. T., occurs frequently in classical Greek as denoting the command or signal given by a general (admiral, or captain of rowers, Thucyd. II. 92), the encouraging shout of the charioteer (Plato, *Phædr.* p. 253 D) or the huntsman (Xenoph. *Cyneget.* VI. 20), or more technically the cry of the κελευστής to the rowers (Eurip. *Iph. T.* 1374), but in most cases has some ref. more or less distinct to the prevailing meaning of the verb: comp. Prov. xxx. 27 (ch. xxiv. LXX), στρατεύει ἀφ' ἑνὸς κελεύσματος εὐτάκτως, and Philo, *de Præm.* § 19, Vol. II. p. 427 (ed. Mang.), ἀνθρώπους . . . . . ἀπῳκισμένους ῥᾳδίως ἂν ἑνὶ κελεύσματι συναγάγοι Θεός. To whom the κέλευσμα is to be referred is somewhat doubtful. The Greek expositors (Chrys. ?) seem to refer it directly to Christ; it appears, however, more plausible to refer it directly to the ἀρχάγγελος, as Christ's minister, and to regard it as a general expression of what is afterwards more distinctly specified by the substantives which follow. The purport of the κέλευσμα it is idle to guess at: it may perhaps be ἐγείρεσθε, ἦλθεν ὁ νυμφίος (Chrys. 1), or more naturally, ἀναστῶσιν οἱ νεκροί (Chrys. 2, Theod.), or perhaps, still more probably, with a strict preservation of the current use of the word, the shout of command of the archangel to the attendant angelical hosts, ἑτοίμους ποιεῖτε πάντας, πάρεστι γὰρ ὁ κριτής, Chrys. 3; comp. Matth. xiii. 41.
On the use of ἐν to denote the concomitant circumstances (Arm. uses its 'instrumental' case), see notes *on Col.* ii. 7, iv. 2. Though with the Aramaic ܒ in our memory, it is not always desirable to over-press ἐν, yet in the present case, it *may* be used, as serving to hint at the κατάβασις, taking place *during* the κέλευσμα, in the sphere of its occurrence; compare notes on ch. ii. 3.
ἐν φωνῇ ἀρχαγγέλου] '*with the voice of the Archangel;*' more specific explanation of the circumstances and concomitants. To refer the ἀρχαγγ. to Christ (Olsh.), or the Holy Spirit (see in Wolf), is obviously untenable: the term is a δὶς λεγόμ. (Jude 9) in the

Χριστῷ ἀναστήσονται πρῶτον, 17 ἔπειτα ἡμεῖς οἱ ζῶντες οἱ περι-

N. T., and designates a leader of the angelical hosts by whom the Lord shall be attended on His coming; compare Matth. xxiv. 31, xxv. 31, 2 Thess. i. 7. With regard to the oblique references of some of the German commentators to the 'jüdischer, nachexilischer Vorstellung' (Lünem, compare Winer, *RWB.* Vol. II. p. 329, ed. 3), it seems enough to say that the apostle elsewhere distinctly alludes to separate orders of angels (see notes and reff. *on Eph.* i. 21, *Col.* i. 16), and that he here as distinctly speaks of a leader of such heavenly beings: to inquire further is idle and presumptuous. σάλπιγγι Θεοῦ] '*trumpet of God;*' not 'tuba Dei, adeoque *magna*,' Beng.,—such a form of Hebraistic superl. not occurring in the N. T., but simply 'the trumpet pertaining to God' (gen. *possess.*), the trumpet used in His service; comp. Rev. xv. 2, and see Winer, *Gr.* § 36. 3, p. 221. The Greek expositors appropriately allude to the use of the trumpet when God appeared on Sinai, Exod. xix. 16; comp. also Psalm xlvii. 5, Isaiah xxvii. 13, Zech. ix. 14. With the Jewish use of the trumpet to call assemblies (Numbers x. 2, xxxi. 6, Joel ii. 1) we have here nothing to do, still less with the speculations of later Judaism as to God's use of a trumpet to awaken the dead (Eisenmenger, *Entd. Jud.* Vol. II. p. 929, adduced by Lünem.): the apostle twice definitely states that the trumpet will sound at Christ's advent (1 Cor. xv. 52), and it infallibly will be so. ἀπ' οὐρανοῦ] '*from heaven*,'—where He now sits enthroned at the right hand of God; see esp. Acts i. 11. καὶ οἱ νεκροὶ κ. τ. λ.] '*and the dead in Christ, etc.;*' consequence and sequel of the ἐν κελεύσματι κ. τ. λ., the καὶ having here a slightly *consecutive* force; comp. notes *on Phil.* iv. 12. The words ἐν Χριστῷ are clearly to be joined with νεκροί, as more specifically designating those about whose share in the παρουσία the Thessalonian converts were disquieted: the general resurrection of *all* men does not here come into consideration; see Winer, *Gr.* § 20. 2, p. 123, comp. West, *Stud. u. Krit.* for 1858, p. 283, and on the omission of the art., notes *on Eph.* i. 15, and Fritz. *Rom.* Vol. I. p. 195. The connection with ἀναστήσονται (Schott) would indirectly assign an undue emphasis to ἐν Χρ. (Lün.), and introduce a specification out of harmony with the context: the subject of the passage is not the means by which (2 Cor. iv. 14), or element in which, the resurrection is to take place, but the respective shares of the holy dead and holy living in the παρουσία of the Lord, considered in relation to *time*. πρῶτον] '*first;*' not with any reference to πρώτη ἀνάστασις, Rev. xx. 5 (Theod., Theophyl., Œcum., al.), but, as the following ἔπειτα suggests, only to the fact that the resurrection of the dead in Christ shall be prior to the assumption of the living. The reading πρῶτοι is found in D¹FG; Vulg., Clarom.; Cyr., Theod. (1), al., and was perhaps suggested by the supposed dogmatical reference to the first resurrection.

17. ἔπειτα] '*then*,'—immediately after the ἀνάστασις of οἱ ἐν Χριστῷ; second act in the mighty drama. The particle ἔπειτα, as its derivation [ἐπ' εἶτα, Hartung, *Partik.* Vol. I. p. 302] and the following ἅμα (see below) both seem to suggest, marks the second event as speedily following on the first, and, like 'deinde' ('de rebus in temporis tractu continuis et proximis,' Hand, *Tursell.* Vol. II. p. 240), specifies not only the continuity but the proximity of the two events; comp. Erfurdt, Soph. *Antig.* 607. οἱ ζῶντες οἱ περιλειπ.] '*we, the living, who are remaining*,' 'we who are being left behind;' see notes on ver. 15.

λειπόμενοι ἅμα σὺν αὐτοῖς ἁρπαγησόμεθα ἐν νεφέλαις εἰς ἀπάντη-

ἅμα σὺν αὐτοῖς] '*at the same time together with them,*' 'simul rapiemur cum illis,' Vulg., Copt., [*euson*]; *i.e.* we shall be caught up with them at the same time that they shall be caught up, ἅμα appy. not marking the mere local coherence, 'all together,' Alf., but, as usually, connection in point of *time* ('res duas vel plures *una* vel *simul* aut esse aut fieri significat,' Klotz, *Devar.* Vol. II. p. 95): comp. Ammon. s. v. ἅμα μέν ἐστι χρονικὸν ἐπίῤῥημα, ὁμοῦ δὲ τοπικόν, and Tittm. *Synon.* I. p. 156, who, however, remarks that in Rom. iii. 12 (LXX) this distinction is not maintained. See notes on ch. v. 10. ἁρπαγησόμεθα ἐν νεφέλαις] '*shall be caught up in clouds;*' certainly not 'in nubes,' Beza, nor even '*auf.* Wolken,' De W., Lün., but, 'in nubibus,' Vulg., Clarom., *i. e.*, 'tanquam in curru triumphali,' Grot,, — the clouds forming the element with which they would be surrounded, and in which they would be borne up to meet their coming Lord; ἐπὶ (?) τοῦ ὀχήματος φερόμεθα τοῦ Πατρός, καὶ γὰρ αὐτὸς ἐν νεφέλαις ὑπέλαβεν αὐτόν [Acts i. 9.], καὶ ἡμεῖς ἐν νεφέλαις ἁρπαγησόμεθα, Chrysost. The transformation specified in 1 Cor. xv. 52, 53 ('compendium mortis per demutationem expunctæ,' Tertull. *de Resurr.* ch. 48, compare Delitzsch, *Psychol.* VII. 5, p. 268 sq.) will necessarily first take place (comp. Pearson, *Creed*, Vol. I. p. 357), upon which the glorified and luciform body will be caught up in the enveloping and upbearing clouds. On the nature of the resurrection body, compare Burnet, *State of Dep.* ch. VII. VIII., and the curious and learned investigations of Cudworth, *Intellect. Syst.* ch. V. 3, Vol. III. p. 310 sq. (ed. Harrison). The forms ἡρπάγην and ἁρπαγήσομαι appear to be later forms (Thom.-Mag. p. 412); but the 'librariorum arbitrium' often leaves it uncertain whether the first or second aor. was the original reading; comp. Pierson, *Mœr.* p. 168 (ed. Koch). εἰς ἀπάντησιν τοῦ Κυρ.] '*to meet the Lord,*' as He is coming down to earth; καὶ γὰρ βασιλέως εἰς πόλιν εἰσελαύνοντος οἱ μὲν ἔντιμοι πρὸς ἀπάντησιν ἐξίασιν, οἱ δὲ κατάδικοι ἔνδον μένουσι τὸν κριτήν, Chrys. The form εἰς ἀπάντησιν (Math. xxv. 1. (*Rec.*), 6, Acts xxviii. 15) seems to have been derived from the LXX, and answers to the Hebrew לִקְרַאת Jud. iv. 18, 22; Alex. ἀπάντ.). It may be associated either, as here, with a defining gen., or with a dative (Acts xxviii. 15), the verbal subst. preserving in the latter case the government of the verb from which it is derived; see Bernhardy, *Synt.* III. 10, comp. Winer, *Gr.* § 31. 3, p. 189. Some authorities [D¹(E¹?) FG; Vulg., Clarom.; Tert., al.] read εἰς ὑπάντησιν τῷ Χριστῷ, but with every appearance of correction in both words.

εἰς ἀέρα] '*into the air,*' 'in aera,' Vulg., Clarom., 'in luftan, Goth., and sim. the other Vv. except Æth. (Pol.), 'in nube;' dependent on ἁρπαγησ. Εἰς ἀέρα is certainly not 'in cœlum' (Flatt), but, as the regular meaning of the word requires, 'into the *air*,' — though perhaps not necessarily (comp. Wordsw.) with any precise limitation to the terrene atmosphere. The ἀήρ, as De W. well observes, marks the way to heaven, and includes the interspace between earth and heaven, with greater or less latitude according to the context; see notes *on Eph.* ii. 2. To question whether the *air* is here represented as the final realm of the faithful (Usteri *Lehrb.* II. 2. B, p. 338, 441) is surely monstrous: the apostle makes here a pause, simply because his design of clearing up the anxieties on the part of his converts is accomplished when he declares that the holy quick and holy dead shall be caught up into the air

σιν τοῦ Κυρίου εἰς ἀέρα· καὶ οὕτως πάντοτε σὺν Κυρίῳ ἐσόμεθα.
18 ὥστε παρακαλεῖτε ἀλλήλους ἐν τοῖς λόγοις τούτοις.

**Ye know that the day of the Lord cometh suddenly. Be watchful and prepared, for God has not appointed us for wrath, but salvation.**

V. Περὶ δὲ τῶν χρόνων καὶ τῶν καιρῶν, ἀδελ-

*simultaneously* to meet the Lord. The great events immediately following Christ's descent to judgment (see Jackson, *Creed*, XI. 12. 1, 2), and his final and eternal union with His saints in the heavenly Jerusalem (Rev. xxi. xxii.), are to be collected from other passages; see Alford *in loc.* καὶ οὕτως κ. τ. λ.] '*and so shall we be ever together with the Lord;*' so, in consequence of this ἁρπάζεσθαι, — the subject of the ἐσόμεθα (Hesych. βιώσομεν) being clearly *both* classes previously mentioned. The force of the σύν, as implying not merely an accompanying (μετά), but a *coherence* with, should not be left unnoticed; see notes *on Eph.* vi. 22.

18. ὥστε] '*So then,*' '*Consequently;*' in consequence of the foregoing revelation. On the force of ὥστε and its connection with the imperative mood, see *on Phil.* ii. 12. παρακαλεῖτε] '*comfort;*' not here 'exhort,' 'teach,' Æth. (both), but, in accordance with the preceding ἵνα μὴ λυπῆσθε (ver. 13), 'consolemini,' Vulg., Clarom., Goth., ܒܝܐܘ Syr., and similarly the remaining Vv. ἐν τοῖς λόγοις τούτοις] '*with these words;*' not 'words of faith,' (Olsh.), but simply 'these words' (τούτοις not without emphasis), — the words in which the apostle delivers to them his inspired message; τοῦτο δὲ ὃ λέγει νῦν, καὶ ῥητῶς ἤκουσε παρὰ τοῦ Θεοῦ, Chrys. on ver. 14. The ἐν is here used in that species of instrumental sense in which the action, etc., of the verb is conceived as *existing in the means;* 'solent Græci pro Latinorum ablativo instrumenti sæpe ἐν præpositionem ponere, significaturi in eâ re, cujus nomini præpositio adjuncta est, vim aut facultatem alicujus rei agendæ sitam esse,' Wunder, Soph. *Philoct.* 60, see exx. in Raphel, *Annot.* Vol. II. p. 549. Thus, in the present case, the παράκλησις may be conceived as contained in the divinely inspired words themselves; comp. Jelf, *Gr.* § 623. 3.

CHAPTER V. 1. Περὶ δὲ τῶν χρόνων κ. τ. λ] '*But concerning the times and seasons,*' scil. of the Lord's coming, τῆς συντελείας, Theoph. The terms χρόνος and καιρὸς are not synonymous: the former denotes time indefinitely, the latter a definite period of time (μέρος χρόνου, ἢ μεμετρημένων ἡμερῶν σύστημα, Thom.-M. p. 489, ed. Bern.), and thence, derivatively, the right or fitting time; comp. Ammon. *de Diff. Voc.* p. 80, ὁ μὲν καιρὸς δηλοῖ ποιότητα..... χρόνος δὲ ποσότητα, and see Tittmann, *Synon.* I. p. 41, where the meaning of καιρὸς is carefully investigated. The force of the plural has been somewhat differently estimated. On the whole, it seems most natural to refer it, not to the length of the periods (Dorner, *de Orat. Christ. Eschat.* p. 73), but simply to the plurality either of the acts or of the moments of the time (Lünem.). There appears no reason to take καὶ here as explanatory (Koch): the two words simply are connected by the copula; comp. Acts i. 7, χρόνους ἢ καιρούς, Eccles. iii. 1, ὁ χρόνος καὶ καιρός, Dan. ii. 21, καιροὺς καὶ χρόνους, Wisdom viii. 8, καιρῶν καὶ χρόνων. οὐ χρείαν ἔχετε] '*ye have no need;*' a παράλειψις, see notes on ch. iv. 9. The reason why there was no need does not seem here to be due to the ἀσύμφορον (Œcum., compare Chrysostom, and Acts i. 7),

φοί, οὐ χρείαν ἔχετε ὑμῖν γράφεσθαι· 2 αὐτοὶ γὰρ ἀκριβῶς
οἴδατε ὅτι ἡμέρα Κυρίου ὡς κλέπτης ἐν νυκτὶ οὕτως ἔρχεται.
3 ὅταν λέγωσιν Εἰρήνη καὶ ἀσφάλεια, τότε αἰφνίδιος αὐτοῖς ἐφίσ-

but, as the next verse suggests, because they had been accurately informed by the apostle, by word of mouth, of all that it was necessary for them to know. On the qualifying and explanatory object-infinitive, see Krüger, *Sprachl.* § 55. 3, comp. § 50. 6. 4, 4.

2. ἀκριβῶς] '*accurately*;' only used once again by the apostle, Eph. v. 15. The use of this adverb, considered exegetically, is very striking. It certainly seems to point to special and definite information on the subject; but whether this was derived from a written Gospel (Wordsw.) or from the oral communications of the apostle cannot possibly be determined. The latter seems much the most probable; comp. 2 Thess. ii. 5. The derivation of ἀκρ. is slightly doubtful; most probably from ἄκρος in a locative form (ἄκρι), and a root BA-, Benfey, *Wurzellex.* Vol. I. p. 158. ἡμέρα Κυρίου] '*the day of the Lord*,' scil. τῆς δεσποτικῆς ἐπιφανείας, Theod.; the day of *our Lord's* coming to judgment (comp. Reuss. *Théol. Chrét.* IV. 21, Vol. II. p. 243), ᾗ ὁ υἱὸς τοῦ ἀνθρώπου ἀποκαλύπτεται, Luke xvii. 30; comp. 1 Cor. i. 8, v. 5, 2 Cor. i. 14, Phil. i. 6, and for the somewhat similar יוֹם יְהוָה, Joel i. 15, ii. 1, Ezek. xiii. 5, al. To refer it to the destruction of Jerusalem (Hamm.), or to include in it τὴν ἰδίαν ἑκάστου ἡμέραν (Theoph., comp. notes *on Phil.* i. 6), is here distinctly at variance with the context, which treats solely and entirely of the Lord's παρουσία. The reading is not quite certain. *Rec.* inserts ἡ with AKL: many Ff.; but though the omission of the ἡ might have been due to the ἡ of the following ἡμέρα, the probability of the insertion (as more definitive) and the preponderance of uncial authority [BDEFG] seem in favor of the omission: *Lachm.*, *Tisch.* ὡς κλέπτης ἐν νυκτί] '*as a thief in the night*,' scil. ἔρχεται; ἐν νυκτὶ not being added as a quasi-epithet to κλέπτης, but belonging to an unexpressed ἔρχεται; see Winer, *Gr.* § 20. 4, p. 126, note. This solemn and regular Scripture simile (comp. Matth. xxiv. 43, Luke xii. 39, 2 Pet. iii. 10, Rev. iii. 3, xvi. 15) does not contain any reference to the *dread* felt with regard to the coming (Schott, compare Alf.), but simply to the τὸ αἰφνίδιον (Theod.): see esp. Rev. *l. c.*, ἥξω ὡς κλέπτης, καὶ οὐ μὴ γνῷς ποίαν ὥραν ἥξω ἐπὶ σέ, and comp. Usteri, *Lehrb.* II. 2. B, p. 337. The addition ἐν νυκτὶ (comp., however, Matth. xxiv. 43, ποίᾳ φυλακῇ) is peculiar to this place, and combined with Matth. *l. c.*, xxv. 6, may have given rise to the ancient tradition of the early church (noticed by Lünem.), that Christ was to come at night (on Easter Eve); compare Lact. *Inst.* VII. 19 ('intempestâ et tenebrosâ nocte'), and Jerome *on Matth.* xxv. 6. οὕτως ἔρχεται] '*so it comes*;' the οὕτως being added to give force and emphasis to the comparison. The pres. ἔρχεται is not for a future (Pelt, al.), nor yet to mark the suddenness of the event (Bengel, Koch), but its fixed nature and prophetic certainty; see Winer, *Gr.* § 40. 2, p. 237, comp. Bernhardy, *Synt.* x 2, p. 371.

3. ὅταν λέγωσιν] '*When they may say*;' certainly not the Jews (Hamm.), nor even their persecutors generally (Chrys.), but all unbelieving and unthinking men; comp. Matth. xxiv. 38, Luke xvii. 27. The true believers were always watching and waiting, knowing the uncertainty and unexpectedness of the hour of the Lord's coming; comp. Matth. xxiv. 44, xxv. 13, Luke xii. 35, 36.

ταται ὄλεθρος ὥσπερ ἡ ὠδὶν τῇ ἐν γαστρὶ ἐχούσῃ, καὶ οὐ μὴ
ἐκφύγωσιν. 4 ὑμεῖς δέ, ἀδελφοί, οὐκ ἐστὲ ἐν σκότει, ἵνα ὑμᾶς ἡ

3. ὅταν λέγωσιν] So *Tisch.* (ed. 1, 2. 7) with AFG; 4 mss.; Syr., Clarom., Goth., Æth. (both); many Lat. Ff (*Griesb., Scholz, De W., Lünem., Alf.*);—and appy. rightly. For though δὲ is well supported,—by BDE; Copt., Syr. (Philox.); Chrys., Theod. ([*Lachm.*], *Koch*), and is not uncommonly displaced for γάρ (see *on Gal.* i. 11), which is here adopted by *Rec.* with KL; most mss.; Vulg., al.; Dam., and some Latin Ff.,—still the tendency to supply expletives is so very decided (Mill, *Prolegom.* p. clvi), and the external authority for the omission so fairly satisfactory, that there seems here no sufficient reason for reversing the judgment of *Tischendorf.*

Εἰρήνη καὶ ἀσφάλεια] '*Peace and safety*,' scil. ἐστίν,—is everywhere present; comp. Ezek. xiii. 10, λέγοντες Εἰρήνη· καὶ οὐκ ἔστιν εἰρήνη. The distinction between these words is obvious: the first [εἴρω, necto, or more probably ΕΡ-, εἴρω, dico; comp. Benfey, *Wurzellex.* Vol. II. p. 7] betokens an inward repose and security; the latter [α, σ-φάλλω; comp. Sanscr. root *phal*, Heb. כָּפַל, Pott. *Etym. Forsch.* Vol. I. p. 238, Donalds. *Crat.* § 209] a sureness and safety that is not interfered with or compromised by outward obstacles. τότε αἰφνίδιος κ. τ. λ.] '*then with suddenness does destruction come upon them*;' αἰφνίδιος not being a mere epithet (adjectivum attributum), 'sudden destr.,' Auth., 'plötzliches Verderben,' De W., but a secondary predication of manner (adjectivum appositum), scil. 'repentinus superveniet,' Vulg., Copt. [*chen ouexopina*], al., and fully emphatic; see esp. Donalds. *Cratyl.* § 303, and Müller, *Kleine Schriften*, Vol. I. p. 310; comp. Winer, *Gr.* § 54. 2, p. 412, and notes *on Col.* ii. 3. The verb ἐφίσταται may be either simply 'imminet,' Beza, or more derivatively 'superveni[e]t,' Vulg. being a 'verbum solemne de rebus hominibusve citius quam quis existimaverit adstantibus,' Schott; comp. esp. Luke xxi. 34. On ὄλεθρος, comp. notes *on* 1 *Tim.* vi. 9. ὥσπερ ἡ ὠδὶν] '*as the birth-pang.*' The true point of the appropriate comparison ('πὲρ vim eam comparativam, quam habet ὡς, usitato more auget atque effert,' Klotz, *Devar.* Vol. II. p. 768) is neither the knowledge that the event is to come (Theod.), nor its nearness (De W.), but, as the context seems clearly to suggest, its *suddenness* and uncertainty; 'inter epulas et risus vel in medio somnio corripitur,' Calv. The form ὠδίν, like the forms ἀκτίν (?), δελφίν, belongs to later Greek; comp. Winer, *Gr.* § 9. 2, p. 61. ἐν γαστρὶ ἐχούσῃ] The regular formula in the N. T., Matth. i. 18, 23, xxiv. 19, Mark xiii. 17, Luke xxi. 23, Rev. xii. 2. The more usual expression in earlier Greek appears to have been ἐν γαστρὶ φέρειν (Plato, *Legg.* VII. p. 792 E, comp. Hom. *Il.* VI. 58), or ἐγκύμων εἶναι or γίγνεσθαι, as in Plato, *Epin.* p. 979 A, al. οὐ μὴ ἐκφύγωσιν] '*they shall in no wise escape*,' not τόν τε πόνον καὶ ὄλεθρον, Œcum., but simply and absolutely; comp. Heb. ii. 3, xii. 25, Ecclus. xvi. 13. On the strengthened negation οὐ μὴ with the subjunctive, see notes and reff. on ch. iv. 15.

4. ὑμεῖς δέ] '*But ye*;' in opposition to the unthinking and unbelieving noticed in the preceding verse: 'occasione acceptâ ex superioribus adhortatur Christianos ad vigilantiam, sobrietatem, et sanctimoniam,' Calv. In the following words it is scarcely necessary to say that ἐστὲ cannot possibly be

ἡμέρα ὡς κλέπτης καταλάβῃ· 5 πάντες γὰρ ὑμεῖς υἱοὶ φωτός

4. ὑμᾶς ἡ ἡμέρα] So *Lachm.* with ADEFG; Vulg., Clarom., appy. Æth. (both); many Lat. Ff. (*Tisch.* ed. 1, *Schott*, *Lünem.*, *Koch*). The simpler order ἡ ἡμέρα ὑμᾶς is adopted by *Tisch.* ed. 2, 7, with BKL; appy. all mss.; Goth., al.; Chrys., Theod., Dam., al. Rec., *Griesb.*, *Alf.*); but appy. with less probability, as the uncial authority is not strong, and the change is just as likely to have been owing to a conformation to the more natural order, as a transposition for the sake of throwing emphasis on the ὑμᾶς.

imperatival (Flatt): both the negative, and the non-occurrence of the imper. ἔστε in the N. T. utterly preclude such a translation. ἐν σκότει] '*in darkness*,' in the element or region of it. The σκότος here mentioned seems to have been suggested by the preceding ἐν νυκτί: it does not mark exclusively either τὸν σκοτεινὸν καὶ ἀκάθαρτον βίον (Chrys., Theoph., Œcum.), as might seem suggested by the succeeding verse, or τὴν ἄγνοιαν (Theod.), as is partially suggested by the preceding verse, but, as the general context requires, *both*, —'statum ignorantiæ et vitii,' Turretin. It was a darkness not only of the mind and understanding (Eph. iv. 18), but of the heart and will (1 John ii. 9); see Andrewes, *Serm.* XIV. Vol. III. p. 371. ἵνα ὑμᾶς κ. τ. λ.] '*in order that the day should surprise you*;' not merely a statement of result, but of the *purpose* contemplated by God in His merciful dispensation implied in οὐκ ἐστὲ ἐν σκότει; see Winer, *Gr.* § 53. 6, p. 408. It may be doubted, however, whether we have not here some trace of a secondary force of ἵνα (see *on Eph.* i. 17), the eventual conclusion being in some degree mixed up with and obscuring the idea of finality; comp. notes *on Gal.* v. 17. With the numerous instances of a secondary final use of ἵνα which the writings of the N. T. (esp. those of St. John, Winer, *Gr.* p. 303) distinctly supply, and a remembrance of the ultimate decline of the particle into the νὰ of modern Greek (Corpe, *Gr.* p. 129), it is prudent to beware in all cases of over-pressing the final force; compare Winer, *Gr.* § 44. 8, p. 299 sq. The 'day' here specified is not specifically the day of judgment [ἐκείνη ἡ ἡμέρα FG; Vulg., Clarom.], but, as the context seems to require, the period of light (De W.), which indeed becomes practically synonymous with the day of the Lord, as bearing salvation (comp. Rom. xiii. 12), and bringing to light the hidden things of darkness (1 Cor. iv. 5).

καταλάβῃ] '*overtake*,' '*surprise*,' ܢܕܪܟ Syr., 'adprehendat.' Clarom., 'gafahai,' Goth.; the κατὰ here not introducing any definite sense of hostility (comp. Koch), but, as usual, being simply *intensive*, and deriving its further shades of meaning from the context: see the good collection of examples in Rost u. Palm, *Lex.* s. v. Vol. I. p. 1623. The reading κλέπτας [*Lachmann*, with AB; Copt.] has not certainly sufficient critical support.

5. πάντες γὰρ] '*for ye all*:' confirmation of the preceding negative statement by a more specific positive declaration. The particle γὰρ, which we can hardly say with Schott is 'haud necessaria ad sententiam,' is omitted by *Rec.*, but on authority [K; majority of mss.] decidedly insufficient. υἱοὶ φωτός] '*sons of light*;' a Hebraistic formula comp. Ewald, *Gr.* § 287) expressing, with considerable emphasis and significance, not merely that they 'belonged to' the light (Alf.), but that they belonged to it in the intimate way of children to a parent,—almost οἱ τὰ τοῦ φωτὸς πράττοντες, Chrys., Theoph.: see Winer, *Gr.*

ἐστε καὶ υἱοὶ ἡμέρας. οὐκ ἐσμὲν νυκτὸς οὐδὲ σκότους. 6 Ἄρα οὖν
μὴ καθεύδωμεν ὡς καὶ οἱ λοιποί, ἀλλὰ γρηγορῶμεν καὶ νήφωμεν.
7 οἱ γὰρ καθεύδοντες νυκτὸς καθεύδουσιν, καὶ οἱ μεθυσκόμενοι

§ 34. 3. b. 2, p. 213, Steiger *on* 1 *Pet.* 14, p. 153, and notes *on Eph.* ii. 2. Somewhat analogous expressions are found in classical Greek, παῖδες σοφῶν, παῖδες ἱερέων κ. τ. λ., but appy. never (as here) in connection with abstract substantives; comp. Blomf. on Æsch. *Pers.* 408.

οὐκ ἐσμὲν νυκτός] '*We belong not to night:*' the genitive idiomatically specifying the domain to which the subjects belong; comp. Acts ix. 2, and see Winer, *Gr.* § 30. 5, p. 176. On the various meanings in which this possessive gen. is connected with εἶναι and γίγνεσθαι, see Krüger, *Sprachl.* § 47. 6. 1 sq., Bernhardy, *Synt.* III. 46, p. 165, and on the very intelligible χιασμός [φῶς, ἡμέρα—νύξ, σκότος], see Jelf, *Gr.* § 904. 3, Madvig, *Lat. Gr.* § 473. a. The reading ἐστὲ [D¹FG; Syr. (not Philox.), Claromon., Goth., al.] is obviously a conformation to the preceding ἐστέ.

6. Ἄρα οὖν] '*Accordingly then;*' exhortation following on the preceding declaration, the illative ἄρα being supported and enhanced by the collective and retrospective οὖν; see notes *on Gal.* vi. 10. In Attic Greek this combination is only found in the case of the interrogative ἆρα, comp. Klotz, *Devar.* Vol. II. p. 181, Herm. *Viger*, No. 292, and Stallb. on Plato, *Republ.* v. p. 462 A.

καθεύδωμεν] '*sleep,*' *i. e.* be careless and indifferent, μὴ ἀμελῶμεν τῶν καλῶν ἔργων, Theoph; comp. Eph. v. 14, and the very pertinent remarks of Beck, *Christ. Lehrwiss.* Vol. I. p. 299 (cited by Koch), on the deepening sleep of the soul under the influence of sin; see also Beck, *Seelenl.* I. 8, p. 18. The οἱ λοιποὶ are here obviously unbelievers, whether careless Jews or ignorant heathens; comp. notes on ch. iv. 13. *Lachm.* omits the καὶ before οἱ λοιποί, but on insufficient external authority [AB; 2 mss.; Amit., al.], and appy. in opposition to St. Paul's prevailing usage: comp. 1 Cor. ix. 5, Eph. ii 3, and above, ch. iv. 13.

νήφωμεν] '*be sober;*' comp. 1 Pet. v. 8. The νήφειν enhances the preceding γρηγορῶμεν; Christians were not only to be wakeful, but have all their senses and capacities in full exercise: ἐν ἡμέρᾳ ἂν γρηγορῇ τις μὴ νήφῃ δέ, μυρίοις περιπεσεῖται δεινοῖς, Chrys. On the regular meaning of this verb, which always appears to be that of 'sobriety,' not that of 'watchfulness' or 'wakefulness' (as perhaps Œcum., ἐπίτασις ἐγρηγόρσεως), see notes *on* 2 *Tim.* iv. 5.

7. οἱ γὰρ καθεύδοντες] '*For they that sleep,*' '*sleepers,*' (Winer, *Gr.* § 45. 7); confirmatory explanation of the preceding exhortation by a reference to the prevailing habits of non-Christian life. At first sight it might seem plausible to give all the words a spiritual reference (Chrys., Theoph., Koch): as however νυκτὸς seems only to mark the period when the actions referred to usually took place, the *literal* and proper meaning is distinctly to be preferred: 'quemadmodum in hoc versu *dormire* ita etiam *ebrium esse* dicitur proprie, tanquam exemplum ejusmodi sentiendi agendique rationis quæ nonnisi hominum sit in caligne nocturnâ lubenter versantium,' Schott; so Lünem. and Alf.

οἱ μεθυσκόμενοι] '*they that are drunken.*' The distinction advocated by Beng., μεθύσκομαι notat actum, μεθύω statum '(comp. Clarom. 'inebriantur—ebri isunt'), seems here more than doubtful. The transition from 'being actually drunk' is so slight (in Rost u. Palm, *Lex* s. vv. both are translated 'berauscht seyn'), that with the preceding καθεύδοντες—καθεύδουσιν before us it seems best to regard them here as simply synonymous.

νυκτὸς μεθύουσιν· [8] ἡμεῖς δὲ ἡμέρας ὄντες νήφωμεν, ἐνδυσάμενοι θώρακα πίστεως καὶ ἀγάπης καὶ περικεφαλαίαν ἐλπίδα σωτηρίας,
[9] ὅτι οὐκ ἔθετο ἡμᾶς ὁ Θεὸς εἰς ὀργήν, ἀλλὰ εἰς περιποίησιν σω-

8. ἡμεῖς δὲ κ. τ. λ.] *'but let us, as we are of the day:'* not exactly 'qui diei sumus,' Vulg., Clarom., but 'quum simus,' Æth. (Platt), Arm., comp. Goth., 'visandans;' the participle not being here used predicatively, but with a slightly causal, or combined 'temporal-causal' force; see Schmalfeld, *Synt. des Gr. Verb.* § 207, comp. Donalds. *Gr.* § 615. On the connection with the gen. with εἰμί, see notes on ver. 5. ἐνδυσάμενοι] *'having put on;'* temporal participle, defining the action contemporaneous with the νήφειν. The apostle now passes into his favorite metaphor of the Christian soldier; Comp. Rom. xiii. 12, 2 Cor. x. 4, and esp. Eph. vi. 11, where not only (as here) the *defensive,* but the offensive portions of the equipment are described. The 'armatura' here consists of the three great Christian virtues, Faith, Love, and Hope, the first and second forming the breastplate (aliter Eph. vi. 14, 16), the third (similarly in Ephes. vi. 17, see notes), the helmet; comp. Reuss, *Théol. Chrét.* IV. 22, Vol. II. p. 259, 260. θώρακα πίστεως] *'a shield of faith,'* or, more probably, *'the shield, etc.'* the second and third substantives, as well-known terms, here dispensing with the article (Winer, *Gr.* § 19. 1), and causing, on the principle of correlation (Middl. *Gr. Art.* III. 6), the governing noun to be also anarthrous. The gen. is that of 'apposition;' see notes and reff. *on Eph.* vi. 14.
καὶ περικεφ. κ. τ. λ.] *'and as a helmet the hope of salvation;* a defence that can never fail. With hope fixed on the ἐπηγγελμένη σωτηρία (Theod.), all the dangers and trials of the present seem light and endurable; καθάπερ γὰρ ἡ περικεφαλαία τὸ καίριον σώζει τῶν ἐν ἡμῖν, τὴν κεφαλὴν περιβάλλουσα καὶ πάντοθεν στεγάζουσα· οὕτω καὶ ἡ ἐλπὶς τὸν λογισμὸν οὐκ ἀφίησι διαπεσεῖν, ἀλλ' ὀρθὸν ἵστησιν ὥσπερ κεφαλήν, οὐδὲν τῶν ἔξωθεν εἰς αὐτὸν πεσεῖν ἐῶσα, Chrys. The gen. σωτηρίας is the gen. *objecti,* that to which it is directed and on which it is fixed, comp. ch. i. 3, Rom. v. 2, and, if necessary, Winer, *Gr.* § 30. 1, p. 167.

9. ὅτι κ. τ. λ] *'because, etc.;'* reason for the use of the foregoing words ἐλπίδα σωτηρίας, expressed both negatively (οὐκ ἔθετο κ. τ. λ.) and positively ἀλλ' εἰς περιπ. κ. τ. λ.: οὐ πρὸς τοῦτο ἐκάλεσεν εἰς τὸ ἀπολέσαι, ἀλλ' εἰς τὸ σῶσαι, Chrys. ἔθετο ἡμᾶς κ. τ. λ.] *'appointed us to anger,'* i. e. to become the subjects of it, to fall under its punitive action. The form τιθέναι (Acts xiii. 47) or θέσθαι εἰς τί (1 Tim. i. 12) appears to have a partially Hebraistic tinge, and to answer to נָתַן, שׂוּם, or שִׁית followed by לְ; comp. Psalm lxvi. 9, Jer. ix. 11, Ezek. xiv. 8, al. On ὀργή, see notes on ch. i. 10. περιποίησιν σωτηρίας] *'the obtaining of salvation,'* ܠܡܩܢܝܢܘܬܐ ܕܚܝ̈ܐ [ad acquisitionem salutis], sim. Vulg., Clarom., Copt. [*tancho,*—here needlessly rendered 'vivificatio;' comp. Mal. iii. 17], 'du gafreideinai ganistais,' Goth.; comp. 2 Thess. ii. 14, εἰς περιποίησιν δόξης. Neither here, Heb. x. 39, nor 2 Thess. *l. c.* is there any reason for departing from this simple and primary meaning of περιποίησις; Hesych. πλεονασμός· κτῆσις, Suid. κτῆσις. Both in Eph. i. 14 (see notes), and 1 Pet. ii. 9, as the context shows, the use is wholly different, and appy. a reflection of the סְגֻלָּה of the O. T. (comp. Acts xx. 28): in 2 Chron. xiv. 13, Pseud.-Plato, *Def.* p. 415 c (see Rost u. Palm, *Lex.* s. v.), the meaning seems rather 'conservatio'; but neither the one (appy. favored by

*τηρίας διὰ τοῦ Κυρίου ἡμῶν Ἰησοῦ Χριστοῦ,* 10 *τοῦ ἀποθανόντος ὑπὲρ ἡμῶν ἵνα, εἴτε γρηγορῶμεν εἴτε καθεύδωμεν, ἅμα σὺν αὐτῷ ζήσωμεν.* 11 *διὸ παρακαλεῖτε ἀλλήλους, καὶ οἰκοδομεῖτε εἷς τὸν ἕνα, καθὼς καὶ ποιεῖτε.*

Œcum., comp. Theod. ἵνα οἰκείους ἀποφήνῃ) nor the other is here either natural or suitable. διὰ τοῦ Κυρίου κ. τ. λ.] Dependent, not on ἔθετο, but on the preceding περιποίησιν σωτηρίας, and specifying the medium by which the σωτηρία was to be obtained. This medium is certainly not 'doctrinam eam quam Christus nobis attulit' (Grot.), nor, in this passage, 'faith in Him' (Lünem.), but, as the next verse seems to show, His atoning death; comp. Eph. i. 7, and notes *in loc.*

10. τοῦ ἀποθ. ὑπὲρ ἡμῶν] '*who died for us;*' specification of the blessed act of redeeming love by which the περιποίησις σωτηρίας has become assured to us; comp. ch. iv. 14. The clause, as Lünem. properly observes, is not causal (ἀποθ would then be anarthrous, comp. Schmalfeld, *Synt.* § 222, 225 (note), and Donalds. *Gr.* § 492), but relative and assertory; 'ne quid de salutis certitudine dubitemus aut de satisfactione soliciti essemus, dicit Christum pro nobis mortuum esse, et pro peccatis nostris satisfecisse, ut salutem consequeremur,' Calv. On the meaning of ὑπὲρ in dogmatical passages, — not *exclusively,* 'in our stead' (Waterl. *Serm.* xxxi. Vol. v. p. 740), see notes and reff. *on Gal.* iii. 13. ἵνα εἴτε κ. τ. λ.] '*in order that whether we wake or sleep;*' holy purpose of the Lord's redeeming death. There is some little doubt as to the exact meaning of the terms καθεύδειν and γρηγορεῖν. It seems clear that they cannot be understood in a simple physical sense (comp. Fell), still less in an ethical sense, as τὸ καθεύδειν was described (ver. 6) as a state incompatible with Christianity. There remains, then, only the supposition that they are used in a metaphorical sense (comp. Psalm lxxxvii. 6, Dan. xii. 2, al.), to which also the following ζήσωμεν seems very distinctly to guide us. The meaning, then, is substantially the same as Rom. xiv. 8, ἐάν τε οὖν ζῶμεν ἐάν τε ἀποθνήσκωμεν, τοῦ Κυρίου ἐσμέν. It is not exact to say that the subjunctive with εἴτε—εἴτε, as here, is not classical (Alf.), for see Plato, *Legg.* XII. p. 958 D (ed. Bekk.). As a general rule, εἴτε is associated with the same moods as εἰ (Klotz, *Devar.* Vol. II. p. 533); as, however, there are cases in which it is now admitted that εἰ can be associated with the subj. ('εἰ cum conjunct. respectum comprehendit experientiæ, expectandumque esse indicat, ut fiat aut non fiat,' Herm. *de Part.* ἄν, II. 7, see Klotz, *Devar.* Vol. II. p. 500 sq.), a similar latitude may rightly be assigned to εἴτε. It seems probable *here* that the subj. is used, in the dependent clause, in a species of conformity with the subj. in the principal clause; comp. Winer, *Gr.* § 41. 2. c, p. 263.

ἅμα σὺν αὐτῷ] '*all together, united with Him,*' not 'together with Him,' Auth.; the ζῆν σὺν Χριστῷ forming the principal idea, while the ἅμα (Heb. יַחְדָּו) subjoins the further notion of aggregation; comp. Rom. iii. 12, and contrast 1 Thess. iv. 17, where the previous specifications of time make the temporal meaning there more plausible. The ζήσωμεν is both more emphatic than ἐσόμεθα (ch. iv. 17), and also serves slightly to elucidate the metaphorical use of the preceding words.

11. διό] '*Wherefore,*' '*On which account;*' not exactly 'quæ cum ita sint' (Alf.), but quamobrem' (see Klotz, *Devar.* Vol. II. p. 173, who correctly assigns the former meaning to οὖν), thereby serv-

Reverence your spiritual rulers; be peaceful and forbearing, and thankful. Quench not the Spirit: and may God sanctify and preserve you.

12 Ἐρωτῶμεν δὲ ὑμᾶς, ἀδελφοί, εἰδέναι τοὺς

ing to place in closer logical connection the foregoing declaration and the present exhortation. On the uses of this particle by St. Paul, see notes *on Gal.* iv. 31. παρακαλεῖτε] '*comfort*,' '*console*,' ܒܝܐܘ [consolamini] Syr. 'consolamini,' Vulg., not 'exhortamini,' Clarom.; the analogy of this verse with ch. iv. 17 (where the contextual argument for the present sense is very strong) appears to require a similarity of translation, more especially as the hortatory tone (ver. 6) seems now to have merged into the consolatory. The exact meaning of this word is frequently somewhat doubtful: it is used more than fifty times in St. Paul's Epp., with several varieties of meaning which can only be decided on by a careful consideration of the context. [Obs. that in notes *on Col.* ii. 2 (ed. 1) 'always' is meant only to apply to passages similar to the one in question, — where in fact there is no doubt about the general meaning, but only its degree of intensity. Expunge, however, the ref. to 1 Thess. iii. 2; see notes *in loc.*] εἷς τὸν ἕνα] '*one the other;*' equivalent in meaning to ἀλλήλους; see exx. in Kypke, *Annot.* Vol. II. p 339, all of which, however, except Theocr. *Idyll.* XXII. 65, are from late authors. Compare οἱ καθ' ἕνα, Eph. v. 33, and the somewhat analogous εἷς πρὸς ἕνα, Plato, *Legg.* I. p. 626 C, al.; see Winer, *Gr.* § 26. 2, p. 156. To regard εἰς as a prep. and to refer τὸν ἕνα to Christ, is in the highest degree forced and improbable; see Lünem. *in loc.*

The metaphorical term οἰκοδομεῖν (1 Cor. viii. 1, x. 23, al.) is derived from the idea, elsewhere both expressed and implied in St. Paul's Epp., that Christians form a ναὸς or οἰκοδομὴ Θεοῦ; see 1 Cor. iii. 9, 16, 2 Cor. vi. 16, Eph. ii. 20, al, and comp. Andrewes, *Serm.* VI. Vol. II. p. 273. καθὼς καὶ ποιεῖτε] '*even as ye also are doing;*' praise and encouragement founded on the actual state of the Thessalonian church; comp. ch. iv. 1, 10. On the force of καὶ in comparative sentences of this kind, see notes *on Eph.* v. 23.

12. Ἐρωτῶμεν δέ] '*Now we ask you;*' transition by means of the δὲ μεταβατικόν (see notes *on Gal.* iii. 8), to their duties towards the rulers of the church, — a subject not improbably suggested by the words immediately preceding. In no case could the precept οἰκοδομεῖτε εἷς τὸν ἕνα be carried out with greater practical benefit to themselves and to the church at large, than in showing respect to their appointed spiritual teachers. εἰδέναι] '*to know,*' '*to regard,*' 'ut rationem ac respectum habeatis,' Est.; not 'to show (by deeds) that you know' (Koch), but simply 'to know,' *i. e.* 'not to be ignorant of,' 'to recognize fully'; this somewhat unusual meaning of εἰδ. being analogous to that of the Heb. יָדַע (see Gesen. *Lex.* s. v. 8), and here approximating in meaning to ἐπιγινώσκειν, 1 Cor. xvi. 18. No instance of a similar or even analogous usage has, as yet, been adduced from classical Greek. τοὺς κοπιῶντας ἐν ὑμῖν] '*those who are laboring among you,*' 'those who are engaged in sacred and ministerial duties; comp. 1 Tim. v. 17, where the more specific ἐν λόγῳ is supplied. On the meaning and derivation of κόπος, κοπιάω, see notes *on* 1 *Tim.* iv. 10. This general designation, as the following explanatory terms seem to suggest, is to be referred to the Presbyters of the Church of Thessalonica (Thorndike, *Prim. Gov.* ch. III. Vol. I. p. 8, A.-C. Libr.), ἐν ὑμῖν obviously having no ethical refer-

κοπιῶντας ἐν ὑμῖν καὶ προϊσταμένους ὑμῶν ἐν Κυρίῳ καὶ νουθε-
τοῦντας ὑμᾶς, 13 καὶ ἡγεῖσθαι αὐτοὺς ὑπερεκπερισσῶς ἐν ἀγάπῃ

ence, ἐν ταῖς καρδ. ὑμῶν (Flatt), still less 'in vobis docendis' (Zanch.), but simply implying 'in vestro cœtu' (Schott), 'inter vos,' Vulg., — with mere local reference to the sphere of the κόπος.

καὶ προϊσταμένους κ. τ. λ.] *'and are presiding over you in the Lord;'* further explanation and specification of the generic κοπιῶντας. The omission of the article plainly precludes any reference of the three participles to three different ministerial classes; the κοπιῶντες are simply regarded under two forms of their spiritual labor, as rulers and practical teachers, and as 'morum magistri,' Grot. Whether these duties were executed by the same or different persons cannot be determined; at this early period of the existence of the Church of Thess. the first supposition seems much the most probable; contrast Eph. iv. 11, 1 Tim. v. 17. The sphere of the προΐστασθαι was to be ἐν Κυρίῳ: οὐκ ἐν τοῖς κοσμικοῖς, ἀλλ' ἐν τοῖς κατὰ Κύριον, Theoph. νουθετοῦντας ὑμᾶς] *'admonishing you,'* 'qui commonent vos,' Vulg.; not simply ܡܠܦܝܢ [docentes] Syr., but ܡܪܬܝܢ admonentes] Syr.-Philox., with reference to the 'exhortationes et *correptiones*' (Est.), which it might be their duty to administer. On the proper meaning of νουθετεῖν, — primarily 'to correct by *word*' (νουθέτησις· λόγος ἐπιτιμητικὸς ἕνεκα ἀποτροπῆς ἁμαρτίας, Zonar. *Lex.* p. 1406), and then derivatively by *deed* (Judges viii. 10), — see Trench, *Synon.* § 32, and the numerous exx. collected by Kypke, *Obs.* Vol. II. p. 339.

13. καὶ ἡγεῖσθαι κ. τ. λ.] *'and to esteem them in love very highly.'* These words appear to admit of two translations according as ἐν ἀγάπῃ is connected (*a*) loosely with all the foregoing words, marking the element (certainly not the cause, Schott 2, 1) in which the ἡγεῖσθαι αὐτοὺς ὑπερεκπερισσῶς is to be put in force, — or (*b*) closely with the preceding ἡγεῖσθαι as specifying and enhancing the general duty implied in the preceding εἰδέναι, ver. 12. Both involve some lexical difficulties, as in (*a*) ἡγεῖσθαι must be regarded as equivalent to πλείονος ἀξιοῦν (Theod.), and in (*b*) ἡγεῖσθαι ἐν ἀγάπῃ must be taken as ἡγεῖσθαι αὐτοὺς ἀξίους τοῦ ἀγαπᾶσθαι (Chrys., Theoph., Œcum.), — solutions, neither of them very strictly defensible. On the whole, the context, the *appy.* similar ἡγεῖσθαί τι ἐν κρίσει, Job xxxv. 2 (Schott), and perhaps the analogous ἐν ὀργῇ ἔχειν τινά, Thucyd. II. 18 (Lünem.), seem to preponderate in favor of (*b*): in ver. 12 the Thess. are exhorted to respect their spiritual rulers, in the present verse also to love them. See Schott., Ols., Lünem, and Alf. The Vv. by preserving carefully the order do not give us any clew to the exact construction adopted. On the cumulative form ὑπερεκπερισσῶς (*Rec.* ὑπερεκπερισσοῦ, but on insufficient authority), comp. notes *on Eph.* iii. 20.

διὰ τὸ ἔργον αὐτῶν] *'for their work's sake;'* on account both of the importance of the work (Heb. xiii. 17) and the earnest and laborious manner in which it was performed; comp. Phil. i. 22, ii. 30. εἰρηνεύετε ἐν ἑαυτοῖς] *'Be at peace among yourselves;'* comp. Mark ix. 50, Rom. xii. 18, 2 Cor. xiii. 11. On this not uncommon use of the reflexive for the reciprocal pronoun (ἀλλήλοις), see Jelf., *Gr.* § 654. 2, Apollon. *de Synt.* II. 27, and for the general principle and limits of the permutation, Kühner on Xenoph. *Mem.* II. 6. 20. Of the converse use (recipr. for refl.) there appears no distinct trace; see Bernhardy, *Synt.* VI. 2. p. 273. The

διὰ τὸ ἔργον αὐτῶν. εἰρηνεύετε ἐν ἑαυτοῖς. 14 Παρακαλοῦμεν δὲ
ὑμᾶς, ἀδελφοί, νουθετεῖτε τοὺς ἀτάκτους, παραμυθεῖσθε τοὺς ὀλι-

reading *αὐτοῖς* [D[1]FG; many mss.; Aug., Vulg., Syr. (both), al.; Chrysost., Theod.], though distinguished by *Griesbach's* highest commendatory mark ('indicat lectionem supparem aut æqualem, immo forsitan præferendam receptæ lectioni'), certainly does not seem to deserve it, as it arose in all probability from the feeling that the short admonition was out of place between the longer *ἐρωτῶμεν δὲ κ. τ. λ.* (ver. 12) and *παρακαλ. δὲ κ. τ. λ.* (ver. 14). Under any circumstances it can scarcely bear the meaning 'pacem habete cum eis,' Vulg., Syr. (comp. Chrysos., Theod.), as this would so much more naturally have been expressed by *εἰρηνεύετε μετ' αὐτῶν*, as in Rom. xii. 18.

14. Παρακαλοῦμεν δὲ] '*Now we beseech you;*' address, neither *πρὸς τοὺς ἄρχοντας* (Chrys.) nor *πρὸς τοὺς διδασκάλους* (Theoph., Œcum.), but, as the *ἀδελφοὶ* suggests, to *all* (Pseud.-Amb., Justin.). The Christian brethren at Thessalonica were not only to be at peace with one another themselves, but also to do their best to cause it to be maintained by others. νουθετεῖτε τοὺς ἀτάκτους] '*admonish the unruly;*' those who do not preserve their *τάξιν*, 'inordinatos,' Beza, 'ungatassans,' Goth. The term *ἄτακτος*, somewhat laxly rendered by Syr. ܡܬܟܫܠܢܐ offendentes], is primarily and properly, as Chrys. suggests, a 'vox militaris' (Xenoph. *Mem.* III. 1. 7, where it is opp. to *τεταγμένος*), and thence derivatively a general epithet to denote a dissolute (Plato, *Legg.* VII. p. 806 C), ill ordered (*περίεργοι καὶ παρὰ τὸ προσῆκον ποιοῦντες*, Bekker, *Anecd.* p. 216), and unruly way of living: *τίνες δέ εἰσιν οἱ ἄτακτοι; πάντως οἱ παρὰ τὸ τῷ Θεῷ δοκοῦν πράττοντες. τάξεως γάρ ἐστι τῆς στρατιωτικῆς ἁρμοδιωτέρα αὕτη ἡ τάξις τῆς ἐκκλησίας*, Chrys. Here the precise reference is probably to the neglect of duties and calling into which the Thessalonians had lapsed owing to mistaken views of the time of the Lord's coming; compare chapter iv. 10, 11, 2 Thess. iii. 6, 11. On the meaning of *νουθετεῖν*, see above on ver. 12, and the exx. collected by Kypke, *Obs.* Vol. II. p. 340.

τοὺς ὀλιγοψύχους] '*the feeble-minded;*' perhaps mainly (as the *παραμυθ.* seems to suggest) in reference to those who were unduly anxious and sorrowful about the state of the *κοιμώμενοι*, ch. iv. 13; *ὀλιγοψύχους τοὺς ἐπὶ τοῖς τεθνεῶσιν ἀμέτρως ἀθυμοῦντας ὠνόμασεν*, Theod.,—who, however, not injudiciously also includes *τοὺς μὴ ἀνδρείως φέροντας τῶν ἐναντίων τὰς προσβολάς*; comp. Theophyl. *ὀλιγόψ. ὁ μὴ φέρων πειρασμόν.* The word *ὀλιγόψ.* is an *ἅπ. λεγόμ.* in the N. T., and appy. of rare occurrence elsewhere, except in the LXX (Isaiah lvii. 15, Prov. xviii. 14, al.; comp. Artemid. *Oneirocr.* III. 5); the more correct and usual term is *μικρόψυχος*, Aristot. *Ethic. Nicom.* IV. 7, Isocr *Panegyr.* p. 76 D.

ἀντέχεσθε τῶν ἀσθενῶν] '*support the weak;*' clearly not the weak in body (Luke x. 9, Acts iv. 9, v. 15, 1 Cor. xi. 30), but the weak in faith, *τοὺς μὴ ἑδραίαν κεκτημένους πίστιν*, Theod.; comp. 1 Cor. viii. 7, 10, so Chrys., Theoph., Œcum., and nearly all modern commentators. In Rom. v. 6, and appy, 1 Cor. ix. 22, the reference seems more inclusive, as marking those who were not Christians, who had not yet received the strength imparted by the Holy Spirit. The verb *ἀντέχεσθαι* (comp. Matth. vi. 24, Luke xvi. 13, and more generically Tit. i. 9) does not so much seem to imply 'observare,' Beng., as *ὑπερείδειν*, Theod., *ὑποστηρίζειν*, Theoph., *ἀντιλαμβάνεσθαι* (Bekker, *Anecd.* p. 408), or

γοψύχους, ἀντέχεσθε τῶν ἀσθενῶν, μακροθυμεῖτε πρὸς πάντας.
15 ὁρᾶτε μή τις κακὸν ἀντὶ κακοῦ τινὶ ἀποδῷ, ἀλλὰ πάντοτε τὸ

15. εἰς ἀλλήλους] So *Lachm.*, *Scholz*, *Tisch.* (ed. 1) with ADEFG; 15 mss.; Syr., Copt., Goth., Clarom., al. (*De W.*, *Koch.*, *Lünem.*, *Griesb.* om. om.). In his later editions *Tisch.* inserts καὶ before εἰς with BKL; great majority of mss.; Syr. (Philox.), Amit.; Chrys., Theod., al. *Rec.*, *Alf.*, *Wordsw.*); but not on satisfactory grounds, as the external authority seems to preponderate for the omission, and the internal arguments (opp. to *Alf.*) would certainly seem rather in favor of its being an interpolation for the sake of specifying, than of its being omitted as unnecessary.

perhaps more exactly 'sustinere,' Clarom. (comp. Goth., Æth.), with a more direct allusion to the primary and physical meaning of the word; comp. notes *on Tit. l. c.*, and see Suicer, *Thesaur.* s. v. Vol. I. p. 371. μακροθυμ. πρὸς πάντας] '*be long-suffering to all;*' not merely to the three classes just mentioned (Theophyl.), but to all, καὶ τοὺς οἰκείους καὶ τοὺς ἀλλοτρίους, Theod.; comp. ver. 15. On the term μακροθυμεῖν opp. to ὀξυθυμεῖν (Eurip. *Androm.* 689], which here serves to mark that gentle and forbearing patience which is so essentially a characteristic of ἀγάπη (1 Cor. xiii. 4), see esp. Basil, *Serm.* [Sym. metaphr.] XIII. Vol. III. p. 784 (ed. Bened. 1839), the good notice in Suicer, *Thesaur.* s. v. Vol. II. p. 293 sq., Röthe, *Theol. Ethik*, § 1056 sq., Vol. II. p. 518 sq., and comp. notes and reff. *on Eph.* iv. 2, 2 Tim. iii. 10. Lastly, πρὸς is not merely 'in regard to,' 'ad omnes,' Vulg., Clarom., 'cum omnibus,' Copt., but more precisely and definitely, *erga:* comp. the Goth. 'viþra,' and see notes *on Gal.* vi. 10.

15. ὁρᾶτε μή τις κ. τ. λ.] '*See that no man render evil, etc.;*' warning against revenge,—yet surely not in the sense that the better among them were to check its outbreaks in others (De W.), but simply that all were to abstain from it; see Lünem. *in loc.* The usual and correct statement that Christianity was the first definitely to forbid the returning evil for evil (see Fritz. *Rom.* xii. 17, Vol. III. p. 91) is called in question by Jowett on the ground that 'Plato knew that it was not the true definition of justice to do harm to one's enemies.' Not to multiply quotations, can this be sustained against *de Legg.* IX. p. 868 B, p. 882, al., where vengeance rather than punishment seems certainly contemplated by the legislator? Individual instances of the recognition of this precept may be found in heathenism (see Pfanner, *Theol. Gen. til.* ch. XI. § 23, comp. Basil, *de Legend. Gent. Libr.* § 5, Vol. II. p. 251, ed. Bened.), but as a general statement the remark of Hermann seems perfectly correct; 'nec laudant Græci si quis iniquis æquus est, sed virtutem esse censent, æquis æquum, iniquum autem iniquis esse,' on Soph. *Philoct.* 679. The formula ὁρᾶν μὴ (Matth. xviii. 10, Mark i. 44) is of less frequent occurrence than βλέπειν μὴ (Mark xiii. 5, Acts xiii. 40, 1 Cor. x. 12, al.), but is more classically usual and correct: for exx. of it in combination with the pres. and aor. subj., see, if necessary, the collection in Gayler, *Partik. Neg.* p. 316 sq. ἀποδῷ] '*render,*' 'usgildai,' Goth. The primary idea conveyed by ἀποδιδόναι, scil. 'ubi quid de aliquâ copiâ das,' and thence 'ubi dando te exsolvis debito' (Winer), here naturally passes into that of 'retribuere,' the κακὸν being represented as something stored up, out of which and with which payment would be made; see Winer, *de Verb. Comp.* IV. p. 12, 13, where this verb is well discussed.

ἀγαθὸν διώκετε εἰς ἀλλήλους καὶ εἰς πάντας. 16 πάντοτε χαί-
ρετε, 17 ἀδιαλείπτως προσεύχεσθε, 18 ἐν παντὶ εὐχαριστεῖτε·

τὸ ἀγαθὸν διώκετε] '*follow after that which is good;*' not here what is 'morally good,' (Lünem.), but, as the antithesis seems rather to require, what is 'beneficial,' what proves good to him who receives it: οὐκ ἀρκεῖ τὸ μὴ ἀποδοῦναι κακὰ ἀντὶ κακῶν, ἀλλὰ χρὴ, φησί, καὶ ἀγαθοῖς ἀμείβεσθαι τὸν κακοποιήσαντα, Theoph., comp. Chrys. Some shade of the same meaning is perhaps apparent in Gal. vi. 10, Eph. iv. 28 (see notes): here, however, it seems more decidedly brought out by the preceding κακόν. On the use of διώκειν (ἐπιτεταμένως σπουδάζειν τι, Theoph.) with abstract substantives or their equivalents, see notes and reff. *on* 2 *Tim.* ii. 22, and for exx. of the same use in classical Greek, see Ast, *Lex. Platon.* s. v. Vol. I. p. 548 sq. The correlative term is καταλαμβάνειν, Phil. iii. 12, and the antithesis φεύγειν, Plato, *Gorg.* p. 507 B.

16. πάντοτε χαίρετε] '*Rejoice alway;*' Phil. iii. 1, iv. 4, comp. 2 Cor. vi. 10; not merely κἂν πειρασμοῖς περιπέσητε (Theoph.),—a limitation not inappropriate in ref. to the recent troubles at Thessalonica, but, at all times,—under all circumstances, and in all dispensations. To the enquiry, 'Why should this be a duty?' (comp. Jowett), it seems sufficient to say with Barrow, in his good sermon on this text,—'if we scan all the doctrines, all the institutions, all the precepts, all the promises of Christianity, will not each appear pregnant with matter of joy, will not each yield great reason and strong obligation to this duty of rejoicing evermore?' *Serm.* XLIII. Vol. II. p. 557; see also sound and comprehensive sermons by Beveridge, *Serm.* CV. Vol. V. p. 62 sq. (A.-C. Libr.), and Donne, *Serm.* CXXX. Vol. V. p. 344 sq. (ed: Alf.). The true originating clause (1 Thess. i. 6) and true sphere (Rom. xiv. 17) of this joy is the Holy Spirit, and its more immediate source, Faith; see notes *on Phil.* i. 25.

17. ἀδιαλείπτως προσεύχ.] '*pray without ceasing;*' a precept naturally following on, and suggested by, the foregoing words; τὴν ὁδὸν ἔδειξε τοῦ ἀεὶ χαίρειν, τὴν ἀδιάλειπτον προσευχὴν καὶ εὐχαριστίαν· ὁ γὰρ ἐθισθεὶς ὁμιλεῖν τῷ Θεῷ καὶ εὐχαριστεῖν αὐτῷ ἐπὶ πᾶσιν ὡς συμφερόντως συμβαίνουσι, πρόδηλον ὅτι χαρὰν ἕξει διηνεκῆ, Theoph. This exhortation to unceasing prayer is distinctly urged by the apostle in other passages (comp. Eph. vi. 18, Col. iv. 2), and is certainly neither to be explained away as 'a precept capable of fulfilment in idea rather than in fact' (Jowett), nor yet, with Bp. Andrewes, to be referred to appointed hours of prayer (*Serm.* VI. Vol. V. p. 354, A.-C. Libr.), but is to be accepted in the simple and plain meaning of the words, and obeyed, as Barrow has well shown, by cherishing a spirit of prayer, and by making devotion the real and true business of a life: see Wordsw. *in loc.*, who appositely cites Barrow, *Serm.* Vol. I. p. 107 sq. Surely the τὸ ὁμιλεῖν τῷ Θεῷ (Theoph.) is one of those things which is real and actual; οὐδὲ τοῦτο τῶν ἀδυνάτων, ῥᾴδιον γὰρ καὶ τῷ ἐσθίοντι τὸν Θεὸν ἀνυμνεῖν, καὶ τῷ βαδίζοντι τὴν τοῦ Θεοῦ συμμαχίαν αἰτεῖν, Theod.; compare Hofmann, *Schriftb.* Vol. II. 2, p. 335. On the duty of constant prayer, see the sound remarks of Hammond, *Pract Catechism*, III. 2, p. 224 (not perfectly decided on this text), and on the power of it compare the noble epilogue of Tertullian, *de Orat.* cap. 29.

18. ἐν παντὶ εὐχαριστεῖτε] '*In everything give thanks;*' not ἐν παντί, scil. καιρῷ, Flatt (comp. Chrys. ἀεί), still less 'in iis quæ vobis bona sunt,' Est., but ἐν παντί, scil. χρήματι, Chrys. *on Phil.*

τοῦτο γὰρ θέλημα Θεοῦ ἐν Χριστῷ Ἰησοῦ εἰς ὑμᾶς. 19 τὸ Πνεῦμα

iv. 6, ܒܟܠ ܡܕܡ Syr., 'in omnibus,' Vulg., Copt.; comp. 2 Cor. ix. 8, ἐν παντὶ πάντοτε, which seems to fix the interpretation, and contrast ἐν μηδενί, Phil. i. 28. On the duty of εὐχαριστία, so often dwelt upon by St. Paul (comp. notes *on Col.* iii. 15), see Beveridge, *Serm.* CVII. Vol. V. p. 76 sq., and on this and on the preceding verses the homily of Basil, *de Grat. Act.* Vol. II. p. 34 (ed. Bened. 1839). τοῦτο γάρ] '*for this,*' scil. τὸ ἐν παντὶ εὐχαρ. (Theoph., Œcum.); not with reference to this and ver. 17 (Grot.), nor to this and the two preceding verses (Alf.), for though the three precepts χαίρετε, προσεύχεσθε, εὐχαριστεῖτε — especially the two latter — are sufficiently homogeneous in character to be included in the singular τοῦτο, yet the peculiar stress, which the apostle always seems to lay on εὐχαρ. (see above), renders the single reference to εὐχαριστία apparently more probable; 'gratiæ sunt in omni re agendæ, quia scimus omnia nobis cooperare ad bonum, Rom. viii. 28,' Cocceius; see Hofmann. *Schriftb.* Vol. II. 2, p. 335. So also Olsh., Bisping, and Lünem., and appy. the majority of recent expositors. After γάρ, *Lachm.* adds ἐστιν with D¹E¹FG; several Vv.; and Lat. Ff., but on insufficient external, and appy. opposing internal evidence. The possible doubt caused by the juxtaposition of τοῦτο and θέλημα would naturally suggest the interpolation of the verb subst.
ἐν Χρ. Ἰησ. εἰς ὑμᾶς] '*in Christ Jesus toward you:*' Christ is here represented not exactly as the medium by which (Theoph. Œcum.), but as the sphere *in which* the θέλημα is evinced and has its manifestation; ἐν ᾧ καὶ τὰ δόξαντα ποιεῖ καὶ ἀναγεννᾷ, Athan. *contr. Arian.* III. 61. Vol. I. p. 610 (ed. Bened. 1698). The objects *towards* whom ('ad vos,' Clarom.) — not 'in whom' (Vulg., Copt.), nor 'in reference to whom' (De W.) — it was so evinced, and to whom it was designed to apply, were the converts of Thessalonica. The reference of θέλημα to the 'decretum divinum de salute generis humani per Christum reparandâ' (see Schott) is grammatically doubtful on account of the omission of the article, and by no means exegetically plausible. The θέλημα seems here suitably anarthrous, as marking εὐχαρ. as one part and portion out of many contemplated in the collective θέλημα τοῦ Θεοῦ; see Lünem. *in loc.*

19. τὸ Πνεῦμα] '*the (Holy) Spirit;*' not merely 'vim divinam Christianis propriam' (Noesselt; comp. Beck, *Seelenl.* p. 37), nor even the gifts of the Spirit as evinced in prophecy (Theod.), nor, more generally, τὴν ἐν αὐτοῖς ἀναφθεῖσαν τοῦ Πνεύματος χάριν (Athan. *ad Serap.* I. 4; see Chrys.), but simply the Holy Spirit, which dwells within in association, with our spirit, and evinces His presence by varied spiritual gifts and manifestations; comp. 1 Cor. xii. 8 sq., and see Waterl. *Serm.* XXI. Vol. V. p. 641. The subject of prayer leads naturally to the mention of the Holy Inspirer of it (comp. Rom. viii. 26, Gal. iv. 6), and thence to the specification of other gifts (προφητείας) which emanate from the same blessed Source. μὴ σβέννυτε] '*Quench not,*' whether in yourselves or in others; contrast 2 Tim. i. 6. The Eternal Spirit is represented as a fire (comp. Andrewes, *Serm.* Vol. III. p. 124, A.-C. Libr.) which it was regarded possible to extinguish, — not, however, in the present case by a βίος ἀκάθαρτος (Chrys.), but, in accordance with the context, — by a studied repression and disregard of its manifestation, arising from erroneous perceptions and a mistaken dread of enthusiasm; compare Neander, *Planting,* Vol. I. p. 202 (Bohn). This is more

μὴ σβέννυτε, 20 προφητείας μὴ ἐξουθενεῖτε· 21 πάντα δὲ δοκι-

21. πάντα δέ] So *Lachm.* and *Tisch.* (ed. I. 7) with BDEFGKL; more than 50 mss.; Vulg., Clarom., Goth., Syr. (Philox.); Clem. (2), Basil, Chrys. (text), al. (*Scholz, Lünem., Alf*). In his second edition *Tisch.* struck out the δὲ with A; appy. many mss.; Syr., Copt., al.; Chrys. (aliquoties), Theod., Œcum., al. (*Rec., De Wette*), — but has now rightly returned to his first ed. On the one hand there is only the internal argument that δὲ was interpolated to help out the connection, on the other hand there is the strong external support, the 'paradiplomatic' argument (comp. Pref. to *Gal.* p. xvii, Scrivener, *Introd.* to *Criticism of N. T.* p. 376) of the ΔΕ having fallen out before the ΔΟ, and lastly, the plausible internal argument that δὲ was omitted to make this sentence equally unconnected with what precede and follow.

distinctly specified in what follows. For several illustrations of the expression, see exx. in Wetst., the most pertinent of which is Galen, *de Theriac.* I. 17, τὸ φάρμακον..... .τὸ ἔμφυτον πνεῦμα ῥαδίως σβέννυσιν. Plutarch, *de Defect. Orac.* § 17, p. 419 B, ἀποσβῆναι τὸ πνεῦμα.

20. προφητείας] '*prophecies;*' not merely announcements of what was to come to pass, but, in accordance with the more extended meaning of προφήτης in the N. T. (see notes *on Eph.* iv. 11), varied declarations of the divine counsels, and expositions of God's oracles, immediately inspired by, and emanating from the Holy Spirit; see Meyer *on* 1 *Cor.* xii. 10, and Fritz *on Rom.* xii. 6. The difference, then, between ordinary διδαχὴ and προφητεία consisted in this, that the latter was due to the immediate influence of the Spirit, the former to an ἐξ οἰκείας διαλέγεσθαι, Chrys.; see Neander, *Planting*, Vol. I. p. 133 (Bohn), and for a comparison between prophecy and speaking with tongues, Thorndike, *Relig. Assemblies*, ch. v. Vol. I. p. 182 sq. (A.-C. Libr.). ἐξουθενεῖτε] '*despise,*' '*set at nought;*' a word used in the N. T. both by St. Paul (Rom. xiv. 3, 10, 1 Cor. i. 28, al.) and St. Luke (xviii. 9, xxiii. 11, Acts iv, 11), and found also in the LXX and later writers. On this, the more orthographically correct but apparently less usual ἐξουδενεῖν (Mark ix. 12, *Lachm., Tisch.*), and ἐξουδενοῦν (LXX, al.: Hesych. ἀποδοκιμάζειν), comp. Lobeck, *Phrynichus*, p. 182. The habit of despising prophecies, here expressly forbidden, most probably arose from instances of πλανῶντες and πλανώμενοι in the Church of Thessalonica, who had brought discredit on this spiritual gift. The deduction of Olsh., that up to the present time St. Paul had no apprehensions of any of the fanaticism which afterwards showed itself among the Thess. (Ep. 2), seems in every way questionable; contrast Neand., *Planting*, Vol. I. p. 203 sq. (Bohn). They were even now in a state of unrest and disquietude (ch. iv. 11 sq.); nay, the very exhortation before us gains all its point from the fact that the more sober thinkers had been probably led by the present state of things to undervalue and unduly reject all the less usual manifestations of the Spirit.

21. πάντα δὲ δοκιμ.] '*but prove all things;*' antithetical exhortation to the foregoing: 'instead of despising and seeking to repress spiritual gifts, let them be manifested, *but* be careful to prove them.' Πάντα must thus have a restricted sense, and be limited to the χαρίσματα previously alluded to; πάντα φησί, δοκιμάζετε, τουτέστι τὰς ὄντως προφητείας, Chrys. A more precise exhortation is given to the Corinthians (1 Cor. xiv. 29),

μάζετε, τὸ καλὸν κατέχετε· 22 ἀπὸ παντὸς εἴδους πονηροῦ ἀπέ-

from which, observing the similar and peculiar subject (προφητεία) here in question, we must conclude that the *present* precept to exercise spiritual discernment applied not so much to the Church at large (Neander, *Planting*, Vol. I. p. 138, Bohn) as more restrictedly to those who had the special gift of διακρίσεις πνευμάτων, 1 Cor. xii. 10. In 1 John iv. 1 (see Waterl. *Serm.* XXVII.) the exhortation is appy. more general, but the points to be tried are more elementary, and more easy to be decided on. On the meaning of the verb δοκιμάζειν, see notes *on Phil.* i. 10, and for an ingenious but improbable explanation of both the word [testing as a coin] and the following verse, Hänsel, *Stud. u. Krit.* 1836, p. 170 sq. τὸ καλὸν κατέχ.] '*hold fast that which is good;*' precept naturally and immediately following on the foregoing: 'exercise the gift of διάκρισις, and having found what is really good, hold to it; τὰ ψευδῆ καὶ τὰ ἀληθῆ μετὰ δοκιμασίας κρίνετε, καὶ τότε τὸ δόξαν ὑμῖν καλόν, τουτέστι τὰς ἀληθεῖς προφητείας κατέχετε, τουτέστι τιμᾶτε, διὰ φροντίδος ποιεῖσθε, Theoph. On the primary meaning and derivation of καλός [καδλός], see Donalds. *Cratyl.* § 334; but observe that in the N. T. it seems equally co-extensive in meaning with ἀγαθός, and frequently, as here, denotes what is simply and morally good; see notes *on Gal.* vi. 9, and comp. Aristot. *Rhetor.* I. 9 (init.), καλὸν μὲν οὖν ἐστίν, ὃ ἂν δι' αὑτὸ αἱρετὸν ὂν ἐπαινετὸν ᾖ. On this whole verse, see an excellent practical sermon by Waterland, *Serm.* XXIII. Vol. V. p. 655 sq.

22. ἀπὸ παντὸς εἴδους κ. τ. λ.] '*abstain from every form of evil;*' general exhortation appended to and suggested by, but not closely connected (De W.) with, what precedes; comp. Neander, *Planting*, Vol. I. p. 204, note (Bohn). In this verse there is some little difficulty depending, first, on the meaning of εἴδους, and secondly, on the construction of πονηροῦ. We will notice these separately. Εἶδος cannot here be 'appearance,' Auth.-Ver., Calv., as this meaning is more than lexically doubtful (compare Luke iii. 22, ix. 29, John v. 37, 2 Cor. v. 7), and even if it could be substantiated, would here be inappropriate, as the antithesis seems plainly not between τὸ καλὸν and any *semblance* of evil, 'quod malum etiamsi non sit, apparet' (Calv.), but what is actually and distinctly such; comp. Wordsw. *in loc.* We therefore adopt the more technical meaning 'species,' 'sort' (Plato, *Epin.* p. 990 E, εἶδος καὶ γένος, *Parmen.* p. 129 C, γένη τε καὶ εἴδη), which is supported by abundant lexical authority (see Rost u. Palm, *Lex.* s. v. and the numerous exx. in Wetstein *in loc.*) and is exegetically clear and forcible; they were to hold fast τὸ καλὸν, and avoid every sort and species (μὴ τούτου ἢ ἐκείνου, ἀλλ' ἁπλῶς παντός, Theoph.) of the contrary. So probably Vulgate, Clarom., 'specie,' and more plainly, Syr. ܨܒܘ [negotio], Copt. *hōb* [re], Æth. *megbār* [agendi ratione], Goth., al., *appy.* the Greek Ff., and nearly all modern commentators. It is more difficult to decide whether πονηροῦ is an adjective or substantive. Most of the ancient Vv. (Syr., Vulg., Copt., Æth.) adopt the former, and so possibly the Greek commentators; the latter, however, preserves more correctly the antithesis, and less infringes (comp. Syr., Copt., al.) on the technical meaning of εἶδος. So De Wette, Lünem., Koch, Alf., and the majority of modern commentators. The absence of the article (Bengel, Middl. *Gr. Art.* p. 378) does not contribute to the decision; as abstract adjectives can certainly be thus constructed, when it is not necessary to mark the wholeness or entirety of what

χεσθε. 23 Αὐτὸς δὲ ὁ Θεὸς τῆς εἰρήνης ἁγιάσαι ὑμᾶς ὁλοτελεῖς, καὶ ὁλόκληρον ὑμῶν τὸ πνεῦμα καὶ ἡ ψυχὴ καὶ τὸ σῶμα ἀμέμπτως

is specified; comp. Heb. v. 14, Plato, *Republ.* II. p. 358 C, *τρίτον εἶδος ἀγαθοῦ*, and see Jelf., *Gr.* § 451. 1. The artificial interpretation of Hänsel (*Stud. u. Krit.* 1836, p. 180 sq.), *εἶδ. πον.* = *κίβδηλον νόμισμα*, founded on the association of this text in several patristic citations with our Lord's traditional saying, *γίνεσθε δόκιμοι τραπεζῖται* (see Suicer, *Thesaur.* Vol. II. p. 1281 sq.), is here adopted by Baumg.-Crus., but rightly rejected by most subsequent expositors. Even if we admit the very doubtful assumption that the simple *εἶδος might* gain from the context the more definite meaning *εἶδος νομίσματος*, the use of *ἀπέχεσθε* in such a form of expression would still be, as De W. observes, appy. unprecedented.

23. **Αὐτὸς δέ**] '*But may He;*' *He* on whom all depends, — in contrast to them and the efforts they might be enabled to make; comp. ch. iii. 12, where, however, the emphasis is somewhat different, and the contrast less definitely marked. **ὁ Θεὸς τῆς εἰρήνης**] '*the God of peace;*' the God of whom peace is a characterizing attribute; the gen. falling under the general category of the gen. of *content* (Scheuerl. *Synt.* § 16. 3, p. 115, comp. notes *on Phil.* iv. 9), and the subst. *εἰρήνη* marking the deep inward peace and tranquillity, which is God's especial gift, and which stands in closest alliance with that holiness which the preceding clauses inculcate. On this meaning of *εἰρήνη*, see notes *on Phil.* iv. 7, and on the various meanings which it may assume in this and similar collocations, see Reuss, *Théol. Chrét.* IV. 18, Vol. II. p. 201. **ὁλοτελεῖς**] '*wholly;*' 'per omnia,' Vulg., — in your collective powers and parts; *ὁλοτ.* marking more emphatically than *ὅλους* that thoroughness and pervasive nature of holiness *ὅλους δι' ὅλων*, Œcum., 'secundum omnes partes,' Cocceius) which the following words specify with further exactness; so distinctly Theoph., *ὁλοτ. δὲ τί ἐστί; τοῦτ' ἔστι, σώματι καὶ ψυχῇ, καὶ ἐφεξῆς δὲ μαθήσῃ.* This seems preferable to the qualitative interpretation, 'ad perfectum,' Clarom., Æth. (Sy. unites both), according to which *ὁλοτελεῖς* would be used proleptically (Syr.-Philox.; comp. notes on ch. iii. 13), but in which the connection between the substance of the first and second portions of the prayer is less close and self-explanatory. The form *ὁλοτελής* is an *ἅπ. λεγόμ.* in the N. T., but occurs occasionally in later Greek; comp. Plutarch, *de Placitis Philos.* § 21, p. 909 B. **καί**] '*and,*' — to specify more exactly; the copula appending to the general prayer one of more *special* details; see Winer, *Gr.* § 53. 3, p. 388, and comp. notes *on Phil.* iv. 12. **ὁλόκληρον κ. τ. λ.**] '*may your spirit, etc., be preserved entire;*' 'not your whole spirit etc.,' Author., Wordsw., compare Syriac; *ὁλόκλ.*, as its position shows, not being an epithet but a secondary predicate; see Donalds. *Cratyl.* § 302, and comp. notes *on Col.* ii. 3. This distinction seems clearly maintained by all the ancient Vv. (except appy. Syr.); some, as Vulg., al., preserving the order of the Greek, others, as Æth., rendering *ὁλόκλ.* by an adverb placed at the end of the clause. The adj. *ὁλόκληρος* is a *δὶς λεγόμ.* in the N. T. (here and James i. 4), and serves to mark that which is 'entire in all its parts, *ἐν οὐδενὶ λειπόμενον* (James *l. c.*), differing from *τέλειος* as rather defining what is *complete*, while the latter marks what has reached its proper end and maturity. In a word, the aspect of the former word is (here especially) mainly *quantitative*, of the latter, mainly *qualitative;* compare

ἐν τῇ παρουσίᾳ τοῦ Κυρίου ἡμῶν Ἰησοῦ Χριστοῦ τηρηθείη.
24 πιστὸς ὁ καλῶν ὑμᾶς, ὃς καὶ ποιήσει.

Trench, *Synon.* § 22, and for exx. see the large collection of Wetst. *in loc.*, one of the most pertinent of which is Lucian, *Macrob.* § 2, εἰς γῆρας ἀφίκεσθαι ἐν ὑγιαινούσῃ τῇ ψυχῇ, καὶ ὁλοκλήρῳ τῷ σώματι; see also Elsner, *Obs.* Vol. II. p. 278. The predicate clearly belongs to all the three substantives, though structurally connected with the first. ὑμῶν τὸ πνεῦμα κ. τ. λ.] '*your body, soul, and spirit;*' distinct enunciation of three component parts of the nature of man: the πνεῦμα, the higher of the two united immaterial parts, being the 'vis superior, agens, imperans in homine' (Olsh.); the ψυχή, 'vis inferior quæ agitur' movetur, (ib.), the sphere of the will and the affections, and the true centre of the personality; see Olshausen, *Opusc.* p. 154, Beck, *Seelenl.* II. 12, 13, p. 30 sq., Schubert, *Gesch. der Seele,* § 48, Vol. II. 495 sq., comp. Vitringa, *Obs. Sacr.* p. 549 sq., and more especially *Destiny of the Creature,* p. 99 – 120, where this text is considered at length, and the scriptural distinction between the πνεῦμα and ψυχὴ discussed and substantiated. It may be remarked that we frequently find instances of an apparent *dichotomy,* 'body and soul' (Matth. vi. 25, x. 28, al.) or 'body and spirit' (1 Cor. v. 3, vii. 34, al.), but such passages will only be found accommodations to the popular division into a material aud immaterial part; the ψυχή, in the former of the exceptional cases, including also the πνεῦμα, just as in the latter case the πνεῦμα also comprehends the ψυχή; see Olsh. *l. c.*, p. 153 note, and contrast the ineffectual denial of Loesner, *Obs.* p. 381. To assert that enumerations like the present are rhetorical (De W.), or worse, that the apostle probably attached 'no distinct thought to each of these words' (Jowett), is plainly to set aside all sound rules of scriptural exegesis. Again, to admit the distinctions, but to refer them to Platonism (Lünem.), is equally unsatisfactory and equally calculated to throw doubt on the truth of the teaching. If St. Paul's words do here imply the trichotomy above described (comp. Usteri, *Lehrb.* p. 384 sq.), then such a trichotomy is infallibly real and true. And if Plato or Philo have maintained (as appears demonstrable) substantially the same views, then God has permitted a heathen and a Jewish philosopher to advance conjectural opinions which have been since confirmed by the independent teaching of an inspired apostle.

ἀμέμπτως] '*blamelessly;*' the adverbial predication of quality appended to τηρηθείη, ὁλόκληρον (see above) involving that of quantity. On the meaning of ἄμεμπτος, 'is in quo nihil desiderari potest,' and its distinction from ἄμωμος, see notes *on Phil.* ii. 15, iii. 6, and Tittm. *Synon.* I. p. 29. ἐν τῇ παρουσίᾳ κ. τ. λ.] Time, — the coming of Christ to judgment, — when the preservation of the ὁλοκληρία is especially to be evinced and found to be realized: comp. notes on ch. ii. 19. On the more exact way in which this ὁλοκληρία may be ascribed to body, soul, and spirit, see *Destiny of Creature,* p. 117.

24. πιστὸς ὁ καλῶν] '*Faithful is He who calleth you,*' 'qui vocat,' Clarom., scil. God the Father; comp. 1 Cor. i. 9, and see notes *on Gal.* i. 6. The tense is neither to be pressed as implying an enduring act (Baumb.-Crus., Bisp.), nor to be regarded as identical with the aor. 'qui vocavit,' Vulg., Goth., but simply to be considered as timeless, and as equivalent to a substantive, 'your Caller;' see notes *on Gal.* v. 8, and Winer, *Gr.* § 45. 7, p. 316. Πιστὸς in ref. to God here implies a faithfulness and true-

Pray for us. Salute the brethren, and cause this Epistle to be read before the Church.

25 Ἀδελφοί, προσεύχεσθε περὶ ἡμῶν.
26 ἀσπάσασθε τοὺς ἀδελφοὺς πάντας ἐν φιλή-
ματι ἁγίῳ. 27 ἐνορκίζω ὑμᾶς τὸν Κύριον, ἀναγνωσθῆναι τὴν

ness to His nature and promises (1 Cor. x. 13, 2 Tim. ii. 13, and hence becomes practically synonymous with ἀληθής, Chrys., Theod.; ἐν γὰρ τῷ ποιεῖν ἃ ἐπαγγέλλεται πιστός ἐστι λαλῶν, Athanas. *contr. Arian.* II. 10, Vol. I. p. 478 (ed. Bened.), see Reuss, *Théol. Chrét.* IV. 13, Vol. II. p. 124. ὃς καὶ ποιήσει] '*who also will do it,*' not exactly 'what I wish' (De W.), nor ἐφ. ᾧ ἐκάλεσεν sc. σώσει (Œcum., Theophyl.), but simply 'that same thing' (Arm.), scil. τὸ ἀμέμπτως ὑμᾶς τηρηθῆναι (Bisp., Lünem.), or, as the identity of subject suggests, τὸ ἁγιάσαι κ. τ. λ. and τὸ τηρηθῆναι κ. τ. λ.,—in a word, the substance of the prayer expressed in the preceding verse. In such cases there is no ellipse of any pronoun; ποιεῖν is merely 'nude positum,' receiving its more exact explanation from the context; comp. Koch *in loc.*, and Schömann on Isæus, *de Apol. Hær.* § 35, p. 372.

25. προσεύχεσθε περὶ ἡμῶν] '*pray for us;*' comp. Eph. vi. 19, Col. iv. 3, 2 Thess. iii. 1. De Wette and Alf. remark that περὶ is here less definite than ὑπέρ; but it is very doubtful whether in this and similar formulæ in the N. T. the difference is really appreciable; see notes *on Eph.* vi. 19, Fritz. *Rom.* Vol. I p. 26, and for the general distinction between the prepositions, notes *on Gal.* i. 4, and *on Phil.* i. 7. The prayer was doubtless intended to include reference both to his own personal state and to the general success of his apostolic work; comp. Cocceius *in loc.* Whether Sylvanus and Timothy are included is perhaps here doubtful; in Eph. *l. c.* where the apostle writes only in his own person, the plural is equally used. *Lachm.*, inserts in brackets καὶ before περὶ ὑμῶν, but on authority [BD[1]; a few mss.; Clarom., Sangerm., Syr. (Philox.), Goth.] scarcely sufficient to warrant even this mode of insertion.

26. ἀσπάσασθε κ. τ. λ.] '*Salute all the brethren;*' concluding exhortation, apparently addressed to the elders of the Church (consider ver. 27). In the parallel passages, Rom. xvi. 16, 1 Cor. xvi. 20, and 2 Cor. xiii. 12 (ἐν ἁγίῳ φιλ., but opp. to AFGL; see Fritz. *on Rom. l. c.*), comp. 1 Pet. v. 14, the exhortation is ἀσπάσασθε ἀλλήλους: ἐπειδὴ φιλήματι αὐτοὺς ἀσπάσασθαι οὐκ ἠδύνατο, ἀπὼν δι' ἑτέρων αὐτοὺς ἀσπάζεται, Chrysost. The Oriental custom of kissing in their greetings (Winer, *RWB* s. v. 'Kuss,' Vol. I. p. 688) is here enhanced with Christian characteristics: it is to be a φίλημα ἅγιον, a φίλημα ἀγάπης, 1 Pet. v. 14, an 'osculum pacis,' Tertull. *de Orat.* cap. 14, a φίλημα μυστικόν, Clem. Alex. *Pædag.* III. 11, Vol. I. p. 301 (ed. Potter),—whether as given after prayer (Just. M. *Apol.* I. 65; comp. *Const. Apost.* II. 57, τὸ ἐν Κυρίῳ φίλημα), or more probably as a token of brotherly love and holy affection,—no idle, meaningless, and merely pagan custom of salutation. On this custom, see more in Bingham, *Antiq.* III. 3. 3, Augusti, *Archäol.* Vol. II. p. 718 sq., Coteler on *Const. Apost. l. c.* and Fritz. *Rom.* xvi. 16. The prep. ἐν may here possibly mark the accompaniment (see *on Col.* iv. 2), but is more naturally taken as simply instrumental; the φίλημα being that in which, so to say, the ἀσπασμὸς was involved; see notes on ch. iv. 18.

27. ἐνορκίζω ὑμᾶς κ. τ. λ.] '*I adjure you by the Lord.*' This very strong form of entreaty has been differently explained. There does not seem sufficient

ἐπιστολὴν πᾶσιν τοῖς ἁγίοις ἀδελφοῖς. **Benediction.** 28 Ἡ χάρις
τοῦ Κυρίου ἡμῶν Ἰησοῦ Χριστοῦ μεθ' ὑμῶν.

27. ἁγίοις ἀδελφοῖς] The reading is very doubtful. *Rec.* and *Scholz* insert ἁγίοις with AKL; mss.; Syr. (both), Vulg., Copt., Goth., Æth. (Platt), Arm.; Chrys., Theod. (*De Wette, Koch*). It is omitted by *Lachm.* and *Tisch.* (ed. 1, 2) with BDEFG; mss.; Clarom., Æth. (Pol.); Ambrst., Damasc. (*Lünem.*, *Alf.*), but rightly restored by *Tisch.* in his last edition. Though the uncial authorities preponderate for the omission, still the strong testimony of the Vv., and the probability that a word, here used somewhat uniquely by St. Paul in adjectival connection with ἀδελφοῖς, should be omitted as superfluous, decide us in favor of the text; comp. Heb. iii. 1. The epithet is certainly not without pertinence in reference to the adjuration and strength of language which marks the verses: all the brethren, viewed generally as Christians, were holy (comp. Numb. xvi. 3), and would especially profit by having this letter read to them.

reason for concluding from ver. 12, 13, with Olsh., that there had been such differences between the elders and the Church of Thess. as to suggest a fear that the Epistle might not be communicated to the Church at large; as the language of those verses is admirably calculated both to bespeak respect to the elders, and to conciliate the Church. That the expression arose from slight distrust combined with a θερμὴ διάνοια towards his converts (Chrys., Theoph.) is improbable; that it was a customary form with St. Paul (Jowett 1), indemonstrable; that the inspired apostle was not master of his words, or did not know their value (Jowett 2), monstrous. We therefore may perhaps fall back on the reason hinted by Theodoret and expanded by recent expositors,—that a deep sense of the great spiritual importance of this Epistle, not merely to those who were anxious about the κεκοιμημένοι (ch. iv. 13) but to *all without exception*, suggested the unusual adjuration; ὅρκον προστέθεικε, πᾶσι τὴν ἐκ τῆς καταγνώσεως ὠφέλειαν πραγματεύων, Theod. The objections of Baur are briefly but satisfactorily answered by Neander, *Planting*, Vol. II. p. 126 (Bohn). The verb ἐνορκ. [*Rec.* has the more usual ὁρκίζω with D²D³FGKL; mss.] is appy. not found elsewhere, and is even wholly omitted in the best modern lexicons.

τὸν Κύριον] Accus. of the person; comp. Mark v. 7, Acts xix. 13, and for the similar construction of ὁρκόω, see Jelf, *Gr.* § 583. 123. On the two forms ὁρκοῦν and ὁρκίζειν, and the prevalence of the former in Attic writers, see Lobeck, *Phryn.* p. 360, 361.

ἀναγνωσθῆναι] '*be read*—as the context suggests—*publicly*;' compare Luke iv. 16, Acts xv. 21, 2 Cor. iii. 15, Col. iv. 16. This meaning ('palam prælegatur,' Schott) is, however, not specially due to the prep. ἀνά, as ἀναγν. is abundantly used without any accessory notion of publicity, but is reflected on the verb by the general tenor of the sentence. The aor. infin. perhaps refers to the single act (Alf.), but must certainly not be pressed, as this tense in the infinitive, especially after verbs of 'hoping,' 'commanding,' etc. (see on ch. iv. 10), is often used in reference not merely to single acts, but to what is either timeless ('ab omni temporis definiti conditione libera et immunis' Stallbaum on Plato, *Euthyd.* p. 140), or simply *eventual*, and dependent on the action expressed by the finite verb; see Scheuerl. *Synt.* § 31. 2. b, p. 320 sq., Winer, *Gr.* § 44. 7. b, p. 296 and esp. Schmalfeld, *Syntax*, §

173. 4, p. 346,—where the different moods of the infin. are carefully considered and contrasted.

28. Ἡ χάρις κ. τ. λ.] The concluding benedictions of St. Paul's Epp. are somewhat noticeably varied. Adopting the best attested readings, we may observe that the shortest form is ἡ χάρις μεθ' ὑμῶν, Col. iv. 18, 2 Tim. iv. 22 (preceded by ὁ Κύριος 'I. X. μετὰ τοῦ πνεύμ. σου), Tit. iii. 25 (μετὰ πάντων ὑμῶν), ἡ χάρ. μετὰ σοῦ 1 Tim. vi. 21; the longest, the familiar benediction 2 Cor. xiii. 13. Of the rest we have *first*, Rom. xvi. 20, 2 Thess. iii. 18, and Rom. xvi. 14) πάντων ὑμῶν), 1 Cor. xvi. 23 (omits ἡμῶν, and appends ἡ ἀγάπη μου μετὰ πάντ. ὑμ. ἐν X. 'I.)—the same as the present; *secondly*, Philem. 25, Gal. vi. 18 (adds ἀδελφοί), Phil. iv. 23 (omits ἡμῶν), in the form ἡ χάρις τοῦ Κυρ. 'I. X. μετὰ τοῦ πνεύματος ὑμῶν; and *lastly*, Eph. vi. 24, in the longer form ἡ χάρις μετὰ πάντων· τῶν ἀγαπώντων τὸν Κύρ. ἡμῶν 'I. X. ἐν ἀφθαρσίᾳ; see Koch *on Philem.* 25, p. 135 sq. The ἀμὴν (*Rec.* with AD²D³EKL; mss.) is appy. rightly omitted by *Lachm.* and *Tisch.* with BD¹ FG; mss.; Clar., Sang., Amit., al., being very probably only a liturgical addition.

# THE

# SECOND EPISTLE TO THE THESSALONIANS.

# INTRODUCTION.

This short but important Epistle was written by the apostle to his converts at Thessalonica, a short time after his First Epistle, and apparently from the same place. If, as seems highly probable, Corinth be regarded as the place from which the First Epistle was written (see *Introd. to Ep.* 1), it is from the same city that we may reasonably suppose the present Epistle to have been written; the same companions (ch. i. 1, comp. 1 Thess i. 1) were still with the apostle (contrast Acts xviii. 18); similar forms and circumstances of trial appear to have been surrounding him (ch. iii. 2, compared with 1 Thess. ii. 16, Acts xviii. 6).

The exact *time* at which the Epistle was written cannot be determined. If the First Epistle was written soon after the arrival of Timothy from Macedonia (ch. iii. 6), and towards the commencement of the apostle's eighteen-month stay at Corinth (Acts xviii. 11), we shall, probably, not be far wrong in placing the date of the Second Epistle towards the end of the first twelve months of the apostle's residence at Corinth (comp. ch. iii. 2 with Acts xviii. 12, and consider ver. 18, ἔτι προσμείνας ἡμέρας ἱκανάς), and thus but a few months after that of the First Epistle. We may thus specify the autumn of A. D. 53 as perhaps an approximately correct date: see Davidson, *Introd.* Vol. II. p. 449.

The circumstances which gave rise to the Epistle seem clearly to have been some additional information which the apostle had received concerning the disquieted state of the minds of his converts. Whether this reached him through the bearer of the First Epistle, or formed the substance of a letter from the elders of the Church of Thessalonica, must remain mere conjecture. This much, however, seems certain, that some letter had been circulated at Thessalonica, purporting to come from the apostle (ch. ii. 2), which, combined probably with some teaching said equally to be derived from St. Paul (comp. notes on ch. ii. 9), had added greatly to the general excitement, and had rendered it necessary for this Second Epistle to be written, and to be vouched for by a clear mark of genuineness (ch. iii. 17). The purport of the letter and the teaching was clearly to the effect that the day of the Lord was at hand; and it does not seem improbable that this might have been based on some expressions in the First Epistle (ch. iv. 15–17, v. 2 sq.), which had been distorted or exaggerated so as better to keep alive the feverish anxiety and unregulated enthusiasm of the converts in this busy city. We may thus perhaps, with Davidson (*Introd.* Vol. II. p. 448), consider it more probable that the Second Epistle was an indirect than a direct result of the First. It was apparently not so much designed to correct innocent misapprehensions of the former Epistle (Paley, al.) as to remove a positively false construction which had been put—whether with a partly good, or mainly bad intent, we know not—both on that Epistle, and on the apostle's general teaching.

The main *subject* of the Epistle, then, was to calm excitement, and to make it perfectly plain that the Lord's second Advent was *not* close at hand, nay, that a mysterious course of events previously alluded to (ch. ii. 5), of which the beginning was confessedly to be recognized (ver. 7), had first to be fully developed. Corrective instruction is thus the chief subject; with this, however, is associated cheering consolation under afflictions (ch. i. 4 sq.), and direct exhortation to orderly conduct (ch. iii. 6), industry (ver. 8 sq.), and quietness (ver. 12).

The *authenticity* and *genuineness* are supported by early and explicit external testimonies (Irenæus, *Hær.* III. 7. 2, Clem.-Alex. *Strom.* V. p. 655, ed. Pott., Tertullian *de Resur. Carn.* cap. 24), and have never been called in question till recently. The objections are however of a most arbitrary and subjective character, and do not deserve any serious consideration. Complete answers will be found in Lünemann, *Einleitung*, p. 163 sq., and Davidson, *Introd.* Vol. II. p. 454 sq.

THE

# SECOND EPISTLE TO THE THESSALONIANS.

---

## CHAPTER I. 1, 2.

Apostolic address and salutation.

ΠΑΥΛΟΣ καὶ Σιλουανὸς καὶ Τιμόθεος, τῇ
ἐκκλησίᾳ Θεσσαλονικέων ἐν Θεῷ πατρὶ
ἡμῶν καὶ Κυρίῳ Ἰησοῦ Χριστῷ. 2 χάρις ὑμῖν καὶ εἰρήνη ἀπὸ
Θεοῦ πατρὸς ἡμῶν καὶ Κυρίου Ἰησοῦ Χριστοῦ.

2. πατρὸς ἡμῶν] The reading is *very* doubtful. *Tisch.* (ed. 2, 7) omits, and *Lachm.* brackets ἡμῶν with BDE; 3 mss.; Clarom., Sangerm.; Theoph.; Ambrst. (ed.), Pel. *Lünem*, *Alf.*). The pronoun is retained in *Rec.* with AFGKL; appy. great majority of mss.; Syr. (both), Aug, Vulg., Goth., Æth. (both), Copt., Arm.; Chrys., Theod., al. (*Griesb.*, but om.), — and appy. rightly; for on the one hand the preponderance of external authority is very decided, and on the other, the probability of an omission either accidentally or intentionally, owing to the ἡμῶν just preceding, is not much less than the probability of an interpolation to conform with other Epistles.

1. Παῦλος καὶ Σιλουανὸς καὶ Τ.] Substantially the same form of salutation as in the First Epistle; see notes *in loc.* The only difference is in the addition ἡμῶν to πατρί, which, contrary to what we might have expected, does not appear to have suggested any variety of reading. For a brief account of Sylvanus and Timothy, who are here, as in the Frst Ep., associated with the apostle as having co-operated with him in founding the Church of Thessalonica, see notes *on* 1 *Thess.* i. 1.

2. χάρις ὑμῖν καὶ εἰρήνη] Regular form of salutation, uniting both the Greek χαίρειν and the Hebrew שָׁלוֹם (Gen. xliii. 23, Judges vi. 23, al.); τὸ χάρις ὑμῖν οὕτω τίθησιν, ὥσπερ ἡμεῖς τὸ χαίρειν ἐν ταῖς ἐπιγραφαῖς τῶν ἐπιστολῶν εἰώθαμεν, Theodos.-Mops. p. 145 (ed. Fritz.): see more in notes *on Gal.* i. 2, Eph. i. 2, and in the long and laborious note of Koch *on* 1 *Thess.* i. 1. The remark of Thom. Aquinas is not without point, 'χάρις quæ est principium omnis boni, εἰρήνη quæ est finale bonorum omnium;' see also notes *on Col.* i. 2. ἀπὸ Θεοῦ πατρὸς ἡμ.] '*from God our Father;*' scil. as the source from which it emanates. In 2 John 3 we find παρὰ

We thank God for your faith and patience. He will recompense you and avenge you. May He count you worthy of His calling.

3 Εὐχαριστεῖν ὀφείλομεν τῷ Θεῷ πάντοτε περὶ ὑμῶν, ἀδελφοί, καθὼς ἄξιόν ἐστιν ὅτι ὑπεραυξάνει ἡ πίστις ὑμῶν, καὶ πλεονάζει ἡ ἀγάπη

in the same combination, but with a difference of meaning that in the present case (in ref. to God) is scarcely appreciable, and depends perhaps entirely on the usage and mode of conception of the writer. St. John, for example, uses παρὰ and ἀπὸ in a proportion a little less than 1 to 3, while St. Paul uses the same prepp. in a proportion of 1 to 5. The general distinction between these prepp. (ἀπό, emanation simply; παρά, eman. from a *personal* source) and the more frequently used ἐκ is well stated by Winer, *Gr.* § 47. b, p. 326 (ed. 6).

καὶ Κυρίου κ. τ. λ.] Scil. καὶ ἀπὸ Κυρίου κ. τ. λ.; not πατρὸς Κυρίου κ. τ. λ., an interpretation rendered highly improbable by the occurrence of πατὴρ without any gen.,—here, according to *Tisch.*, [*Lachm.*], with less doubt Gal. i. 3, 1 Tim. i. 2, and with no var. 2 Tim. i. 2, Tit. i. 4; see notes *on Eph.* i. 3. On the reading, see critical note.

3. Εὐχαρ. ὀφείλομεν] '*We are bound to return thanks*,' scil. St. Paul, Sylvanus, and Timothy. Though we must be cautious in pressing the plural in every case, yet in the present, remembering the relation in which Sylv. and Tim. stood to the Church of Thess., it can hardly be overlooked: see notes *on* 1 *Thess.* i. 2. On this use of εὐχαριστεῖν in the sense of χάριν ἔχειν, see notes *on Phil.* i. 3, and for the constructions of εὐχαρ., notes *on Col.* i. 12. περὶ ὑμῶν] '*concerning you*;' with no very appreciable difference from ὑπὲρ (Eph. i. 16) in the same formula; see notes *on* 1 *Thess.* i. 2, v. 25, and for the distinction between these prepositions in cases where they appear less interchangeable, see *on Gal.* i. 4, and *on Phil.* i. 7.

καθὼς ἄξιόν ἐστιν] '*as it is meet*;' not, on the one hand, a mere parenthetical addition to the preceding εὐχαρ. ὀφείλ. ('ut par est,' Beza), nor yet on the other, an emphatic statement of the 'modus eximius' (Schott; καὶ διὰ λόγων καὶ δι' ἔργων, Theoph. 2) in which such an εὐχαριστία ought to be offered, but simply a connecting clause between the first member of the sentence and the distinctly causal statement ὅτι ὑπεραυξάνει κ. τ. λ. which follows, and with which καθὼς ἄξιον κ. τ. λ. stands in more immediate union. Thus, as Lünemann well observes, while the ὀφείλομεν states the duty of the εὐχαριστία on its *subjective* side, καθὼς κ. τ. λ. subjoins the *objective* aspects. Few probably will hesitate to prefer this simple and logical explanation to any assumption so injurious to the inspired writer as that of a tautology designed to supply the place of emphasis (Jowett). ὅτι will thus be not relatival to ܕ [quod] Syr.-Pesh., but distinctly causal, 'quoniam,' Vulg., Clarom., Æth. (both), Goth., Syr.-Philox.,—in close union with the clause immediately preceding. It may be remarked that few particles in St. Paul's Epp cause a more decided discrepancy of interpretation than ὅτι. Between the merely objective (Winer, *Gr.* § 53. 9, p. 398) and the strictly causal force (Winer, *Gr.* § 53. 8, p. 395) of the particle, it is not only often very difficult to decide, but in several passages (*e. g.* Rom. viii. 21) exegetical considerations of some moment will be found to depend on the decision; comp. notes *on* 1 *Thess.* iv. 16.

ὑπεραυξάνει] '*increaseth above measure*;' an ἅπ. λεγόμ. in the N. T. and not very common elsewhere, comp. Andoc. *contr. Alcib.* p. 32 (ed. Steph.), τοὺς ὑπεραυξανομένους. The predilection of St. Paul for emphatic compounds of ὑπὲρ has been noticed and briefly illustrated

ἑνὸς ἑκάστου πάντων ὑμῶν εἰς ἀλλήλους, 4 ὥστε ἡμᾶς αὐτοὺς ἐν ὑμῖν ἐγκαυχᾶσθαι ἐν ταῖς ἐκκλησίαις τοῦ Θεοῦ ὑπὲρ τῆς ὑπομονῆς

on *Eph.* iii. 20; see also Fritz. *Rom.* v. 20, Vol. I. p. 351. It may be observed that ὑπεραυξάνει appears associated with πίστις as conveying more distinctly the idea of organic evolution and growth (comp. Matth. xvii. 20, Luke xvii. 6), while with ἀγάπη a term is used which expresses more generally the idea of spiritual enlargement, and of extension toward others; comp. notes *on* 1 *Thess.* iii. 12. ἑνὸς ἑκάστου κ. τ. λ.] *of every one of you all toward each other;*', not without distinctive emphasis, — first, in specifying that this ἀγάπη was not merely general, but individually manifested (ἴση ἦν παρὰ πάντων ἡ ἀγάπη εἰς πάντας, Theoph.), and secondly, in showing that it was not restricted in its exhibitions to those who loved them, but extended to all their fellow-Christians at Thessalonica; ὅταν μερικῶς ἀγαπῶμεν, οὐκ ἀγάπη τοῦτο ἀλλὰ διάστασις· εἰ γὰρ διὰ τὸν Θεὸν ἀγαπᾷς, πάντας ἀγάπα. Theoph. On this verse see five practical sermons by Manton, *Works*, Vol. IV. p. 420—458 (Lond. 1698).

4. ἡμᾶς αὐτούς] '*we ourselves*,' — as well as others, whether among you or elsewhere, who might call attention to your Christian progress more naturally and appropriately than those who felt it, humanly speaking, due to their own exertions, but who, in the present case, could not forbear. De Wette compares 1 Thess. i. 8, but it may be doubted whether St. Paul had here that passage very distinctly in his thoughts. To refer ἡμᾶς αὐτοὺς to St. Paul himself, in contrast to his associates included in the preceding plural verbs (Schott), seems distinctly illogical; and to leave open the possibility that this may be only an instance of 'false emphasis or awkwardness of expression' (Jowett), can only be characterized as a subterfuge at variance with all fair, sound, and reasonable exegesis. The distinction between ἡμεῖς αὐτοὶ (in which the emphasis falls on the ἡμεῖς) and αὐτοὶ ἡμεῖς (in which it falls more on the αὐτοί; comp. 1 Thess. iv. 9) is illustrated by Krüger, *Sprachl.* § 51. 2. 8. ἐν ὑμῖν ἐγκαυχᾶσθαι] '*boast in you;*' you were the objects of it, and the sphere, or rather substratum of its manifestation; comp. Winer, *Gr.* § 48. a. p. 345, and see notes *on Gal.* i. 24. The somewhat rare form ἐγκαυχᾶσθαι is found a few times in the LXX, *e. g.* Psalm lii. 1, cvi. 47, al., in eccles. writers, and in Æsop, *Fab.* CCCXLII. p. 139 (ed. Schneider). The reading is not by any means certain; *Rec.* with DE(FG καυχήσασθαι) KL; mss.; many Ff., reads καυχᾶσθαι; but the probability that the change to the simpler and more common form is due to the corrector, seems in this case so *very* great that the reading of *Lachm.* and *Tisch.*, though only with AB, 17, may perhaps with critical correctness be considered to deserve the preference. ἐν ταῖς ἐκκλ. τοῦ Θεοῦ] '*in the Churches of God*,' scil. in Corinth and its neighborhood, where the apostle was at the time of writing this Ep.; comp. Acts xviii. 11, and see Wieseler, *Chronol.* p. 254 sq. The remark of Chrys. ἐνταῦθα δείκνυσι καὶ πολὺν παρελθόντα χρόνον· ἡ γὰρ ὑπομονὴ ἀπὸ χρόνου φαίνεται πολλοῦ, οὐκ ἐν δύο καὶ τρισὶν ἡμέραις, — must be received with reservation; as there seems no reason for thinking that the Epistle was written later than the spring of 54 A. D., perhaps even a few months earlier; compare Lünem. *Einleit.* p. 160. ὑπομ. ὑμῶν καὶ πίστεως] '*your patience of faith;*' precise subjects of the apostle's boasting. There is no ἓν διὰ δυοῖν in these words, scil. ὑπομονῆς ἐν πιστεί, Grot., — ever a doubtful and pre-

ὑμῶν καὶ πίστεως ἐν πᾶσιν τοῖς διωγμοῖς ὑμῶν καὶ ταῖς θλίψεσιν
αἷς ἀνέχεσθε, 5 ἔνδειγμα τῆς δικαίας κρίσεως τοῦ Θεοῦ, εἰς τὸ

carious assumption (see Fritz *on Matth.* p. 853—858, Ex. IV., where this grammatical formula is well considered), nor does πίστις here imply 'fidelis constantia,' Beng., 'Treue,' Lünem., — a doubtful meaning of πίστις in the N. T., especially when the more usual meaning has just preceded (ver. 3) in reference to the same subjects. The Thessal. evinced *faith* in its proper and usual sense, in bearing up in their tribulations, and *believing* on Him while bearing His cross. On the meaning of ὑπομονή (here almost taking the place of ἐλπίς, Neand. *Planting*, p. 479, Bohn), which in the N. T. seems ever to imply not mere 'endurance,' but 'brave patience,' see notes *on* 1 *Thess.* i. 3, and comp. *on* 2 *Tim.* ii. 10 πᾶσιν seems clearly to belong only to διωγμοῖς; the article would otherwise have been omitted before θλίψεσιν. The distinction between the two words appears sufficiently obvious: διωγμὸς is the more special term ('injurias complectitur, quas Judæi et ethnici Christianis propter doctrinæ Christi professionem imposuerunt,' Fritz.) θλίψις the more general and comprehensive; see Fritz. *Rom.* viii. 35, Vol. II. p. 221.

αἷς ἀνέχεσθε] '*which ye are enduring*,' 'quas sustinetis,' Vulg., Clarom.; ordinary and regular attraction (Winer, *Gr.* § 24. 1, p. 147) — for ὧν ἀνέχ., if we follow the analogy of 2 Cor. xi. 1, 2 Tim. iv. 3, — or for ἃς ἀνέχ., if we follow the more usual structure of the verb in classical Greek. In the N. T. ἀνέχομαι is associated most commonly with *persons*, and but rarely with things; in both cases, however, it is constructed with a gen., while in earlier Greek its construction, esp. with persons, is comparatively rare except in the accus.; see Rost u. Palm, *Lex.* s. v. Vol. I. p. 227. The present tense shows that the application is still going on, and is no way at variance with 1 Thess. i. 6, ii. 14 (contrast Baur, *Paulus*, p. 488, notes), which refer to an earlier persecution that appears to have partially subsided before the 1st Epistle was written The present allusion, as Lünem. rightly observes, is to some fresh outbreak. On this verse and on the remaining verses of the chapter, see sixteen practical sermons by Manton, *Works*, Vol. v. p 393—514 (Lond. 1698).

5. ἔνδειγμα κ. τ. λ.] '(*which is*) *a token* or *proof of the righteous judgment, etc.*;' appositional clause to the whole foregoing sentence, and practically equivalent to ὅ τι ἐστιν ἔνδειγμα κ. τ. λ.; comp. Phil. i. 28 [where observe the comparatively slight difference between the two verbals], and see Fritz. *Rom.* xii. 1, Vol. I. p. 16. The apposition here seems to be not accusatival (Rom. xii. 1, 1 Tim. ii. 6), but nominatival, ἔνδειγμα not referring merely to the clause that more immediately involves the verb, but to all the preceding words, τῆς ὑπομονῆς ......ἀνέχεσθε: the endurance of all their persecutions and afflictions in patience and faith formed the ἔνδειγμα τῆς δικαίας κρίσεως τοῦ Θεοῦ; comp. Rom. viii. 3, and see Winer, *Gr.* § 59. 9, p. 472. The reference of ἔνδειγμα to the Thess. ('ipsi Thessal. adversa sustinentes intelligi possunt esse exemplum justi judicii Dei,' Est.) is grammatically plausible, but both logically and exegetically improbable and unsatisfactory: the proof of the righteous judgment of God was not to be looked for in the Thessalonians themselves, but in their acts and their patient endurance. τῆς δικαίας κρίσεως] '*the just judgment*,' that will be displayed at the Lord's second coming (comp. ver. 7), when they who have suffered with and for the Lord will also reign with Him; comp. 2 Tim. ii. 12.

καταξιωθῆναι ὑμᾶς τῆς βασιλείας τοῦ Θεοῦ, ὑπερ ἧς καὶ πάσχετε, 6 εἴπερ δίκαιον παρὰ Θεῷ ἀνταποδοῦναι τοῖς θλί-

To refer the δικαία κρίσις solely to present sufferings, as perfecting and preparing the Thessal. for future glory (Olsh.), is to miss the whole point of the sentence: the apostle's argument is that their endurance of suffering in faith is a token of God's righteous judgment and of a future reward, which will display itself in rewarding the patient sufferers, as surely as it will inflict punishment on their persecutors; ἴστε σαφῶς τῶν κινδύνων τὰ ἆθλα, καὶ τὴν τῶν οὐρανῶν προσδέχεσθε βασιλείαν, τοῦ ἀγωνοθέτου τὴν δικαίαν ἐπιστάμενοι ψῆφον, Theod. εἰς τὸ καταξιωθ.] '*that ye may be counted worthy;*' general direction of the δικαία κρίσις and object to which it tended. This infinitival clause has been associated with three different portions of the preceding sentence; (*a*) with αἷς ἀνέχεσθε, scil. 'quas afflictiones sustinetis eo fine et fructu ut..... efficiamini digni regno Dei,' Est.; (*b*) with ἔνδειγμα—Θεοῦ, scil. 'quæ perseverantia vestra judicii divini justissimi olim futuri pignori inservit, quod hoc attinet, ut digni judicemini,' Schott 2; (*c*) with δικαίας κρίσεως, so as to mark either (1) the result to which it tended, Lünem., or (2) the aim which it contemplated, De Wette. Of these, while (*a*) causes the really important member ἔνδειγμα κ. τ. λ. to relapse into a mere parenthesis, and (*b*) infringe on the almost regular meaning of εἰς τὸ with the infin., (*c*) preserves the logical sequence of clauses and the usual force of εἰς τὸ with the infin. Whether, however, the *result* or the *aim* is here specified is somewhat doubtful. The decidedly predominant usage in St. Paul's Epp. of εἰς τὸ with the inf. suggests the latter (Winer, *Gr.* § 44. 6, p. 295, Meyer *on Rom.* i. 20, note): as, however, there seems some reason for recognizing elsewhere in the N. T. a secondary final force of εἰς τό (see notes *on* 1 *Thess.* ii. 12), we may perhaps most plausibly, in the present case, regard the καταξιωθῆναι κ. τ. λ. not purely as the purpose, 'in order to,' Alf., but rather as the object to which it *tended:* the general direction and tendency of the κρίσις was that patient and holy sufferers should be accounted worthy of God's kingdom.

βασιλείας τοῦ Θεοῦ] '*the kingdom of God;*' His future kingdom in heaven, of which the Christian here on earth is a subject, but the full privileges of which he is to enjoy hereafter; see notes *on* 1 *Thess.* ii. 12, and comp. Bauer's treatise there alluded to, *de Notione Regni Div. in N. T.* p. 120 sq. ὑπὲρ ἧς καὶ πάσχετε] '*for which ye are also suffering;*' not exactly 'pro quo consequendo,' Est., but, with a more general reference, 'in behalf of which,' 'for the sake of which,'—the ὑπὲρ marking the object for which ('in commodum cujus,' Usteri, *Lehrb.* II. 1. 1, p. 116) the suffering was endured (comp. Acts v. 41, Rom. i. 5, see Winer, *Gr.* § 48. 1, p. 343), while the καὶ with a species of consecutive force supplies a renewed hint of the connection between the suffering and the καταξιωθῆναι κ. τ. λ. On this force of καί, see Winer, *Gr.* § 53 3, p. 387, and comp. *on* 1 *Thess.* iv. 1. The clause thus contains no indirect assertion that sufferings established a *claim* to the kingdom of God (ἀπὸ τοῦ πάσχειν προπορίζεται ἡ βασιλεία τῶν οὐρανῶν, Theoph.), but only confirms the idea elsewhere expressed in Scripture that they formed the *avenue* which led to it (οὕτως δεῖ εἰς τὴν βασιλείαν εἰσιέναι, Chrys.), and that the connection between holy suffering and future blessedness was mystically close and indissoluble; comp. Acts xiv. 22, Rom. viii. 17. On the general aspects of suffering in the N. T., see *Destiny of Creature*, p. 35—42.

6. εἴπερ δίκαιον] '*if so be that it is*

βουσιν ὑμᾶς θλίψιν 7 καὶ ὑμῖν τοῖς θλιβομένοις ἄνεσιν
μεθ' ἡμῶν, ἐν τῇ ἀποκαλύψει τοῦ Κυρίου Ἰησοῦ ἀπ' οὐρανοῦ

*righteous;*' confirmation, in a hypothetical form, of the preceding declaration of the justice of God, derived from His dealings with their persecutors. The εἴπερ thus involves no doubt (οὐκ ἐπὶ ἀμφιβολίας τέθεικεν, ἀλλ' ἐπὶ βεβαιώσεως, Theod.), but only, with a species of rhetorical force, regards as an assumption ('εἴπερ usurpatur de re quæ esse sumitur,' Hermann, *Viger* No. 310) what is really felt to be a certain and recognized verity; τίθησι τὸ 'εἴπερ,' ὡς ἐπὶ τῶν ὡμολογημένων, Chrys. On the force of εἴπερ, see Klotz, *Devar.* Vol. II. p. 528, and on its distinction from εἴγε, comp. notes *on Gal.* iii. 4. The word δίκαιον evidently points back to the δικαία κρίσις in ver. 5, not with any antithetical allusion to the grace of God (comp. Pelt), but in simple and immediate reference to His justice as regarded under the analogies of strict human justice (εἰ γὰρ παρὰ ἀνθρώποις τοῦτο δίκαιον, πολλῷ μᾶλλον παρὰ τῷ Θεῷ, Chrys.), and as inferred from His own declarations: comp. Rom. ii. 5, Col. iii. 24, 25. παρὰ Θεῷ] '*before God,*' '*with God,*' 'apud Deum,' Vulg. ܩܕܡ ܐܠܗܐ. [coram Deo] Syr.; the secondary idea of locality ('motion connected with that of closeness,' Donalds. *Cratyl.* § 177) being still *faintly* retained in the notion of judgment as at a tribunal, *e. g.* Herod. III. 160, παρὰ Δαρείῳ κριτῇ; comp. Gal. iii. 11, and see Winer, *Gr.* § 48. d, p. 352. On the meaning of ἀνταποδιδόναι, see notes *on 1 Thess.* iii. 9. τοῖς θλίβουσιν κ. τ. λ.] '*to those that afflict you, affliction;*' the 'jus talionis' exhibited in its clearest form: the θλίβοντες are requited with θλίψις, the θλιβόμενοι with ἄνεσις. Theoph. subjoins the further comparison; οὐχ ὥσπερ δὲ αἱ ἐπαγόμενοι ὑμῖν θλίψεις πρόσκαιροι, οὕτω καὶ αἱ τοῖς θλίβουσιν ὑμᾶς ἀντεπαχθησόμεναι παρὰ Θεοῦ πρόσκαιροι ἔσονται, ἀλλ' ἀτελεύτητοι· καὶ αἱ ἀνέσεις ὑμῖν τοιαῦται.

7. τοῖς θλιβομένοις] '*who are afflicted;*' passive, clearly not middle, 'qui pressuram toleratis,' Beng., as the antithesis would thus be marred, and the illustration of the 'jus talionis' rendered somewhat less distinct.

ἄνεσιν μεθ' ἡμῶν] '*rest with us;*' rest in company with us, who are writing to you, and who like you have been exposed to suffering; see ch. iii. 2. To give ἡμεῖς a general reference (De W.) would not be strictly true, and would impair the encouraging and consolatory character of the reference; ἐπάγει τὸ μεθ' ὑμῶν, ἵνα κοινωνοὺς αὐτοὺς λάβῃ καὶ τῶν ἀγώνων καὶ στεφάνων τῶν ἀποστολικῶν, Œcum. Ἄνεσις is similarly used in antithesis to θλίβεσθαι and θλίψις, 2 Cor. vii. 5, viii. 13; it properly implies a relaxation, as of strings, and in such combinations stands in opposition to ἐπίτασις; comp. Plato, *Republ.* I. p. 349 E, ἐν τῇ ἐπιτάσει καὶ ἀνέσει τῶν χορδῶν. It here obviously refers to the final rest in the kingdom of God; and forms one of the elements of its blessedness considered under simply negative aspects; comp. Rev. xiv. 13. ἐν τῇ ἀποκαλ. κ. τ. λ.] '*at the revelation of the Lord Jesus;*' predication of time when the ἀνταπόδοσις shall take place. The term ἀποκάλυψις (1 Cor. i. 7, comp. Luke xvii. 30) is here suitably used in preference to the more usual παρουσία, as perhaps hinting that though now hidden, our Lord's coming to judge both the quick and the dead will be something real, certain, and manifest; νῦν γάρ, φησί, κρύπτεται, ἀλλὰ μὴ ἀλύετε· ἀποκαλυφθήσεται γάρ, καὶ ὡς Θεὸς καὶ δεσπότης, Theoph. ἀπ' οὐρανοῦ] Predication of place: it is from heaven, from the right hand of God, where He is now sitting, that the Lord will come:

μετ' ἀγγέλων δυνάμεως αὐτοῦ 8 ἐν φλογὶ πυρὸς, διδόντος ἐκδίκη-

8. φλογὶ πυρός) So *Lachm.* with BDEFG; 71; Vulg., Clarom., Syr., Goth, al.; Iren. (interpr.), Maced., Theod. (comment.?), Œcum.; Tertull. (*Scholz.*, *Tisch.* ed. 1, *Lünem.*, *Wordsw.*). In ed. 2, 7, *Tisch.* adopts πυρὶ φλογὸς with AKL; nearly all mss.; Syr.-Philox. (marg.); Chrys., Theod. (text), Dam., al. (*Rec.*, *Alf.*) but appy. not on sufficient evidence. Though a change from the less usual to the more natural form of expression is far from improbable; still either erroneous transcription or a reminiscence of the well-known passage, Exod. iii. 2, might have led to the inverted form. In this uncertainty the preponderance of external evidence ought certainly to decide us.

compare 1 Thess. iv. 16, and Pearson, *Creed*, Art. VII. Vol. I. p. 346 (ed. Burton). μετ' ἀγγέλων δυνάμ. αὐτοῦ] '*accompanied with the angels of His power*;' predication of manner; the Lord will come accompanied with the hosts of heaven, which shall be the ministers of His will and the exponents and instruments of His power. The gloss of Theoph. and Œcum. 2, δυνάμεως ἄγγελοι, τουτέστι δυνατοί, followed by Auth., al., but found in none of the better Vv. of antiquity, is now properly rejected by app. all modern commentators. The gen. appears simply to fall under the general head of the *gen. possessivus*, and serves to mark that to which the ἄγγελοι appertained, and of which they were the ministers; comp. Bernhardy, *Synt.* III. 44, p. 161, Winer, *Gr.* § 34. 3. b. p. 211 (note). The Syr. practically inverts the clause, sc. ܥܡ ܚܝܠܐ ܕܡܠܐܟܘܗܝ [cum virtute Angelorum suorum], and may have suggested the equally incorrect and inverted paraphrase of Michaelis, 'das ganze Heer seiner Engel;' the former, however, is corrected in Syr.-Philox., and the latter has been properly rejected by all recent expositors. On the force of μετὰ in this combination, see notes *on* 1 *Thess.* iii. 13.

8. ἐν φλογὶ πυρός] '*in a flame of fire*,' *i. e.*, encircled by, encompassed by; continued predication of the manner of the ἀποκάλυψις; 'in libris V. T. sæpenumero ignis et flamma commemoratur, ubi de præsentiâ et efficacitate Numinis divini singulari modo patefaciendâ, præsertim de judicio divino, sermo est, Exod. iii. 2 sq., Malach. iv. 1, Dan. vii. 9, 10,' Schott. The addition thus serves not only to express the majesty of the Lord's coming, but is noticeable as ascribing to the Son the same glorious manifestations that the Old Testament ascribes to the Father. The Syriac (Pesh.), Æth. (Platt), and, if the punctuation can be trusted, some of the other Vv. (comp. Theoph. 1) connect this clause with διδόντος ἐκδίκ., as an instrumental clause (Jowett actually unites both interpr.), but without plausibility; the attendant heavenly hosts and the encircling fire seem naturally to be associated as the two symbols and accompaniments of the divine presence.

διδόντος ἐκδίκ.] '*awarding vengeance*;' scil. τοῦ Κυρίου Ἰησ., not in connection with πυρός, which would not only be a halting and unduly protracted structure, but would wholly mar the symmetry of the two clauses of manner. The formula διδόναι ἐκδίκ. only occurs here in the N. T., but is occasionally found elsewhere; see Ezek. xxv. 14, and compare (ἀποδιδ. ἐκδ.) Numb. xxxi. 3. No exx. of its occurrence have been adduced from classical Greek; ἐκδίκ. ποιήσασθαι is found in Polyb. *Hist.* III. 8. 10. τοῖς μὴ εἰδόσιν Θεόν] '*to those who know not God*,' who belong

σιν τοῖς μὴ εἰδόσιν Θεὸν καὶ τοῖς μὴ ὑπακούουσιν τῷ εὐαγγε-
λίῳ τοῦ Κυρίου ἡμῶν Ἰησοῦ· 9 οἵτινες δίκην τίσουσιν, ὄλεθρον

to a class marked by such characteristics; first of the two classes who will be the future objects of the divine wrath, 'qui in ethnicâ ignorantiâ de Deo versantur' (Beng.), — in a word, the Heathens. On the peculiar force of the subjective negation, see notes *on* 1 *Thess.* iv. 5, and comp. Winer, *Gr.* § 55. 5, p. 428 sq. τοῖς μὴ ὑπακ. κ. τ. λ.] '*who obey not the Gospel of our Lord Jesus;*'; second class of those who afflicted the Thess. converts, those whose characteristic was disobedience generally, and especially to the Gospel (Rom. x. 16), — in a word, the unbelieving Jews. It is somewhat singular that a scholar usually so sound as Schott should have felt a difficulty at the division into two classes: surely the article before μὴ ὑπακ. renders such a view all but certain; see Winer, *Gr.* § 19. 5, p. 117, Green, *Gram.* p. 215. Even in seeming exceptions to the rule (Matth. xxvii. 3, Luke xxii. 4, al.) it may be fairly questioned whether the writer did not, in these particular cases, really intend the two classes to be regarded as separate, though otherwise commonly united. The reading is slightly doubtful; *Rec.* adds, and *Lachm.* inserts in brackets Χριστοῦ with AFG; mss.; Vulg., Clarom., Goth., al. Though the omission of Χρ. does not characterize this Ep. as it does the first (see *on* 1 *Thess.* iii. 13), the external authority [BDEKL; 25 mss.; Copt., al.; many Ff.] seems decidedly to preponderate for the omission.

9. οἵτινες] '*men who;*' reference by means of the qualitative rel. pronoun to the two preceding classes. If we revert to the distinctions stated in the notes *on Gal.* iv. 24, it would seem that ὅστις is here used, not in a causal sense with ref. to the *reason* for τίσουσιν (Lünem., Alford — who, however, mix up two usages), but *explicatively* ('who truly'), or even simply *classifically*, with ref. to the class or category to which the antecedents are referred and to the characteristics which mark them; see notes *on Gal.* ii. 4, and *on Phil.* ii. 20. The brief distinction of Krüger (*Sprachl.* § 50. 8), that ὃς has simply an objective aspect, ὅστις one qualitative and generic, will in most cases be found useful and applicable. For other and idiomatic usages, see Ellendt, *Lex. Sophocl.* s. v. Vol. II. p. 381 sq., and comp. Schæfer, notes *on Demosth.* Vol. II. p. 531.

δίκην τίσουσιν] '*shall pay the penalty.*' This formula does not occur elsewhere in the N. T. (compare, however, δίκην ὑπέχειν, Jude 7), but is sufficiently common in both earlier and later Greek, and is copiously illustrated by Wetst. *in loc.* ὄλεθρον αἰώνιον] '*eternal destruction;*' accus. in apposition to the preceding δίκην. All the sounder commentators on this text recognize in αἰώνιος a reference to 'res in perpetuum futuræ' (Schott), and a testimony to the eternity of future punishment that is not easy to be explained away: ποῦ τοίνυν οἱ Ὠριγενιασταί, οἱ τέλος τῆς κολάσεως μυθούμενοι; αἰώνιον ταύτην ὁ Παῦλος λέγει, Theoph.; comp. Pearson, *Creed*, Art. XII. p. 465 (ed. Burton). In answer to the efforts of some writers of the present day to give αἰώνιος a *qualitative* aspect, let it briefly be said that the earliest Greek expositors never appear to have lost sight of its *quantitative* aspects; ἀκριβέστερον ἔδειξε τῆς τιμωρίας τὸ μέγεθος αἰώνιον ταύτην ἀποκαλέσας, Theod. For further remarks on this subject, see notes and reff. in *Destiny of the Creature*, p. 158—164, and for a discussion of the grave question of the eternity of divine punishments, Erbkam, in *Stud. u. Krit.* for 1838, p. 422 sq.

αἰώνιον ἀπὸ προσώπου τοῦ Κυρίου καὶ ἀπὸ τῆς δόξης τῆς ἰσχύος
αὐτοῦ, 10 ὅταν ἔλθῃ ἐνδοξασθῆναι ἐν τοῖς ἁγίοις αὐτοῦ καὶ θαυ-

The reading of *Lachm.* ὀλέθριον [with A; 2 mss.; Ephr., Chrys. (ms.); Tert.] is far too feebly supported to deserve much consideration. ἀπὸ προσώπου τοῦ Κυρ.] '*removed from the presence of the Lord.*' These words have received three different explanations, corresponding to the three meanings, temporal, causal, and local, which may be assigned to the preposition. Of these, ἀπὸ can scarcely be here (*a*) temporal (ἀρκεῖ παραγενέσθαι μόνον καὶ ὀφθῆναι τὸν Θεόν, καὶ πάντες ἐν κολάσει καὶ τιμωρίᾳ γίνονται, Chrys., compare Theoph., Œcum.), as the subst. with which it is associated seems wholly to preclude anything but a simple and quasi-physical reference. Equally doubtful is (*b*) the causal translation; for though ἀπὸ may be thus associated with neuter and even passive verbs, as marking the *personal* source whence the action *originates* (see exx. in Winer, *Gr.* § 47. a. p. 332, comp. Thiersch, *de Pentat.* II. 15, p. 106), yet, on the other hand, such a connection in the present case would involve the assumption that προσώπου τοῦ Κυρ. was a periphrasis for the personal τοῦ Κυρίου (Acts iii. 19, cited by De W., owing to the dissimilar nature of the verbs, is no parallel), and merely equivalent to 'a præsente Domino' (compare Pelt), — a resolution of the words in a high degree precarious and doubtful. We therefore adopt (*c*) the simply *local* translation, according to which ἀπὸ marks the idea of 'separation from' (Olsh., Lünem.), *emkedma* ['de devant'] Æth., while προσώπου Κυρ. retains its proper meaning, and specifies that perennial fountain of blessedness (compare Psalm xv. 11, Matth. xviii. 10, Rev. xxii. 4), to be separated from which will constitute the true essence of the fearful 'pœna damni' (Jackson, *Creed*, XI. 20. 9): see further details in Schott and Lünem. *in loc.*, by both of whom this view is well maintained. ἀπὸ τῆς δόξης τῆς ἰσχ.] '*from the glory of His might,*' not 'His mighty glory,' Jowett, — a most doubtful paraphrase, but, the glory arising from, emanating from His might (gen. *originis*, comp. notes *on* 1 *Thess.* i. 6), the δόξα being regarded, as it were, the result of the exercise of His ἰσχύς, and as that sphere and halo of glory which environs its manifestations. The assumption of De Wette that in this clause ἀπὸ has a causal force is perfectly gratuitous.

10. ὅταν ἔλθῃ] '*when He shall have come;*' specific statement of the time in which the preceding δίκην τίσουσιν shall be brought about and accomplished; τότε γὰρ τοῦ κριτοῦ τὴν δικαίαν ψῆφον θαυμάσουσιν ἅπαντες, Theod. On the force of ὅταν with the *aor.* subj. as referring to an objectively possible event, which is to, can, or must take place at some single point of time distinct from the actual present, but the exact epoch of which is left uncertain, see Winer, *Gr.* § 42. 5, p. 275, and esp. Schmalfeld, *Synt.* § 121, where the nature of the construction is well discussed. The most natural and idiomatic mode of translation is briefly noticed in notes to *Transl.* ἐνδοξασθῆναι ἐν τοῖς ἁγίοις] '*to be glorified in* (*the persons of*) *His saints;*' infinitive of design or purpose, — not equivalent to ὥστε κ. τ. λ. (Jowett), from which it is grammatically distinguishable as involving no reference to mode or degree; see notes *on Col.* i. 22, where both formulæ are briefly discussed. The verb itself is a δὶς λεγόμ. in the N. T. (here and ver. 12), and, with the exception of the LXX (Exod. xiv. 4, Isaiah xlv. 25, xlix. 3, al.) and eccl. writers, is of rare occurrence. The prep. seems

μασθῆναι ἐν πᾶσιν τοῖς πιστεύσασιν, ὅτι ἐπιστεύθη τὸ μαρτύριον
ἡμῶν ἐφ' ὑμᾶς, ἐν τῇ ἡμέρᾳ ἐκείνῃ. 11 Εἰς ὃ καὶ προσευχόμεθα

here very distinctly to mark—not the mere locality 'among His saints' (Michael.), still less the instruments or media of the glorification (ἐν διά ἐστί, Chrysost., Beng.), but the *substratum* of the action, the mirror as it were (Alf.), in which and on which the δόξα was reflected and displayed; comp. Exod. xiv. 14, Isaiah xlix. 3, and see notes *on Gal.* i. 24 Lastly, the ἅγιοι do not here appear to refer to the Holy angels, but, as the tacit contrasts and limitations of the context suggest, to the risen and glorified company of believers; contrast 1 Thess. iii. 13, where πάντες, and the absence of all notice of the unholy, suggest the more inclusive reference

θαυμασθῆναι κ. τ. λ.] '*to be wondered at in all them that believed;*' scil. owing to the reflection of His glory and power which is displayed in those that believed on Him while they were on earth; 'obstupescent, Christum in credentibus tam magnum et gloriosum esse,' Cocceius. The aor. πιστεύσασιν [*Rec.* πιστεύουσιν, but in opp. to all the MSS., many Vv. and Ff.] is here suitably used in connection with the period referred to: at that time the belief of the faithful would belong to the past; compare Wordsw. *in loc.* For exx. of this pass. use of θαυμάζω, see Kypke, *Obs.* Vol. II. p. 342. ὅτι ἐπιστεύθη κ. τ. λ.] '*because our testimony to you was believed;*' parenthetical clause taking up the preceding πιστεύσασιν, and giving it a more distinct reference to those (ἐφ' ὑμᾶς) to whom he was writing. The μαρτύριον ἡμῶν is the testimony relating to Christ (μαρτ. τοῦ Χρ., 1 Cor. i. 6), the message of the Gospel (μαρτύριον δὲ κήρυγμα προσηγόρευσε, Theod.) delivered by the apostle and his associates (gen. *originis* or *causæ efficientis*, Scheuerl. *Synt.* § 17, notes *on 1 Thess.* i. 6), the destination of which is specified in the same enunciation; comp. Col. i. 8, τὴν ὑμῶν ἀγάπην ἐν πνεύματι, where, as here, the anarthrous prepositional member gives the whole clause a more complete unity of conception; see notes *l. c.*, and Winer, *Gr.* § 30. 2, p. 123. On the prep. ἐπί, which here seems to mark the mental direction of the μαρτύριον (compare Luke ix. 5), and commonly involves some idea of 'nearness or approximation (Donalds. *Crat.* § 172), see Winer, *Gr.* § 49. l, p. 363 sq. ἐν τῇ ἡμέρᾳ ἐκ. is most naturally joined with θαυμασθῆναι κ. τ. λ., to which it is joined as a predication of *time*, reiterating and more precisely defining the foregoing temporal clause, ὅταν ἔλθῃ κ. τ. λ. Some of the older Vv., *e. g.* Syr., Æth., Goth., appear to have joined these words with what precedes, but are compelled either to regard the aor. ἐπιστ. as equivalent to a future ([Syriac], Syr., but not Philox.) or to assign meanings to ἐν ἐκείνῃ ἡμέρᾳ, scil. 'de illo die,' Menoch., cum spe retributionis in illo die percipiendæ,' Est., that are neither grammatically nor exegetically defensible. The position of ἐν τῇ ἡμ. is confessedly somewhat unusual, but perhaps may have been designed still more to impress on the readers the exact and definite epoch when all was to be realized.

11. Εἰς ὃ] '*Whereunto*,' 'with expectations directed to which,' to its realization and fruition; not equivalent to δι' ὅ (Authoriz., Schott), nor even to ὑπὲρ ὅ (compare De W.), but simply, with the primary force of the prep., definitive of the *direction* taken, as it were, by the longing prayers of the apostle and his associates; see Winer, *Gr.* § 49. a, p. 354, Donalds. *Cratyl.* § 170, and comp. Col. i. 29, but observe that the verb with

πάντοτε περὶ ὑμῶν, ἵνα ὑμᾶς ἀξιώσῃ τῆς κλήσεως ὁ Θεὸς ἡμῶν καὶ πληρώσῃ πᾶσαν εὐδοκίαν ἀγαθωσύνης καὶ ἔργον πίστεως ἐν

which it is there associated (κοπιῶ) gives the prep. a somewhat stronger and more definite meaning. **καὶ προσευχόμεθα**] '*we also pray;*' beside merely longing or merely directing your hopes, we also avail ourselves of the definite accents of prayer, the καὶ *gently* contrasting the προσεύχ. with the infusion of the hope and expectation involved in the preceding words and especially echoed in the parenthetical member. On this use of καί, see notes *on Phil.* iv. 12, and on the use of περὶ with προσεύχ., see notes *on* 1 *Thess.* v. 25, and *on Col.* i. 3. **ἵνα ὑμᾶς κ. τ. λ.**] '*that God may count you worthy of your calling;*' subject of the prayer blended with the purpose of making it; ἵνα having here, as not uncommonly in this combination, its secondary and weakened force; comp. Col. iv. 3, 1 Thess. iv. 1, and notes *on Eph.* i. 17, and *on Phil.* i. 9. The verb ἀξιοῦν occurs a few times in the N. T. (Luke vii. 7, 1 Tim. v. 17, Heb. iii. 3, al.), and regularly in the sense of '*esteeming* or counting ἄξιος' ('dignari,' Vulg., Clarom.), not of *making* so (comp. Syr. ܢܫܘܐܟܘܢ, Copt., al.), a meaning not lexically demonstrable; compare Rost u. Palm, *Lex.* s. v. The context is urged by Olsh., on the ground that the call had been already received: κλῆσις, however, though really the initial act (comp. 1 Thess. ii. 12), includes the Christian course which follows (Eph. iv. 1), and its issues in blessedness hereafter; κλῆσιν οὖν ἐνταῦθα λέγει τὴν διὰ τῶν πράξεων βεβαιουμένην, ἥτις καὶ κυρίως κλῆσις ἐστι, Theoph., see notes *on Phil.* iii. 14, and comp. Reuss, *Théol Chrét.* IV. 15, Vol. II. p. 145. **πληρώσῃ πᾶσαν κ. τ. λ.**] '*fulfil, bring to completion, every good pleasure of goodness;*' 'ut expleat omnem dulcedinem honestatis, h. e. ut plenam et perfectam, quâ recreemini, honestatem vobis impertiat,' Fritz, *Rom.* x. 1, Vol. II. p. 372, note. The meaning of these words is not perfectly clear. The familiar use of εὐδοκεῖν, εὐδοκία, in ref. to God (Eph. i. 5, 9, Phil. ii. 13), suggests a similar reference in the present case (Œcum., in part Theoph., Beng., al.); to this, however, there is (1) the exegetical objection, that ἀγαθωσύνη, though occurring 4 times in St. Paul's Epp. (Rom. xv. 14, Gal. v. 22, Eph. v. 9), is never applied to God, and (2) the more grave contextual objection, that the second member ἔργον πίστεως, equally undefined by any pronoun, certainly refers to those whom the apostle is addressing. It seems safest then to refer the present member to *the Thessal.;* εὐδοκία marking the good pleasure they evinced, and the defining gen. ἀγαθωσύνης (gen. *objecti*, Krüger, *Sprachl.* § 47. 7. 1, — not of *apposition*, Alf.) the element in which it was so manifested, or more exactly, the object to which the action implied in the derivative subst. was especially directed; see Scheuerl. *Synt.* § 17. 1, p. 126. The attempt to refer the expression partly to God and partly to the Thessal. (Olsh., comp. Theoph.), or to regard the operation of the believer and that of the Spirit as blended and confused (Jowett), is in a high degree precarious and unsatisfactory. On the meaning of εὐδοκία, see the good note of Fritz. *Rom.* x. 1, Vol. II. p. 369 sq., and on the meaning of ἀγαθωσύνη (moral goodness) and its distinction from ἀγαθότης, notes *on Gal.* v. 22. **ἔργον πίστεως**] '*the work of faith,*' the work which is the distinctive feature of it; ἔργον being that which marks, characterizes, and evinces the vitality of the πίστις, almost 'the activity of faith,' not, however, merely as

δυνάμει, 12 ὅπως ἐνδοξασθῇ τὸ ὄνομα τοῦ Κυρίου ἡμῶν Ἰησοῦ ἐν ὑμῖν καὶ ὑμεῖς ἐν αὐτῷ, κατὰ τὴν χάριν τοῦ Θεοῦ ἡμῶν καὶ Κυρίου Ἰησοῦ Χριστοῦ.

τὴν ὑπομονὴν τῶν διωγμῶν, Theoph., but ὑπομονὴν as exhibited in the various circumstances of Christian life and duty. On the exact meaning and construction of these words, see notes *on* 1 *Thess.* i. 3, and comp. Reuss, *Théol. Chrét.* IV. 19, Vol. II. p. 205. ἐν δυνάμει] '*with power*,' *i. e.* powerfully,—specification of manner annexed to the verb πληρώσῃ, with which it is associated with a practically adverbial force; compare Rom. i. 4, Col. i. 29, and see Bernhardy, *Synt.* v. 7, p. 209. The analogous use of σὺν (comp. Scheuerl. *Synt.* § 22. b, p. 180) is appy. not found in the N. T.

12. ὅπως ἐνδοξασθῇ] '*in order that the name of etc., be glorified;*' reiteration of the *purpose* (not merely *result*, ἐνδοξασθήσεται, Theoph.), stated generally in verse 10, in special reference to the converts of Thessalonica. It is not easy to state the exact difference between the present use of ὅπως (used comparatively rarely by St. Paul; only six times excluding quotations), and the corresponding one of ἵνα. To speak somewhat roughly, it may be perhaps said that the relatival compound ὅπως (Donalds. *Cratyl.* § 196) involves some obscure reference to *manner*, while ἵνα (appy. connected with the reflexive ἵ, or the pronoun of the second person, comp. Donaldson *Cratyl.* § 139) may retain some tinge of its primary reference to locality. The real, practical differences, however, are these, (*a*) that ὅπως has often more of an *eventual* aspect; (*b*) that it is used with the future and occasionally associated with ἄν,—both which constructions are inadmissible with the *final* ἵνα; see Klotz, *Devar.* Vol. II. p. 629, 630. τὸ ὄνομα τοῦ Κυρ.] is not a mere periphrasis for ὁ Κύριος, but specifies that character and personality as revealed to, and acknowledged by men; comp., but with caution, Bretschn. *Lex.* s. v. ὄνομ. 6, p. 291, and comp. *on Phil.* ii. 10. The assertion of Jowett *in loc.*, that these words have 'no specific meaning,' cannot be sustained, and is language in every way to be regretted.

The addition Χριστοῦ (*Rec.*, [*Lachm.*], with AFG; mss.; many Vv.; Chrys.) is rightly rejected by *Tisch.* with BDE KL; majority of mss.; Clarom., Sangerm., Copt., Sahid., al.; Theod. (ms.), Œcum., al. ἐν αὐτῷ) '*in Him*'; not in reference to ὄνομα τοῦ Κυρ. (Lünem.), but to the immediately preceding Ἰησοῦ. The exact notion of reciprocity (comp. *on Gal.* vi. 14) would be best maintained by the former reference; but, as Alf. correctly observes, the present expression is used far too frequently and exclusively in ref. to union in our Lord *Himself*, to justify any change in the present application of the words.

κατὰ τὴν χάριν] '*in accordance with the grace;*' the χάρις is the 'norma' according to which the glorification took place, and thence, by an intelligible transition, that to which it is to be referred as a *consequence*; ἡ χάρις αὐτοῦ δι' ἡμῶν πάντα κατορθοῖ, Œcum.; comp. notes *on Phil.* ii. 3, and *on Tit.* iii. 5.

τοῦ Θεοῦ ἡμῶν κ. τ. λ.] This is one of the passages supposed to fall under Granville Sharpe's rule (compare Middl. *Gr. Art.* p. 56, ed. Rose), according to which Θεὸς and Κύριος would refer to the same person. Is may be justly doubted, however, owing to the peculiar nature of Κύριος (Winer, *Gr.* § 19. 1, p. 113), whether this can be sustained in the present case; see esp. Middleton, p. 379 sq., and comp. Green, *Gram.* p. 216.

Be not disquieted concerning the Lord's coming. The Man of Sin, as ye know, must first be revealed; and then shall be destroyed by the Lord.

II. Ἐρωτῶμεν δὲ ὑμᾶς, ἀδελφοί, ὑπὲρ τῆς
παρουσίας τοῦ Κυρίου ἡμῶν Ἰησοῦ Χριστοῦ
καὶ ἡμῶν ἐπισυναγωγῆς ἐπ' αὐτόν, 2 εἰς τὸ μὴ

CHAPTER II. 1. Ἐρωτῶμεν δέ] '*Now we beseech you;*' transition, by means of the δὲ μεταβατικόν (see *on Gal.* iii. 8), from the apostle's prayers for his converts to what he claims of them, and the course of conduct he exhorts them to follow. On the meaning of ἐρωτᾶν, see notes *on* 1 *Thess.* iv. 1. ὑπὲρ is here certainly not introductory of a formula of adjuration (Vulg., perhaps Æth. [*baenta,*—often so used], Beza, al.), as such a meaning, though grammatically tenable (Bernhardy, *Synt.* v. 21, p. 244,—partially, but appy., without full reason, objected to by Winer), is by no means exegetically probable, and is without precedent in the language of the N. T. The more natural interpretation is to regard the prep. as approximating in meaning to περί (Winer, *Gr.* § 47. 1, p. 343; comp. Krüger, *Sprachl.* § 68. 28. 3), but still distinct from it, as involving some trace of the idea of benefit to, or furtherance of, the παρουσία; see notes *on Phil.* ii. 13, and comp. Wordsw. *h. l.* The subject of the παρουσία had been misunderstood and misinterpreted, and its *commodum* was what the apostle wished to promote. ἡμῶν ἐπισυν. ἐπ' αὐτόν] '*our gathering together unto Him,*' scil. in the clouds of heaven, and when he comes to judge the quick and dead; see 1 Thess. iv. 17, and compare Matth. xxiv. 31, Mark xiii. 27. The subst. ἐπισυναγωγή only occurs once again in the N. T. (Heb x. 25), in ref. to Christian worship (comp. 2 Macc. ii. 7), and seems confined to later writers. The meaning assigned by Hammond, 'the greater liberty of the Christians to assemble to the service of Christ, the greater freedom of ecclesiastical assemblies,' is due to his reference of the present παρουσία τοῦ Κυρίου to God's judgment on the Jews. The relation of the two Epp. seems totally to preclude such a reference: if in 1 Thess. iv. 15 the words refer to the final day of doom (Hammond), the allusion here must certainly be the same.

ἐπ' αὐτόν] '*unto Him;*' comp. Mark v. 21, συνήχθη ὄχλος πολὺς ἐπ' αὐτόν; the preposition marking the point to which the συναγωγή was directed, and losing its idea of superposition in that of approximation to or juxtaposition; compare Donalds. *Cratyl.* § 172. The difference between the present usage and that of πρὸς in the same combination is perhaps no more than this, that while πρὸς points more to the *direction* to be taken, ἐπὶ marks more the *point* to be reached.

2. εἰς τὸ μὴ κ. τ. λ.] '*that ye should not be soon shaken,*' 'ut non cito moveamini,' Vulg., Clarom.; object and aim of the ἐρωτᾶν, with perhaps some included reference to the subject of it; compare 1 Thess. iii. 10, and notes *on* 1 *Thess.* ii. 12. The verb σαλεύω, as its derivation shows [σάλος, connected with ΣΑΛ-, and with Sanscr. form *sal*, Benfey, *Wurzellex.* Vol. I. p. 61], marks that agitated and disquieted state of mind, which, in the present case, was due to wild spiritual anticipations: comp. Acts xvii. 13, and see exx. in Elsner, *Obs.* Vol. II. p. 283. The ταχέως does not seem to refer to the period since St. Paul's presence with them, or to the date of the First Epistle, but simply to the time when they might happen to hear of it; the reference being rather *modal* ('præcipitanter,' De W.) than purely temporal; 'si id crederent facili momento quassaretur ipsorum fides,' Coc-

ταχέως σαλευθῆναι ὑμᾶς ἀπὸ τοῦ νοὸς μηδὲ θροεῖσθαι, μήτε διὰ πνεύματος μήτε διὰ λόγου μήτε δι' ἐπιστολῆς ὡς δι' ἡμῶν, ὡς ὅτι

ceius. ἀπὸ τοῦ νοός] *'from your mind,'* 'a vestro sensu,' Vulg.; certainly not 'a sententiâ seu doctrinâ,' Est., but simply 'statu mentis solito,' Schott I, — their ordinary, sober, and normal state of mind, παρατραπῆναι ἀπὸ τοῦ νοὸς, ὃν μέχρι τοῦ νῦν εἴχετε ὀρθῶς ἱστάμενον, Theoph.; comp. xiv. 5, and Beck, *Seelenl.* § 18. 1, p. 51. The construction is what is usually termed *prægnans,* scil. 'ita concuti ut demovearis,' Schott; comp. Rom. vi. 7, ix. 3, 2 Tim. iv. 18, al., and Winer, *Gr.* § 66. 2, p. 547. The reading is scarcely doubtful; DE, several Vv. and some Ff. supply ὑμῶν, but this seems obviously only introduced to make clear the reference and meaning of νοός. μηδὲ θροεῖσθαι] *'nor yet be troubled;'* stronger expression than the foregoing, introduced by the slightly ascensive μηδέ; see notes *on* 1 *Thess.* ii. 3 (*Transl.*). The verb θροέω [derived from ΘΡΕΟΜΑΙ, and connected with τρέω; comp. Donalds. *Cratyl.* § 272] properly implies 'clamorem tumultuantem edere' (Schott), and thence, by a natural transition, that *terrified* state (ταραχίζεσθαι, Zonaras), which is associated with, and gives rise to, such kind of outward manifestations. In later writers, μὴ θροηθῇς comes to mean little more than μὴ θαυμάσῃς, Lobeck, *Phryn.* p. 676. The reading of *Rec* μήτε [with D³EKL; several Ff.] is rightly rejected by *Lachm.* and *Tisch.* on the preponderating external authority ABD¹F (four times μηδὲ) G; Orig. This adjunctive negative was probably suggested by the following μήτε, the true relation of the negatives not having been properly understood. μήτε διὰ πνεύματος] *'neither by spirit;'* scil. of prophecy; διὰ προφητείας· τινὲς γὰρ προφητείαν ὑποκρινόμενοι ἐπλάνων τὸν λαόν, ὡς ἤδη παρόντος τοῦ Κυρίου, Theoph. The second negation is here, by means of the three times repeated μήτε, divided into three members; see exx. and illustrations in Winer, *Gram.* § 55. 6, p. 437, where the distinctive character of μηδὲ and μήτε, their meaning, and sequence are well delineated. μήτε διὰ λόγου may be either regarded, (*a*) as an independent member distinguished both from what precedes and follows, or (*b*) may be connected more closely with the third negative member, both being associated with ὡς δι' ἡμῶν. In the former case, λόγου forms a species of antithesis to πνεύματος as denoting oral teaching, less marked by supernatural or prophetic characteristics (διδασκαλίας ζώσῃ φωνῇ γενομένης, Theoph.); in the latter the λόγου is in antithesis to ἐπιστολῆς, as marking what the apostle had communicated by word of mouth, in contradistinction to what he had written; μὴ πιστεύειν . . . . . μήτε εἰ πλασάμενοι ὡς ἐξ αὐτοῦ γραφεῖσαν ἐπιστολὴν προφέροιεν, μήτε εἰ ἀγράφως αὐτὸν εἰρηκέναι λέγοιεν, Theodos. Of these (*b*) seems slightly the most probable, especially as λόγος and ἐπιστολὴ are found similarly combined in v. 15. To extend ὡς δι' ἡμῶν to the first clause, either partially (Jowett), or completely (Nösselt), seems illogical; oral or written communications might be ascribed to the absent apostle, but the πνεῦμα could only have been recognized working in him (De W.) when he was with them; comp. Lünem. *in loc.*

ὡς δι' ἡμῶν] *'as by us,'* represented to come from us as its *mediate* authors; the ὡς as usual marking the erroneous *aspects* under which the λόγος or ἐπιστολὴ was designed to be regarded: 'particula ὡς substantivis, participiis, totisque enuntiationibus præposita, rei veritate sublatâ, aliquid *opinione, errore, simulatione* niti declarat,' Fritz. *Rom.* ix. 32, Vol. II. p.

ἐνέστηκεν ἡ ἡμέρα τοῦ Κυρίου. 3 μή τις ὑμᾶς ἐξαπατήσῃ κατὰ
μηδένα τρόπον· ὅτι ἐὰν μὴ ἔλθῃ ἡ ἀποστασία πρῶτον καὶ ἀποκα-

360, compare notes *on Eph.* v. 22. It seems impossible to understand these words otherwise, especially when coupled with the notice in ch. iii. 17, than as implying that not only oral but *written* communications, definitely ascribed to St. Paul, were not only conceived (Jowett) but actually *known* by the apostle to have been lately circulated in the Church of Thess.: καὶ γὰρ καὶ ἐπιστολὰς πλάττοντες ὡς παρὰ Παύλου σταλείσας ἐκύρουν ἃ ἔλεγον, Theoph., compare Neander, *Planting*, Vol. I. p. 204 (Bohn). When we consider the extreme disquietude and anxieties that appear to have prevailed in the Church of Thessal. in ref. to the παρουσία τοῦ Κυρίου, there appears nothing strange in the supposition, that even within a less time than a year since the apostle had last written, fictitious letters should have obtained currency among them. To refer the expression with Hammond, al., to portions of the First Epistle which had been misunderstood, seems distinctly to infringe on the simple meaning of ὡς δι' ἡμῶν.

ὡς ὅτι ἐνέστ. κ. τ. λ.] '*as that, to the effect that, the day of the Lord is now commencing, already come;*' subject of the pretended communication introduced by ὡς, which, as before, represents the statement not as actual, but *as so represented*, as the notion which was designed to be propagated; see Winer, *Gr.* § 65. 9, p. 544, Meyer *on* 2 *Cor.* xi. 21, and exx. in Kypke, *Observ.* Vol. II. p. 268. The verb ἐνέστηκεν is somewhat stronger than ἐφέστ (2 Tim. iv. 6), and seems to mark, not only the nearness but the actual presence and *commencement* of the ἡμέρα τοῦ Κυρίου; 'magna hoc verbo propinquitas significatur; nam ἐνεστὼς [Rom. viii. 38, 1 Cor. iii. 22] est *præsens*,' Beng. comp. notes *on Gal.* i. 4, Hammond *in loc.* and see the numerous exx. in Rost u. Palm, *Lex.* s. v. Vol. I. p. 929. The ἡμέρα τοῦ Κυρ. thus approximates in meaning to παρουσία τοῦ Κυρ., and like it includes, beside the exact epoch of the Lord's appearance, the course of events immediately preceding and connected with it; comp. Reuss, *Théol. Chrét.* IV. 21, Vol. II. p. 230, 243.

3. μή τις ὑμᾶς ἐξαπ.] '*Let no one deceive you in any way;*' not only in any of the three ways before specified (Theoph., Œcum.), but, with a more completely inclusive reference,—*in any way*, or by any artifice whatever; πάντα κατὰ ταὐτὸν τὰ τῆς ἀπάτης ἐξέβαλεν εἴδη, Theod. On the form ἐξαπατᾶν, comp. notes *on* 1 *Tim.* ii. 14.

ὅτι ἐὰν μὴ ἔλθῃ] '*because (the day will not arrive) unless there come;*' slight grammatical irregularity owing to the omission of a member involving the finite verb, οὐ γενήσεται ἡ παρουσία τοῦ Κυρ., Theoph., or ἡ ἡμέρα οὐκ ἐνστήσεται, which can easily be supplied by the reader; see Winer, *Gr.* § 64. 7, p 528, comp. Donalds. *Gr.* § 583. β, note. The most natural punctuation seems, not a comma before ὅτι as in *Lachm.*, *Tisch.*, *Buttm.*, but a colon, as in *Mill*, and as suggested by Lünemann.

ἡ ἀποστασία] '*the falling away*,' the definite religious apostasy that shall precede the coming of Antichrist, and of which it is not improbable that the apostle had informed them by word of mouth; see ver. 5, and comp. Green, *Gram.* p. 155. It is hardly necessary to say that ἀποστασία is not an abstract for a concrete term (αὐτὸν καλεῖ τὸν ἀντίχριστον ἀποστασίαν, Chrys.; so Theod., Theoph., Œcum. 1), nor again a political (Nösselt), or politico-religious (Kern) falling away, whether past or future, but simply, in accordance with the appy. regular use of the word (Acts xxi. 21, compare

λυφθῇ ὁ ἄνθρωπος τῆς ἁμαρτίας, ὁ υἱὸς τῆς ἀπωλείας, 4 ὁ ἀντι-

2 Chron. xxix. 19, 1 Macc. ii. 15), that *religious* and *spiritual* apostasy ('diabolicam apostasiam,' Iren. *Hær.* v. 25. 1), that falling away from faith in Christ (ἀπὸ Θεοῦ ἀναχώρησιν, Œcum.), of which the revelation of Antichrist shall be the concluding and most appalling phenomenon; comp. Luke xviii. 8. The paulo-post future view, according to which the ἀποστασία refers to the revolt of the Jews from the Romans (Schoettg. *Hor. Hebr.* Vol. I. p. 840), is thus opposed to the appy. technical meaning of the word, while that of Hammond, who mainly refers it to the lapse to Gnosticism, fails to exhibit its generic reference, and to exhaust its prophetic significance.

On the form of the word ἀποστ. (a later form for ἀπόστασις), see Lobeck, *Phryn.* p. 528. ἀποκαλυφθῇ] '*be revealed*,'— a very noticeable expression: as the Lord's coming is characterized as an ἀποκάλυψις (ch. i. 7), so is that of Antichrist. Even as he is now spiritually present in His Church, to be personally revealed more gloriously hereafter, even so the power of Antichrist is now secretly at work, but will hereafter be made manifest in a definite and distinctive bodily personality. The καὶ has here appy. its *consecutive* force (see *on* 1 *Thess.* iv. 1); the revelation of Antichrist was the aggravated issue and accumulated outcoming of the ἀποστασία. ὁ ἄνθρ. τῆς ἁμαρτίας] '*the man of Sin*,' the fearful child of man (obs. the distinct term ἄνθρ.) of whom Sin is the special characteristic and attribute, and in whom it is as it were impersonated and incarnate; ἄνθρωπον δὲ αὐτὸν ἁμαρτίας προσηγόρευσεν, ἐπειδὴ ἄνθ. ἐστι τὴν φύσιν, πᾶσαν ἐν ἑαυτῷ τοῦ διαβόλου δεχόμενος τὴν ἐνέργειαν, Theod. On this gen. of the 'predominating quality,' which is commonly classed under the general head of the *gen. possessivus*, see Scheuerlein, *Synt.* § 16. 3, p. 115, Winer, *Gr.* § 34. 3. b, p. 211, 213. ὁ υἱὸς τῆς ἀπωλ.] '*the son of perdition*;' he who stands in the sort of relation to it that a son does to a father, and who falls under its power and domination, 'cujus finis est interitus [Phil. iii. 19],' Cocceius; see John xvii. 12, where this awful term is applied to Judas, and comp. *Evang. Nicod.* cap. 20, where it is applied to Satan; see Thilo, p. 708. The transitive (Pelt), or mixed trans. and intransitive meaning (ὡς καὶ αὐτὸς ἀπολλύμενος καὶ ἑτέροις πρόξενος τούτου γινόμενος, Theod. comp. Œcum.) seems appy. phraseologically doubtful; comp. Winer, *Gr.* § 34. 3. b, p. 213, and notes *on* 1 *Thess.* v. 5.

4. ὁ ἀντικείμενος] '*he that opposeth*,' '*the adversary*,' ܗܘ ܕܣܩܘܒܠܐ ܗܘ [qui adversarius est] Syr., comp. Copt., Æth.; participial substantive defining more nearly the characteristics of Antichrist; comp. Winer, *Gr.* § 45. 7, p. 316. The adversary, though assimilating one of the distinctive features of Satan (שָׂטָן), is clearly not to be confounded with him whose agent and emissary he is (ver. 9), but, in accordance with the almost uniform tradition of the ancient Church, is *Antichrist*,— no mere set of principles ('vis spiritualis evangelio contraria,' Pelt) or succession of opponents (Jowett, comp. Middleton, *Gr. Art.* p. 383, and Wordsw. *in loc.*), but one single personal being, as truly man as He whom he impiously opposes; τίς δὲ οὗτός ἐστιν; ἆρα ὁ σατανᾶς· οὐδαμῶς. ἀλλ' ἄνθρωπός τις πᾶσαν αὐτοῦ δεχόμενος τὴν ἐνέργειαν, Chrys., see Wieseler, *Chronol.* p. 261, Hofmann, *Schriftb.* II. 2, Vol. II. p. 617. The patristic references will be found in the Excursus of Lünem. p. 204, and at length in Alford, *Prolegom.* p. 56. The object of the opposition (ἀντι-), it

κείμενος καὶ ὑπεραιρόμενος ἐπὶ πάντα λεγόμενον Θεὸν ἢ σέβασμα,

need scarcely be said, can be none other than *Christ*,— He whose blessed name is involved in the more distinctive title (ἀντίχριστος) of the adversary, and to whom that son of perdition, as Origen well says, is κατὰ διάμετρον ἐναντίος, *contra Cels.* VI. 64. The present grammatical connection, which (see above) is as old as Syr., is rightly adopted by De W., Lünem., and most modern commentators: the absence of the art., urged by Pelt, only shows that the ὑπεραιρόμενος ἐπὶ πάντα κ. τ. λ. is not a different person from the ἀντικείμενος, but by no means specifies that both are to be united in connection with ἐπὶ πάντα κ. τ. λ.; comp. Winer, *Gr.* § 19. 4, 5, p. 116, 117. In a case like the present, the article really performs a kind of double duty; it serves to turn ἀντικ. into a substantive, and also indicates that the two participles refer to the same individual.

καὶ ὑπεραιρόμ. κ. τ. λ.] '*and (who) exalteth himself above (and against) every one called God*,' scil. every one so called, whether 'eum qui verissime dicitur Deus' (Schott), or those esteemed so by the heathen; the participle being prefixed to avoid seeming to place on a level or include in a common designation—τὸν Θεὸν and the so-called gods of paganism; comp. 1 Cor. viii. 5, λεγόμενοι θεοί, Eph. ii. 11. The verb ὑπεραιρ. occurs twice in 2 Cor. xii. 7, and serves to mark the haughty exaltation (ὑψωθήσεται καὶ μεγαλυνθήσεται ἐπί πάντα θεόν, καὶ λαλήσει ὑπέρογκα, Dan. xi. 36), while ἐπὶ with its general local meaning ('supra,' Vulg., 'ufar,' Goth.) of 'motion with a view to superposition' (Donalds. *Gr.* § 483), involves the more specific and ethical one of opposition: comp. Matth. x. 21, and Winer, *Gr.* § 49. 1, p. 363 sq.

ἐπὶ πάντα λεγόμ. Θεόν] This characteristic of impious exaltation is in such striking parallelism with that ascribed by Daniel to 'the king that shall do according to his will' (ch. xi. 36), that we can scarcely doubt that the ancient interpreters were right in referring both to the same person,— Antichrist. The former portion of the prophecy in Daniel is appy. correctly referred to Antiochus Epiphanes, but the concluding verses (ver. 36 sq.) seem only applicable to him of whom Antiochus was merely a type and shadow; comp. Jerome *on Dan.* xi. 21, and see Prideaux, *Connection*, Part II. Book 3 (*ad fin.*). If this be correct, we may be justified in believing that other types of Antichrist may have appeared, and may yet appear, before that fearful being finally come. If asked to name them, we shrink not from pointing to this prophecy, and saying, that in whomsoever these distinctive features be found,— whosoever wields temporal, or temporal and spiritual power, in any degree similar to that in which the Man of Sin is here described as wielding it,— he, be he pope or potentate, is beyond all doubt a distinct type of Antichrist. From such comparisons the wisest and most catholic writers have not deemed it right to shrink; see Andrewes, *Serm.* VI. Vol. IV. p. 146 sq., and compare the reff. at the end of Wordsworth's long and important note on this passage.

ἢ σέβασμα] '*or (that is) an object of worship*,' scil. of divine worship,— an expansion of the preceding πάντα λεγόμενον Θεόν. The special interpretation of Bengel, founded on the connection of σέβασμα and σεβαστός, 'Cæsaris majestas et potestas Romæ maxime conspicua,' is wholly at variance with the prevailing use of the word (Acts xvii. 23, Wisdom xiv. 20, xv. 17, Bel 27, see Suicer, *Thesaur.* s. v. Vol. II. p. 942), and still more so with the generic terms of the prophecy.

ὥστε αὐτὸν καθ.] '*so that he sitteth down*;' his arrogance

ὥστε αὐτὸν εἰς τὸν ναὸν τοῦ Θεοῦ καθίσαι, ἀποδεικνύντα ἑαυτὸν ὅτι ἐστὶν Θεός. 5 Οὐ μνημονεύετε ὅτι ἔτι ὢν πρὸς ὑμᾶς ταῦτα

rises to such an impious height as to lead to this uttermost act of unholy daring; 'ὥστε minus hic consilium quam sequelam innuere videtur,' Pelt. The verb καθίσαι is here not transitive (1 Cor. vi. 4, Eph. i. 20), but in accordance with its nearly regular usage in the N. T, *intransitive;* comp. Thom.-Mag. p. 486 (ed. Bern.). The pronoun is thus not reflexive (Grot.), but is introduced and placed prominently forward to mark the individualizing arrogance ('hic ipse, qui quævis sancta et divina contemnit,' Schott) of this impious intruder. The interpolation ὡς (FG[1] ἵνα) Θεόν, adopted by *Rec.* with D[3]EFGKL; mss.; Syr. (Philox with an asterisk), Ar. (Polygl.); Chrys., al., is rightly rejected by *Lachm.*, *Tisch.*, with ABD[1]; 10 mss.; Clarom., Vulg., Goth.(?), Copt., Sah., Æth., Armenian; Origen (3), and many Ff. Though the uncial testimony is strong for the insertion, the authority of Vv. and Ff. is weak, and the probability of an explanatory gloss here very great.

εἰς τὸν ναὸν τοῦ Θεοῦ] '*in the temple of God;*' literally 'into,' with the not uncommon pregnant force of the preposition in connection with ἵζειν, καθέζεσθαι κ. τ. λ.; comp. Winer, *Gr.* § 50. 4, p. 368 sq., Buttm. *Mid.* p. 175. The exact meaning of these words has been greatly contested. Is it (*a*) merely a figurative or metaphorical expression (1 Cor. iii. 17, comp. Eph. ii. 21) for the Church of Christ, τὰς πανταχοῦ ἐκκλησίας (Chrys.), according to the views of most of the interpreters of the fourth century? Or is it (*b*) the actual temple of God at Jerusalem (Matth. xxvi. 61), which prophecy seems to declare shall be restored (Ezek. xxxvii. 26; see Todd *on Antichr.* p. 218), as proposed by Irenæus (*Hær.* v. 30. 4), and as adopted, though with varying modes of explanation, by the majority of recent German commentators? If called upon to decide absolutely, the *combination* (opp. to Alf.) of local terms and the possibly traditional nature of the interpr. of Irenæus must decidedly sway us to (*b*). It may be asked, however, in so wide a prophecy, whether we are wise in positively excluding (*a*). May it not be possible that a haughty judicial or dictatorial session in the Church of Christ may be succeeded by and culminate in a literal act of ineffable presumption, to which the present words may more immediately, though not exclusively, refer? Combined, or partially combined, interpretations are ever to be regarded with suspicion, but in a *prophecy* of this profound nature they appear to have some claim on our attention.

ἀποδεικνύντα κ. τ. λ.] '*exhibiting himself that he is God;*' not merely 'a god,' Copt., or even 'tanquam sit Deus,' Vulg. (compare Syr), but ܕܐܠܗܐ ܗܘ [quod sit Deus] Syr.-Philox.,—with a studied reference to the execrable assumption of an unconditioned glory, dignity, and independence, which will characterize the God-opposing session of the son of perdition: so, with an effective *paraphrase*, Æth., 'et dicet omnibus, Ego sum Deus.' The participle thus does not mark the 'conatus' (πειρώμενον ἀποδεικνύναι, Chrys.,—this it must be from the nature of the case,—but the continuing nature of the act, the impious *persistence* of this developed outcoming of frightful and intolerable selfishness; see Müller *on Sin*, Book I. 3. 2, Vol. I. p. 145, comp. Book V. Vol. II. p. 480 (Clark). For examples of this use of ἀποδεικνύναι, see Loesner, *Obs.* p. 384, and for the force of the compound ἀποδ. ('spectandum aliquid proponere'), Winer, *de Verb. Comp.* IV. p. 16.

5. Οὐ μνημονεύετε] '*Remember ye not;*' emphatic, reminding them, with

ἔλεγον ὑμῖν; 6 καὶ νῦν τὸ κατέχον οἴδατε, εἰς τὸ ἀποκαλυφθῆναι
αὐτὸν ἐν τῷ ἑαυτοῦ καιρῷ. 7 τὸ γὰρ μυστήριον ἤδη ἐνεργεῖται

some degree of implied blame, of the definite oral communications which had been made to them during the apostle's first visit; ἰδοὺ γὰρ καὶ παρόντος ἤκουσαν ταῦτα λέγοντος, καὶ πάλιν ἐδεήθησαν ὑπομνήσεως, Chrys. πρὸς ὑμᾶς] '*with you;*' so 1 Thess. iii. 4. On this combination of πρὸς with the acc. and verbs implying rest, see notes *on Gal.* i. 8, iv. 18. The ταῦτα is clearly the substance of the two preceding verses.

6. καὶ νῦν τὸ κατέχ. οἴδ.] '*and now what restraineth ye know.*' The difficulty of these words is twofold, (1) *lexical*, turning on the meaning of νῦν, (2) *exegetical*, in reference to the explanation that is to be given of τὸ κατέχον. With regard to the first, the temporal particle subsequently connected with ὁ κατέχων (ver. 7), and the preceding ἔτι (ver. 5), both seem decidedly to suggest the *temporal* use of νῦν (Wieseler, *Chronol.* p. 259 note; the order of the words, however, and the context seem so very distinctly in favor of the *logical* use (Hartung, *Partik.* νῦν, 2. 2, Vol. II. p. 25, see notes *on* 1 *Thess.* iii. 8), that on the whole that meaning is to be preferred; see esp. Lünem. *in loc.* who has brought appy. valid arguments against the temporal meaning. Properly to investigate (2) would far outstrip the limits of this commentary. It may be said, however, briefly,—that after most anxious consideration, a modification of the current patristic view seems much the most plausible. The majority of these early writers referred the restraining influence to the Roman Empire, 'quis nisi Romanus status,' Tertull. *de Resurr.* cap. 24: so Chrys., Theoph., Œcum., Cyril of Jerusalem, al. In its literal meaning, this cannot now be sustained without artificial and unhistorical assumptions; if, however, we refer the τὸ κατέχον to what really formed the groundwork of that interpretation,—the restraining power of *well-ordered human rule*, the principles of *legality* as opposed to those of ἀνομία,—of which the Roman Empire was the then embodiment and manifestation, we shall probably not be far from the real meaning of the very mysterious expression. Of the numerous other views, we may notice the opinion of Theod. and Theod.-Mops., that the τὸ κατέχον is ὁ τοῦ Θεοῦ ὅρος, as certainly being at first sight plausible; but to this, the ἕως ἐκ μέσου γένηται introduces an objection that seems positively insuperable. Further information will be found in the Excursus of Pelt (who, however, adopts the view of Theod.), p. 185 sq., in the thoughtful note of Olsh., the discussion of Lünem. p. 204 sq., the useful summary of Alford, *Prolegom.* p. 55 sq., and the good note of Wordsw. *in loc.*; comp. also Hofmann, *Schriftb.* II. 2, Vol. II. p. 613 sq. εἰς τὸ ἀποκαλ.] '*that he should be revealed;*' purpose contemplated in the existence of the restraining principle. This ἀποκάλυψις was not to be immediate (οὐκ εἶπεν ὅτι ταχέως ἔσται, Chrys.), or fortuitous, but was to be deferred till the ὁ ἑαυτοῦ καιρός,—the season appointed and ordained by God. On the (correct) insertion of ἐν, see notes *on Ephes.* ii. 12

7. τὸ γὰρ μυστήρ.] '*For the mystery of lawlessness;*' confirmatory explanation of the preceding statement: the mystery of iniquity, it is true, is at work; but its full manifestation cannot take place till the removal of the restraining power. On this sort of mixed explanatory and argumentative force of γάρ, see notes *on Gal.* iv. 22. The meaning of μυστήριον τῆς ἀνομ. is somewhat doubtful. Considered merely grammatically, the gen. does not seem to be that of the *agent* (Theod.), or that of

τῆς ἀνομίας, μόνον ὁ κατέχων ἄρτι ἕως ἐκ μέσου γένηται·

*apposition* (Lünem., and Alford,—who, however, seems to mix it up with a gen. *continentis*), but simply a gen. *definitivus* (comp. Madvig, *Synt.* § 49) or gen. of the 'characterizing principle or quality' (Scheuerl. *Synt.*) 16. 3, p. 115), — the mystery, of which the characterizing feature, or, so to say, the *active principle*, was ἀνομία; comp. Joseph. *Bell. Jud.* I. 24. 1, τὸν Ἀντιπάτρου βίον οὐκ ἂν ἁμάρτοι τις εἰπὼν κακίας μυστήριον. The transition from this gen. to that of (ethical) *content* is so easy and natural, that it is often difficult to decide whether the gen. belongs to that category or that of the possess. gen.; see Scheuerl. *l. c.* The genitival relation of μυστήρ. τῆς εὐσεβείας is often somewhat plausibly contrasted with the present expression (Andrewes, *Serm.* III. Vol. I. 34), but seems really different; see notes *on* 1 *Tim.* iii. 9. This mystery of ἀνομία is no personality, scil. Antichrist, or any real or assumed type of Antichrist (Νέρωνα ἐνταῦθά φησιν, Chrys.), but all that mass of uncombined, and so to say, unorganized ἀνομία, which, though at present seen only in detail and not *revealed* in its true proportions, is even now (ἤδη) aggregating and energizing, and will hereafter (ἐν τῷ ἑαυτοῦ καιρῷ) find its complete development and organization in the person and power of Antichrist. On the meaning of μυστήριον, — here placed emphatically forward as in tacit antithesis to ἀποκαλυφθ. ver. 6, 8, — see notes *on Ephes.* v. 32, and comp. Sanderson, Serm. IX. (ad Aul.), Vol. I. p. 227 (ed. Jacobs.).

ἀνομίας] '*lawlessness;*' in appropriate and illustrative antithesis to the principle of order and legality involved in the apparent meaning of τὸ κατέχον. On the meaning of ἀνομία ('in quâ cogitatur potissimum legem non servari,' Tittm.) and its distinction from ἀδικία, see Tittm. *Synon.* I, p. 48, and compare notes *on Tit.* ii. 14.

ἐνεργεῖται] '*is working,*' 'operatur,' Vulg., ܫܪܝ ܠܡܬܥܒܕܘ [incipit efficax esse] Syr. comp. Æth.; clearly not passive, 'efficax redditur' Schott), which would not only be here inappropriate, but in opposition to the prevailing use of the word in the N. T.; see notes *on Gal.* v. 6, and on the different constructions of the word, notes *on ib.* ii. 8.

μόνον ὁ κατέχων κ. τ. λ.] '*only until he that now restraineth shall be removed;*' rhetorical change of the usual order; see exx. in Winer, *Gr.* § 61. 3, p. 405 (ed. 6), and comp. Gal. ii. 10, μόνον τῶν πτωχῶν ἵνα μνημονεύωμεν, where the emphatic words are similarly attached to the semi-elliptical μόνον. As, however, in Gal. *l. c*, so here, it is not necessary to supply definitely any verb to complete the ellipsis ('tantum ut qui tenet nunc teneat,' Vulg., comp. Auth.), still less to connect μόνον with what precedes (Kypke, *Obs.* Vol. II. p. 342). The μόνον belongs to ἕως, and simply states the limitation involved in the present working of the μυστήριον τῆς ἀνομίας: it is working already, but only with unconcentrated action until the obstacle be removed, and Antichrist be revealed. So rightly as to structure, Chrys., ἡ ἀρχὴ ἡ Ῥωμαϊκὴ ὅταν ἀρθῇ ἐκ μέσου, τότε ἐκεῖνος ἥξει. The only other plausible structure is the supplement of ἐστι, but the objection of Lünem., that a word in the present case of such real importance could scarcely be omitted, seems reasonable and valid. The greatest difficulty is, however, the change of gender in the designation of the restraining principle. Perhaps the simplest view is to regard it, not as a studied designation of a single individual (*e. g.* St. Paul, Schott, p. 249), or of a collection of such

8 καὶ τότε ἀποκαλυφθήσεται ὁ ἄνομος, ὃν ὁ Κύριος Ἰησοῦς ἀνα-
λώσει τῷ πνεύματι τοῦ στόματος αὐτοῦ καὶ καταργήσει τῇ ἐπιφα-

8. ὁ Κύριος Ἰησ.] So *Lachm.* and *Tisch.* ed. 1, 7, with $AD^1E^1FGL^2$; 10 mss.; Syr. (both), Vulg., Clarom., Copt, Æth. (both), Arm.; Orig., Hippol., Ath., al.; Tertull., Hieron. (*Scholz, Lünem., Alf., Wordsw.*). In his second ed., *Tisch.* omitted Ἰησοῦς with $BD^3E^2KL^1$; great majority of mss.; Arab (Polygl.); Orig. (1), Maced., Cyr. (Hieros.), Theod. (1), al.; Vig. (*Rec.*), — authority of some weight, but decidedly inferior to that in favor of the insertion. He now rightly reverts to the better-attested reading.

(*e. g.* the saints at Jerusalem, Wieseler, *Chronol.* p. 273, or, more plausibly, the succession of Roman emperors, Wordsworth), but merely as a *realistic* touch, by which what was previously expressed by the more abstract τὸ κατέχον is now, as it were, represented as concrete and personified; comp. Rom. xiii. 4, where the personification is somewhat similarly introduced after, and elicited from a foregoing abstract term (ἐξουσίαν). ἄρτι is to be closely connected with ὁ κατέχων, and simply refers to time regarded as present *to the writer.* On the derivation and meaning of the word, see notes *on* 1 *Thess.* iii. 6. ἕως ἐκ μέσου γένηται] On this connection of ἕως with the subjunctive without ἄν, — a construction especially characteristic of later writers, see Winer, *Gr.* § 41. 3, p. 266. The distinction acutely drawn by Herm. (*de Partic.* ἄν, II. 9, p. 109) between such formulæ as μίμνετε ἕως θάνω (de moribundo) and ἕως ἂν θάνω (de eo qui non ita propinquam sibi putaret mortem esse), and repeated by Klotz (*Devar* Vol. II. p. 568), cannot with safety be applied in the N. T.; nor can we with distinct probability ascribe the omission of ἂν to any idea of design supposed to be involved in the sentence, as suggested by Green, *Gram.* p. 64, note. We have only an instance of that obliteration of finer shades of distinction which characterizes the later and decadent Greek. The phrase ἐκ μέσου γίγνεσθαι is illustrated by Wetstein and Kypke (*Obs.* Vol. II. p. 343); it indicates the removal of any obstacle, of anything ἐν μέσῳ ὂν (Xenoph. *Cyrop.* v. 2. 26, cited by Lünemann), leaving the manner of the removal wholly undefined; comp. ἀρθῇ (*Lachm., Tisch*) ἐκ μέσου, 1 Cor. v. 2, Isaiah lvii. 2.

8. καὶ τότε] '*and* THEN,'—*then* when ὁ κατέχων shall have been removed; the primary emphasis clearly falling on the particle of time, the secondary and subordinate on ἀποκαλυφθήσεται. ὁ ἄνομος] '*the lawless one;*' identical with the foregoing ὁ ἄνθρωπος τῆς ἁμαρτ., the changed designation serving appropriately to echo the preceding term (ἀνομία), which defines more nearly the evil principle that the Man of Sin will especially develop; '*Exlex ille,* qui nullis legum vinculis coerceri vult, sed omnia jura divina et humana suo ipsius arbitrio subjicit,' Vorst, ap. Pol. *Syn.* ὃν ὁ Κύριος κ. τ. λ.] '*whom the Lord Jesus shall consume with the breath of his mouth:*' relative sentence describing, with a consolatory glance forward to the final issue, the ultimate fate of Antichrist; καὶ τί μετὰ ταῦτα; ἐγγὺς ἡ παραμυθία· ἐπάγει γάρ, ὃν ὁ Κύριος κ. τ. λ., Chrys. The forcible expression τῷ πνεύμ. τοῦ στόμ. has received different explanations. It has been referred (*a*) by the Greek commentators to the words of power (φθέγξεται μόνον, Chrys.; comp. Theod., Theodosius-Mops., al.) issuing from the

νείᾳ τῆς παρουσίας αὐτοῦ, 9 οὗ ἐστιν ἡ παρουσία κατ' ἐνέργειαν
τοῦ Σατανᾶ ἐν πάσῃ δυνάμει καὶ σημείοις καὶ τέρασιν ψεύδους,

Lord's lips; (*b*) by Athan. (*ad Serap.* I. 6, p. 655), Theoph. 2, al., to the Holy Spirit; but is most simply regarded, (*c*) as a vivid declaration of the glorious and invincible power of the coming Lord, 'cui sufficiat halitus oris quo ἄνομος ille perdatur,' Schott; comp. Isaiah xi. 4 (of which these words may have been a partial reminiscence), Wisdom xi. 20, and the pertinent quotations from Rabbinical writers collected by Wetst. *in loc.*: on the word καταργέω, comp. notes *on Gal.* v. 4. The reading is doubtful: ἀναλεῖ is adopted by *Lachm.* with ABD[1]? (FG; 67* ἀνέλοι); above ten mss.; Orig. 1, Hippol., Maced., but is suspicious as a possible conformation to Isaiah xi. 4. We retain therefore ἀναλώσει [D[3]EKL; great majority of mss.; Origen (1), Basil (1), Theod. (2), al.] with *Rec.*, *Tisch.*, (ed. 2, 7), and most recent commentators.

τῇ ἐπιφανείᾳ τῆς παρ.] '*with the manifestation of His coming;*' not with a semi-theological reference to the *glorious* manifestation ('illustratione,' Vulgate, 'brightness,' Auth.-Ver., 'vi salutari,' Kypke, *Obs.* Vol. II. p. 343) of Christ at His second coming (comp. notes *on* 1 *Tim.* vi. 14, and *on Tit.* ii. 3, where τῆς δόξης is definitely added), but with simple reference to His visible coming ('aspectu adventus sui,' Clarom., Æth.) and actual local appearing; στήσει τὴν ἀπάτην καὶ φανεὶς μόνον, Chrys., Theoph.

9. οὗ ἐστιν ἡ παρουσία] Return to the time and subject of Antichrist's coming, after the anticipatory allusion to his final overthrow; the οὗ resuming and re-echoing the ὃν of verse 8. The (ethical) present ἐστὶν marks the certainty of the future event; see Winer, *Gr.* § 40. 2, p. 237, Bernhardy, *Synt.* x. 2. p. 371. κατ' ἐνέργ. τοῦ Σατ.] '*according to the working of Satan;*' 'not here in consequence of' (De W., comp. notes on ch. i. 12), but, in accordance with the more usual force of κατά, 'in agreement and correspondence with' an ἐνέργεια such as belongs to, and might be looked for from Satan; comp. notes *on Eph.* i. 19, and *on Col.* i. 29. ἐν πάσῃ δυνάμ. κ. τ. λ.] '*in all power and signs and wonders of falsehood,*'—in every form of (see notes *on Eph.* i. 8) power, signs, and wonders, leading to and tending to develop ψεῦδος: ἐν being no 'nota dativi' (Olsh.), but marking the *sphere* and *domain* of this [ἀντι]παρουσία (comp. *on* 1 *Thess.* i. 5), and both πάσῃ (comp. Winer, *Gr.* § 59. 5, p. 466) and the gen. being associated with all the three substantives. The exact nature of the genitival relation is not perfectly certain: ψεύδους may be regarded as (*a*) a gen. of the *origin*, (*b*) of the *characterizing quality* or essence (see notes on ver. 7), or lastly, (*c*) of 'the point in view' (Scheuerl. *Synt.* § 18, p. 129). Of these (*a*) is by no means probable; but between (*b*) and (*c*) it is very difficult to decide. Perhaps the object specified in ver. 11, and the analogy of ἀπάτη ἀδικίας (ver. 10), scil. 'fraus quæ ad improbitatem spectat' (Schott I, Winer, *Gr.* § 30. 2, p. 170), may here incline us to the latter; so Chrys. 2, εἰς ψεῦδος ἄγουσι. For exx. of these more lax connections of the gen., see Winer, *Gr.* § 30. 2. β, p. 169. The three substantives might seem to be climactic; it was not only in an element of power (see *on* 1 *Thess.* i. 5), but one of signs, and further, one of prodigies, that the working of Satan took place; as, however, we find a varied order (Acts ii. 22), and as the difference between σημεῖα ('res insolitas quibus Deus *aliquid significet*,' Fritz.) and τέρατα ('quæ ut inusitata *observari* soleant,' *ib.*) is less in

10 καὶ ἐν πάσῃ ἀπάτῃ ἀδικίας τοῖς ἀπολλυμένοις, ἀνθ' ὧν τὴν

the things themselves than in the mode of regarding them, we may perhaps most naturally consider the substantives as studiedly accumulated, so as to give force and expansion to the description.; comp. Bornemann, *Schol. in Luc.* p. xxx. On the meaning of the last two words, and the derivation of τέρας [τηρέω, comp. Benfey. *Wurzellex.* Vol. II. p. 238], see the elaborate note of Fritz. *Rom.* xv. 19, Vol. III. p. 270. The form σημεῖον appears closely connected with σῆμα (θηματ-), and thence with ΘΕΩ, τίθημι; see Pott, *Etym. Forsch.* Vol. II. p. 592.

10. καὶ ἐν πάσῃ κ. τ. λ.] '*and in all (kind of) deceit of iniquity;*' generic and comprehensive term appended by the collective καὶ to the foregoing list of more special details; comp. Winer, *Gr.* § 53. 3, p. 388, and notes *on Phil.* iv. 12. On the genitival relation, see above, ver. 9, and Winer, *Gr.* § 30. 2, p. 170, and on the meaning of ἀδικία ('de quâcunque improbitate dicitur, quatenus τῷ δικαίῳ repugnat,' Tittm.), notes *on* 2 *Tim.* ii. 19. The addition of the art. [*Rec.* with DEKL; mss.; Hippolitus, Chrysost., Theod.] is rejected by *Lachm.*, *Tisch.* on the higher authority of ABFG; mss.; Orig. (6), Cyr.-Hieros.

τοῖς ἀπολλυμένοις] '*for those that are perishing;*' dat. *incommodi*, belonging to the general head of the dative of *interest;* see Krüger, *Sprachl.* § 48. 4. The more exactly specifying τοῖς ἀπολλ. has no reference to any 'decretum reprobationis' (comp. even Pelt, 'damnationi a Deo devoti'), but either like ἐστὶν marks the certainty of the event ('qui certissime sunt perituri,' Turretin), or perhaps, more simply, with merely a temporal parallelism, points to those who 'are perishing' at the time in contemplation,—not too without reference to the present existence (comp. ver. 7) of such a class (1 Cor. i. 18, 2 Cor. ii. 15, iv. 3), of which those here specified will be the continuance and development. The consolatory nature of the tacit limitation is not overlooked by the Greek commentators; μὴ φοβηθῇς ἀγαπητέ, ἀλλ' ἄκουε λέγοντος αὐτοῦ· ἐν τοῖς ἀπολλ. ἰσχύει, οἵ, εἰ καὶ μὴ παρεγένετο ἐκεῖνος, οὐκ ἂν ἐπείσθησαν, Chrys. The reading is somewhat doubtful: ἐν is prefixed by *Rec.* with D[3]EKL; mss.; Syr. (both); Orig. (1), al., but is rightly rejected by *Lachm.*, *Tisch.*, both with preponderant external authority [ABD[1]FG; Vulgate, Clarom., Copt., Æth. (both), Sah., al.; Orig. (5), Cyr.-Hieros., Iren.], and as a probable interpolation to remove a supposed difficulty of construction.

ἀνθ' ὧν] '*for that,*' 'in requital for which' (τί οὖν τὸ κέρδος, Chrys.), Luke i. 20, xii. 3, xix. 44, Acts xii. 23, comp. Lev. xxiv. 20; explanatory statement of the cause of the judicial dispensation of God, and of the justness and deservedness of their punishment. On this meaning of ἀνθ' ὧν ('propterea quod'), see Herm. *Viger*, No. 33, Winer, *Gr.* § 48. a, p. 326, and for exx. see the list collected by Wetst. *on Luke* i. 20, and Raphel, *Annot.* Vol. I. p. 442.

τὴν ἀγάπην τῆς ἀληθ.] '*the love of the truth;*' not charitatem veram,' Anselm (cited by Corn. a Lap.), but 'the love felt for the truth,' 'dilectionem veritatis,' Pseud.-Ambr.,—ἀληθ. not being a gen. of *quality*, but the simple and common gen. *objecti;* comp. Winer, *Gr.* § 30, p. 167, Krüger, *Sprachl.* § 47. 7. 1 sq. It seems somewhat perverse in Jowett to deny that this implies any higher degree of alienation from the truth than the less distinctive οὐκ ἐδέξαντο τὴν ἀλήθ.; surely it is one thing not to receive the truth,—an unhappy state that might be referable to a mental obliquity for which some excuse might be found,—and another to receive *no*

ἀγάπην τῆς ἀληθείας οὐκ ἐδέξαντο εἰς τὸ σωθῆναι αὐτούς. 11 καὶ
διὰ τοῦτο πέμπει αὐτοῖς ὁ Θεὸς ἐνέργειαν πλάνης, εἰς τὸ πιστεῦσαι
αὐτοὺς τῷ ψεύδει, 12 ἵνα κριθῶσιν πάντες οἱ μὴ πιστεύσαντες
τῇ ἀληθείᾳ ἀλλ' εὐδοκήσαντες ἐν τῇ ἀδικίᾳ.

*love* of it, to be open to no desire to seek it, to be worse than indifferent to it; 'ubi veritas summopere amabilis, ibi se quodammodo amor veritatis insinuat,' Cocceius. The prosopopœia (ἀγάπην ἀληθ. τὸν Κύριον κέκληκεν) adopted by Theod., Theoph., and Œcum., is artificial, and unsupported by analogy.

εἰς τὸ σωθῆναι] '*that they might be saved;*' object that would have been naturally contemplated in their reception of it; and which was negatived and disregarded by the contrary course; 'non ita sibi chari fuerunt ut cogitarent de vitâ æternâ,' Cocceius.

11. καὶ διὰ τοῦτο] '*And for this cause;*' almost 'so for this cause,' καὶ serving to mark the correspondence between the judgments and the course of conduct that had provoked them, and perhaps involving partly a consecutive, and partly a contrasting force; compare notes *on Phil.* iv. 12.

πέμπει] '*doth send;* not so much an ethical (see ver. 9) as a direct present; the mystery of iniquity is even *now* at work (ver. 7), and is even now calling down on itself the punishment of judicial obduracy. There is no need for explaining away πέμπει (συγχωρήσει φανῆναι τὴν πλάνην, Theod., compare Theod.-Mops., Theoph., Œcum.), nor is it right merely to ascribe it to a form of thought in the age of the apostle (Jowett), nor enough to say merely that 'whatever God permits He ordains,' Alford. The words are definite and significant; they point to that 'judicial infatuation' (Waterl. *Serm.* Vol. v. p. 486,— differently, however, Vol. IV. p. 363) into which, in the development of His just government of the world, God causes evil and error to be unfolded, and which He brings into punitive agency in the case of all obstinate and truth-hating rejection of His offers and calls of mercy; comp. Müller, *Doctr. of Sin*, Book v. Vol. I. p. 471 (Clark), and see two able Sermons on this text by South, *Serm.* Vol. II. p. 192—228. The reading πέμψει [*Rec.* with D[3]EKL; mss.; majority of Vv., and many Ff.] is rightly rejected by most modern editors, being inferior in uncial authority to πέμπει [ABD[1]FG: 67; Amit., Orig. (3) al.], and a correction of it that would easily suggest itself.

ἐνέργειαν πλάνης] '*an (effective) working of delusion;*' not πλάνην ἔνεργον, Œcum.,— here a most questionable solution of the governing subst. (see Winer, *Gr.* § 34. 3, p. 211), but, in accordance with δυνάμει κ. τ. λ. ψεύδους, of which ἐνέργ. πλάνης is a kind of summary,— 'a working which tends to enhance and develop πλάνη,' the gen. being (as in verse 9) that of 'the point of view;' τὰ ἔργα ἃ ποιεῖ ['Αντίχρ.] εἰς τὸ πλανῆσαι, Theophilus. On the meaning of πλάνη ('error,' Vulg.), see notes *on* 1 *Thess.* ii. 3, and *on Eph.* iv. 14.

εἰς τὸ πιστεῦσαι κ. τ. λ] '*to the intent that they should believe the lie,*' scil. the falsehood implied in the preceding words οὗ ἐστὶν—ἀδικίας (Green, *Gram.* p. 141), not falsehood generally, as Middl. *Gr. Art.* p. 383 (ed. Rose); clause stating the purpose of God ('non meram sequelam,' Schott), in His judicial act of sending to them the ἐνέργ. πλάνης. He sends a power of a nature designed to work out the appointed issue, and to bring about a state which involves its own chastisement. On the force of εἰς τὸ in sentences similar to the present, see Meyer *on Rom.* i. 20.

12. ἵνα κριθῶσιν πάντες] '*that*

**We ought to thank God that He hath chosen and called you. Hold what we delivered unto you; and may God stablish you.**

13 Ἡμεῖς δὲ ὀφείλομεν εὐχαριστεῖν τῷ Θεῷ
πάντοτε περὶ ὑμῶν, ἀδελφοὶ ἠγαπημένοι ὑπὸ
Κυρίου, ὅτι εἵλατο ὑμᾶς ὁ Θεὸς ἀπ' ἀρχῆς εἰς

*they may all be judged;*' more remote *purpose* involved in the preceding words εἰς τὸ πιστεῦσαι κ. τ. λ, with which this clause seems more naturally in connection than directly with the preceding πέμπει. The preceding εἰς τὸ κ. τ. λ. renders a reference to *result* ('quo fiet, ut,' Schott) here distinctly untenable. It need scarcely be said that κριθῶσιν is not *per se* 'might be damned,' Auth. (ἵνα κατακριθῶσι, Chrys.), but simply 'might be judged,' 'judicentur,' Vulg., the further idea of an unfavorable judgment being supplied by the *context;* compare κρῖμα, 1 *Tim.* iii. 6, and see notes *in loc.* The reading is doubtful: *Tischend.* reads ἅπαντες with AFG; mss.; Orig. (2), Cyr.: *Rec.* and *Lachm.* adopt πάντες with BDEL; mss.; Orig. (1), many Ff. The evidence for the latter reading seems preponderant. εὐδοκήσαντες ἐν τῇ ἀδικ.] '*took pleasure in unrighteousness.*' On the meaning of εὐδοκεῖν ('re aut personâ delectari,' Fritz.), compare notes *on* 1 *Thess.* ii. 8, but see esp. the elaborate note of Fritz. *Rom.* x. 1, Vol. II. p. 369 sq. The reading is not quite certain; ἐν is retained by *Rec.* and *Tisch.* ed. 2, 7 [with AD³EKL; great majority of mss.; Syr. (both), Copt., Æth. (both), al.; Orig. (2), Chrys., Theod.], but rejected by *Lachm., Tisch.* ed. 1 [with BD¹FG; 7 mss.; Vulgate, Clarom., Sahid.; Origen (2) Hippolitus, al.], — appy. however, with less probability, as the construction with the simple dat. is not found in the N. T., and as the omission of the particle may here have been easily suggested by a desire to preserve a parallelism of clauses.

13. Ἡμεῖς δέ] '*But we,*' scil. the apostle and his companions, Silvanus and Timothy (ch. i. 1), not St. Paul alone (Jowett),—placed by means of the oppositive δὲ in contrast with those alluded to in the foregoing verses. ὀφείλομεν] '*are bound,*' Auth., 'oportet,' Copt. [*sempsha*]; the verb ὀφείλειν, as in ch. i. 3, expressing the duty on its *subjective* side, 'das innerlich Gedrungenfühlen,' Lünem. On the connection of εὐχαριστεῖν with περί, and on the meaning of the verb, see notes and reff. *on* 1 *Thess.* i. 2. ἀδελφοὶ κ. τ. λ.] So, similarly, 1 Thess. i. 4, ἀδελφοὶ ἠγαπημένοι ὑπὸ Θεοῦ,—except that Κυρίου here, as nearly always in St. Paul's Epp., refers to our Lord, not to God the Father. Though *love*, as Alf. remarks, is in this sort of collocation somewhat more usually referred by St. Paul to the First Person of the blessed Trinity (ver. 16, Eph. ii. 4, al.), yet such references to the Second Person are by no means without precedent; comp. Rom. viii. 37, Eph. v. 2, 25. ὅτι εἵλατο ὑμᾶς] '*that He chose you;*' objective sentence ('quod,' Vulg., ?, Syr.), stating the matter and grounds, surely not 'the reason,' Alf. (comp. Æth., Auth.) of the εὐχαριστία; see 1 Thess. ii. 13, 1 Cor. i. 14, and on objective sentences generally, or as they are sometimes termed, 'expositive' sentences, consult Schmalfeld, *Synt.* § 163 sq., Donalds. *Gr.* § 584 sq. The verb αἱρεῖσθαι is an ἅπ. λεγόμ. in St. Paul's Epp. in reference to the divine ἐκλογή, the more regular term being ἐκλέγεσθαι (1 Cor. i. 27, 28, Eph. i. 4); comp. 1 Thess. i. 4, and Reuss, *Théol. Chrét.* IV. 14, Vol. II. p. 133 sq. The Alexandrian form εἵλατο (see Lobeck, *Phryn.* p. 183) is rightly adopted by *Lachm., Tisch.*, and most modern editors, with greatly preponderating authority [ABDEFGL; mss.; Theodos. (ms.)]. On these forms in the N. T.,

σωτηρίαν ἐν ἁγιασμῷ Πνεύματος καὶ πίστει ἀληθείας,
14 εἰς ὃ
ἐκάλεσεν ὑμᾶς διὰ τοῦ εὐαγγελίου ἡμῶν, εἰς περιποίησιν δόξης τοῦ

see *Tisch. Prolegom* p. lvi. (ed. 7), and the somewhat opposing comments of Scrivener, *Introd. to N. T.* VIII. 6, p. 416. ἀπ' ἀρχῆς] '*from the beginning*,' scil. of all things, 'from eternity; so 1 John i. 1, ii. 13, but not elsewhere in St. Paul's Epp., where the more distinctive formulæ ἀπὸ καταβολῆς κόσμου (Eph. i. 4), πρὸ τῶν αἰώνων (1 Cor. ii. 7), πρὸ χρόνων αἰωνίων (2 Tim. i. 9), and more restrictedly, ἀπὸ τῶν αἰώνων (Eph. iii. 9), are used to express the same or a similar idea. The reference to the beginning of the gospel-preaching (Michaelis, al.) is rightly rejected by Schott and Lünem., as requiring some supplement, either immediately connected with ἀρχή (Phil. iv. 15), or obviously involved in the context (1 John ii. 7, 24). Finally, the reading ἀπαρχὴν (*Lachm.*, *Tischend.* I) has fair external support [BFG; mss.; Vulg.], but is so distinctly inferior in external authority to ἀπ' ἀρχῆς [ADEKL; nearly all mss. and Vv.; Gr. and Lat. Ff.], and involves such a tacit opposition to actual history (the Thessalonians were *not* the first believers in Macedonia), that we can here scarcely hesitate in our choice.

ἐν ἁγιασμῷ Πνεύματος] '*in sanctification of the Spirit*,' scil. wrought by, and affected by the Spirit; Πνεύματος being the gen. of the *causa efficiens* (see notes *on* 1 *Thess.* i. 6), and referring not to man's spirit (Schott), but to the personal Holy Spirit. No argument can be founded on the omission of the article, as in the first place such omissions are not rare with Πνεῦμα, and secondly, it might here be due to the common principle of correlation; comp. Middl. *Gr. Art.* III. 3. 7, p. 49 (ed. Rose]. The prep. ἐν *may* be instrumental (Chrysost., Lünem., al.), but is perhaps more naturally taken in its usual sense as denoting the spiritual state *in* which the εἵλατο εἰς σωτηρίαν was realized; see Winer, *Gr.* § 50. 5, p. 370, who, in ed. 5, refers it less exactly to σωτηρία. The assumption of De Wette, that ἐν is here equivalent to εἰς, is well refuted by Lünem., who justly urges the obscuring effect this would have on the preceding εἰς σωτηρίαν.

πίστει ἀληθείας] '*belief in the truth*;' ἀληθείας not being a gen. of quality (πίστεως ἀληθοῦς, Chrys.), but simply the gen. *objecti*, see Winer, *Gr.* § 30. 1, p. 167, and comp Phil. i. 27.

14. εἰς ὅ] '*whereunto*,' scil. εἰς σωτηρίαν ἐν ἁγιασμῷ κ. τ. λ., not 'ad electionem atque animum quo eâdem digni evadimus' (Pelt), as the historical ἐκάλεσεν naturally stands in connection, not with the election which had taken place ἀπ' ἀρχῆς, but with those issues contemplated by the εἵλατο, which had their commencements in *time*. So rightly Theoph., εἰς τοῦτο γὰρ ἐκάλεσεν ὑμᾶς, φησιν, εἰς τοῦτο; ποῖον εἰς τὸ σωθῆναι διὰ (?) τοῦ ἁγιασμοῦ καὶ τῆς πίστεως. The reading of *Lachm.*, ἐκάλεσεν ἡμᾶς, has the support of ABD[1]; a few mss.; Clarom., Sangerm., and,— as ὑμᾶς *might* have been a conformation to the preceding ὑμᾶς,— is *plausible* but hardly sufficiently supported by external authority to be admitted with confidence.

διὰ τοῦ εὐαγγ. ἡμῶν] '*by means of our Gospel*,' scil. 'the Gospel we preached,' that which involved the ἀκοὴν which is the antecedent of πίστις; comp. Rom. x. 17, and Usteri, *Lehrb.* II. 2. 2, p. 267. On the exact genitival relation of ἡμῶν, see notes *on* 1 *Thess.* i. 5.

εἰς περιποίησιν δόξης] '*to the obtaining of the glory of our Lord J. C.*,' 'in acquisitionem gloriæ,' Vulg., Coptic, comp. Æth. 'ut vivatis in gloriâ Domini;' more exact specification of the preceding εἰς σωτηρίαν (ver. 13), the term

Κυρίου ἡμῶν Ἰησοῦ Χριστοῦ. 15 ἄρα οὖν, ἀδελφοί, στήκετε, καὶ
κρατεῖτε τὰς παραδόσεις ἃς ἐδιδάχθητε εἴτε διὰ λόγου εἴτε δι'

περιποίησις giving the σωτηρία the aspect of a κτῆσις (Hesych., Suid.), and that of a glory of which Christ was — not the *author* (Pelt), but, in accordance with the analogy of Scripture — the Lord and *possessor;* see John xvii. 24, comp. Rom. viii. 17. See esp. notes *on* 1 *Thess.* v. 9, where this meaning of περιπ. is briefly investigated. Of the two other interpretations of περιπ.,— (*a*) active, with reference to God, scil. ἵνα δόξαν περιποιήσῃ τῷ υἱῷ αὐτοῦ, Œcum.; and (*b*) passive (comp. Eph. i. 14), δόξης being resolved into an adj., scil. 'gloriosa possessio,' Est. 2,— the first is grammatically, the second contextually doubtful. In the case of (*a*) we must have had the usual dative of 'interest,' not (as here) a gen. of possession; in the case of (*b*) the seeming parallelism with 1 Thess. v. 9 would be destroyed, and the object of the καλεῖν would really become the glorification of our Lord (so expressly Syr.

ܕܬܗܘܘܢ ܫܘܒܚܐ ܠܡܪܢ

[ut gloria sitis Domino]), not the future reserved for the Thess. on which the illative exhortation of v. 15 (ἄρα οὖν seems logically to depend; comp. Lünem. *in loc.*

15. ἄρα οὖν κ. τ. λ.] '*Accordingly then, brethren, stand* (*firm*);' exhortation following on the preceding declaration of the gracious purpose of God, — the illative ἄρα being supported by the collective οὖν; see notes *on Galat.* vi. 10, and references *on* 1 *Thessalonians* v. 6. On the present derivative meaning of στήκετε (*per*state, Beza, μὴ καταβλῆθετε, Œcum.; compare 1 Thess. v. 8), here suitably used in retrospective antithesis to σαλευθῆναι (ver. 2), see notes *on Phil.* i. 27. This verb, as has before been noticed, only occurs in St. Paul's Epp. (7 times) and in Mark xi. 25. It occurs only once in the LXX, Exod. xiv. 13 (*Alex.*, *Complut.*). κρατεῖτε τὰς παραδόσεις] '*hold fast the instructions;*' practically synonymous with 1 Cor. xi. 2, τὰς παραδόσεις κατέχετε. These παραδόσεις (Mark vii. 3, Gal. i. 14, al.) probably related, — not, as in 1 Cor. *l. c.* (see Meyer *in loc.*), to matters both of doctrine *and* discipline, but, as the more specific ἐδιδάχθητε and the general tenor of the context (comp. ver. 5) suggest, solely to the former, κανόνα διδασκαλίας, Theod. The polemical and controversial use of the term, hinted at even by Chrysostom, is brought forward by Damasc. (*de Imag.* I. 23, Vol. I. p. 518, Paris, 1712), and enforced by most writers of the Rom. Church (comp. *Canon. Conc. Trid.* Sess. IV. p. 15, ed. Tauchn.), but distinctly without plausibility. No reference to any ἐκκλησιαστικὸν φρόνημα Euseb. *Hist. Eccl.* v. 27; (comp. Möhler, *Symbolik*, § 38, p. 361) can fairly be elicited from the words. The apostle, as the following clause most distinctly shows, is referring to some definite and lately-given communications on the doctrine which he had specially made to the Thessalonians (comp. 1 Cor. *l. c.*, καθὼς παρέδωκα) by word of mouth and in his former letter. For the most ingenious modern defence of the Romanist doctrine of tradition, see Möhler, *Symbolik*, *l. c.* p. 361—365. ἃς ἐδιδάχθητε] '*which ye were taught.*' For examples of this well-known construction, see Winer, *Gr.* § 32. 5, p. 204, and for the general theory of the connection of the accus. with the passive verbs, Schmalfeld, *Syntax*, § 25, p. 29 sq.

εἴτε διὰ λόγου κ. κ. λ.] '*whether by word or by our epistle,*'— ἐπιστολῆ ἡμῶν (gen. *auctoris*), not an ἐπιστολὴ ὡς δι' ἡμῶν, ver. 2. We can hardly say with Gom. (cited and approved by Pelt, compare Schott) — 'εἴτε non disjungit, sed

ἐπιστολῆς ἡμῶν· 16 αὐτὸς δὲ ὁ Κύριος ἡμῶν Ἰησοῦς Χριστὸς
καὶ ὁ Θεὸς καὶ πατὴρ ἡμῶν, ὁ ἀγαπήσας ἡμᾶς καὶ δοὺς παράκλησιν

conjungit et copulat;' it rather subdivides the general ἐδιδάχθητε into the two special modes in which διδαχὴ is usually and regularly conveyed; comp. 1 Cor. xiii. 8, and Meyer *in loc.*

16. αὐτὸς δέ ὁ Κύρ.] '*but may our Lord Himself;*' concluding prayer (πάλιν εὐχὴ μετὰ παραίνεσιν· τοῦτο γάρ ἐστιν ὄντως βοηθεῖν, Chrys.) the δὲ contrasting the succeeding prayer with the foregoing exhortation, and the αὐτὸς giving force and dignity to the mention of our Lord as compared with the preceding ἡμῶν; comp. 1 Thess. iii. 11, v. 23, where, however, the connection is less close, and the contrasting force, both of the particle and the pronoun, somewhat less emphatic. Our Lord is probably put first in the enumeration (2 Cor. xiii. 13), contrary to the apostle's usual habit of writing, either on account of the recent mention of our Lord in ver. 14, or from the feeling that it was by His grace alone that they could have strength to carry into practice the preceding exhortations; 'per gratiam Christi venitur ad Patris amorem,' Bengel *on* 2 *Cor. l. c.* This unusual order is not left unnoticed by Chrys. and the Greek expositors; τῇ τῆς τάξεως ἐναλλαγῇ τὴν ὁμοτιμίαν δεικνύει, Theodor. The reading is somewhat doubtful. *Lachm.* inserts ὁ before Χριστός [with A], brackets it before Θεός [BD[1] omit], and puts it in the place of καὶ before πατήρ [with BD[1]FG; mss.; some Vv. and some Lat. Ff.]. In such cases of variation it is difficult to speak with precision, but, on the whole, the reading of the text (*Rec.*, *Tisch.*, Alf.) seems best attested. ὁ Θεὸς καὶ πατὴρ ἡμῶν] '*God and our Father.*' On the meaning of this august title, see notes *on Gal.* i. 4, and on the simply copulative force of καί, compare the observations in notes *on* 1 *Thess.* iii. 11. ὁ ἀγαπήσας κ. τ. λ. seems to refer only to God the Father. The union of Father and Son, esp. as shown by the subsequent singular verb, is confessedly so mystically close that it is difficult to speak with complete confidence (Alf., but see *ib.* on ver. 16), still the usual reff. of ἀγάπη to the Father (see on ver. 16) may incline us here to the more exclusive reference. The arbitrary ref. of the first of the two participles to Christ, and of the second to God the Father (Baum.-Crus.) is almost obviously untenable.

παράκλησιν αἰωνίαν] '*eternal consolation;*' not appy. with any specially qualitative reference to an ἐλπίδα τῶν μελλόντων (Chrysostom, Theoph.), but mainly in a *temporal* sense, in contrast to the transitory and fleeting nature of earthly joys (Olshausen): the ἐλπὶς τῶν μελλόντων is embodied in the ἐλπίδα ἀγαθήν, 'la perspective d'un heureux avenir,' Reuss, *Théol. Chrét.* IV. 9. Vol. II. p. 85; comp., though with a slightly different reference, τὴν μακαρίαν ἐλπίδα, Tit. ii. 13. ἐν χάριτι] '*in grace;*' adjunct of manner, not to both preceding participles (ἀγαπ. being more usually undefined, Rom. viii. 37, Gal. ii. 20, al.), but to δούς (Schott, and appy. Chrys., Œcum.), the ἐν, as usual, defining the sphere and element in which the love is evinced and the consolation vouchsafed. In cases like the present the line of demarcation between the above reference to ethical locality and the instrumental use (χάριτι, Chrys.) is really very shadowy. It can scarcely be doubted that such a use has arisen from the inclusive nature of the Aramaic ב, and it is well not to be unduly narrow in interpretation; still, in most of the expressions similar to the present there is a theological idea, — an idea of an *encompassing element* of grace and love, which it seems desirable to retain; comp. notes *on* 1 *Thess.* ii. 8.

αἰωνίαν καὶ ἐλπίδα ἀγαθὴν ἐν χάριτι, 17 παρακαλέσαι ὑμῶν τὰς καρδίας καὶ στηρίξαι ἐν παντὶ ἔργῳ καὶ λόγῳ ἀγαθῷ.

Finally, pray for the advance of the Lord's word, and for us. He will stablish you; and may He guide your hearts.

III. Τὸ λοιπόν, προσεύχεσθε, ἀδελφοί, περὶ ἡμῶν, ἵνα ὁ λόγος τοῦ Κυρίου τρέχῃ καὶ

17. παρακαλέσαι] '*comfort;*' opt. and sing., as in 1 Thess. iii. 11, where see notes. The apostle does not say merely ὑμᾶς, but ὑμῶν τὰς καρδίας (comp. Col. ii. 2); it was the καρδία, the seat of their feelings and affections (comp. notes *on* 1 *Tim.* i. 5, Beck, *Seelenl.* III. 24, p. 92 sq.), the καρδία that was so full of hope and fear about the future, that the apostle prayed might receive comfort. The meaning, ܢܒܝܐ [consoletur] Syr. (comp. Æth.), seems thus in the present case more suitable than 'exhortetur,' Vulg., as a translation of παρακαλέσαι; see notes *on* 1 *Thess.* v. 11. στηρίξαι] '*Establish* (*you*);' βεβαιῶσαι, ὥστε μὴ σαλεύεσθαι μηδὲ παρακλίνεσθαι, Chrys.; comp. 1 Thess. iii. 2. The obvious supplement ὑμᾶς is inserted by *Rec.* with D[3]E[2]KL; mss., but rightly rejected by *Lachm.* and *Tisch.* with very decidedly preponderating uncial authority. ἐν παντὶ ἔργῳ κ.τ.λ.] '*in every good work and word;*' both παντὶ and ἀγαθῷ being obviously connected with the two intervening substantives. The slightly unusual order [*Rec.*, however, λόγ. κ. ἔργ.,—but only with FGK; mss.] has apparently caused the Greek commentators (silet Theod.) to assign the doubtful meaning δόγματα to the simple word λόγῳ. This is by no means probable; the association with ἔργῳ (comp. Fritz. *Rom.* xv. 18, Vol. III. p. 268), and still more the inclusive παντί, seem both decisive for the ordinary meaning. It is singular that Chrys. (so Theoph.) should have here taken ἐν as instrumental; clearly the ἔργον καὶ λόγος is not the means *by* which, but the elements *in* which, the στηριγμὸς takes place.

CHAPTER III. 1. Τὸ λοιπόν] '*Finally,*' 'as to what remains to be said;' similar in meaning to λοιπόν (1 Thess. iv. 1), but owing to the article, slightly more specific. On the grammatical difference between this formula and the gen. τοῦ λοιποῦ, see notes *on Gal.* vi. 17. προσεύχεσθε περὶ ἡμῶν] '*pray for us;*' ἄνω αὐτὸς εὐξάμενος ὑπὲρ αὐτῶν νῦν αἰτεῖ εὐχὴν παρ' αὐτῶν, Œcum. On the formula προσεύχομαι περί, and its practical equivalence to προσεύχομαι ὑπέρ, see notes *on Col.* i. 3. ἵνα ὁ λόγος κ.τ.λ.] Subject of the prayer blended with the purpose of making it, as so often in St. Paul's Epp.; see notes *on Eph.* i. 17. This prayer of the apostle, as Chrys. has well observed, was not ἵνα μὴ κινδυνεύῃ (εἰς τοῦτο γὰρ ἔκειτο), but that his Lord's word (comp. 1 Thess. i. 8) might speed onward and be glorified. As ever, his prayer did not involve one single selfish element. τρέχῃ καὶ δοξάζηται] '*may have free course and be glorified;*' 'currat et clarificetur,' Vulg., *i. e.* may find no obstacles and hindrances (ἀκωλύτως συντρέχῃ, Theod., προκόπτῃ, Damasc.) in its onward course (contrast 2 Tim. ii. 9, δέδεται), and be manifested, felt, and acknowledged in its true power and glory by all; compare chap. i. 12, but not, as usually cited, Acts xiii. 48,—where, as De W. rightly observes, the word has a somewhat weaker force, more nearly approaching to 'laudare,' comp. Schneider on Xen. *Anab.* v. 9. 32. The middle force adopted by Pelt, 'laudem sibi paret,' is not supported by the usage of the N. T., nor is it at all accurate to say that ἀπὸ would have been more naturally used if the verb had been passive. If

δοξάζηται καθὼς καὶ πρὸς ὑμᾶς, [2] καὶ ἵνα ῥυσθῶμεν ἀπὸ τῶν ἀτόπων καὶ πονηρῶν ἀνθρώπων· οὐ γὰρ πάντων ἡ πίστις. [3] πισ-

any other prep. had been used, it would have been ὑπὸ (Matth. vi. 2, Luke iv. 15), or ἐν (John xvii. 10); πρός, however, is perfectly suitable, as denoting the locality reached where the glorification took place. On the use of πρὸς with verbs implying rest, etc., see notes *on Gal.* i. 18. καθὼς καὶ πρὸς ὑμᾶς] '*even as it is also with you;*' the καὶ gently contrasting them with others where a similar reception had taken place, and the clause 'tacitâ laude' (Est.) reminding them of their previous and present receptivity; comp. 1. Thess. i. 6 sq.

2. καὶ ἵνα ῥυσθῶμεν] '*and that we may be delivered,*' that we may by our freedom co-operate in this advance of God's word. To find here a mere shrinking of the flesh on the part of the apostle from the dangers that awaited him (Jowett), is to assign to the apostle a character that never belonged to him, and which such passages as Rom. xv. 31 (see only ver. 32, which shows the true reason) and 2 Cor. i. 8, *most certainly* do not substantiate. How much keener are the perceptions of the older commentators; διπλῆ μὲν ἡ αἴτησις εἶναι δοκεῖ, μία δὲ ὅμως ἐστί. τῶν γὰρ πονηρῶν ἀνθρώπων ἡττωμένων, ἀκωλύτως καὶ ὁ τοῦ κηρύγματος συντρέχει λόγος, Theod. τῶν ἀτόπων κ. τ. λ.] '*perverse and wicked men,*' or, in the more derivative sense of the term ἄτοπος,—'iniquis et malis hominibus,' Claromanus; compare Syriac ܒ̈ܝܫܐ ܘܥܘ̈ܠܐ [malorum et perversorum], where the order seems changed. The word ἄτοπος, frequently used by Plato, and in connection with καινός (*Rep.* III. p. 405 D), θαυμαστός (*Legg.* I. p. 646 B), and ἀήθης (*Tim.* p. 48 B, *Legg.* VII. p. 797 A), properly signifies ὁ μὴ ἔχων τόπον (Suid. s. v.), and thence derivatively, as the same lexicographer observes, κακός, μοχθηρός (see Bekker *Anecd.* p. 460, Hesych. πονηρός, αἰσχρός), with concomitant ideas of 'mischief,' etc., according to the context; comp. Acts xxviii. 6, Philo, *Leg. Alleg.* III. § 17, ἄτοπος λέγεται εἶναι ὁ φαῦλος, ἄτοπον δέ ἐστι κακὸν δύσθετον (Vol. I. p. 98, ed. Mang.), and the examples collected by Kypke, *Obs.* Vol. II. p. 145 sq. Who these men were is somewhat doubtful. The most natural supposition is, that they were perverse and fanatical Jews (not Christians, on account of what follows) at Corinth, who were then opposing the word of God and the apostle's ministry of it; comp. Acts xviii. 12 sq. and Wieseler, *Chronol.* p. 256. The remark of Tertullian seems to have ever been very true in reference to the early Church,—'synagogus Judæorum, fontes persecutionum,' *adv. Gnost. Scorp.* ch. 10. οὐ γὰρ πάντων ἡ πίστις] '*for the faith doth not pertain unto all men;*' reason for the foregoing clause, and the mention of those alluded to in it. The definite ἡ πίστις can here only refer to 'faith' in the Christian sense (τὸ πιστεῦσαι, Œcum.), and perhaps Syr. ܗܝ ܗܝܡܢܘܬܐ: the expansion of Schott, 'fides sincera et constans,' in contrast to false Christians (ψευδάδελφοι, Gal. ii. 4), seems inconsistent with the use of the simple unqualified substantive. For exx. of this not uncommon use of the possessive gen., see Krüger, *Sprachl.* § 47. 6. 8, and comp. Acts i. 7, Winer, *Gr.* § 30. 5, p. 176. Wetstein *in loc.* cites the well-known proverbial saying, οὐ παντὸς ἀνδρὸς ἐς Κόρινθον ἐσθ' ὁ πλοῦς, cited by Suidas s. vv. οὐ παντός, Vol. II. p. 1220 (ed. Bern.)

3. πιστὸς δέ κ. τ. λ.] '*But faithful is the Lord;*' antithesis to the member

τὸς δέ ἐστιν ὁ Κύριος, ὃς στηρίξει ὑμᾶς καὶ φυλάξει ἀπὸ τοῦ πονηροῦ. 4 πεποίθαμεν δὲ ἐν Κυρίῳ ἐφ' ὑμᾶς, ὅτι ἃ παραγγέλ-

immediately preceding, with a paronomasia, or rather play on the word, suggested by the preceding πίστις; comp. 2 Tim. ii. 13, and see exx. in Winer, *Gr.* § 68. 2, p. 561, where the distinction is drawn between simple paronomasia and a play on words (Wortspiel) where a fresh or slightly changed meaning is introduced. There seems no reason for departing, either here or verse 4, from the usual reference of ὁ Κύριος to the second person of the blessed Trinity; comp. notes on ch. ii. 13. The reading adopted by *Lachm.*, ὁ Θεός [AD[1]FG; Vulg. (not Amit.), Armen. (marg.); Latin Ff.], seems clearly a correction, and a conformation to the more usual formula, 1 Cor. i. 9, x. 13, 2 Cor. i. 18.

ὃς στηρίξει] *'who shall stablish you,'* not perhaps without a faint explanatory force in the relative, 'being one who will, etc.;' comp. notes *on* 1 *Tim.* ii. 4, and *on Col.* i. 25, 27. The form στηρίσει (found in B) is noticed by Winer, *Gr.* § 15, p. 82, and is not without analogy in Alexandrian Greek. ἀπὸ τοῦ πονηροῦ] *'from the Evil One.'* Here as elsewhere in the N. T., it is extremely doubtful whether τοῦ πονηροῦ refers to evil in the abstract (see Rom. xii. 9), or to the Evil One (1 John v. 18, compare Eph. vi. 16, and notes *in loc.*). The context alone must decide; and this in the present case, in spite of the reference to ch. ii. 17, στηρίξαι ἐν παντὶ ἔργῳ καὶ λόγῳ, urged by Lünem. and repeated by Alf., seems rather in favor of the masculine,—(1) in consequence of the seeming ref. to the Lord's prayer, where the Greek comm. (whose opinion in such points deserves full consideration) adopt the masc.,—and (2) from the tacit personal antithesis suggested by the preceding Κύριος. The ancient Vv., whose testimony would here have been of considerable importance, do not seem to afford us any *sure* indications of the view they adopted. The Syr., we may observe, uses the same word both here and 1 John v. 18, where the meaning is not doubtful.

4. πεποίθαμεν δὲ ἐν Κυρ] *'Yea, we have trust in the Lord;'* declaration of the apostle's trust in his converts,—the δὲ subjoining with a faint antithesis to the simple future just preceding ('ei quæ jam significata est, similis notio quodam modo opponitur,' Klotz, *Devar.* Vol. II. p. 361) the apostle's present trust and convictions, and paving the way for the exhortations in ver. 6 sq.; καὶ τοῦτο εἰς προτροπὴν αὐτῶν τέθεικεν, ἵνα μαθόντες οἵας ἔχει δόξας περὶ αὐτῶν τοῖς ἔργοις βεβαιώσωσι ταύτας, Theod. This πεποίθησις, as ever, was ἐν Κυρίῳ: it was not only a trust in His φιλανθρωπία (Chrys.), but a trust *in Him* as the blessed *sphere* and element in which alone it could be truly felt and entertained: see Phil. ii. 19, and notes *on Eph.* iv. 17, vi. 1.

ἐφ' ὑμᾶς] *'in regard of you;'* the preposition marking the ethical direction of the πεποιθέναι; comp. Matth. xxvii. 43, 2 Cor. ii. 3, and see Winer, *Gr.* § 49, l. p. 363. It is very difficult to draw clear lines of demarcation between the ethical uses of πρός, ἐπί, and εἰς, in combinations like the present. To speak somewhat generally we may perhaps say that πρὸς with the acc. commonly indicates simple ethical *motion* (comp. Donalds. *Crat.* § 169, 171); ἐπὶ with the same case, mental *direction* with an idea of *approximation* (Donalds. *Crat.* § 172), and a more defined expression of the *erga* (Luke vi. 35) or *contra* (Matth. x. 21); εἰς direction or destination with the idea of having actually *reached* the object (compare Krüger, *Sprachl.* § 68. 21. 5, and notes *on Philem.* 5), and with a wider and more inclusive notion of general behavior however characterized. For the distinctions

λομεν καὶ ποιεῖτε καὶ ποιήσετε. 5 ὁ δὲ Κύριος κατευθύναι ὑμῶν
τὰς καρδίας εἰς τὴν ἀγάπην τοῦ Θεοῦ καὶ εἰς τὴν ὑπομονὴν τοῦ
Χριστοῦ.

between εἰς, πρός, and κατά, see notes *on Tit.* i. 1. ὅτι ἃ παραγγέλλ.] '*that the things which we command:*' objective or expositive sentence (Donalds. *Gr.* § 584, see notes on ch. ii. 13), stating the matter of the apostle's confidence. The ἃ παραγγέλλ., — clearly not '*quæ præcipimus*,' Pelt, — here refers most naturally to the commands which the apostle is now in the act of giving to his converts, and links the present verse in an easy and natural way with ver. 6.

καὶ ποιεῖτε κ. ποιήσ. belongs to the apodosis of the sentence, καὶ — καὶ presenting both ποιεῖτε and ποιήσ. simultaneously in a single predication; see notes *on* 1 *Tim.* iv. 10. The reading is slightly doubtful. *Lachm.* reads παραγγέλλομεν [ὑμῖν καὶ ἐποιήσατε καὶ] ποιεῖτε, but the authority for καὶ ἐποιήσ. [BFG; Boern.] is perhaps scarcely sufficient to warrant even the bracketed introduction. The case of ὑμῖν [*Rec.* with AD³EFGKL; many mss.; Syr., Aug., Goth., al.] is different. Though so strongly attested, the omission [*Tisch.* with BD¹; 17. 67**; Clarom., Sangerm., Vulg., al.; Chrys. (comm. 2), many Lat. Ff.] still seems to deserve the preference on *critical* grounds, the ὑμῖν being so very natural a conformation to ver. 6.

5. ὁ δὲ Κύρ. κατευθ.] '*But may the Lord direct your hearts;*' repetition of the apostle's prayer, introduced in the form of a gentle antithesis (δὲ) to what precedes, — 'I doubt you not, my confidence is in the Lord; may He, however, vouchsafe His blessed aid;' ἀμφοτέρων ἡμῖν χρεία, καὶ προθέσεως ἀγαθῆς καὶ τῆς ἄνωθεν συνεργείας, Theod. The appearance of τοῦ Χριστοῦ in the concluding member of the verse has led Basil (*de Spir. Sanct.* cap. 21, πάντως ἂν εἴρητο· ὁ δὲ κ. τ. λ. εἰς τὴν ἑαυτοῦ ἀγάπην), Theod. Theophilus, Œcum., and, recently, Wordsw., to refer ὁ Κύριος to the Holy Spirit. This, however, is unnecessary, and indeed contrary to the language of the N. T.; Κύριος appy. not being so applied even in the debatable passage, 2 Cor. iii. 18, see Meyer *in loc.* On the compound κατευθύνειν (εὐθυπορεῖν, Theoph.), see notes *on* 1 *Thess.* iii. 11, and on the meaning of καρδία in such combinations (here, the centre of the active will and its *practical* applications), see Delitzsch, *Bibl. Psych.* IV. 12, p. 202, Beck, *Seelenl.* III. 24, p. 94, 95.

εἰς τὴν ἀγ. τοῦ Θεοῦ] '*into the love of God;*' principle to which and into which the apostle prays that his converts may be guided. The only doubt is whether τοῦ Θεοῦ is a gen. *subjecti*, under the more specific form of a gen. *auctoris*, scil. 'amor quem Deus hominum quasi infundit animis,' Pelt, — or simply a gen. *objecti*, 'amor erga Deum,' Beng., τὸ ἀγαπῆσαι αὐτόν, Theoph. The latter seems most natural; the love of God is indeed the 'virtutis Christianæ fons limpidissimus,' 'Schott:' see Matth. xxii. 37. τὴν ὑπομ. τοῦ Χρ.] '*the patience of Christ.*' The meaning of these words is also slightly doubtful, owing to the different aspects in which the gen. may be regarded. Analogy with what precedes would suggest (*a*) a genitive *objecti*, 'waiting for Christ' (Auth., Chrys. 2, Theoph. 2) but would introduce a meaning of ὑπομ. that is apparently not lexically defensible, and certainly is contrary to the usage of the N. T. Of the other meanings, (*b*) the gen. *auctoris* or *causæ efficientis* (Pelt) is plausible, but appy. less simple than the more inclusive *possessive* gen. (Lünem., Alf.), 'patience such as Christ exhibited;' ἵνα ὑπομένωμεν ὡς ἐκεῖνος ὑπέμεινεν

Avoid all disorderly brethren, and imitate us. We charge such to labor, and bid you mark them that disobey. The Lord give you peace.

6 Παραγγέλλομεν δὲ ὑμῖν, ἀδελφοί, ἐν ὀνόματι τοῦ Κυρίου Ἰησοῦ Χριστοῦ, στέλλεσθαι ὑμᾶς ἀπὸ παντὸς ἀδελφοῦ ἀτάκτως περιπατοῦν-

Chrys. 1, Theod. 1, comp. 1 Pet. ii. 21. On the meaning of the word ὑπομονή, see notes *on* 1 *Thess*. i. 3. The addition of the art. (*Rec*. ὑπομ.) has the support of all the MSS. and very many Greek Ff.

6. Παραγγέλλομεν δέ] '*Now we command you;*' transition by means of the δὲ μεταβατικὸν (notes *on Gal*. iii. 8) to the more distinctly *preceptive* portion of the Epistle. In what follows, the exhortations of the former Epistle (ch. iv. 11, 12, v. 14) are repeated and expanded with more studied distinctness of language, it being probable that the evils previously alluded to had advanced among some members of this Church to a still more perilous height. The words ἐν ὀνόματι κ. τ. λ. give the παραγγελία a greater force and solemnity; οὐχ ἡμεῖς ταῦτα λέγομεν ἀλλ' ὁ Χριστός, Chrys.: see 1 Cor. v. 4, and comp. Acts iii. 6, xvi. 18. The addition ἡμῶν after Κυρίου (*Rec*., [*Lachm*.], with AD[3]E[2]FG KL; mss.). though well supported, is appy. rightly rejected by *Tischend*. with BD[1]E[1]; Clarom., Sangerm.; Cypr. (1), as a likely interpolation.

στέλλεσθαι ὑμᾶς κ. τ. λ] '*that ye withdraw yourselves from;*' object-infin., stating the substance of the παραγγελία. The verb στέλλειν [derived from a root ΣΤΑ-, Pott, *Etym. Forsch*. Vol. I. p. 197] properly signifies 'collocare,'—thence, with a not improbable figurative reference (τὰ ἱστία, Rost u. Palm, *Lex*. s. v. Vol. II. p. 1529), 'cohibere,' 'comprimere,' and reflexively, 'se subtrahere,' Vulg, Clarom., ܕܬܗܘܘܢ ܦܪܝܩܝܢ [ut sitis distantes] Syriac, 'gascaidai þ izvis,' Goth., sim. Copt., al.; comp. Mal. ii. 5, ἀπὸ προσώπου ὀνόματός μου στέλλεσθαι [where the Heb. נִחַת seems to suggest a tinge of the still further derivative meaning 'præ *metu* se subducere;' Hesych. φοβεῖται, στέλλεται], Gen. viii. 1 (Aquil.), and with an acc., 2 Cor. viii. 20, στελλόμενοι τοῦτο, rightly translated by Vulg. 'devitantes hoc;' add also Gal. ii. 12, ὑπέστελλεν ἑαυτόν, Heb. x 38, ὑποστείληται. For further exx., see Elsner, *Obs*. Vol. II. p. 283, Kypke, *Obs*. Vol. II. p. 344, Loesner, *Obs*. p. 387, where this verb is copiously illustrated.

ἀτάκτως περιπ.] '*walking disorderly;*' comp. 1 Thess. v. 14, τοὺς ἀτάκτους. On this use of the verb περιπατεῖν (περιπ. τουτέστι, βιοῦντος, Chrys.), as indicating the general course of a life in its habitual and practical manifestations, see reff. *on* 1 *Thess*. iv. 12, and comp. notes *on Phil*. iii. 18.

κατὰ τὴν παράδοσιν] '*according to the lesson* or *instruction;*' παράδοσις (comp. ch. ii. 15) including both the oral (comp. ver. 10, 1 Thess. iv. 11) and written (1 Thess. iv. 11, 12) instructions which the apostle had delivered to his converts. To refer this to a παράδοσιν τὴν διὰ τῶν ἔργων, as Chrys. and the Greek expositors, is to infringe on what follows, where this mode of teaching is distinctly specified.

ἣν παρελάβοσαν] '*which they received*,' scil. those included in the foregoing παντὸς ἀδελφοῦ, which has here the character of a collective substantive. The main difficulty is the reading. *Lachm*. adopts παρελάβετε with BFG; 3 mss.; Goth., Syr. (Philox.), al.,—but scarcely with plausibility, as the change would have been so easily suggested by the seeming difficulty of construction in the plural. The same may be said of *Rec*. παρέλαβε, which, however, has scarcely any external authority. The choice, then, seems to lie between παρέλαβον [*Scholz*, with D[2]D[3]EKL; mss.; Greek Ff.] and the text [*Griesb*, *Tisch*., with A; Bas., and ἐλάβοσαν, D[1]]. Of these,

τος καὶ μὴ κατὰ τὴν παράδοσιν ἣν παρελάβοσαν παρ' ἡμῶν.
7 αὐτοὶ γὰρ οἴδατε πῶς δεῖ μιμεῖσθαι ἡμᾶς, ὅτι οὐκ ἠτακτήσαμεν
ἐν ὑμῖν, 8 οὐδὲ δωρεὰν ἄρτον ἐφάγομεν παρά τινος, ἀλλ' ἐν κόπῳ

the tendency to grammatical correction coupled with the known existence (Sturz, *de Dial. Alex.* p. 60, Matth. *Gr.* § 201. 5) and prevalence, even to a late period (Lobeck, *Phryn.* p. 349), of the form -οσαν in the 3rd plur. of the imperf. and second aor., may perhaps induce us to acquiesce in the not improbable, though weakly supported παρελάβοσαν; so Olsh., Lünem., Alf., and Wordsworth.

7. αὐτοὶ γὰρ κ. τ. λ.] *'For yourselves know;'* confirmation of the wisdom and pertinence of the foregoing exhortation, and more especially of the modal clause immediately preceding, by an appeal to their own knowledge and observation. The Thessalonian converts knew 'of themselves' πῶς δεῖ κ. τ. λ., and needed not that the apostle should inform them. πῶς δεῖ μιμεῖσθαι ἡμ.] *'how ye ought to imitate us;'* a simple and intelligible 'brachylogy.' The more natural sequence would have been πῶς δεῖ περιπατεῖν καὶ ἡμᾶς μιμεῖσθαι, but the more brief mode of expression is probably designedly chosen, as throwing emphasis on the μιμεῖσθαι, and giving the whole appeal more point and force. It is somewhat doubtful whether the plural is to be referred to St. Paul alone, or to the apostle and his associates. By a comparison with 1 Thess. ii. 9, where the ref. seems to the latter, we shall most probably be justified in adopting the same view in the present case.

ὅτι οὐκ ἠτακτήσαμεν] *'in that we behaved not disorderly.'* This is apparently one of those cases in which the causal sentence approaches somewhat nearly,—not so much to the *modal* (comp. Æth. *kama* [sicut, quemadmodum], Peile, 'how') as to the *relative* (comp. Syr. ܕܠܐ ܗܠܟܢ, [qui non ambulavimus]) or to the *expositive* sentence, with both of which it has some logical and grammatical affinity; comp. Winer, *Gr.* § 60. 6, p. 479. It was not precisely 'because' St. Paul and his associates οὐκ ἠτάκτησαν, as 'seeing that,' 'in that' such was the case, that the Thess. came to know how (quali ratione vivendi,' Beng.) to imitate them. In a word, the εὐταξία was not so much a cause, as a *causa sine quâ non* of the knowledge. This use of ὅτι, which might perhaps be termed its 'sub-causal' or 'secondary causal' use, apparently deserves some attention, esp. in the N. T.

The verb ἀτακτεῖν is an ἅπ. λεγόμ. in the N. T., and here practically synonymous with περιπατεῖν ἀτάκτως, ver. 11: it occurs occasionally in classical Greek, sometimes in a more restricted reference to τὰ στρατιωτικά, *e. g* Demosth. *Olynth.* III. p. 31, τοὺς ἀτακτοῦντας ('qui disciplinam militarem labefactant,' Wolf), sometimes, as here, with a more general reference, *e. g.* Xenoph. *Cyrop.* VIII. 1. 22; see Kypke, *Obs.* Vol. II. p. 345.

8. δωρεὰν ἄρτον ἐφάγ.] *'ate (our) bread for nought.'* Δωρεὰν is an adverbial accusative implying either 'sine justâ causâ,' Gal. ii. 21 (see notes), or, as here, 'gratis,' Vulg., ܡܓܢ, Syr.—the true idea of λαμβάνειν δωρεὰν being 'ita accipere ut nihil referas, nullâ prægressâ causâ accipiendi,' Tittmann *Synon.* II. p. 161. The formula ἄρτον φαγεῖν appears to be Hebraistic (comp. אָכַל לֶחֶם, Gen. xliii. 25, 2 Sam. ix. 7, 10, al.), implying really little more than the simple verb φαγεῖν (1 Cor. ix. 4), but, like all these Hebraistic terms, being full of force and expressiveness; comp. Winer, *Gr.* § 3, p. 26 sq. ἐν κόπῳ καὶ μόχθῳ] *'in toil and travail,'* scil. ἄρτον ἐφάγομεν; adjunct of manner, involving a tacit opposition to the preceding δωρεάν. On

καὶ μόχθῳ, νύκτα καὶ ἡμέραν ἐργαζόμενοι, πρὸς τὸ μὴ ἐπιβαρῆσαί
τινα ὑμῶν· 9 οὐχ ὅτι οὐκ ἔχομεν ἐξουσίαν, ἀλλ' ἵνα ἑαυτοὺς τύπον
δῶμεν ὑμῖν εἰς τὸ μιμεῖσθαι ἡμᾶς. 10 καὶ γὰρ ὅτε ἦμεν πρὸς ὑμᾶς,

the meaning and derivation of these words, and the apparent distinction between them, see notes *on* 1 *Thess.* ii. 9.

νύκτα καὶ ἡμ. κ. τ. λ.] '*laboring during night and day;*' participial explanation of the preceding ἐν κόπῳ καὶ μόχθῳ, more remotely dependent on the foregoing ἐφάγομεν; see Winer, *Gr.* § 45. 6. b, 314. Lünem. and Alford connect the participial clause closely with ἐν κόπῳ καὶ μόχθῳ, according to which ἐργ. would have a more distinctly modal force. This is perfectly admissible; the emphatic position of δωρεάν, however, appy. suggests the sharper antithesis which the separation of the members here seems to introduce. The reading νυκτὸς καὶ ἡμέρας [*Lachmann* with BFG; 5 mss.; Chrys. (ms.), Dam.] seems to be more than doubtful, — the change being probably suggested either by a desire to modify the hyperbole of the expression, or, more probably, to bring the text into conformation with 1 Thess. ii. 9; comp. iii. 10. On the phrase itself, see notes *on* 1 *Thess. l. c.*, and *on* 1 *Tim.* v. 5.

πρὸς τὸ μὴ ἐπιβ.] '*with the view of not being burdensome to any of you;*' object contemplated in the νύκτα καὶ ἡμ. ἐργαζ. On the word ἐπιβαρ., see notes *on* 1 *Thess.* ii. 9, where precisely the same words are used in ref. to the same subject.

9. οὐχ. ὅτι] '*not that;*' limitation of what precedes, to prevent the preceding declaration being misapprehended and misapplied; the apostle conserves his ministerial right and privilege of receiving, if need be, support from his converts; comp. 1 Cor. ix. 4 sq. On the use of this formula ('ex dialecticis, ut ita dicam formulis Paulo solemnibus,' Pelt), which is found several times in St. Paul's Epp. (2 Cor. i. 24, iii. 5, Phil. iii. 12, iv. 11, 17), see Hartung, *Partik.* Vol. II. p. 154, and notes *on Phil.* iii. 12.

ἐξουσίαν] '*power,* '*right,*' scil. τοῦ μὴ ἐργ. (De W.), or, more naturally, τοῦ δωρεὰν φαγεῖν ἄρτον (Lünem.), — the latter being the principal statement of the preceding verse. The word ἐξουσία ('jus, licentia, auctoritas aliquid faciendi,' Schott) is used exactly similarly, 1 Cor. ix. 12.

ἑαυτούς] '*ourselves;*' with reference to the apostle and his associates. On this use of ἑαυτοὺς for ἡμᾶς αὐτούς, ὑμᾶς αὐτούς, see Winer, *Gr.* § 22. 5, p. 136, and for exx. in classical Greek, Krüger, *Sprachl.* § 51. 2. 15.

εἰς τὸ μιμ. ἡμᾶς] '*that ye should, to the intent that, ye imitate us;*' not merely an objective member, but, as usual, specifying the object and purpose of the ἑαυτ. τύπον διδόναι; comp. Winer, *Gr.* § 44. 6, p. 295.

10. καὶ γάρ] '*For also,*' '*for besides;*' second confirmation of the wisdom and pertinence of the preceding warning that they ought to avoid those that were walking disorderly, — the γὰρ being co-ordinate with the preceding γὰρ in ver. 7, and the καὶ having appy. a *conjunctive* force, and serving to connect this argumentative clause with that in ver. 7, and thus more thoroughly to substantiate the κατὰ τὴν παράδ. ἣν κ. τ. λ. Lünemann, followed by Alf., makes καὶ *ascensive,* and refers it to τοῦτο παρηγγέλλ., as bringing out an additional element in the reminiscence. This is somewhat forced: καὶ γὰρ has two usages in the N. T., — one in which the *conjunctive* force of καὶ prevails ('etenim,' Beza), the other ('nam etiam;' nam et,' Vulg., — but not Clarom., which omits 'et') in which the *ascensive* force is predominant; see Winer, *Gr.* § 53. 8, p. 397, and notes *on Phil.* ii. 27. The latter has been undoubtedly far too often overlooked in the

τοῦτο παρηγγέλλομεν ὑμῖν, ὅτι εἴ τις οὐ θέλει ἐργάζεσθαι, μηδὲ
ἐσθιέτω. 11 ἀκούομεν γάρ τινας περιπατοῦντας ἐν ὑμῖν ἀτάκτως,
μηδὲν ἐργαζομένους ἀλλὰ περιεργαζομένους. 12 τοῖς δὲ τοιούτοις

12. ἐν Κυρ. Ἰησ. Χρ.] So *Lachm.*, *Tisch.* ed. 1, 7, with ABD¹E¹FG (D¹E¹ Χρ.); 4 mss.; Vulg., Clarom., Goth., Copt., al.; Dam. (1); Lat. Ff (*Lünem.*, Alford). In his second edition *Tischend.* reads διὰ τοῦ Κυρ. ἡμῶν Ἰησ. Χρ. with D³E²KL; nearly all mss.; Syr. (both; insert ἡμῶν), al.; Chrys., Theod., Dam. (1), Theoph., Œcum. (*Rec.*, *Griesb.*, *Schott*, *De W.*), but has now rightly returned to the reading of his first ed. As, however, the internal arguments are very nearly balanced,—the διὰ being perhaps as likely to have been introduced in consequence of Rom. xv. 30 and the more usual παρακ. διά, as the ἐν to have been derived from 1 Thess. iv. 1,—we seem bound to follow the best attested reading.

N. T. (comp. Fritz. *Rom.* Vol. II. p. 433), but is not to be obtruded in a passage like the present, where the context (contrast 1 Thess. iii. 4) and sequence of argument seem somewhat decidedly in favor of the *conjunctive* use. On the use of πρὸς with εἶναι and verbs implying rest (παρ' ὑμῖν, μεθ' ὑμῶν, Theoph.), compare notes *on Gal.* i. 18, and see above, ch. ii. 4, 1 Thess. iii. 4.

τοῦτο]. '*this*,'—that follows; the pronoun being placed emphatically forward to direct attention to the succeeding declaration; comp. Winer, *Gr.* § 23. 5, p. 145. The partially proverbial statement which follows is illustrated by Wetstein *in loc.*, and Schoettg. *Hor. Hebr.* Vol. I. p. 850: the most pertinent quotation seems *Bereschith*, XIV, 12, 'R. Hunna dixit: fecit eum servum manumissum coram se ipso, ut si non laboret, non manducet.' The exhortation is expressed in the form of a kind of 'enthymeme' (Whately, *Logic*, II. 3. 7, p. 121), the portion to be supplied being 'atqui quilibet edit; ergo quilibet laborato,' Beng. On the use of οὐ following εἰ, when the negative is closely united with the verb, see notes *on* 1 *Tim.* iii. 5, and the exx. collected by Gayler, *de Part. Neg.* ch. v. p. 9 sq.

11. ἀκούομεν γὰρ κ.τ.λ.] '*For we hear that there are some walking, etc.;*' ground for the reiteration of the apostle's previous παραγγελία. In cases like the present the predicative participle is not merely equivalent to an infinitive mood, but is idiomatically used as marking the state or action as now in existence, and, as such coming before the observation of the writer; see Winer, *Gr.* § 45. 4, p. 308 sq.,—where there is a good collection of examples; comp. also Schmalfeld, *Synt* § 217. 2, p. 437, and esp. the able tract of Weller (*Bemerk. zum Gr. Synt.* Meining., 1845), where the distinctions between the finite verb with ὅτι, with the infin., and with the participle, are carefully stated, and illustrated by numerous examples. μηδὲν ἐργαζ. ἀλλὰ περιεργ.] '*doing no work, but being busy-bodies,*' 'nihil operantes, sed curiose agentes, Vulg., Clarom., ܡܕܡ ܠܐ ܦܠܚܝܢ ܐܠܐ ܠܣܪ̈ܝܩܬܐ [nihil quidquam operantur nisi vana] Syr.; more exact specification of the preceding περιπατοῦν. ἐν ὑμῖν ἀτάκτως by means of a forcible paronomasia; comp. [Demosth.] *Phil.* IV. p. 150, ἐξ ὧν ἐργάζῃ καὶ περιεργάζῃ, and Quintil. *Inst. Orat.* VI. 3. 54, 'non agere dixit, sed satagere.' The verb περιεργ. is an ἅπαξ λέγομ. in the N. T., and serves to mark the ἀνόνητον πολυπραγμοσύνην (Theod.), the 'pravam curiositatem et sedulitatem' (Pelt), which marked the actions of those to whom the apostle referred; comp. περί-

παραγγέλλομεν καὶ παρακαλοῦμεν ἐν Κυρίῳ Ἰησοῦ Χριστῷ, ἵνα
μετὰ ἡσυχίας ἐργαζόμενοι τὸν ἑαυτῶν ἄρτον ἐσθίωσιν. 13 ὑμεῖς

εργοι, 1 Tim. v. 13, and see the good notice of this verb in Suicer, *Thesaur.* s. v. Vol. II. p. 670.

12. τοῖς δὲ τοιούτοις] '*Now to such as these;*' the article with τοιοῦτος marking the whole class of persons so specified, and having such characteristics as those previously mentioned; see Krüger, *Sprachl.* § 50. 4. 6, Jelf, *Gr.* § 453. β, and notes *on Gal.* v. 21. καὶ παρακαλοῦμεν] '*and exhort* (*them*)', ܘܡܬܟܫܦܝܢ ܡܢܗܘܢ [et petimus ab iis] Syr.,—τοὺς τοιούτους Schott), or, more simply, αὐτούς (Lünem.), being here supplied zeugmatically, as it is called, to παρακαλ., which is only found with the *accus.* This παράκλησις is ἐν Κυρ. Ἰησ. Χρ.; it is in Him that it has its proper force and efficacy; see notes *on* 1 *Thess.* iv. 1, where παρακαλεῖν is enhanced by the same addition. The reading is doubtful, but that retained in the text seems to deserve the preference; see critical note. μετὰ ἡσυχίας] '*with quietness;*' in opposition to the busy and meddlesome course of life followed by the περιπατοῦντες ἀτάκτως, and περιεργαζόμενοι; see 1 Thess. iv. 11. The preposition μετὰ serves to point to, not the 'causa instrumentalis' (Kypke, *Obs.* Vol. I. p. 143), but the *concomitant* of their working,—that which was associated with it, and characterized their 'modus operandi; comp. Winer, *Gr.* 47. h, p. 337. On the derivation of ἡσυχία and its probable distinction from the less common ἠρεμία, see notes *on* 1 *Tim.* ii. 2. τὸν ἑαυτῶν ἄρτον] '*their own bread,*'—'their own' (τὸν ἐξ οἰκείων πόνων, Chrys.), not without emphasis; they were not to seek it at the hands of others (comp. ver. 8), they were not 'alienâ vivere quadrâ,' Juven. *Sat.* v. 2. The sentiment is well illustrated by Schoettg. and Wetst. *in loc.* from the Rabbinical writings, out of which the following deserves citation; 'quo tempore homo panem proprium edit, animo composito ac sedato est; si vero panem parentum aut liberorum comedit, non animo tam sedato est, ne dicam de pane peregrino,' Aboth R. Nathan, cap. 30.

13. ὑμεῖς δέ, ἀδελφοί] '*But ye, brethren;*' renewal of his address to those who were 'recte animati' (Schott), and lived orderly, after the example which he had set them. Such the apostle urges to pursue their course, and not from faintness to fall into idle, and eventually meddlesome and unquiet habits, like those he had just been condemning. μὴ ἐγκακ. καλοπ.] '*be not weary in well doing.*' The exact meaning of καλοποιεῖν has been somewhat differently estimated. Several modern writers, following the hint, though not the exact interpretation (μὴ μὴν περιίδητε λιμῷ διαφθαρέντας) of Chrys., Theoph. assign to the verb the idea of 'conferring benefits;' the connection between this and the preceding verse arising from the gentle contrast between the duty of living by their own labor, and the still further duty of conferring benefits on others; see Calv. *in loc.* As this meaning, however, seems lexically doubtful, see Lev. v. 4 (*Cod. Coisl.*, where καλοπ. stands in antithesis to κακοποιῆσαι), and as the more generic 'recte agere' (comp Syriac ܠܡܥܒܕ ܫܦܝܪܐ) is perfectly in harmony with the context, it seems best here, as in the very similar passage Gal. vi. 9, to give καλὸν its less restricted meaning. What this καλὸν exactly is, lies in the specifications of the context. On the form ἐγκακεῖν [*Lachm.*, *Tisch.* (ἐνκ.), with ABD¹], and the somewhat doubtful ἐκκακεῖν [*Rec.*] see the remarks and distinctions in notes *on Gal.* vi. 9.

14. τῷ λόγῳ ἡμῶν κ. τ. λ.] '*our*

δέ, ἀδελφοί, μὴ ἐγκακήσητε καλοποιοῦντες. 14 εἰ δέ τις οὐχ ὑπα-
κούει τῷ λόγῳ ἡμῶν διὰ τῆς ἐπιστολῆς, τοῦτον σημειοῦσθε καὶ μὴ

*word conveyed by the Epistle;'* ܠܡ̈ܠܝܢ ܗܠܝܢ ܕܒܐܓܪܬܐ [sermonibus nostris istis qui sunt in epistolâ]. It is doubtful whether διὰ τῆς ἐπιστολῆς is to be joined (*a*) with the following verb σεμειοῦσθε, or (*b*) with the preceding subst. τῷ λόγῳ, scil. τῷ διὰ τῆς ἐπιστολῆς ἀποσταλέντι, Œcumen. The former is adopted by Æth. (Polygl.), Beng., Pelt, Winer, (*Gr.* § 18. 9. 3, p. 108), and others, either ($a_1$) in the simple sense, 'notate in epistolâ,' Æth., scil. 'in epistolâ ad me scriptâ illum suis notis depingite,' Grot.,—τῆς ἐπιστολῆς referring to the letter which St. Paul would, in that case, receive from the Thess. (see Winer); or ($a_2$) in the more artificial sense, *hâc* epistolâ freti severius tractate,' Pelt (comp. Beng.),—τῆς ἐπιστολῆς in that case referring to the present epistle. Of these last mentioned, ($a_2$) seems clearly forced and improbable, while ($a_1$), though somewhat more plausible, lies open to the contextual objection, that the present order of words would tend to throw an emphasis on διὰ τῆς ἐπιστ. which cannot be accounted for, and further, to the still graver exegetical objection, that a letter would seem uncalled for after the precept in ver. 6, where the course to be pursued by the Thess. is already stated. We retain then (*b*) with Syr., not improbably Vulg., Copt., Goth. [the exact order of the Greek is preserved], Chrys. (appy.), Theoph., Œcum., and most modern expositors. The objection founded on the omission of the art. before λόγῳ is not of weight, as διὰ τῆς ἐπιστ. is so associated with τῷ λόγῳ ἡμ. as to form with it only a single idea; see exx. in Winer, *Gr.* § 20. 2, p. 123. It may be observed that this is one of those cases in which the use of the art. in the N. T. seems slightly to differ from that of the best Attic Greek. While in the latter the article is rarely omitted, except after verbal substantives (Krüger, *Sprachl.* § 50. 9. 9), or where the structural connection of the prepositional member with what precedes is palpably close, this omission of the art. in the N. T. is so far from unusual, that its insertion usually implies some degree of emphasis; see Fritz. *Rom.* iii. 25, Vol. I. p. 195 (note).

σημειοῦσθε] *'mark,'*—scil. by avoiding his company (comp. ver. 6), as more fully specified in the words following. So paraphrastically Syr. ܢܬܦܪܫ ܡܢܟܘܢ [separetur a vobis] compare Æth.-Platt. The verb σημειοῦν is an ἅπ. λεγόμ. in the N. T.; it properly implies 'signo distinguere' (Schott), *e. g.* ἐπιστολὰς σφραγῖδι, Dion. Hal. *Antiq.* IV. 57, and thence in the middle 'sibi notare aliquid' Polyb. *Hist.* XXII. 11. 12),—more correctly, according to the Atticists, ἀποσημαίνεσθαι (Thomas-Mag. p. 791, Herodian, p. 420, ed. Koch), or, as here, with a more intensive force, 'notâ (censoriâ) notare;' the middle having what has been termed its 'dynamic' character, Krüger, *Sprachl.* § 52. 8. 4. For a large list of verbs of this class, see Schmalfeld, *Synt.* § 35, p. 44 sq., and compare notes *on Col.* iv. 1.

μὴ συναναμίγνυσθε] *'keep no company with;'* present, pointing to the course they were to follow. The double compound συναναμίγν. (Athen. *Deipn.* VI. 68, p. 256 A) appears used in a sense little differing from the simpler and more usual συμμίγν., and probably only in accordance with that noticeable tendency of later Greek to double composition; compare notes *on Gal.* iii. 13. The reading is doubtful; *Lachm.*, (*Griesbach* om. om.) omits καὶ with ABD³E; 17; Clarom., Sangerm., Goth., Copt.; Chrys.; Tert., al.,—and reads συναναμίγνυσθαι with ABD¹(DE συναναμίσγεσθαι); 17 (?); Clarom., Sangerm., Copt., and perhaps

συναναμίγνυσθε αὐτῷ, ἵνα ἐντραπῇ. 15 καὶ μὴ ὡς ἐχθρὸν ἡγεῖσθε,
ἀλλὰ νουθετεῖτε ὡς ἀδελφόν. 16 αὐτὸς δὲ ὁ Κύριος τῆς εἰρήνης
δῴη ὑμῖν τὴν εἰρήνην διὰ παντὸς ἐν παντὶ τρόπῳ. ὁ Κύριος μετὰ
πάντων ὑμῶν.

Goth., Tert.,—but appy. on evidence scantly sufficient; esp. when the change to the infin. might have been suggested by a desire to mark more distinctly the meaning of the unusual verb σημειοῦσθε. On the whole, then, it seems safest to retain the reading of *Rec.* [D[1]FGKL; nearly all mss.; Vulg., Boern., Syriac (both), Æth. (both), al.; Basil, al.], with *Tisch.* ed. 2, and most modern editors. ἐντραπῇ] '*be shamed,*' 'ut confundatur,' Vulg.; passive,—not with a middle sense, 'ad se ipsum quasi redire,' Pelt (comp. Grot., 'ut pudore tactus ad mentem meliorem redeat),—a meaning for which there seems no sufficient reason either here or Tit. ii. 8, see notes *in loc.* The active occurs in 1 Cor. iv. 14.

15. καὶ is not 'here instead of ἀλλά' (Jowett; comp. De Wette, 'aber'),—a most precarious statement,—but, with its usual and proper force, subjoins to the previous exhortation a further one that was fully compatible with it, and in fact tended to show the real principle on which the command was given: it was not punitive, but corrective. ὡς ἐχθρόν] '*as an enemy,*' 'in the light of an enemy;' the ὡς being used (here almost pleonastically, Plato, *Gorg.* p. 473 A) to mark the *aspect* in which he was (not) to be regarded; comp. notes on ch. ii. 2, and see *on Col.* iii. 23.

16. αὐτὸς δὲ κ. τ. λ.] '*But may the Lord Himself;*' the δὲ (as in 1 Thess. v. 23) putting in slight antithesis the prayer with the foregoing exhortation, and the αὐτὸς enhancing the dignity of the subject; comp. notes on ch. ii. 16, where, however, the antithesis is somewhat more distinctly marked. On the meaning of the word εἰρήνη, not merely 'concord' (ὥστε μηδαμόθεν ἔχειν φιλονεικίας ἀφορμήν, Chrys.), but *peace* in its widest and Christian sense,—the deep tranquillity of a soul resting on God, see notes *on Phil.* iv. 7, and on the nature of the gen. *ib.* iv. 9, comp. also *on* 1 *Thess.* v. 23,—but observe that Κύριος can more readily be associated with the gen. as allied in meaning to verbs that regularly govern that case; comp. Krüger, *Sprachl.* § 47. 26. 8. διὰ παντὸς κ. τ. λ.] '*continually, in every manner,*'—'at all times' (Matth. xviii. 10, Acts ii. 25, Rom. xi. 10, comp. Ast, *Lex. Platon.* Vol. III. p. 63), and in every possible mode of its manifestation, 'in omnibus quæ facitis,' Æth.-Pol.; ὥστε πρὸς αὐτὸν εἰρηνεύειν, καὶ πρὸς ἀλλήλους καὶ τῆς τῶν ἐναντίων ἐπιβουλῆς ἀπηλλάχθαι; Theod. The second mode is, however, but slightly in the contemplation of the apostle, as there is nothing in the Ep. to make us think that τὸ εἰρηνεύειν πρὸς ἀλλήλους had been seriously endangered or violated. The reading ἐν παντὶ τόπῳ, adopted by *Lachm.* with A[1]D[1]FG; 17. 49; Vulg., Clarom., Goth.; Chrys. [but see the note of Montfaucon], seems to have been suggested by the not uncommon occurrence of the formula (1 Cor. i. 2, 2 Cor. ii. 14, 1 Tim. ii. 8), and perhaps partially by the foregoing allusion to *time.* The reading of the text is strongly supported [A[2]BD[3]EKL; nearly all mss.; Syr. (both), Copt., al.; Theod., Dam.], and seems in every way more suitable to the context.

17. Ὁ ἀσπασμὸς κ. τ. λ.] '*The salutation of me Paul with mine own hand;*' comp. 1 Cor. xvi. 21, and Col. iv. 18, where see notes on the quasi-appositional genitive Παύλου. These words appy. form the commencement of the autograph salutation with which the apostle

**Autograph salutation and benediction.**

17 Ὁ ἀσπασμὸς τῇ ἐμῇ χειρὶ Παύλου, ὅ
ἐστιν σημεῖον ἐν πάσῃ ἐπιστολῇ· οὕτως γράφω· 18 ἡ χάρις τοῦ
Κυρίου ἡμῶν Ἰησοῦ Χριστοῦ μετὰ πάντων ὑμῶν. ἀμήν.

18. Ἀμήν] This is omitted by *Tisch.* (*Griesb.* om. om.) with B; 17. 44. 67**. 116; Harl. Tol.; Chrys. (ms.); Ambrst.,—but apparently rightly retained by *Rec.* and *Lachm.* Though even a probable liturgical interpolation, it still cannot be safely extruded when so *strongly* supported by external authority

attests the genuineness and authenticity of the Epistle (comp. notes *on Gal.* vi. 11), the two verses having apparently both been written by the apostle,—not merely ver. 18 (τὸ ἡ χάρις κ. τ. λ. ἀντὶ τοῦ ἐῤῥῶσθαί σε γράφειν εἰώθει, Theod., al.), which, as Lünem. rightly observes, could hardly be termed a direct ἀσπασμός. ὅ] '*which thing;*' not, by an attraction (see exx. Winer, *Gr.* § 24. 3, p. 150) to the following σημεῖον, 'which greeting,' but more simply and naturally in reference to the preceding words, and to the general fact of their being written τῇ ἐμῇ χειρὶ Παύλου. These autograph lines formed a σημεῖον that the Ep. was not ὡς δι' αὐτοῦ (ch. ii. 2), but was truly and genuinely his own inspired composition. ἐν πάσῃ ἐπιστολῇ] '*in every epistle;*' appy. with reference to every future epistle (τῇ πρὸς οὕστινας δήποτε, Theoph. 2) which the apostle might hereafter deem it necessary so to authenticate,—not merely those he might have contemplated writing *to Thessalonica* (Theoph. 1, Lünem.); for consider 1 Cor. xvi. 21, and Col. iv. 18. If it be urged that these last mentioned are the only Epistles in which the autograph attestation seems to have found a place, it may be reasonably answered that the πάσῃ must be understood relatively of every Epistle that was sent in such a way or under such circumstances as to have needed it. All the other Epistles (except 1 Cor., Col., which have the σημεῖον, and 1 Thess., which was sent before circumstances proved it to be necessary) are fairly shown both by De Wette and by Alford *in loc.* to have either been delivered by emissaries (2 Corinth., Phil.), to bear marks (Gal. vi. 11, and perhaps the doxology in Rom., Eph.), or to be of such a general character (Rom. ? Eph. ? and those to individuals) as to have rendered such a formal attestation unnecessary. οὕτως γράφω] '*so I write;*' scil. in such characters as verses 17 and 18 appeared written with. The suppositions that the apostle here inserted some words (τό, ἀσπάζομαι ὑμᾶς, ἢ τό, ἔῤῥωσθε, ἤ τι τοιοῦτον, Œcum.), or adopted a monogram ('conjunctis scilicet apte literis Π et Λ,' according to Zeltner, *de Monogr. Pauli,* Altorf, 1721; see contra, Wolf *in loc.*), or lastly, 'singulari et inimitabili picturâ et ductu literarum expressisse illud, *gratia,* etc.' (Beng.),—seem all far too artificial to deserve serious consideration. The οὕτως simply and naturally points to the *visible* and *recognizable* difference between the handwriting of the transcriber and of the apostle.

18. ἡ χάρις κ. τ. λ.] The same form of benediction as at the end of 1 Thess. (where see notes), except that the inclusive and significant πάντων is here added,—'all,'—even those who had deserved and received the apostle's censure (compare μετὰ πάντων, ver. 16) were to share in his benediction and farewell prayer; see Pelt *in loc.*, who however joins with it the less probable supposition, 'ne rixæ [none of which appear to have existed] disceptationesque Thessalonicenses turbarent.'

# TRANSLATION.

# NOTICE.

THE following revised translation will be found in accordance with the principles previously laid down in former portions of this work. Experience seems satisfactorily to show, that change is undesirable except where our admirable Version is *incorrect*, *inexact*, *insufficient*, *obscure* (Pref. to *Gal.* p. xx.), or *inconsistent* with itself in renderings of less usual words or forms of expression (Notice to Transl. of *Past. Epistles*). The last form of correction is perhaps the most difficult to adjust satisfactorily, as our last Translators expressly state that they have not been careful to preserve throughout their work a studied uniformity of translation, and consequently as any attempt to do this regularly would only reverse the principles on which they acted, independently of being frequently spiritless and monotonous. Still in the same epistle, and especially in the same context, it is so obviously desirable to be consistent, that here at least changes will have to be introduced. It must, however, always rest with individual judgment, whether the word or expression in question is of such a character as to demand uniformity, or whether it is best left to take its hue from the context. That I have been always judicious in my decisions is much too presumptuous to hope. but I have still striven to make them with a clear recognition of the general principles that characterize the noble Version which I am presuming to revise.

That these points may be more fully considered, and that my opinion, where seemingly capricious or precipitate, may be more completely tested, I have made a few additions to the notes in the shape of reasons for the changes adopted, and I have further sought to add to the common stock of principles of revision a brief record of my own humble experiences and my own many difficulties. Sincerely and earnestly do I trust that the revision of our Authorized Version may be undertaken in its own good time, and that that time is not indefinitely remote, still year after year I am made more sensibly to feel that this can only be done by a frank and modest avowal, on the part of every one who has gained any experience, of the real difficulties that attend on the work,—difficulties far more numerous than the inexact and often presumptuous criticism of the day is at all aware of.

I have carefully considered the Revised Translation of these Epistles published by the American Bible Union (Trübner, London, 1856), and have in a few cases been benefited by its suggestions, still, as I have said more fully in my Preface, I venture to reiterate the opinion that this laborious work is at present very far from what we may imagine to be the model of a national Revision.

THE

# FIRST EPISTLE TO THE THESSALONIANS.

---

## CHAPTER I.

PAUL, and Silvanus, and Timothy, unto the church of the
Thessalonians in God the Father and the Lord Jesus Christ.
Grace *be* unto you, and peace.
2 We give thanks to God always for you all, making mention of
you in our prayers; 3 remembering without ceasing your work of
faith and toil of love and patience of hope in our Lord Jesus
Christ, in the presence of God and our Father; 4 knowing, breth-
ren beloved of God, your election; 5 because our gospel came not

CHAP. I. 1. *Timothy*] So *Wiclif, Cran., Rhem.:* 'Timotheus,' *Auth.* See notes *on Col.* i. 1 (Transl.). *In God*] So *Wicl., Tynd., Cov.* (both), *Cran., Rhem.:* '*which is* in God,' *Auth., Gen., Bish.,* — an unnecessary and inexact addition, not adopted by *Auth.* in the parallel passage, 2 Thess. i. 1. *And the Lord, etc.*] Sim. *Rhem.,* 'and our Lord, etc.;' 'and in the Lord, etc.' *Auth.* and remaining Vv. The addition of 'in' seems unnecessary, and is best reserved for those cases where it is expressed in the Greek, or where, as in 1 Tim. vi. 9 (see notes), there are contextual reasons for its introduction. The mistakes caused by such insertions are well noticed by Blunt, *Lectures on Par. Priest,* p. 56. *And peace*] *Auth.* adds '*from God our Father, and the Lord Jesus Christ.'

3. *Toil*] Sim. *Wiclif,* 'traueile;' 'labor,' *Auth.* and the remaining Vv. except *Gen.,* 'diligent love.' Though 'labor of love' from the alliteration has become familiar to the ear, it still seems desirable here to maintain the more strict translation of κόπος; see notes. *In the presence*] So *Auth.* ch. ii. 19: 'in the sight,' *Auth.* and the other Vv. except *Wicl., Cov.* (both), *Rhem.,* 'before.' It is of but little moment which of these translations is adopted; but as the expression ἔμπρ. τοῦ Θεοῦ is only used by St. Paul in this Epistle, it should be similarly translated throughout.

4. *Beloved of God*] So *Tynd., Cov.* (both), *Cran., Rhem.,* and similarly *Wicl.:* 'beloved, your election of God,' *Auth.,* and sim. *Gen., Bish.*

5. *Because*] 'For,' *Auth.* and all the Vv. except *Rhem.,* 'that.' *Even as*] 'As,' *Auth.* and all the other Vv. It is almost impossible to lay down any exact rule for the translation of καθώς. Whether the lighter 'as,' or the more

unto you in word only, but also in power, and in the Holy Ghost,
and in much assurance; even as ye know what manner of men we
became among you for your sake. [6] And ye became followers of
us, and of the Lord, having received the word in much affliction,
with joy of the Holy Ghost; [7] so that ye became an ensample to
all that believe in Macedonia and Achaia. [8] For from you hath
sounded forth the word of the Lord not only in Macedonia and
Achaia, but in every place your faith to God-ward has gone forth;
so that we need not to speak anything. [9] For they themselves
report of us what manner of entering in we had unto you, and
how ye turned to God from idols to serve the living and true God;
[10] and to wait for His Son from heaven, whom He raised from the
dead, *even* Jesus, which delivereth us from the coming wrath.

expressive and perhaps more literal 'even as,' or 'according as,' is to be adopted, must appy. be left wholly to the context, and to individual judgment. *We became*] 'We were,' *Auth.* and the other Vv. except *Tynd.*, 'we behaued oure selves;' *Cov.* (Test.), 'we haue bene.'

6. *Followers*] So *Auth.* and all the Vv. Though 'imitators' would be more exact, it is perhaps hardly necessary to displace the present idiomatic and perfectly intelligible translation. Return then to the present rendering in Eph. v. 1 (*Transl.* ed. 1). *Received*] So *Auth.* and all the other Vv. Some modern Versions endeavor to make a distinction between δεξάμενοι and παραλαβόντες (ch. ii. 13), *e. g.* 'accepted—received;' it seems doubtful, however, both whether there is any *real* distinction in the Greek, and also whether the proposed translation adequately represents it.

7. *Became an ensample*] So *Cov.* (Test.), and sim. *Wicl.*, 'ben made an ensaumple,' *Rhem.*, 'were made a paterne:' 'were ensamples*,' *Auth.*; 'were an ens.,' *Tynd.*, *Cov.*, *Cran.*; 'were as ens.,' *Gen.*, *Bish.* *And in Achaia*] 'And *Achaia,' *Auth.*

8. *Hath sounded forth*] 'Sounded out,' *Auth.* and the Vv. except *Wicl.*, 'is pupplischid;' *Cov.* (Test.), 'is...... noysed out;' *Rhem.*, 'was bruited.' The perfect ought always to be observed in translation. Though idiom may occasionally require the aorist to be translated with the usual sign of the perfect, the converse is extremely rare; compare 2 Cor. i. 9. *Has gone forth*] So *Wicl.*, and sim. *Cov.* (Test.), 'is gone oute;' 'is spread abroad,' *Auth.*, *Cov.* (*Cran.*, *Bish.*, omit 'is'); 'spred her silfe abroad,' *Tynd.*, *Cran.*; 'is proceded,' *Rhem.* *But*] 'But *also,' *Auth.*

9. *Report*] So *Rhem.*: 'shew,' *Auth.* and the remaining Vv. *From heaven*] So *Auth.* and the other Vv. except *Wicl.* 'from heuenes;' *Cov.* (Test.), 'from the heauens.' Many modern Vv. observe both the article and the plural, but with the familiar usage of the word before us in the N. T. (*e. g.* Matth. vi. 9, Luke xi. 2), it seems in general passages like the present both harsh and unnecessary to be thus literally precise.

10. *Which delivereth*] So *Tynd.*, *Cov.*, *Cran.*, *Gen.*, *Bish.* 'which delivered,' *Auth.*; sim. *Wicl.*, 'whych hath drawen us oute;' *Cov.* (Test.), who hath deliuered.' *The coming wrath*] 'The wrath to come,' *Auth.* and all the other Vv. except *Wicl.*, 'wraththe to comynge.'

## CHAPTER II.

For yourselves know, brethren, our entering in unto you, that
it hath not been vain: 2 but after that we had suffered before, and
had been shamefully entreated, as ye know, at Philippi, we were
bold of speech in our God, so as to speak unto you the gospel of God
in much conflict. 3 For our exhortation is not of error, nor yet of

CHAP. II. 1. *Know brethren*] So, in the same order, *Tynd.*, *Gen.*, *Bish.*, *Rhem.*: 'brethren,' know,' *Auth.* and sim. the remaining Vv. There seems here no reason for departing from the order of the original. *Hath not been*] 'Was not,' *Auth.* This correction should also have appeared in the notes: correct therefore accordingly. *Vain*] So *Wicl.*, *Rhem.*: 'in vain,' *Auth.* and the remaining Vv.

2. *But after*] 'But *even after,' *Auth.* *Had been shamefully, etc.*] 'Were shamefully, etc.' *Auth.*, and so too *Tynd.*, *Cran.*, *Gen.*, *Bish.* The other Vv. slightly vary the transl. of the part.; some, as *Cov.*, giving προπαθόντες a causal force, and converting ὑβρισθέντες into a finite verb; others, as *Cov.* (Test.) *Rhem.*, retaining the purely participial transl. If the view taken in the notes be correct, it seems best to regard both participles as *temporal*, and to express it by the usual idiomatic resolution into the English pluperf. On the transl. of the aor. part. when associated with the finite verb, see notes on *Phil.* ii. 30 (Transl.). *Bold of speech*] 'Bold,' *Authorized* and the remaining Vv. except *Wicl.*, 'hadden trist;' *Cov.* (Test.), 'were boldened;' *Rhem.*, 'had confidence:' see notes *in loc.* *So as to speak*] 'To speak,' *Auth.* and the remaining Vv. The introduction seems necessary to exhibit the nature of the (explanatory) infinitive, and to avoid tautology. *In much*] So *Wicl. Cov.* (Test.), *Cranmer*, *Rhem.*; 'with much,' *Auth.* and the remaining Vv. There is some difference in the translation of ἀγῶνι: *Auth.* here adopts 'contention;' *Tynd.*, *Cov.*, *Cran.*, *Gen.*, *Bish.*, 'striving;' *Wicl.*, 'bisynesse;' *Cov.* (Test.), *Rhem.*, 'carefulnesse.' Apparently the translation adopted by *Auth.* in Col. ii. 1, may here be suitably repeated.

3. *Is not*] So *Wicl.*: '*was* not,' *Auth.* and the remaining Vv. *Error*] So *Wicl.*, *Cov.* (Test.), *Rhem.*: 'deceit,' *Auth.*, *Bish.*; 'to bring you to erroure,' *Tynd.*, *Cov.*, *Cran.*; 'not to use deceite,' *Gen.* *Nor yet*] So *Tynd.*, *Cov.*, *Cran*, *Gen.*: 'nor,' *Auth.*, *Cov.* (Test.), *Bish.*; 'neither,' *Wicl.*; 'nor of,' *Rhem.* There is some little difficulty in the choice of an appropriate rendering in the different cases of continued negation. Perhaps the following distinctions of translation may be found generally satisfactory in application. (1) Μὴ — μηδὲ or οὐ — οὐδὲ will commonly admit the translation (*a*) 'not — neither,' when the two words or clauses to which the negation is prefixed are simply parallel and coördinate; *e. g.* Matth. vii. 6; (*b*) 'not — nor,' when there is some sort of connection in thought, or accordance in meaning, in the words or clauses with which the negatives are associated, *e. g.* ch. v. 5; (*c*) 'not — nor yet,' where there is less accordance, and where the latter clause has somewhat of a climactic character, *e. g.* Phil. ii. 16, and see notes to *Transl.* (2) Μὴ — μηδὲ — μηδέ, 'not — nor — nor' (John i. 13), where the terms are similar or non-ascensive, or 'not' followed by 'nor — nor yet,' as perhaps Col. ii. 21 (but see notes), or

impurity, nor in guile: 4 but according as we have been approved
of God to be put in trust with the gospel, even so we speak; not
as pleasing men, but God, which trieth our hearts. 5 For neither
at any time used we speech of flattery, as ye know, nor a cloke
of covetousness; God *is* witness; 6 neither seeking glory of men,
neither of you nor of others, though we might have used author-
ity, as Christ's apostles. 7 But we were gentle in the midst of
you, like as a nurse cherisheth her own children; 8 so, being af-
fectionately desirous of you, had we good will to impart unto you,

by 'nor yet—nor,' as here, according as the dissimilarity or climactic force is mainly exhibited in the second or in the third term. (3) Μὴ — μήτε — μήτε, 'not —neither—nor;' where the first negation, so to say, bifurcates, and is expanded into two similar clauses introduced each by the adjunctive μήτε; comp. 1 Tim. i. 7. In cases where there are three or more repetitions of μήτε, our Authorized Version appears generally to continue (3) with repetitions of 'neither;' comp. Matth. v. 34, Luke ix. 3. *Impurity*] 'Uncleanness,' *Auth.* and the remaining Vv. except *Gen.*, 'wickedness.' The present use of the term 'uncleanness' is perhaps insufficiently inclusive; see notes.

4. *According as*] 'As,' *Auth.* and all the other Vv. As has been before observed, the introduction of the 'according' or 'even,' must depend on the general hue of the passage: here it seems necessary. *Have been approved*] Sim. *Wiclif*, 'ben preued;' *Rhem.*, 'were approved:' 'were allowed,' *Auth.* and the remaining Vv. except *Coverd.*, 'are allowed.'

5. *Speech of flattery*] Somewhat similarly *Wicl.*, 'word of glosynge;' *Rhem.*, 'word of adulation:' 'flattering words,' *Auth.* and the remaining Vv.

6. *Neither seeking, etc.*] So *Wicl.*, and sim. *Cov.* (Test.), *Rhem.*, 'nor seeking:' 'nor of men sought we glory,' *Auth.*, and similarly the remaining Vv., except that they more correctly adopt 'neither' at the commencement of the clauses. In some cases, especially in St. Paul's Epp., it is almost impossible to give an idiomatic translation without converting the participle into a finite verb (comp. Rom. xiv. 9 sq.): here, however, there appears no such necessity. *Nor*] So rightly *Cov.* (both), *Bish.*, *Rhem.*: 'nor yet,' *Auth.* and the remaining Vv. except *Wicl.*, 'nether.' *Though we might, etc.*] Similarly *Cran.*, 'when we myght have bene in auctorite:' 'when we might have been burdensome,' *Auth.*, 'whanne .... we myghten haue be in charge,' *Wicl.*; 'when we myght have bene chargeable,' *Tynd.*, *Cov.* (both), *Gen.*, *Bish.*; 'whereas we might have been a burden,' *Rhem.* *Christ's apostles*] So *Wicl.*: 'the Apostles of Christ,' *Auth.* and the remaining Vv.

7. *In the midst of*] So *Cov.* (Test.) *Rhem.*, and similarly *Wicl.*: 'among,' *Auth.* and the remaining Vv. *Like as*] So *Cov.*: 'even as,' *Auth.* and the other Vv. except *Wicl.*, *Cov.* (Test.), 'as if.' *Her own*] 'Her,' *Auth.* and the remaining Vv.; but see notes.

8. *Had we good will*] So somewhat similarly *Tynd.*, *Cran.*, *Gen.*, *Bish.*, 'our good will was;' *Cov.*, 'wolde with good wyll:' 'we were willing,' *Auth.*; 'wolden haue bitake to you,' *Wicl.*; 'wolde delyuer,' *Cov.* (Test.); 'would gladly deliuer,' *Rhem.* *Impart*] Similarly with a *present* infin., *Cov.*

not the gospel of God only, but also our own souls, because ye
became very dear unto us. 9 For ye remember, brethren, our
toil and travail: working night and day, that we might not be
burdensome unto any of you, preached we unto you the Gospel of
God. 10 Ye are witnesses, and *so is* God, how holily and justly
and unblameably we behaved ourselves to you that believe; 11 even
as ye know how in regard of EVERY ONE of you we *did so*, as a
father toward his own children, exhorting you and encouraging
*you*, and charging *you*, 12 that ye should walk worthy of God, who
is calling you into His own kingdom and glory.
13 For this cause we also thank God without ceasing, that when

(Test.), *Rhem.:* 'have imparted,' *Auth.;* 'haue bitake,' *Wicl.;* 'have dealte,' *Tynd.*, *Cov.*, *Cran.*, *Gen.*, *Bish.* *Became*] Similarly *Wicl.*, 'ben made;' *Coverd.* (Test.), 'were become;' *Rhem.*, 'are become;' 'were,' *Auth.* and the remaining Vv. *Very dear*] Similarly *Wicl.*, *Rhem.*, 'moost dere;' *Cov.* (Test.), 'moost beloued:' 'dear,' *Auth.* and remaining Vv.

9. *Toil*] 'Labour,' *Auth.* and the other Vv. except *Wicl.*, 'trauel.' *Working*] So *Coverd.* (Test.), *Rhem.:* 'for *labouring,' *Auth.;* 'for . . . we worchid,' *Wicl.;* 'for we laboured,' *Tynd.*, *Cran.*, *Gen.*, *Bish.;* 'for . . . . . . wroughte we,' *Cov.* *That we might not, etc.*] Somewhat similarly *Wicl.*, 'that we schulden not greue;' 'because we would not be chargeable,' *Auth.*, *Tynd.* ('greveous'), *Cov.*, *Cran.*, *Gen.*, *Bish.;* 'lest we shulde be chargeable,' *Cov.* (Test.); 'lest we should charge,' *Rhem.* *Preached we*] 'We preached,' *Auth.*, *Cov.* (Test.), *Rhem.;* the other Vv. connect the clause with 'and.' The inversion seems to give a slight force, and to keep in more immediate connection the participle and its finite verb.

10. *So is God*] So *Tynd.*, *Cov. Cran.*, *Gen.:* 'God *also*,' *Auth.*, *Bish.;* 'God and ye,' *Wicl.;* 'and God,' *Cov.* (Test.), *Rhem.* *To you*] So *Wicl.*, *Rhem.:* 'among you,' *Auth.* and the remaining Vv. except *Cov.* (Test.), 'by you.'

11. *Even as*] 'As,' *Auth.* and all the other Vv. *How in regard of, etc.*] 'How we exhorted and comforted and charged every one of you,' *Auth.*, and, with a similar use of the finite verb, *Wicl.*, *Tynd.*, *Cov.*, *Gen.*, *Bish.* Of the remaining Vv., *Cov.* (Test.) and *Rhem.* convert the *last* participle only into a finite verb, while *Cran.* alone preserves in all three the participial translation, and in a manner appy. similar to that in the text, 'how that we bare soch affeccyon unto euery one of you, as a father doth unto chyldren, exhortyng, confortyng, and beseechyng you that, etc.' This also seems the more correct position of the clause ὡς πατὴρ κ. τ. λ., except that it somewhat interferes with the easy run of the sentence. *Encouraging*] 'Comforting,' *Auth.* and all the other Vv., though not all with the participle. *His own*] As above, ver. 7: 'his,' *Auth.* and the other Vv. except *Cran.*, which omits the pronoun.

12. *Should*] So *Wicl.:* 'would,' *Auth.* and all the remaining Vv. *Is calling*] 'Hath called,' *Auth.* and all the other Vv. except *Wicl.*, 'that clepid.' *Into*] So *Wicl.*, *Rhem.;* 'unto,' *Auth.* and the remaining Vv. *His own*] 'His,' *Auth.* and all the other Vv.

13. *We also, etc.*] Similarly *Cov.*

ye received from us the word of preaching *that is* of God, ye
received not the word of men, but, as it is in truth, the word of
God, which worketh also in you that believe. 14 For ye, brethren,
became followers of the churches of God which are in Judæa in
Christ Jesus, in that ye also suffered like things of your own coun-
trymen, even as they of the Jews; 15 who killed both the LORD
JESUS and the prophets, and drove us out, and please not God,
and are contrary to all men, 16 hindering us from speaking to the

(Test.), *Rhem.* (omits 'do'), 'do we also giue thankes:' 'also thank we God,' *Auth., Gen., Bish.; Wicl., Tynd., Cov.* omit 'also;' 'thanke we God also,' *Cran.* *That when*] So *Bish.*: 'because when,' *Auth., Cov.* (Test.); 'for whanne,' *Wicl.*; 'because that when,' *Tynd., Cov., Cran., Gen., Rhem.* *The word of, etc.*] Very similarly, *Coverd.* (both), *Bish.*, 'the worde of the preachinge of God:' 'the word of God which ye heard of us,' *Auth.*; 'the word of the herynge of God,' *Wicl., Rhem.*; 'the word wherewith God was preached,' *Tynd., Gen.*; 'the word (wherewith ye learned to know God),' *Cran.* *Received not*] 'Received it not as,' *Auth.* and all the other Vv. except *Wicl.*, 'ye token it not, as.' *Worketh*] So all the other Vv.: 'effectually worketh,' *Auth.* The force of ἐνεργεῖσθαι, 'ex se vim suam exercere,' is not easy to be expressed in English: 'to work,' seems hardly sufficient on the one hand; 'to work effectually,' somewhat too strong on the other. The most exact translation is perhaps 'to evince (its) working,' but is not in harmony with the tone of our Authorized Version.

14. *Are in Judæa*] So *Wicl., Cov.* (Test.), and sim. *Rhem.*: 'in Judæa are,' *Auth.* and the remaining Vv. *In that*] Similarly *Gen., Bish.*, 'because:' 'for,' *Auth.* and the remaining Vv. except *Cov.*, 'so that.' *Suffered*] 'Have suffered,' *Auth.* and all the other Vv. *They*] So *Wicl., Coverd.* (Test.), *Rhem.*; 'they have,' *Auth., Bish.*; 'we ourselves have suffered,' *Tynd., Cran.*; 'as they have suffered,' *Cov., Gen.*

15. *Killed both*] So, in respect of order, *Wicl., Coverd.* (Test.): 'both killed,' *Auth., Gen., Rhem.*; 'as they killed the Lord,' *Tynd., Cran., Bish.*, and sim. *Cov.* *The prophets*] '*Their own,' *Auth.* *Drove us out*] 'Have persecuted us,' *Auth.* and the other Vv. except *Wicl.*, 'persueden us;' *Cov.* (Test.), 'haue persued us.' *Please*] So *Cov., Rhem.*, and similarly *Coverd.* (Test.), 'do not please:' 'they please,' *Auth., Wicl.* and sim. *Tynd.*, and remaining Vv., 'God they please not.'

16. *Hindering us from speaking*] Somewhat similarly *Cran., Bish.*, 'and hynder us:' 'forbidding us to speak,' *Auth., Wicl., Cov.* (both); 'and forbid,' *Tynd., Gen.*; 'prohibiting us to speak,' *Rhem.* *In order to fill*] 'To fill,' *Auth.* *But*] 'For,' *Auth.* and all the other Vv. *Is come*] So *Auth.* and all the other Vv. except *Wicl.*, 'cam.' This certainly seems one of those cases in which our English aorist does not convey the full force of the Greek, but remands the event too unequivocally to the past. While the Greek ἔφθασε states the fact, but is simply *silent* as to 'quam late pateat id quod actum est' (see notes), the English 'came' seems to *express* it, and to imply too distinctly that the event plainly belongs with all its issues to the past. *Very end*] Sim. *Wicl.*, 'in to the ende;' *Cov.* (Test.), 'untyll ye ende;' *Rhem.*, 'to the end:' 'to the

Gentiles that they might be saved, — in order to fill up their sins alway. But the wrath is come upon them to the *very* end.

17 But we, brethren, having been torn from you for a short time,
in presence, not in heart, the more abundantly endeavored to see
your face with great desire. 18 On which account we would fain
have come unto you, even I Paul, both once and again, — and
Satan hindered us. 19 For what *is* our hope, or joy, or crown of

uttermost,' *Auth.*, and similarly *Tynd.*, *Cran.*, *Gen.*, 'even to the utmost;' *Cov.*, 'already unto ye utmost;' *Bish.*, 'to the utmost.' The translation adopted in the text perhaps more precisely conveys the φθάνειν εἰς τέλος than the more qualitative and appy. adverbial 'to the uttermost;' see notes.

17. *Having been torn*] 'Being taken from you,' *Auth.*; 'disolat fro you,' *Wicl*; 'as we are kept from you,' *Tynd.*, *Cov.* ('haue bene'), *Cran.*, *Gen.*, *Bish.* ('were'); 'deprived of you,' *Rhem.* It is almost impossible to represent in English without a paraphrase the highly expressive ἀπορφανισθέντες, which serves so forcibly to convey not only the separation and severance of the Apostle from his converts, but also his desolate and *bereaved* state while so separated. The present translation adopted by Murdoch (*Transl. of Syr. N. T.*), Peile, and others, seems to come as near perhaps to this meaning as any single word that has yet been suggested. *The more abundantly end.*] 'Endeavoured the more abundantly,' *Auth.*; 'hiyed more plenteousli,' *Wicl.*; 'enforsed the more,' *Tynd.*, *Cran.*, *Gen.*, *Bish.*; 'haisted the more,' *Cov.*; 'haysted more spedely,' *Cov.* (Test.); 'hastened the more abundantly,' *Rhem.* Though all the Vv. thus put the adverb after, and not before the verb, the latter order is perhaps still to be preferred, as throwing the emphasis more distinctly on the 'more abundantly.' It may be observed that much caution must be used in adjusting the order of the words in English with regard to emphasis; for while in Greek the emphatic word seems always to have the precedence, the attentive reader will often observe that the contrary is the case in English. In the position of the verb and adverb, however, the two languages seem mainly coincident. The discrepancy between the *English* and the *Greek* position of emphasis has been far too much neglected by modern revisers, who too often seem to think that in all cases the most complete faithfulness is attained by rigidly following the order of the original; see, for example, the canons laid down by Wade, *Notes on the Rev. Transl. of St. John*, p. iv.

18. *On which account*] '*Wherefore,' *Auth.* *Would fain*] 'Would,' *Auth.* and all the other Vv. Few words cause more difficulty to the translator of the N. T. than the verb θέλω: 'wish' is commonly much to weak, 'desire' not always exact, and 'will' and 'would' often liable to be mistaken for mere auxiliaries. In many cases our Auth. Revisers appear to have availed themselves of the past tense 'would' as a very suitable and idiomatic translation of the present θέλω; compare Rom. vii. 15 sq. Here, however, it would be open to the misconception above alluded to. *Both once*] 'Once,' *Auth.* and all the other Vv. *And*] 'But,' *Auth.* and all the other Vv.

19. *Boasting*] 'Rejoicing,' *Auth.* and the other Vv. except *Wicl.*, *Cov.* (Test.), *Rhem.*, 'glory.' *Or are*] 'Are,' *Auth.* and the other Vv. except *Wicl.*,

boasting? Or *are* not ye too it in the presence of our Lord Jesus
at His coming? 20 Verily ye are our glory and joy.

## CHAPTER III.

WHEREFORE when we could no longer forbear, we thought it
good to be left behind at Athens — alone; 2 and sent Timothy,
our brother and fellow-worker with God in the gospel of Christ, to
establish you, and to exhort in behalf of your faith 3 that no man
be disquieted in these afflictions: for yourselves know that we are
appointed thereunto. 4 For verily, when we were with you, we
told you before that we are to be afflicted; as also it came to pass,
and ye know. 5 For this cause, when I too could no longer forbear,

'whether ye ben not.' It is frequently difficult to decide whether, in interrogations introduced by ἢ οὐχί, the ἢ is to be regarded as only giving a greater vividness and abruptness to the question, almost 'What! are not, etc.,' or as really retaining its proper disjunctive force. In the present case, and in more, perhaps than are usually so regarded, the latter seems the most correct view.

*Ye too it*] So, as regards the introduction of 'it,' *Tynd.*, *Cov.* (both), *Cran.*, *Gen.*, *Bish.*; all, however, except *Bish.* ('euen you'), neglect the καί: 'even ye,' *Auth.*; 'ye,' *Wicl.*; 'you,' *Rhem.* *Jesus*] 'Jesus *Christ,' *Auth.*

20. *Verily*] Similarly *Tynd.*, *Cov.*, *Cran.*, *Gen.*, *Bish.*, 'yes ye are:' 'for,' *Auth.* and remaining Vv.

CHAP. III. 1. *Left behind*] 'Left,' *Auth.*; 'dwelle,' *Wicl.*; 'remayne,' *Tynd.*, *Cov.* (both), *Cran.*, *Gen.*, *Bish.*, *Rhem.*

2. *Timothy*] 'Timotheus,' *Auth.*: see ch. i. 1. *And fellow-worker with God*] 'And *minister of God, and our fellow-labourer,' *Auth.* *Exhort*] 'Comfort *you,' *Auth.* and the other Vv. except *Wicl.*, 'be taught;' *Coverd.* (Test.), *Rhem.*, 'exhort.' *In behalf of*] '*Concerning,' *Auth.*

3. *Be disquieted*] 'Should be moved,' *Auth.* and the other Vv. except *Wicl.*, *Coverd.* (Test.), *Rhem.*, 'be moved.' *In*] So *Wicl.*, *Tynd.*, *Coverd.* (both), *Cran.*, *Rhem.*: 'by,' *Auth.*; 'with,' *Gen.*, *Bish.*

4. *Are to be afflicted*] 'Should suffer tribulation,' *Auth.* and the other Vv. except *Wicl.*, *Cov.* (Test.), *Bish.*, *Rhem.*, which adopt the plural 'tribulations.' *As also*] So *Rhem.*: 'even as,' *Auth.* and the remaining Vv.

5. *I too*] Sim. *Cov.* (Test.), *Rhem.*, 'I also:' 'I,' *Auth.* and remaining Vv. except *Wicl.*, 'I Poul.' *In order to know*] 'To know,' *Auth.*, *Wicl.*, *Coverd.* (Test.), *Rhem.*; 'that I myght have knowledge,' *Tynd.* and the remaining Vv. *Haply*] So *Tynd.*, *Cov.* (both), and sim. *Wiclif*, 'peradventure;' *Rhem.*, 'perhaps:' 'by some means,' *Auth.*, *Cran.*; 'in any sort,' *Gen.*, *Bish.* *Have tempted*] So *Auth.*, *Cov.* (Test.), *Rhem.* ('hath'): 'had,' *Tynd.* and the remaining Vv. Neither translation is quite exact, or strictly idiomatic; the English perfect, however, seems here to approach more nearly to the present use of the Greek aorist than the pluperfect, and perhaps, owing to the peculiar form of the expression in the original, may be

I sent in order to know your faith, lest haply the tempter have
tempted you, and our labor should prove in vain.
6 But now when Timothy came to us from you, and brought us
the good tidings of your faith and your love, and that ye have good
remembrance of us always, longing to see us, as we also *to see*
you, — 7 for this cause, were we comforted, brethren, over you in
all our distress and affliction by your faith: 8 since now we live, if
ye stand fast in the Lord. 9 For what thanks can we render to
God for you, for all the joy which we joy for your sakes in the
presence of our God; 10 night and day praying very exceedingly

considered as admissible in point of English. *Should prove*] 'Be,' *Auth.*: 'be made,' *Wicl.*, *Rhem.*; 'had bene bestowed,' *Tynd.*, *Cov.*, *Cran.*, *Gen.*; 'become,' *Cov.* (Test.); 'had been,' *Bish.* It seems here perhaps unnecessary to adopt the more strict translation of κόπος, as the phrase is semi-proverbial, and does appear to place in prominence that idea of 'molestus labor,' which in other passages is often distinctly traceable in κόπος, and is necessary to be preserved; see notes on ch. i. 3,

6. *Timothy*] 'Timotheus,' *Auth.*: see ch. i. 1. *To us from you*] So *Wicl.*, *Cov.* (Test.), *Rhem.*; 'from you unto us,' *Auth.* and the remaining Vv., — a departure from the order of the Greek for which there does not here seem any satisfactory reason. *Your love*] So *Cov.*, *Cran.*, and sim. *Tynd.*, *Gen.*, *Bish.*, 'love:' 'charity,' *Auth.*, *Wicl.*, *Cov.* (Test.), *Rhem.* On this correction see notes *on* 1 *Tim.* i. 5 (Transl.). *Longing*] 'Desiring greatly,' *Auth.*; 'desiryngе,' *Wicl.* and the other Vv.: the ἐπι- is not intensive; see notes.

7. *For this cause*] 'Therefore,' *Auth.* and the remaining Vv. *Were we*] 'We were,' *Auth.* and similarly the remaining Vv. The transposition seems to keep the sentence a little closer together, and is frequently adopted in *Auth.* *Brethren*] So, in this place, *Rhem.*: *Auth.* and remaining Vv. append it to 'therefore.' In this case it seems more exact to retain the order of the Greek. *Distress and affliction*] '*Affliction and distress,' *Auth.*

8. *Since*] 'For,' *Auth.* and the other Vv. except *Rhem.*, 'because.' Here the particle ὅτι seems scarcely to have so full a force as 'because,' and yet to be somewhat stronger than 'for,' — which, as a general rule, it seems desirable to reserve as the translation of γάρ.

9. *Render to God*] So *Cov.* (Test.), *Rhem.*, and similarly *Wicl.*, 'gilde to God:' 'render to God again,' *Auth.*; 'recompence to God,' *Tynd.* and the remaining Vv. *Which*] Similarly *Tynd.*, *Cran.*, *Gen.*, 'that:' 'wherewith,' *Auth.*, *Cov.* (Test.), *Bish.*, *Rhem.*; 'in which,' *Wicl.* *In the presence of*] 'Before,' *Auth.*; see notes on ch. i. 3.

10. *Very exceedingly*] 'Exceedingly,' *Auth.* and the other Vv. except *Wicl.*, 'more plenteousli;' *Rhem.*, 'more abundantly.' *May*] So *Cov.* (Test.), *Rhem.*: 'might,' *Auth.* and the remaining Vv. *Supply, etc.*] 'Might perfect that which is lacking in,' *Auth.*, and similarly *Tynd.* ('fulfil'), *Gen.* (ib.), *Bish.* ('accomplish'), 'fulfille the thingis that failen,' *Wicl.*; 'fulfyll the thynges that are,' *Cov.* (Test.), *Cran.* ('which'); 'accomplish those things that want of,' *Rhem.*

that we may see your face and supply the lacking measures of your faith?

11 Now may God Himself and our Father, and our Lord Jesus Christ, direct our way unto you: 12 but you may the Lord make to increase and abound in your love one toward another and toward all *men*, even as we also *do* toward you; 13 to the end he may stablish your hearts unblamable in holiness in the presence of God and our Father, at the coming of our Lord Jesus with all His saints.

## CHAPTER IV.

FURTHERMORE then, brethren, we beseech you and exhort *you* in the Lord Jesus, that as ye received of us how ye ought to walk and to please God, as indeed ye ARE walking, *so* ye would abound still more. 2 For ye know what commandments we gave you by the Lord Jesus. 3 For this is the will of God, *even* your

11. *May God*] *Auth.* and the other Vv. omit 'may,' which however seems to add perspicuity to the sentence.

12. *But you may the Lord*] 'And the Lord make you, etc.,' *Auth.*, and similarly the other Vv. except *Cov.*, which adopts 'but,' and *Cran.*, which omits δέ, and incorrectly adopts a future in translation, 'the Lord also shall, etc.' Though there is perhaps some little awkwardness in the prominence given to the pronoun, it seems required to convey to the English reader the antithesis of the original; see notes. *Your love*] So *Wicl.*, *Cov.* (Test.), *Rhem.*: 'love,' *Auth.* and the remaining Vv. *We also*] So *Rhem.*, and similarly *Wicl.* 'also we:' *Cov.* (Test.), 'we do also:' 'we,' *Auth.* and the remaining Vv.

13. *In the presence of*] 'Before,' *Auth*; see notes on ch. i. 3. *God and our Father*] So *Wicl.*, *Cov.* (Test.), *Rhem.*: 'God, even our Father,' *Auth.*; 'God oure Father,' *Tynd.* and the remaining Vv. On the best mode of translating this august formula, see notes on *Gal.* i. 4 (Transl.). *Jesus*] 'Jesus* Christ,' *Auth.*

CHAPTER IV. 1. *Furthermore*] So *Auth.* and the remaining Vv. except *Wicl.*, 'fro hennesforward;' *Rhem.*, 'for the rest.' This translation of λοιπὸν is perhaps not exactly literal, but seems sufficiently approximate: 'finally' would here be hardly appropriate, and 'for the rest' (*Rhem.*), though literal, both harsh and awkward. *Brethren, we*] So *Rhem.*, *Cov.* (Test.), and similarly *Wicl.*: *Auth.* and remaining Vv. insert it after 'you,'—but not in accordance with the Greek order. *In the Lord*] So *Wicl.*, *Tynd.*, *Cov.* (Test.), *Gen.*, *Bish.*, *Rhem.*: 'by the Lord,' *Auth.*, *Cov.*, *Cran.* *Received*] 'Have received,' *Auth.* and all the other Vv. *As indeed ye are walking*] *Auth.** omits. *Still more*] 'More and more,' *Auth.* and the other Vv. except *Wicl.*, 'the more;' *Cov.* (Test.), 'be more plentyfull;' *Rhem.*, 'abounde more.'

3. *To wit, that ye abstain*] Sim. *Wicl.*,

sanctification, to wit, that ye abstain from fornication, — 4 that
every one of you know how to get himself his own vessel in sancti-
fication and honor, 5 not in the lustfulness of desire, even as the
Gentiles also which know not God; 6 that no *man* go beyond and
overreach HIS BROTHER in the matter: because that the Lord *is*
the avenger of all these things, as also we before told you and did
solemnly testify. 7 For God called us not for uncleanness, but in
sanctification. 8 Wherefore then, he that rejecteth, rejecteth not
man, but God, who also gave HIS HOLY SPIRIT unto you.

*Cov.*, *Rhem.*, 'that ye (*Rhem.*, 'you') absteyne:' 'that ye should abstain,' *Auth.*, *Cran.*; 'and that ye shuld abstayne,' *Tynd.*, *Gen.*, *Bish.*; 'that ye abstayne yourselues,' *Cov.* (Test.)

4. *Know*] So *Cov.*, and sim. *Wicl.*, 'kunne:' 'should know,' *Auth.* and the remaining Vv. except *Rhem.*, 'may know.' *Get himself his own*] 'Possess his,' *Auth.*, *Cov.* (Test.), *Bish.*, *Rhem.*; 'wilde' [wield], *Wicl.*; 'kepe his,' *Tynd.*, *Cov.*, *Cran.*, *Gen.*

5. *Lustfulness of desire*] 'Lust of concupiscence,' *Auth.* and the other Vv. except *Wicl.*, *Rhem.*, 'passioun of lust.' *Gentiles also*] Similarly *Cov.* (Test.), 'the hethen also:' 'Gentiles,' *Auth.*, and similarly, as respects the omission of 'also,' the remaining Vv.

6. *Overreach*] 'Defraud,' *Auth.*; 'ouer go,' *Wicl.*, *Rhem.*; 'goe to farre,' *Tynd.*, *Cov.*; 'passe,' *Cov.* (Test.); 'oppress,' *Cran.*, *Gen.*, *Bish.* *The matter*] '*Any* matter,' *Auth.*, *Gen.*, *Bish.*; 'chaffaringe,' *Wicl.*; 'bargayning,' *Tynd.*, *Cov.* (both), *Cran*; 'in businesse,' *Rhem.* *All these things*] So *Wicl.*, *Coverd.* (Test.), *Rhem.*, 'all such,' *Auth.*; 'all suche thynges,' *Tynd.* and the remaining Vv. *As also, etc.*] 'As we also have forewarned you and testified,' *Auth.*; 'as we bifor seiden to you and han witnessid,' *Wicl.*; 'as we told you before tyme and testified,' *Tynd.*; 'as we haue sayde and testified unto you aforetyme,' *Cov.*; 'as we haue sayde unto you before and haue wytnessed,' *Cov.* (Test.); 'as we tolde you before and testifyed,' *Cran.*, *Gen.* ('before tyme'); 'as we have told you before time and have testified,' *Bish.*; 'as we haue foretold you and haue testified,' *Rhem.* The slight change to 'did testify' is for the sake of preserving a sort of rhythm; comp. notes on *Phil.* ii. 16 (Transl.).

7. *Called us not*] Similarly *Wicl.*, 'clepid not us:' 'hath not called us,' *Auth.* and the remaining Vv. *For*] 'Unto,' *Auth.* and the other Vv. except *Wicl.*, *Rhem.*, 'in to;' *Cov.*, 'to.' *In sanctification*] 'Unto holiness,' *Auth.* and the other Vv. except *Wicl.*, 'in to holyness;' *Cov.* (Test.), 'unto halowyng;' *Rhem.*, 'into sanctification.'

8. *Wherefore then, etc.*] 'He therefore that despiseth despiseth,' *Auth.* and the other Vv. except *Wicl.*, *Rhem.*, 'therefore he that dispisith thes thingis;' *Cov.* (Test.), 'wherfore he that despyseth these thynges despyseth,' and *Gen.*, *Rhem.*, which also insert 'these things' after the first 'despiseth.' *Also gave*] So *Wicl.*: 'hath also given,' *Auth.*; 'hath sent,' *Tynd.*, *Cran.*, *Gen.*. 'hath geuen,' *Cov.*: 'also hath geuen,' *Cov.* (Test.), *Rhem.*; 'hath euen given you,' *Bish.* *His Holy Spirit unto you*] 'Unto *us His Holy Spirit,' *Auth.*; 'His Holi Spirit in us,' *Wicl.*, Cov. (Test.), *Rhem.*; 'His Holy Sprete among you,' *Tynd.*, *Cran.*; 'His Holy Spirit in to you,' *Cov.*; 'you

9 Now as touching brotherly love, ye need not that I write unto
you; for ye yourselves are TAUGHT of God to love one another:
10 for indeed ye do it toward all the brethren that are in the whole
of Macedonia. But we beseech you, brethren, to abound still
more, 11 and to study to be quiet, and to do your own business, and
to work with your own hands, according as we commanded you;
12 in order that ye may walk becomingly toward them that are
without, and may have lack of nothing.

13 Now we would not have you to be ignorant, brethren, con-
cerning them that are sleeping, that ye sorrow not, even as the
rest which have no hope. 14 For if we believe that Jesus died and
rose again, even so those laid to sleep through Jesus will God
bring with Him. 15 For this we say unto you in the word of the

His Holy Sprite,' *Gen.*; 'you His Holy Spirit,' *Bish.*

9. *Now*] 'But,' *Auth.* and all the other Vv.

10. *For indeed*] 'And indeed,' *Auth.*; 'for,' *Wicl.*, *Cov.* (Test.); 'ye and that thinge verely,' *Tynd.*, *Cov.* (omits 'verely'), *Cran.*, *Gen.*, *Bish.*; 'yea and you doe it,' *Rhem.* *That*] 'Which,' *Auth.* and the other Vv. except *Wicl.*, *Coverd.* (Test.), *Rhem.*, which omit the relative. *The whole of*] 'All,' *Auth.* and the other Vv. except *Cov.* (Test.), 'whole Maced.' *To abound still more*] 'That ye increase more and more,' *Auth.*, *Tynd.*, *Cov.* ('yet more and more'), *Cran.*, *Bish.*; 'that ye abounde more,' *Wiclif*, *Rhem.*; 'that ye be more abundaunte,' *Cov.* (Test.); 'that ye excel more and more,' *Gen.*

11. *To study*] 'That ye study,' *Auth.* and the other Vv. except *Wicl.*, 'and taken kepe;' 'that ye endeuoure,' *Coverd.* (Test.); 'that you employ your indeuour,' *Rhem.* *According as*] 'As,' *Auth.* and all the other Vv.

12. *In order that*] 'That,' *Auth.* and the other Vv. except *Wiclif*, *Rhem.*, 'and that.' *Becomingly*] 'Honestly,' *Auth.* and all the other Vv. The translation 'seemly' deserves consideration, but is appy. open to the objection that, in point of strict etymology, such a form of the *adverb* is somewhat doubtful; see Trench, *on Auth. Vers.* ch. II. p. 31.

13. *Now we*] 'But I,' *Auth.*; 'for—we,' *Wicl.*; 'but we,' *Cov.* (Test.); 'and we,' *Rhem.*: *Tynd.*, *Coverd.* ('we'), *Cran.*, *Gen.*, *Bish.* omit δὲ in translation. *That are sleeping*] Very similarly *Cov.* (Test.), 'that be slepynge:' 'which are *asleep,' *Auth.*, *Bish.*; 'men that dreume,' *Wiclif*; 'which are fallen asleep,' *Tynd.*, *Cov.*, *Cran.*, *Gen.*, 'that sleepe,' *Rhem.* *The rest*] 'Others,' *Auth.*, *Rhem.*; 'other,' *Wiclif*, *Tynd.*, *Coverd.*, *Cran.*, *Gen.*, *Bish.*; 'ye other,' *Cov.* (Test.).

14. *Those laid to sleep through Jesus*] 'Them also which sleep in Jesus,' *Auth.*, *Gen.*, *Bish.* (omits 'also'); 'them that been deed bi Jesus,' *Wicl.*; 'them also which slepe by Jesus,' *Tynd.*, *Cov.*, *Cran.*; 'them that haue slept,' *Cov.* (Test.), *Rhem.*

15. *In the word*] So *Wicl.*, *Tynd.*, *Cov.*, *Cran.*, *Gen.* ('words'), *Rhem.*: 'by the word,' *Auth.*, *Bish.*; 'on the worde,' *Cov.* (Test.),—a translation that deserves consideration. *Living and are remaining behind*] 'Which are alive and remain,' *Auth.*: 'that lyuen that ben lefte,' *Wicl.*: 'which live and are re-

Lord, that we which are living *and* are remaining behind unto the
coming of the Lord shall in no wise prevent them which are
asleep: 16 because the Lord Himself shall descend from heaven
with a shout, with the voice of the archangel, and with the trump
of God, and the dead in Christ shall rise first; 17 THEN we which
are living *and* are remaining behind shall be caught up at the same
time with them in clouds, to meet the Lord in the air; and so shall
we ever be with the Lord. 18 So then comfort one another with
these words.

## CHAPTER V.

BUT concerning the times and the seasons, brethren, ye have no

mayninge,' *Tynd., Cov., Gen., Bish.;* 'that lyue whych remayne,' *Cov.* (Test.); 'whych shall lyue, and shall remayne,' *Cran;* 'which liue, which are remaining,' *Rhem.* It is not easy to give these words a perfectly accurate and perfectly idiomatic translation: 'we the living, the remaining, etc.,' would be accurate, but bald; 'we the living who are, etc.,' somewhat harsh and appositional. We therefore may perhaps not unwisely retain the 'and,' and also (with *Auth.*) omit the second οἱ in translation, as tending to overload the sentence.

*Shall in no wise*] 'Shall not,' *Auth.* and all the other Vv. Great caution is required in the translation of οὐ μὴ in the N. T., as in some cases it appears very doubtful whether any emphatic negation is really contemplated by the writer, and whether the formula was not due to that general tendency to strengthened negation which is often observable in later Greek. Perhaps the simplest and best rule is to be guided by the context,—which here seems to require the stronger form of translation. If it be thought necessary to alter the now obsolete 'prevent,' we may perhaps have recourse to the more modern 'precede;' archaisms, however, as such, are not altered in this revision.

16. *Because*] 'For,' *Auth.* and all the other Vv. In the following words it is perhaps doubtful whether, as in *Rhem.*, the Greek order might not be advantageously retained. It tends, however, to throw appy. a greater stress on καταβήσεται ἀπ' οὐρανοῦ than is conveyed by the original.

17. *Are living, etc.*] 'Are alive *and* remain,' *Auth.;* 'that lyuen and ben lefte,' *Wicl.;* 'which live and remain,' *Tynd., Cov., Gen., Bish.;* 'that lyue whyche are left ouer,' *Cov.* (Test.); 'which shall lyue (euen we which shall remayne),' *Cran.;* 'we that liue, that are left,' *Rhem.* The slight addition 'behind' seems suggested by the compound περιλείπεσθαι, the prep. perhaps marking the idea of overplus, and thence, in the present context, of a continuance on earth and survival; comp. Herod. I. 82.

*At the same time*] 'Together,' *Auth., Wicl., Cov.* (Test.); 'with them also,' *Tynd., Coverd., Cran., Gen., Bish.;* 'withal,' *Rhem.* On the translation of ἅμα, see notes. *In clouds*] So *Wicl.;* 'in the clouds,' *Auth.* and the remaining Vv. except *Cov.* (Test.), 'into the ayre.'

18. *So then*] 'Wherefore,' *Auth.* and the other Vv. except *Wicl., Rhem.*, 'therfor.'

CHAPTER V. 1. *Concerning*] 'Of,'

need to be written unto. 2 For yourselves know perfectly that the
day of the Lord so cometh as a thief in the night. 3 For when
they shall say, Peace and safety; then doth destruction come sud-
denly upon them, as travail upon a woman with child; and they
shall in no wise escape. 4 But ye, brethren, are not in darkness,
that the day should overtake you as a thief. 5 For ye all are sons
of light, and sons of the day: we are not of the night, nor of
darkness. 6 Accordingly then let us not sleep, even as *do* the
rest; but let us watch and be sober. 7 For they that sleep sleep
in the night; and they that are drunken are drunken in the night.
8 But let us, as we are of the day, be sober, having put on the
breastplate of faith and love, and as an helmet, the hope of salva-
tion; 9 because God did not appoint us to wrath, but to obtain

*Auth.* and all the other Vv. *To be written unto*] 'That I write unto you,' *Auth.* and the other Vv. (*Wicl.* 'to') except *Coverd.*, 'it is no nede to wryte unto you;' *Cov.* (Test.), 'that we do wryt unto you;' *Rhem.*, 'that we write to you.'

3. *Doth destruction come suddenly*] 'Sudden destruction cometh,' *Auth.*; 'sudeyn deeth schal come,' *Wicl.*; 'commeth on the soden destr.,' *Tynd.*; 'shall soden destr. come,' *Coverd*, *Cran.*, *Rhem.*; 'shall a soden destr. come,' *Cov.* (Test.); 'commeth on them soden destr.,' *Gen.*; 'shall come upon them sudden destr.,' *Bish.* *In no wise*] 'Not,' *Auth.* and all the other Vv.; see notes on ch. iv. 15 (Transl.).

4. *The*] 'That,' *Auth.* and the other Vv. except *Wicl.*, 'the ilke;' *Rhem.*, 'the same.' It may be doubted whether the text is here so explicit as *Auth.*; the translation, however, of the article by a pronoun is so very hazardous, and so erroneous in principle, that the cases are but very few in which idiom or perspicuity can be admitted so far to prevail over the literal rendering.

5. *For ye all are*] '*Ye are all,' *Auth.* Independent of the insertion of γάρ, which is required by uncial authority, it seems also better to give 'all' a prominence corresponding to that of the πάν-τες in the Greek. *Sons* (bis)] Sim. *Wicl.*, 'the sones — sones;' 'the children,' *Auth* and the remaining Vv. except *Cov.*, which omits the article in both cases, and *Rhem.*, which omits it in the second.

6. *Accordingly then*] 'Therefore,' *Auth.* and all the other Vv. *Even as*] '*As,' *Auth.* and the other Vv. except *Rhem.*, 'as also.' *The rest*] 'Others,' *Auth.*, *Rhem.*; 'other,' *Tynd.* and the remaining Vv. except *Cov.* (Test.), 'the other.'

7. *Are drunken*] 'Be drunken,' *Auth.* and the other Vv. except *Rhem.*, 'be drunke.'

8. *As we are*] 'Who are,' *Auth.*; 'that ben,' *Wicl.*; 'which are,' *Tynd.*, *Cov.*, *Cran.*, *Gen.*, *Bish.*; 'that are,' *Cov.* (Test.), *Rhem.* *Having put on*] 'Putting on,' *Auth.*; 'clothid in,' *Wicl.*; 'armed with,' *Tynd.*, *Coverd.* (both), *Cran.*, *Gen.*, *Bish.*; 'hauing on,' *Rhem.* *As an helmet*] So *Tynd.*, *Gen.*: 'for an helmet,' *Auth.*, *Cran.*, *Bish.*; 'in the helme of,' *Wicl.*; 'with ye helmet of,' *Cov.*; 'the helmet the hope, etc.,' *Cov.* (Test.); 'a helmet the hope of,' *Rhem.*

9. *Because*] 'For,' *Auth.* and all the

salvation through our Lord Jesus Christ, 10 who died for us, that,
whether we wake or sleep, we should together live with him.
11 Wherefore comfort each other, and edify one the other, even as
also ye do.

12 Now we beseech you, brethren, to regard them which labor
among you, and preside over you in the Lord, and admonish you;
13 and to esteem them very highly in love for their work's sake.
Be at peace among yourselves. 14 Moreover, we exhort you,
brethren, admonish the unruly, comfort the feebleminded, support
the weak, be long suffering toward all *men*. 15 See that none ren-
der evil for evil unto any *man;* but alway follow after that which
is good, toward one another and toward all *men*. 16 Rejoice alway;
17 pray without ceasing; 18 in every thing give thanks: for this is

other Vv. *Did not appoint*] 'Hath not appointed,' *Auth.* and the other Vv. except *Wicl.*, 'puttid not us.' *Through*] So *Cov.* (Test.): 'by,' *Auth. Wicl., Rhem.;* 'by the meanes of,' *Tynd., Cov., Cran., Gen., Bish.*

10. *Together live*] 'Live together,' *Auth.* and all the other Vv.; see notes.

11. *Each other*] 'Yourselves together,' *Auth., Tynd., Cov., Cran.;* 'ye to gidre,' *Wicl.;* 'one another,' *Cov.* (Test.), *Gen., Bish., Rhem.* *The other*] 'Another,' *Auth.* and the other Vv. except *Wicl.*, 'ech other.'

12. *Now*]. So *Bish.:* 'and,' *Auth., Wicl., Cov.,* (Test.), *Rhem.; Tynd., Cov., Cran., Gen.* omit. *Regard*] 'Know,' *Auth.* and all the other Vv. *Preside over*] 'Are over,' *Auth., Bish.;* 'ben souereyns to,' *Wicl.;* 'have the oversight,' *Tynd., Cov., Cran., Gen.;* 'haue oversight,' *Coverd.* (Test.); 'gouerne,' *Rhem.*

13. *Be at peace*] *Auth., Tynd., Cov.; Cran., Gen., Bish.* prefix 'and;' 'haue ye pees,' *Wicl.;* 'and haue peace,' *Cov.* (Test.); 'haue peace,' *Rhem.*

14. *Moreover*] 'Now,' *Auth.;* 'and,' *Wicl., Cov.* (Test.), *Rhem.:* the rest omit. *Admonish the unruly*] Sim. *Bish.*, 'admonish them that are unruly;' *Rhem.*, 'admonish the unquiet:' 'warn them that are unruly,' *Auth., Tynd., Cov., Cran., Gen.;* 'repreue ye unpesible men,' *Wicl.;* 'rebuke the restless, *Cov.* (Test.). *Longsuffering*] 'Patient,' *Auth.* and all the other Vv.

15. *None*] So *Auth.* and the other Vv. except *Wicl., Cov.* (Test.), 'no man.' It may be remarked that *Auth.* and the older Vv. appy. always adopt the form 'none,' not 'no one.' *Alway*] So *Cov.* (Test.), and sim. *Rhem.*, 'alwaies:' 'ever,' *Auth.* and the other Vv. except *Wicl.*, 'euermore.' *Follow after*] 'Follow,' *Auth.* and the other Vv. except *Wicl.*, 'sue;' *Cov.* (Test.), 'followe — upon;' *Rhem.*, 'pursue.' *Toward one another*] So ch. iii. 12 (*Auth.*): '*both among yourselves,' *Auth.* and the other Vv. except *Wicl.*, 'eche to other;' *Coverd.* (Test.), 'one unto another;' *Rhem.*, 'towards eche other.' *Toward*] So *Bish., Rhem.;* 'to,' *Auth.* and the remaining Vv. except *Coverd.* (Test.), 'unto,'

16. *Alway*] So *Cov.* (both), *Rhem.:* 'evermore,' *Auth., Wicl.;* 'euer,' *Tynd.*, and the remaining Vv.

18. *Toward you*] So *Tynd., Coverd.* (both), *Cran., Gen.:* 'concerning you,' *Auth., Bish.:* 'in alle you,' *Wicl., Rhem.*

the will of God in Christ Jesus toward you. 19 Quench not the Spirit; 20 despise not prophesyings: 21 but prove all things; hold fast that which is good. 22 Abstain from every form of evil. 23 But may the God of peace Himself sanctify you wholly; and may your spirit and soul and body be preserved whole without blame in the coming of our Lord Jesus Christ. 24 Faithful *is* He that calleth you, who also will do *it*.

25 Brethren, pray for us. 26 Salute all the brethren with an holy kiss. 27 I adjure you by the Lord that this epistle be read unto all the holy brethren.

28 The grace of our Lord Jesus Christ *be* with you.

21. *But prove*] '*Prove,' *Auth.*.

22. *Every form*] Similarly *Gen.*, 'all kynde:' 'all appearance,' *Auth.*, *Bish.*, *Rhem.*, sim. *Cran.*; 'al yuel spice.' *Wicl.*; 'all suspicious thinges,' *Tynd.*, *Cov.*; 'all euel lykenesse,' *Cov.* (Test.).

23. *But may the God, etc.*] Sim. *Rhem.*, 'and the God of peace Himself:' 'and the very God of peace,' *Auth.*; 'and God himsilf of pees,' *Wicl.*; 'the very God of peace,' *Tynd.*, *Cov.* (both), *Cran.*; 'that God of peace,' *Gen.*; 'now the very God of peace, *Bish.* *May*] '*I pray God*,' *Auth.* and the other Vv. except *Wicl.*, *Cov.* (Test.), *Rhem.*, which omit the words. *Your spirit*] 'Your whole spirit,' *Auth.* and the other Vv. except *Wicl.*, 'your spirit be kept hool:' see notes. *Whole without blame*] 'Blameless,' *Auth.*, *Cov.* (both), *Bish.*; 'without playnt,' *Wicl.*; 'be kept fautlesse,' *Tynd.*, *Gen.*; 'so that in nothing ye maye be blamed,' *Cran.*; 'without blame may be, etc.,' *Rhem.* *In*] So *Wicl.*, *Cov.* (Test ), *Cran.*, *Rhem.*; 'unto,' *Auth.*, *Tynd*, *Cov.*, *Gen*, *Bish.*

26. *Salute*] So *Rhem.*; 'greet,' *Auth.* and the remaining Vv.

27. *Adjure*] So *Rhem.*, and sim. *Wicl.*, 'conjure:' 'charge,' *Auth.* and the remaining Vv.

28. *With you*] *Auth.* adds '*Amen.'

THE

# SECOND EPISTLE TO THE THESSALONIANS.

## CHAPTER I.

PAUL, and Silvanus, and Timothy, unto the church of the
Thessalonians in God our Father and the Lord Jesus
Christ. [2] Grace *be* unto you and peace, from God our Father
and the Lord Jesus Christ.
[3] We are bound to give thanks to God always for you, brethren,
as it is meet, because that your faith increaseth exceedingly, and
the love of every one of you all toward each other ABOUNDETH;
[4] so that we ourselves make our boast in you in the churches of
God, for your patience and faith in all your persecutions and the
afflictions that ye are enduring; — [5] *which is* a token of the right-
eous judgment of God, that ye may be counted worthy of the

CHAP. I. 1. *Timothy*] 'Timotheus,' *Auth.* and the other Vv. except *Wicl.*, 'Tymothe;' *Rhem.*, 'Timothee:' see notes *on Col.* i. 1 (Transl.).

2. *Grace be unto*] So *Cov.* (Test.), *Cran.*: 'Grace unto you,' *Auth.*; 'grace to you,' *Wicl.*, *Rhem.*; 'grace be with you,' *Tynd.*, *Cov.*, *Bish.*; 'grace be to you,' *Gen.*

3. *Give thanks to*] So *Cov.* (Test.), *Rhem.*, and *Auth.* in 1 Thess. i. 2: 'thank,' *Auth.* and the remaining Vv. except *Wicl.*, 'do thankyngis.'

*Increaseth*] So *Cov.* (both), *Rhem.*: 'groweth,' *Auth.* and the remaining Vv. except *Wicl.*, 'wexith.' *Love*] So *Tynd.*, *Cov.* (both), *Cran.*, *Gen.*, *Bish.*: 'charity,' *Auth.*, *Wicl.*, *Rhem.*; comp. notes *on* 1 *Tim.* i. 5 (Transl.).

4. *Make our boast in*] Similarly *Cov.*, 'make our boast of;' *Cran.*, 'boast of:' 'glory in,' *Auth.*, *Wicl.*, *Rhem.*; 'rejoice of,' *Tynd.*, *Cov.* (Test.), *Gen.*, *Bish.* *The afflictions*] 'Tribulations,' *Auth.* and the other Vv. except *Cov.* (both), 'troubles.'

5. *Token*] So *Tynd.*, *Cov.*, *Cran.*, *Gen.*, *Bish.*; 'manifest token,' *Auth.*; 'ensaumple,' *Wicl.*, *Cov.* (Test.), *Rhem.* *Are also suffering*] 'Ye also suffer, *Auth.* and the other Vv. except *Wicl.*, *Cov.* (Test.), 'ye suffre;' *Rhem.*, 'also you suffer.' The change appears to have two advantages, first, that it more distinctly preserves the association of καὶ and πάσχετε, and secondly, that it conveys more fully the present and continuing nature of the trials of the Thessalonians.

kingdom of God, for which ye are also suffering. [6] If so be that
it is righteous with God to recompense to them that afflict you
affliction; [7] and to you who are afflicted, rest with us, at the reve-
lation of the Lord Jesus from heaven with the angels of His power
[8] in flame of fire, rendering vengeance to them that know not
God, and that obey not the gospel of our Lord Jesus Christ.
[9] Who shall suffer punishment, *even* eternal destruction apart from
the presence of the Lord, and from the glory of His power;
[10] when He shall come to be glorified in His saints, and to be
admired in all them that believe (because our testimony to you-

6. *If so be that*] So *Auth.* in Rom. viii. 9, 17, 1 Cor. xv. 15, 2 Cor. v. 3, 1 Pet. ii. 3: 'seeing,' *Auth.;* 'if nethe-less,' *Wicl.;* 'it is verely,' *Tynd., Cran.;* 'for it is,' *Cov., Bish.;* 'if at the leest,' *Cov.* (Test.); 'for it is verely,' *Gen.;* 'if yet,' *Rhem.* *Afflict you, affliction*] 'Tribulation to them that trouble you,' *Auth.* and the other Vv. (*Cov.* 'unto') except *Rhem.*, 'tribulation to them that vexe you.' The change seems to preserve more clearly the antithesis, and also to bring more into prominence the 'lex talionis' that is tacitly referred to.

7. *Afflicted*] 'Troubled,' *Auth.* and the other Vv. except *Rhem.*, 'vexed.' *At the revelation of the Lord Jesus*] Sim. *Cov.* (Test.), 'unto the reuelation, etc.;' *Rhem.*, 'in the revelation, etc.:' 'when the Lord Jesus shall be revealed,' *Auth.;* 'in the schewynge of, etc.,' *Wicl.;* 'when the Lord Jesus shall shewe him silfe,' *Tynd., Cov., Cran., Gen., Bish.* *The angels of His power*] So *Cov.* (both), *Cran., Rhem.*, and sim. *Wicl.*, 'aungels of His vertu:' 'His mighty angels,' *Auth., Tynd., Gen., Bish.*

8. *In flame of fire*] So *Rhem.* and similarly *Wicl., Coverd.* (Test.), 'the flawme of fire:' 'in flaming fire,' *Auth., Tynd., Gen., Bish.;* 'with flam-inge fyre,' *Cov., Cran.* *Rendering*] So *Tynd., Gen., Bish.;* 'taking,' *Auth.;* 'schall geue,' *Wicl.;* 'to geue,' *Cov.;* 'geuynge,' *Coverd.* (Test.), *Rhem.;* 'shall rendre,' *Cran.*

9. *Suffer punishment, even*] 'Shall be punished with,' *Auth.* and the other Vv. except *Wicl., Cov.* (Test.), *Rhem.*, 'schulen suffre.' *Eternal*] So *Rhem.:* 'everlasting,' *Auth.* and the remaining Vv. Though really the change is here unimportant, it is still perhaps best to translate this word uniformly, except where the context seems specially and *exclusively* to imply *simple* duration. In the present case the αἰώνιος is equally qualitative and quantitative. *Apart from*] 'From,' *Auth.* and all the other Vv.

10. *Shall come*] So *Auth.* and all the other Vv. There is some little difficulty in the translation of ὅταν with the aor. subj. Perhaps, as a general rule, it may be said that when the exact rendering 'shall have,' is inapplicable (see notes on *Tit.* iii. 12, *Transl.*), we may conveniently adopt in translation the *present* (indic. or conj.) when the reference to the actual futurity of the subsequent event is less specially contemplated (comp. Matth. xxi. 40, Mark iv. 29, al.), and *future* when, as here, such a reference is more distinct and prominent. *To you-ward*] Sim. *Bish.*, 'toward you,' and somewhat sim. *Tynd.;* 'that we had unto you;' *Cov.*, 'unto you;' *Cran.*,

ward was believed) in that day. [11] Whereunto we also pray always for you, that our God may count you worthy of your calling, and fulfil every good pleasure of goodness and the work of faith with power; [12] that the name of our Lord Jesus Christ may be glorified in you, and ye in Him, according to the grace of our God and the Lord Jesus Christ.

## CHAPTER II.

Now we beseech you, brethren, touching the coming of our Lord Jesus Christ, and our gathering together unto Him, [2] that ye be not quickly shaken from your *sober* mind, nor be troubled, neither by spirit, nor by word nor by letter as from us, to the effect that the day of Christ is now come. [3] Let no man deceive

'that we had to you:' 'among you,' *Auth.;* 'is bileued on you,' *Wicl.;* 'wytnesse upon you,' *Coverd.* (Test.), 'was beleued of you,' *Gen.;* 'testimony concerning you,' *Rhem.*

11. *Whereunto we also*] 'Wherefore also we,' *Auth.* and similarly *Tynd., Cov., Cran., Gen.,* which omit 'also,' and *Bish.,* which inverts ('wee also'); 'in which thing also we,' *Wicl., Cov.* (Test.) ('the whych'); 'wherein also we,' *Rhem.* *May*] So *Bish.:* 'would,' *Auth.;* 'wyll,' *Cov.* (Test.), *Cran.;* the remaining Vv. omit the auxiliary. *Your*] '*This,*' *Auth., Cran., Gen.;* 'His,' *Wicl., Cov.* (Test.), *Bish., Rhem.;* 'the,' *Tynd., Cov.* *Every good pleasure of*] 'All the good pleasure of *His,*' *Auth., Bish., Rhem.* 'all the wille of His,' *Wicl., Coverd.* (Test.); 'all delectation of,' *Tynd., Cov., Cran.;* 'all the fre benevolence of His,' *Gen.*

CHAPTER II. 1. *Touching*] 'By,' *Auth.* and all the other Vv.; see notes. *And our*] So *Cov.* (Test.): 'and by our,' *Auth., Bish.;* 'and of oure,' *Wicl., Rhem.;* 'and in that we shall assemble,' *Tynd., Cov., Cran., Gen.*

2. *Quickly*] 'Soon,' *Auth., Wicl., Cov.* (Test.); 'sodenly,' *Tynd., Cov., Cran., Gen., Bish.;* 'easily,' *Rhem.* *From your sober mind*] Similarly *Wicl.,* 'fro youre witte;' *Tynd., Cov., Cran., Gen., Bish.,* 'from youre mynde;' 'from youre meanynge,' *Coverd.* (Test.); 'from your sense,' *Rhem.: Auth.* alone adopts the incorrect 'in mind.' *Nor*] So *Cov.* (Test.), *Cran., Bish., Rhem.:* 'or,' *Auth.;* 'neither,' *Wicl.;* 'and be not,' *Tynd., Cov., Gen.* *To the effect that*] 'As that,' *Auth.,* 'as if,' *Wicl.;* 'as though,' *Tynd.,* and the remaining Vv. This slight change seems to make the meaning a little more perspicuous. *Now come*] 'At hand,' *Auth.* and the other Vv. except *Wicl.,* 'be nyg.'

3. *In any way*] 'By any means,' *Auth.* and the other Vv. except *Wicl.,* 'on ony maner.' *Because the day will not come*] 'For that day shall not come,' *Auth., Bish.;* 'for but discencioun come first,' *Wicl.;* 'for the Lord cometh not excepte,' *Tynd., Cov.* (both); 'for the Lord shall not come except,' *Cran.;* 'for the day of Christ shal not come,' *Gen.;* 'for unless there come, etc.,' *Rhem.* *The falling away*] 'A falling away.'

you in any way; because *the day will not come*, except there come
the falling away first, and the Man of Sin be revealed, the son of
perdition; 4 he that opposeth, and exalteth himself against every
one called God or an object of worship; insomuch that he sitteth
down in the temple of God, displaying himself that he is God.
5 Remember ye not, that, when I was yet with you, I told you
these things? 6 And now ye know what restraineth, that he may
be revealed in HIS OWN time. 7 For the mystery of lawlessness is
ALREADY working, *yet* only until he who now restraineth be taken
out of the way. 8 And THEN shall the Lawless One be REVEALED,

*Auth.*; 'discencioun,' *Wicl.*; 'a revolt,' *Rhem.*; 'a departynge,' *Tynd.*, and the remaining Vv. except *Cov.* (both), which alone of these Vv. preserve correctly the force of the article. *The man*] So *Wicl.*, *Rhem*: 'that man,' *Auth.*, *Coverd.*, *Bish.*; 'that synfull man,' *Tynd.* and the remaining Vv.

4. *He that opposeth*] 'who opposeth,' *Auth.*; 'that is adversarie,' *Wiclif*, 'which is an adversarie,' *Tynd.*, *Coverd.*, *Cran.*, *Gen.*, *Bish.*, *Rhem.*: 'which withstandeth;' *Cov.* (Test.). It will thus be seen that most of the Vv. rightly recognize the substantival character of ὁ ἀντικείμενος, and unite ἐπὶ πάντα κ. τ. λ. solely with the latter participle. *Against every one*] 'Above all that is,' *Auth.*, *Tynd.*, *Cov.* (both), *Cran.*, *Gen.*, *Rhem.*; 'oure alle thing that is,' *Wicl.*; 'agaynst all that is,' *Bish.* *An object of worship*] 'That is worshipped,' *Auth.* and the other Vv. except *Cov.*, 'God's seruyce.' *Insomuch*] So *Cov.* (Test.): 'so,' *Auth.* and the remaining Vv. *That He*] 'That he *as God,' *Auth.* *Displaying*] 'Shewing,' *Auth.*, *Coverd.* (Test.), *Bish.*, *Rhem.*; 'and schewe,' *Wicl.*, *Tynd.*; 'and boasteth himselfe,' *Cov.*, *Cran.*; 'and beare in hand that,' *Gen.*

6. *Restraineth*] 'Withholdeth,' *Auth.* and the other Vv. except *Cov.* (Test.), 'doth withhold;' *Rhem.*, 'letteth.' There does not seem any reason for supplying the pronoun 'him,' as Scholef. (*Hints*, p. 116, ed. 3): we seem bound to preserve the mysterious indefiniteness of the original. *May*] So *Cov.* (Test.), *Rhem.*; 'might,' *Auth.* and the remaining Vv. except *Wicl.*, 'be.' *His own*] 'His,' *Auth.* and all the other Vv.

7. *Lawlessness*] 'Iniquity,' *Auth.*, *Bish*, *Rhem*; 'wickednes,' *Wicl.*; 'that iniquitie,' *Tynd.*, *Cov.* (Test.); 'the iniquyte,' *Cov.*, *Cran.*, *Gen.* It seems desirable here to retain this more rigidly literal translation as serving more clearly to indicate the essential character of τὸ κατέχον. *Is already working*] 'Doth already work,' *Auth.*, *Cran.*, *Gen.*, *Bish.*; 'worchith now,' *Wicl.*; 'doeth he all readie work,' *Tynd.*; 'worketh already,' *Cov.*; 'doth worke allreadye,' *Coverd.* (Test.); 'now—worketh,' *Rhem.* *Yet only until, etc.*] Similarly *Cov.*, *Cran.*, 'tyll he which now onely letteth:' 'only he who now letteth *will let* until he,' *Auth.*; 'oonli that he that hooldith now, holde til he,' *Wicl.*; 'which onlie loketh, untill it be,' *Tynd.*; 'onely that he that holdeth let hym holde now untill he,' *Cov.* (Test.); 'only he which now letteth, *shal* let til he,' *Gen.*; 'only he which nowe withholdeth (shall let) till he,' *Bish.*; 'only that he which now holdeth, doe hold,' *Rhem.* The insertion of 'yet' may perhaps be admitted as slightly clearing up the elliptical formula.

8. *The lawless One*] 'That Wicked.'

whom the Lord shall consume with the breath of His mouth, and
shall destroy with the appearance of His coming; 9 whose coming
is after the working of Satan in all power and signs and wonders
of falsehood, 10 and in all deceit of unrighteousness for them
that are perishing; because they received not the love of the
truth, that they might be saved. 11 And for this cause doth God
send them a working of delusion that they should believe the lie;
12 that they may all of them be judged who believed not the truth,
but had pleasure in unrighteousness.

*Auth., Tynd., Coverd., Cran.;* 'the ilke wickid,' *Wicl.;* 'the wicked,' *Coverd.* (Test.); 'that wicked man,' *Gen. Bish.;* 'that wicked one,' *Rhem.* *Breath*] So *Coverd.* (Test.): 'spirit,' *Auth.* and the remaining Vv. *Appearance*] So *Tynd., Cov.* (both), *Cran., Gen.:* 'brightness,' *Auth., Bish.;* 'lightnynge,' *Wicl.;* 'manifestation' *Rhem.* The regular translation of this word in *Auth.* is 'appearing' (1 Tim. vi. 14, 2 Tim. i. 10, iv. 1, 8, Tit. ii. 13), but is here slightly changed to avoid the juxtaposition of two participial substantives.

9. *Whose*] So *Rhem.: Auth.* prefixes '*even him*,' and so the remaining Vv. except *Wicl., Cov.* (Test.), 'hym whose.' *In*] So *Wicl., Cov.* (Test.), *Rhem.:* 'with,' *Auth.* and the remaining Vv. *Wonders of falsehood*] 'Lying wonders,' *Auth., Coverd.* (Test.), *Gen., Bish., Wicl.;* 'wondris fals;' 'lyinge power, signes and wonders,' *Tynd., Coverd.* ('power and'), *Cran.;* 'lying signes and wonders,' *Rhem.*

10. *And in*] So *Wicl., Tynd, Cov.* (Test.), *Gen., Rhem.;* 'and with,' *Auth., Cov., Cran., Bish.* *Deceit*] So *Wicl.*, and similarly *Cov.* (Test.), 'deceatfulnesse:' 'deceivableness,' *Auth.* and the remaining Vv. except *Rhem.*, 'seducing.' *For them*] 'In them,' *Auth.;* 'to hem,' *Wicl., Rhem.;* 'amonge them,' *Tynd., Coverd., Cran., Gen., Bish.;* 'unto them,' *Cov.* (Test.). *Are perishing*] 'That perish,' *Auth.* and all the other Vv.

11. *Doth God send*] 'God *shall send.' *Auth.* and the other Vv. except *Coverd.* (Test.), 'shall God sende;' *Rhem.*, 'God wil send.' *A working*] As in ver. 9, and as in *Wicl., Coverd.* Test. ('the'): 'strong delusion,' *Auth.* and the remaining Vv. except *Rhem.*, 'the operation of errour.' Though in both cases the introduction of the adjective 'effectual' seems partly borne out by the context, it is still, lexically considered, somewhat too strong as a purely literal rendering. It would thus seem perhaps better to strike out 'effectual' in Eph. iii. 7, iv. 16, Col. ii. 12, or to retain it only in italics. These are, however, points which it is very difficult to adjust, for if the one translation is too strong, the other certainly seems somewhat too weak: 'energy,' as adopted by some translators, is appy. too modern. *The lie*] So *Cov.* (Test.); 'a lie,' *Auth.;* 'lesynge,' *Wiclif;* 'lyes,' *Tynd., Cov. Cran., Gen., Bish.;* 'lying,' *Rhem.*

12. *That they may all of them*] 'That *they all might,' *Auth.;* 'that all be,' *Wicl.;* 'that all they might,' *Tynd., Cov., Cran., Gen., Bish.;* 'that all they may,' *Cov.* (Test.); 'that al may,' *Rhem.* The two slight changes are made to preserve the reading ἅπαντες, and the correct sequence of tenses; comp. Latham, *Engl. Lang.* § 539 (ed. 4).

13 But we are bound to give thanks to God alway for you, brethren beloved of the Lord, that God chose you from the beginning to salvation in sanctification of the Spirit and belief in the truth:
14 whereunto he called you by our gospel, to the obtaining of the glory of our Lord Jesus Christ.
15 Accordingly, then, brethren, stand fast and hold the traditions which ye were taught, whether by word, or by our epistle.
16 But may our Lord Jesus Christ Himself, and God and our Father, which loved us, and gave *us* eternal consolation and good hope in grace,
17 comfort your hearts, and stablish *you* in every good work and word.

## CHAPTER III.

FINALLY, brethren, pray for us, that the word of the Lord may

13. *To God alway*] 'Alway to God,' *Auth.* and in sim. order the Vv. except *Wicl.*, 'do thankyngis euermore to God;' *Cov.*, 'unto God;' *Coverd.* (Test.), 'geue God thankes alwaye;' *Rhem.*, 'giue thankes to God alwaies. There does not here seem any necessity for leaving the order of the original. *That*] So *Wicl.*. *Cov.* (Test ), *Rhem.*; 'because,' *Auth.*, *Coverd.*; 'for because that,' *Tynd.*, *Cran.*, *Gen.*; 'because that,' *Bish.* *Chose you*] So *Wiclif*, 'chees:' 'hath from the beginning chosen,' *Auth.* and the remaining Vv. except *Coverd.* (Test.), *Rhem.*, which read ἀπαρχὴν [so too *Wicl.*], but equally insert the 'hath.' *In sanctification*] So *Rhem.*, and sim. *Cov.* (Test.), 'in the s.:' 'through sanctification,' *Auth.*, *Bish.*; 'in halowinge,' *Wicl.*; 'thorow sanctifyinge,' *Tynd.*, *Cran.*, *Gen.*; 'in the sanctifyenge,' *Cov.* *In the truth*] 'Of the truth,' *Auth.*, *Cran.*, *Rhem.*; 'of truth.' *Wicl.*, *Cov.*, (Test.) *Gen.*, *Bish.*; 'beleuynge the trueth', *Tyn.*, *Cov.* ('of the').

15. *Accordingly then*] 'Therefore,' *Auth.* and all the other Vv. *Traditions*] So *Auth.* with *Wicl.*, *Cov.* (Test.), *Rhem.* The other Vv. vary: 'ordinaunces,' *Tynd.*, *Cov.*, *Cran.*; 'instructions,' *Cov.*, *Gen.*, *Bish.* *Were taught*] 'Have been taught,' *Auth.*, *Bish.*; 'han lerned,' *Wicl.* and the remaining Vv. *By our*] So *Wicl.*, *Cov* (Test.), *Bish.*, *Rhem.*: 'our,' *Auth.*; 'by pistle,' *Tynd.* and the remaining Vv.

16 *But may*] 'Now,' *Auth.* *God and our Father*] So *Rhem.*: 'God even our Father,' *Authorized* and sim. *Bish.*, 'our God even the Father;' 'God our Father,' *Wicl.* and the remaining Vv. except *Cov.* (Test.), 'oure God and Father.' On the translation of this solemn title, compare notes *on Gal.* i. 4 (Transl.). *Loved*] So *Wicl.*: 'hath loved,' *Auth.* and the remaining Vv. *Gave*] So *Wicl.*: 'hath given,' *Auth.* and the remaining Vv. *Eternal*] So *Wicl.*: 'everlasting,' *Auth.* and the remaining Vv.; see notes on ch. i. 9, and correct Gal. vi. 8, 1 Tim. i. 16. *In grace*] So *Wicl.*, *Cov.* (Test.), *Rhem.*: 'through,' *Auth.* and the remaining Vv.

17. *Stablish you*] *Auth.* retains '*you' in Roman type, but contrary to the best mss. authority; see notes. *Work and word*] '*Word and work,' *Auth.*

CHAP. III. 1. *Free course*] In the best authenticated copies of *Auth.*, 'free' is

have free course, and be glorified, even as *it is* also with you:
2 and that we may be delivered from perverse and wicked men;
for it is not all that have Faith. 3 But faithful is the Lord, who
shall stablish you, and keep *you* from the Evil One. 4 Yea we
have confidence in the Lord touching you, that ye both do and
will do the things which we command. 5 But may the Lord direct
your hearts into the love of God, and into the patience of Christ.
6 Now we command you, brethren, in the name of our Lord
Jesus Christ, that ye withdraw yourselves from every brother walk-
ing disorderly, and not after the tradition which they received of
us. 7 For yourselves know how ye ought to follow us: in that we
behaved not disorderly among you; 8 neither ate we bread of any

in italics, but perhaps may be fairly considered as involved in the translation of τρέχῃ. *Also with you*] So *Bish.*, and similarly *Cran.* (omits 'even'), *Rhem.*, (omits '*it is*'): *Auth.* and the remaining Vv. omit 'also.'

2. *Perverse*] 'Unreasonable,' *Auth.* and the other Vv. except *Wicl.*, 'noyous;' *Cov.* (Test.), *Rhem.*, 'importunate.' *It is not all, etc.*] 'All men have not faith,' *Auth.* and the other Vv. except *Wicl.*, 'feith is not of all men;' *Cov.* (both), 'fayth is not every mans.'

3. *But faithful is the Lord*] 'But the Lord is faithful,' *Auth.* and the other Vv. except *Wicl.*, 'the Lorde is trewe;' *Rhem.*, 'our Lord is faythful.' Independently of the change of order agreeing better with that of the original, the paronomasia caused by the juxtaposition of πίστις and πιστὸς is more distinctly preserved. *The Evil One*] 'Evil,' *Auth.* and all the other Vv.; see notes.

4. *Yea we*] 'And we,' *Auth.*, *Wicl.*, *Bish.*, *Rhem.*; 'but we,' *Cov.* (Test.); the rest, *Tynd.*, *Cov.*, *Cran.*, *Gen.*, omit δὲ in translation. *Command*] 'Command *you,' *Auth.*

5. *But may the Lord*] 'And the Lord,' *Auth.* and the other Vv. except *Cov.*, which omits δὲ in translation.

*Patience of Christ*] So *Wicl.*, *Tynd.*, *Cov.* (both), *Cran.*, *Rhem.*: 'patient waiting for Christ,' *Auth.*; 'weating for of Christ,' *Gen.*, *Bish.*

6. *Walking*] So *Cov.* (Test.), *Rhem.*: 'that walketh,' *Auth.*, *Tynd.*, *Cov.*, *Gen.*, *Bish.*; 'that wandrith,' *Wicl.*; 'that behaveth himself,' *Cran.*. Though the meaning is practically the same, it still seems desirable in translation, when consistent with our idiom, to mark the anarthrous participle. *Tradition*] So *Auth.*, *Rhem.*: 'techynge,' *Wicl.*; 'institution,' *Tynd.*, *Coverd.*, *Cran.*; 'ordinaunce,' *Coverd.* (Test.); 'instruction,' *Gen.*, *Bish.* If any change be thought necessary, the last of these translations is perhaps to be preferred.
*They received*] '*He received,' *Auth.*

7. *In that*] 'For,' *Auth.* and all the other Vv.; see notes.
*Behaved not disorderly*] 'Behaved not ourselves disorderly,' *Auth.*; 'we weren not unpeisible,' *Wicl.*; 'behaved not ourselves inordinately,' *Tynd.*, *Cov.*, *Cran.*, *Gen.*, *Bish.*; 'we were not restless,' *Cov.* (Test.); 'we haue not been unquiet,' *Rhem.*

8. *Ate we bread of any man*] Sim. *Wicl.*, 'eten breed of ony man;' *Rhem.*, 'haue we eaten bread of any man;' 'did we eat any man's bread;' *Auth.*,

man for nought, but with toil and travail, working night and day,
that we might not be burdensome to any of you: 9 not that we
have not power, but to make ourselves an ensample unto you that
ye should follow us. 10 For also when we were with you, THIS we
commanded you, that if any will not work, neither let him eat.
11 For we hear that there are some walking among you disorderly,
working at nothing, but being busybodies. 12 Now them that are
such we command and exhort in the Lord Jesus Christ, that with
quietness they work, and eat THEIR OWN bread. 13 But ye, breth-
ren, be not weary in well doing. 14 But if any man obey not our

and similarly *Cov.* (Test.), 'the bread of ony man;' 'toke we breed of eny man,' *Tynd.*, *Coverd.*, *Cran.*, *Gen.*, *Bish.* It seems desirable here to invert the order of the Greek that δωρεάν, which occupies the emphatic place in Greek, may occupy the same place in English, — that place being not uncommonly in our language *the last.* *But with toil, etc.*] 'But wrought with labour,' *Auth.* and the other Vv. (*Bish.* 'we wrought') except *Wicl.*, 'but in traueil and werynesse worchiden;' *Cov.* (Test), 'but labouring night and day in weeryness;' *Rhem.*, 'but in labour and in toil night and day working.' *Burdensome*] Similarly *Rhem.*, 'lest we should burden:' 'chargeable,' *Auth.*, *Coverd.*, *Cran.*, *Gen.*, *Bish.*; 'that we greeieden noon,' *Wicl.*; 'we wolde not be grevous,' *Tynd.*; 'lest we shulde charge,' *Cov.* (Test.).

9. *Not that*] 'Not because,' *Auth.*; 'not as,' *Wicl.*; 'not but that,' *Tynd.*, *Cov.*, *Cran.*, *Gen.*, *Bish.*; 'not as though,' *Cov.* (Test.), *Rhem.* *That ye should follow*] Somewhat similarly *Rhem.*, 'for to:' 'to follow,' *Auth.* and the remaining Vv. except *Wicl.*, 'to sue.'

10. *For also*] So *Wicl.*, *Rhem.*, and sim. *Cov.* (Test.): 'for even,' *Auth.*, *Bish.*; 'and when,' *Cov.*; the rest, *Tynd.*, *Cran.*, *Gen.*, omit καὶ in translation. *Will not*] So *Wicl.*, *Cov.* (Test.), *Rhem.*: 'would not,' *Auth.* and the remaining Vv. *Neither let him*] So *Rhem.*, and sim. *Wiclif*, 'nether ete he:' 'neither should he,' *Auth.*; 'that the same shuld not,' *Tynd.*, *Cov.* (omits 'that'). *Cran.* (ib.), *Gen.*; 'let him not,' *Cov.* (Test.); 'that he should not,' *Bish.*

11. *Walking*] 'Which walk,' *Auth.* and the other Vv. except *Wicl*, 'that somme among you gon in rest;' *Cov.* (Test.), 'to be walkyng;' *Rhem.*, 'that walke;' also comp. notes on ver. 6. *Working at nothing*] Similarly *Coverd.* (Test.), *Rhem.*, 'working nothing:' 'working not at all,' *Auth.*, *Cran.*; 'and no thing worchen,' *Wicl.*; 'and worke not at all,' *Tynd.*, *Cov.*, *Gen.*, *Bish.* *Being busybodies*] So *Cran.*: 'are busybodies,' *Auth.*, *Tynd.*, *Cov.*, *Gen.*, *Bish.*; 'don curiousli,' *Wicl.*; 'using curiosite,' *Coverd.* (Test.); 'curiously meddling,' *Rhem.*

12. *In the*] '*By our,' *Auth.*

14. *But if*] So *Cov.*: 'and if,' *Auth.*, *Rhem.* If 'but' be objected to in consequence of the preceding 'but' in ver. 13, it would then seem better with *Tynd.* and the remaining Vv. to omit it in translation. *Obey not*] So *Auth.* and the other Vv. except *Wicl.*, 'obeieth not;' *Cov.* (Test.), 'doth not obey.' At first sight the latter translation might seem preferable, but considered strictly, it would seem to imply that such would probably be the case (see Latham, *Eng. Lang.* § 537, ed. 4), whereas the Greek εἰ with the indic. 'per se nihil significat

word by this epistle, mark that man, and keep no company with
him, that he may be shamed. [15] And count *him* not as an enemy,
but admonish *him* as a brother. [16] But may the Lord of peace
Himself give you peace continually, in every way. The Lord be
with you all.

[17] THE SALUTATION OF ME PAUL WITH MINE OWN HAND WHICH
IS A TOKEN IN EVERY EPISTLE: SO I WRITE. [18] THE GRACE OF
OUR LORD JESUS CHRIST BE WITH YOU ALL. AMEN.

præter conditionem' (Klotz, *Devar.* Vol. II. p. 455). It may thus be best, as a general rule, only to adopt the indicative in English where either (*a*) the context or circumstances of the case corroborate the likelihood of the assumed case, or (*b*) where the speaker appears to regard it as a matter of fact. The possibility of inserting after 'if' the words, 'as is matter of fact,' or, 'as seems matter of fact,' will commonly facilitate decision. *This epistle*] So *Auth.*; 'oure worde bi epistil,' *Wicl.*: all the other Vv. join τῆς ἐπιστολῆς with σημειοῦσθε, and translate τῆς by the English indef. art. This, perhaps, may remain as one of the *few* cases in which idiom and euphony may justify us in retaining the pronominal translation: Scholefield (*Hints*, p. 118, ed. 3) proposes 'our epistle,' but this is scarcely suitable after the preceding 'our word,' where the 'our' is a translation of ἡμῶν, and would thus seem to imply that it was repeated before τῆς ἐπιστολῆς. *Mark*] So *Wiclif*: 'note,' *Auth.*, *Bish.*, *Rhem.*; 'sende us worde of him,' *Tynd.*, *Cov.*, *Cran.*, *Gen.*; 'shewe [us] the same,' *Cov.* (Test.). *Keep*] 'Have,' *Auth.* and the other Vv. except *Wicl.*, 'comyne ye not;' *Rhem.*, do not companie with.' *Shamed*] So *Wicl.*: 'ashamed,' *Auth.* and the remaining Vv. except *Rhem.*, 'be confounded.'

15. *And*] So *Wicl.*, *Tynd.*, *Cran.*, *Rhem.*: 'yet,' *Auth.* and the remaining Vv.

16. *But may*] 'Now—give,' *Auth.*, *Gen.*, *Bish.*; 'and—geue,' *Wiclif*, *Rhem.*; *Tynd.*, *Cov.* (both), *Cran.*, omit δὲ in translation. *Continually in every way*] 'Always by all means,' *Auth.* and the other Vv. except *Wicl.*, 'everlasting pees in al place;' *Cov.* (Test.), *Rhem.*, 'euerlastynge peace in euery place.'

17. *Me Paul*] So *Tynd.*, *Coverd.*, *Cran.*, *Gen.*, *Bish.*: 'Paul,' *Auth.*; 'be the hond of Poul,' *Wiclif*; 'with myne owne hande Paul,' *Coverd.* (Test.), *Rhem.* ('Paules'). *A token*] Similarly *Rhem.*, 'a signe:' 'the token,' *Auth.* and the remaining Vv. except *Wicl.*, 'whiche signe.'

THE END.